Walter Besant, Edward Henry Palmer

Jerusalem, the city of Herod and Saladin

Walter Besant, Edward Henry Palmer

Jerusalem, the city of Herod and Saladin

ISBN/EAN: 9783743333765

Manufactured in Europe, USA, Canada, Australia, Japa

Cover: Foto ©ninafisch / pixelio.de

Manufactured and distributed by brebook publishing software (www.brebook.com)

Walter Besant, Edward Henry Palmer

Jerusalem, the city of Herod and Saladin

From a Photograph by C. F. Tyrwhitt Drake, Esq.] THE DOME OF THE ROCK. [Frontispiece.

JERUSALEM,

THE CITY OF HEROD AND SALADIN.

BY

WALTER BESANT, M.A.,
CHRIST'S COLLEGE, CAMBRIDGE.
AUTHOR OF "STUDIES IN EARLY FRENCH POETRY," ETC., ETC., ETC.

AND

E. H. PALMER, M.A.,
LORD ALMONER'S PROFESSOR OF ARABIC IN THE UNIVERSITY OF
CAMBRIDGE, AND FELLOW OF ST. JOHN'S COLLEGE.
AUTHOR OF THE "DESERT OF THE EXODUS."
ETC., ETC., ETC.

LONDON:
RICHARD BENTLEY AND SON,
NEW BURLINGTON STREET,
Publishers in Ordinary to Her Majesty.
1871.
[*The Right of Translation is reserved.*]

LONDON
PRINTED BY WILLIAM CLOWES AND SONS, STAMFORD STREET
AND CHARING CROSS.

PREFACE.

VERY few words are needed to introduce this volume. It is intended to give a history of the city of Jerusalem from about the year 30 to the present time. This period includes the siege and capture by Titus, the last revolts of the Jews, the Christian occupation of three hundred years, the Mohammedan conquest, the building by the Mohammedans of the Dome of the Rock, the Crusades, the Christian kingdom, the reconquest of the city, and a long period of Mohammedan occupation, during which no event has happened except the yearly flocking of pilgrims to the Church of the Sepulchre, and an occasional quarrel among the monks.

There are here, surely, sufficient materials for the historian if only he knows how to use them.

For the modern period, that of the Christian kingdom, two sources of information exist, one, the contemporary and later chronicles of the Crusaders, written either in Latin or Langue d'Oil, and the other, the Arabic historians themselves. I have written my own part of the book from the former; to my colleague is due all that part (the Mohammedan Conquest, the chapter on Saladin, &c.) which has been taken from Arabic writers. Most of this has the great advantage of being entirely new, and now for the first time introduced to English readers. For my own share in the work, I claim no other novelty than the presentation of facts as faithfully as I could gather them, at first hand, and from the earliest writers.

There is nothing sacred about the actors in this long story we have to tell, and we have not thought it necessary to endeavour to invest them, as is generally done by those who write on Jerusalem, with an appearance of sanctity, because they fought for the City of Sacred Memories, or because they bore the Cross upon their shoulders. We have, on the other hand, endeavoured to show them as they were, men and women actuated by mixed motives, sometimes base, sometimes noble, sometimes interested, sometimes pure and lofty: but always men and women, never saints. The Christians in the East were as the Christians in the West, certainly never better, more often worse. If we have succeeded in making a plain tale, divested of its customary pseudoreligious trappings, interesting and useful, our design is satisfied.

One word more. There may be found, owing to the double source from which our pages are derived, certain small discrepancies in the narrative. We have not cared to try and reconcile these. Let it be remembered that the one narrative is Christian, the other Mohammedan.

W. B.

October, 1871.

CONTENTS.

CHAPTER I.
Introductory 1

CHAPTER II.
The Siege of Jerusalem 19

CHAPTER III.
From Titus to Omar 47

CHAPTER IV.
The Mohammedan Conquest 66

CHAPTER V.
The Christian Pilgrims 112

CHAPTER VI.
The First Crusade 141

CHAPTER VII.
King Godfrey 190

CHAPTER VIII.
King Baldwin I. 211

CHAPTER IX.
King Baldwin II. 236

CHAPTER X.
King Fulke 259

CHAPTER XI.
King Baldwin III. and the Second Crusade . . 269

CHAPTER XII.
King Amaury 298

CHAPTER XIII.
King Baldwin the Leper 335

CHAPTER XIV.
King Guy de Lusignan 344

CHAPTER XV.
Richard Cœur de Lion and the Third Crusade . . 362

CHAPTER XVI.
Saladin 372

CHAPTER XVII.
The Mohammedan Pilgrims 417

CHAPTER XVIII.
The Chronicle of Six Hundred Years . . . 443

CHAPTER XIX.
Modern Jerusalem 466

APPENDIX.
On the Position of the Sacred Sites 478

Index 489

JERUSALEM.

THE CITY OF HEROD AND SALADIN.

CHAPTER I.

INTRODUCTORY.

It is our object to write a book which may serve as a historical account, complete so far as it goes, of the principal events with which Jerusalem is concerned, from the time when its history, as connected with the Bible, ceases, till the present; that is to say, from the year A.D. 33 downwards. But it is difficult to take up the thread of the story at this date, and we are forced either to go as far back as Herod the Great, or to begin our narrative with the events which preceded the siege of Jerusalem by Titus. No date seems to us more ready to our hand than that of the death of Herod Agrippa. Even then we may seem beginning to tell a thrice told tale. The revolt of the Jews, their defeat of Cestius, the siege of Titus, are surely, it may be objected, too well known to require telling again. They are not well known, though they have been told again and again, and told with ten times the force, the vigour, the originality which we can put into these pages. But they are told here again because our central figure is Jerusalem. We have to show her first, in all her pride, the joy of the Jews, the visible mark of their greatness; and then we have to follow her through two thousand years of varying fortune, always before the eyes of the world,—

B

always the object of tender pity and reverence,—always the centre of some conflict, the scene of some religious contention. Frequent as were the sieges of the city in the olden days, they have been more frequent since. Titus took Jerusalem, Barcochebas took it, Julius Severus took it, Chosroes, Heraclius, Omar, the Charezmians, Godfrey, Saladin, Frederick, all took it by turns,—all after hard fighting, and with much slaughter.

There is not a stone in the city but has been reddened with human blood; not a spot but where some hand-to-hand conflict has taken place; not an old wall but has echoed back the shrieks of despairing women. Jew, Pagan, Christian, Mohammedan, each has had his turn of triumph, occupation, and defeat; and were all those ancient cemeteries outside the city emptied of their bones, it would be hard to tell whether Jew, or Pagan, or Christian, or Mohammedan would prevail. For Jerusalem has been the representative sacred place of the world; there has been none other like unto it, or equal to it, or shall be, while the world lasts; so long as men go on believing that one spot in the world is more sacred than another, because things of sacred interest have been done there, so long Jerusalem will continue the Holy City. That this belief has been one of the misfortunes of the human race, one of the foremost causes of superstition, some of the pages which follow may perhaps help to show. But, in our capacity as narrators only, let us agree to think and talk of the city apart, as much as may be, from its sacred associations, as well as from its ecclesiastical history.

The fatal revolt of the Jews, which ended in the fall of their city and the destruction of their Temple, was due, among many other causes, to the teaching of Judas the Galilæan acting on minds inflated with pride in the exaggerated glories of the past, looking to national independence as the one thing needful, and wholly ignorant of the power and resources of the mighty empire which held them in subjection. Judas, himself in spirit a worthy descendant of the Maccabæans, had taught that Jehovah was the only King of the Jews, who were his chosen people; that submission to a foreign yoke involved not only national degradation, but treason to the lawful powers; that tribute, the badge and sign of slavery, ought to be refused at any cost. "We have no Lord and master but God," was the cry of his party. With that cry he and his followers assembled to do battle against the world: with that cry on their lips they died. But the cry and its idea did not die; for from that time a fourth sect was among the Jews, more powerful than all the rest put together, containing the great mass of the people, who had no education to give them common sense, and whose ignorance added fuel to the flames of a religious enthusiasm almost without parallel in the history of the world. The Pharisees and the Sadducees still continued for a time in the high places; the Essenes still lived and died apart from the world, the Shakers of their time, a small band with no power or influence; but all around them was rising a tide destined to whelm all beneath the waves of fanaticism. The followers of Judas became the Zealots and the Sicarii of later times: they were those who looked daily for the Messiah; whom false Christs led astray by thousands; who thought no act too daring to be attempted in this sacred cause, no life too valuable to be sacrificed: they were those who let their countrymen die of starvation by thousands while they maintained a hopeless struggle with Titus.

When Herod Agrippa died, his son, who was only seventeen years of age, was in Rome; and, as he was too young to be entrusted with the conduct of the turbulent province of Judæa, Cuspius Fadus was sent there as Governor. He found that Agrippa had allowed the robbers who always infested the country east of Jordan to gain head. He put them down with a strong arm, and turned his attention to things of domestic importance. By the permission of Vitellius, the custody of the sacred robes had been surrendered to the High Priest. Cuspius Fadus ordered that they should be restored to the fortress of Antonia. The Jews appealed to Cæsar, and, by the intercession of young Agrippa, they carried their point, and retained the possession of the robes. Under Fadus, one Theudas, whom Josephus calls a magician, persuaded multitudes of the Jews to go with him to the Jordan, which he pretended would open its waters to let him pass. Cuspius Fadus sent out a troop of cavalry, who took Theudas alive, cut off his head, and brought it to Jerusalem. Under Cuspius, too, occurred a great famine in Judæa, which was relieved by the generosity of Queen Helena of Adiabene, the proselyte.*

When Fadus either died or was recalled, Tiberius Alexander, a renegade Jew, nephew of Philo, succeeded him for a short time. It is not stated how long he continued in power. His only recorded act is the crucifixion of two of the sons of Judas the Galilæan. In his turn Tiberius was replaced by Ventidius Cumanus, and the first symptoms of the approaching madness broke out. The fortress of Antonia commanded the Temple area, and communicated with the Temple itself by means of cloisters. On those days of public festivals when the fanaticism of the people was most likely to break out and cause mischief, a strong guard was always placed in Antonia, in full view of the people, to overawe them with good behaviour. Most unfortunately, on one occasion, immediately after the arrival of Cumanus, one of the soldiers of the guard expressed his contempt for the religious ceremonies by an indecent gesture. The rage

* The story of Queen Helena is told by Josephus, 'Antiq.' xx. 2, 3, 4, and in Milman, 'Hist. of the Jews,' ii. p. 200; and see also, for the whole of this period, Williams's 'Holy City,' vol. i. p. 150 et seq.

of the people knew no bounds; they declared that Cumanus had himself ordered the affront to be committed. The governor bore their reproaches with patience, only urging them not to disturb their festival by riotous conduct. As, however, they still continued clamouring, he ordered his whole garrison to proceed to Antonia. Then a panic ensued. The mob, thinking they were about to be attacked by the soldiers, turned and fled, trampling on each other in the narrow passages. Many thousands perished in this way, without a blow being struck. And while they were still mourning over this disaster, another happened to them. Some of the very men who had raised the first tumult, probably countrymen on their way home, fell on and robbed Stephanus, a slave of the Emperor. Cumanus, obliged to punish this, sent soldiers to bring in the chief men of the village. One of the soldiers tore up a book of the Law with abuse and scurrility. The Jews came to Cumanus, and represented that they could not possibly endure such an insult to their God. Cumanus appeased them for the time by beheading the soldier who had been guilty of the offence.

The animosities of the Samaritans and the Jews were the cause of the next disturbances. The Galilæans always used the roads which passed through the Samaritan territory in their journeys to and from the Temple. Faction fights naturally often took place. In one of these, of greater magnitude than the generality, a good many Galilæans were killed: the Jews came to Cumanus and complained of what they were pleased to call murder. Cumanus took the part of the Samaritans, and actually went to their aid, after the Jews called in the assistance of a robber chieftain, and helped them to defeat the Galilæans. It is difficult to see what else they could do. Both parties appealed to Cæsar. Cumanus was recalled: his military tribune was beheaded, decision was given in favour of the

Jews: all this, no doubt, was done with a full knowledge of the dangerous and the turbulent nature of the people, and with a view to preserving the peace.

Claudius Felix was sent in place of Cumanus, a freedman, brother of Pallas the favourite of the Emperor, magnificent, prodigal, luxurious, and unscrupulous. He found the country in the worst state possible, full of robbers, and impostors. These sprung up everyday, and were everyday caught and destroyed; no doubt most of them men whose wits were utterly gone in looking for the Messiah, until they ended in believing themselves to be the Messiah. These poor creatures, followed by a rabble more ignorant and more mad than themselves, went up and down the distracted country, raising hopes which were doomed to disappointment, and leading out the wild countrymen to meet death and torture when they looked for glory and victory. One of the impostors, an Egyptian, probably an Egyptian Jew, brought a multitude up to the Mount of Olives, promising that at his word the walls of the city should fall down, and they themselves march in triumphant. He came, but instead of seeing the walls fall down, he met the troops of Felix, who dispersed his people, slaying four hundred of them.

To Felix belongs the crime of introducing the Sicarii into the city of Jerusalem. Wearied with the importunities of the high priest, Jonathan, who exhorted him continually to govern better, or at all events to govern differently, and reproached him with the fact that it was through his own influence that Felix obtained his office, he resolved to rid himself of a friend so troublesome, by the speediest and surest method, that of assassination. The Sicarii were not, like the hired bravoes of the middle ages, men who would commit any murder for which they were paid. It appears, on the contrary, that they held it a cardinal point of faith to murder those, and only those, who seemed to stand in the way of their cause. Now their cause was that of the sect which had grown out of Judas's teaching, the zealots. These Sicarii mingling with the crowd of those who went up to worship, carrying daggers concealed under their garments, fell upon Jonathan the High Priest, and murdered him.* This done they went on slaying all those who were obnoxious to them, even in the Temple itself. "And this," says the historian, "seems to me the reason why God, out of his hatred to the wickedness of these men, rejected our city: and as for the Temple, he no longer esteemed it sufficiently pure for him to inhabit therein, but brought the Romans upon us, and threw a fire upon the city to purge it: and brought upon us, our wives, and children, slavery,—as desirous to make us wiser by our calamities." And now the voice of discord was heard even among the priests themselves, who had hitherto preserved a certain sobriety. Between the chief priests and "the principal men of the multitude of Jerusalem," a feud broke out. Each side had its followers: they cast, we are told, not only reproachful words, but also stones at each other. And the chief priests, robbing the threshingfloors and appropriating all the tithes to themselves, caused many of the poorer priests to die of want.

Then occurred the first outbreak in Cæsarea. This town was about equally divided between the Syrians and the Jews, the former claimed the pre-eminence on the ground that Herod the founder, though himself a Jew, had built the splendid temples and statues by which the city was evidently intended to be a Grecian city, upon the site of Strato's Tower; while the Jews argued that as the founder was a Jew, the city was evidently Jewish, and ought not to be ruled except by Jews. The dispute, as was always the case, came to the arbitrament of arms, in which the Jews got the best of it. Then

---

* Milman says, in the Temple itself, which does not appear from the account of Josephus, who expressly says that, after this, they had the boldness to murder men in the Temple itself.

Felix came himself, with a strong force, and brought them to their senses. But as the dispute still went on, he sent representatives on both sides to Nero the Emperor, who ruled in favour of the Greeks or Syrians. Here, the decision of the Emperor appears to have been just. Herod, the founder of Cæsarea, had clearly not intended to found a city for the further propagation of a sect to which he indeed belonged, regarding it, nevertheless, with the toleration of a cultivated Roman, as only one sect out of many. The Jews accepted the decision in their usual way: they only became more turbulent. Agrippa's own dispute with his own countrymen was decided, however, in their favour, no doubt from politic considerations. He had built an upper room in his palace, where, lying on his couch, he could look over into the Temple and watch the sacrifices. Some of the priests discovering this, made out that it was an intrusion into the necessary privacy of their religious ceremonies, and hastily ran up a wall to prevent being overlooked. Festus, who had now succeeded Felix, ordered it to be pulled down; but, most probably at the instigation of Agrippa, whose popularity might be at stake, he gave permission to appeal to Nero. Ismael, the high priest, went, accompanied by the keeper of the Treasury. They carried their point: the wall was allowed to stand, but Ismael was detained in Rome, and Agrippa appointed and deprived three high priests in succession—Joseph, Annas, and Jesus son of Dammai. The firm, strong hand of Festus was meantime employed in putting down robbers, and regulating the disturbances of the country. Unhappily for the Jews, while he was so engaged, he was seized with some illness and died. Albinus succeeded him. As for Albinus, Josephus tells us that there was no sort of wickedness named but he had a hand in it. "Not only did he steal and plunder every one's substance, not only did he burden the whole nation with taxes, but he permitted the relations of such as were in prison for robbery to redeem them for money; and nobody remained in the prisons as a malefactor but he who gave him nothing .... The principal men among the seditious purchased leave of Albinus to go on with their practices: and every one of these wretches was encompassed with his own band of robbers. Those who lost their goods were forced to hold their peace, when they had reason to show great indignation at what they had suffered; those who had escaped were forced to flatter him, that deserved to be punished out of the fear they were in of suffering equally with the others."

This, however, is a vague accusation, and is found in the 'Wars of the Jews,' where Josephus is anxious to represent the revolt of the people as caused by the bad government of the Romans. From the 'Antiquities' we learn that it was Albinus's wish to keep the country in peace, with which object he destroyed many of the Sicarii. Unfortunately for himself, he formed a great friendship with Ananias the high priest; and when Eleazar, son of Ananias, fell into the hands of the Sicarii, he consented to release ten of his own prisoners for his ransom. This was a fatal measure, because henceforth the Sicarii, if one of their number fell into trouble, and got taken by the Romans, caught a Jew and effected an exchange. Thus the prisons were emptied.

At this time the Temple was finished, and eighteen thousand workmen found themselves suddenly out of employment. Terrified at the prospect of this starving mob being added to their difficulties (for the streets of Jerusalem were already filled with bands of armed men, partisans of deposed high priests), the citizens asked Agrippa to rebuild the Eastern Cloisters, the splendid piece of work which had been built originally by Solomon along that east wall which still stands overlooking the valley of the Kedron. But Agrippa, whose interest in the turbulent city was very small, already meditated departure to some safer quarter, and was spending all the money he had to spare at Beyrout, where he built a theatre, and collected a gallery of sculptures. But he conceded something to his petitioners, and allowed them to pave the city with stone.

Albinus disappears from the history, and Gessius Florus, who exchanged a scourging with whips for a scourging with scorpions, ruled in his place. Cestius Gallus, a man of equal rapacity with himself, ruled in Syria. One cannot read Josephus without, in the first place, suspecting that he wilfully exaggerates the wickedness of the Roman rulers; that he does so in the case of Albinus is clear, as we have shown from comparing the account given in the 'Antiquities' with that given in the 'Wars.' But even if he only exaggerates, and making allowance for this, were men of special inhumanity and rapacity chosen for those very qualities to rule the country? And if not, if Gessius Florus and Albinus be fair specimens of the officers by whom Rome ruled her provinces and colonies, by what mysterious power was this vast empire kept from universal revolt?

"Upon what meat had this their Cæsar fed,
That he was grown so great?"

The Jews, however, were not the people to brook illtreatment; and when they took arms against the Romans it was not as if their case seemed to themselves hopeless. They had, it is true, the western world against them; but they had the eastern world behind them, a possible place of refuge. And though they armed against the whole Roman Empire, it must be remembered that the forces at the command of the Emperor were not overwhelming; that they were spread over Africa, Egypt, Spain, Gaul, Britain, Greece, and Italy; that only a certain number could be spared; and that the number of the Jews in Syria amounted probably to several millions. When Cestius Gallus was in Jerusalem at the time of the Passover he ordered the lambs which were sacrificed to be counted. They came to two hundred and fifty-five thousand six hundred. It was reckoned that this represented a total of three millions present in Jerusalem and camped round about it, assisting at the festival. Probably not more than half, perhaps not more than a quarter of the whole number of the people came up. However this may be, it is certain that Palestine was very densely populated; that there were great numbers of Jews in Alexandria, Asia Minor, and Italy; that at any signal success those would have flocked to the standard of revolt; and that had the nation been unanimous and obedient to one general, instead of being divided into sects, parties, and factions, the armies of Vespasian and Titus would have been wholly unable to cope with the rebellion, and the independence of the Jews would have been prevented only by putting forth all the power of the Roman Empire. This was shown later on in the revolt of Barcochebas, a far more serious revolt than this of the zealots, though not so well known, because it was attended with no such signal result as the destruction of the Temple, and because there was no Josephus in the camp of the enemy taking notes of what went on.

The object of Florus, we are told, was to drive the people to revolt. This we do not believe. It could not have been the policy of Florus to drive into revolt a dangerous and stubborn people, whose character was well known at Rome, whom the Emperor had always been anxious to conciliate. His object may have been, undoubtedly was, to enrich himself as speedily as possible, knowing that revolt was impending and inevitable, and anxious to secure himself a provision in case of his own recall or banishment. Until that provision was secured it would have been fatal for Florus that the revolt should break out.

The first disturbances took place at Cæsarea, when the

Greeks, exulting in Nero's decision, were daily more and more insulting to the Jews. The latter had a synagogue, round which was an open space of ground which they wished to purchase. The owner refused to sell it, and built mean shops upon it, leaving only a narrow passage whereby the Jews could pass to their place of worship. One John, a publican, went to Florus, and begged him to interfere, offering at the same time a bribe of eight talents, an enormous sum, which shows that this was more than an ordinary squabble. Florus went away, leaving them to fight it out; and the Greeks added fresh matter of wrath to the Jews by ostentatiously sacrificing birds in an earthen vase as they passed to the synagogue. The significance of this act was that the Greeks loved to tell how the Jews had been all expelled from Egypt, on account of their being leprous. Arms were taken up, and the Jews got the worst of the fray. They withdrew to a place some miles from the town, and sent John to Florus to ask for assistance. John ventured on a reminder about the eight talents, and was rewarded by being thrown into prison. Then Florus went on to Jerusalem, where the wildest tumults raged in consequence of this affront to religion. Alarmed at the symptoms of revolt, he sent messengers beforehand to take seventeen talents out of the sacred treasury, on the ground that Cæsar wanted them. Then the people ran to the Temple, and called upon Cæsar by name, as if he could hear them, to rid them of this Florus. Some of them went about with baskets begging money for him as for a man in a destitute and miserable condition.

The next day news came that Florus was advancing to the city, and the people thought they had better go out and speak him fair. But he was not disposed to receive their salutation, and so sent on Capito, a centurion, with fifty soldiers, bidding them go back and not pretend to receive him as if they were delighted to see him among them again. And he rode into the city, the people being all expectation of what would happen the next day. And in the morning the tribunal of Florus was erected before the gates of his palace. The high priest was summoned to attend, and ordered to give up those who had led the tumult. He urged in extenuation that he did not know the ringleaders, that the act of a few hot-headed youths ought not to be visited on the whole city, and that, in short, he was very sorry for the whole business, and hoped Florus would overlook it. Florus gave orders to his soldiers to pillage the upper market; they did so, scourging, pillaging, and murdering. Berenice, the sister of Agrippa, came herself, barefoot, with shorn head and penitential dress, before Florus, urging him to have pity. But the inexorable Roman, bent on revenge, allowed the soldiers to go on.

Next day he sent again for the high priest, and told him that as a sign of the loyalty of the people, and their sorrow for the late tumults, he should expect them to go forth and meet the two cohorts who were advancing to Jerusalem with every sign of joy. The seditious part of the citizens refused. Then the chief priests, with dust upon their heads and rent garments, brought out the holy vessels and the sacerdotal robes, with their harpers and harps, and implored the people not to risk a collision with the Romans. They yielded, and went out to welcome the cohorts. But the soldiers preserved a gloomy silence. Then some of the more fiery Jews, turning on the Romans, began to abuse Florus. The horsemen rode at them and trampled them down, and a scene of the wildest uproar took place at the gates as they pressed and jostled each other to get in. Then the troops marched straight on Antonia, hoping to get both the fortress and the Temple into their hands. They got into Antonia, when the Jews cut down some part of the cloisters which connected the fort with the Temple. Florus tried to join them, but his men could not pass through the streets, which were crammed with Jews. And next day Florus retired to Cæsarea, leaving only one cohort behind, and the city boiling and seething with rage and madness. And now, indeed, there was little hope of any reconciliation. Both Florus and the Jews sent statements of their conduct to Cestius Gallus, and begged for an investigation. And it must have been now, if at all, that Florus became desirous of fanning the embers of discontent into a flame and making that a war which had only promised to be a disturbance. But nothing can be discovered to prove that Josephus's assertions as to his motives are based on fact. It is easy, of course, to attribute motives, but hard to prove them. Nothing advanced by Josephus proves more than that Florus was rapacious and cruel, and the people discontented and turbulent. Cestius sent Neapolitanus, one of his officers, to report on the condition of the city. Agrippa joined him. The people came sixty furlongs out of the town to meet them, crying and lamenting, calling on Agrippa to help them in their miseries, and beseeching Neapolitanus to hear their complaints against Florus. The latter they took all round the city, showing him that it was perfectly quiet, and that the people had risen, not against the Romans, but against Florus. Then Neapolitanus went into the Temple to perform such sacrifices as were allowed to strangers, and commending the Jews for their fidelity, went back to Cestius. Agrippa came next. Placing his sister Berenice, doubtless a favourite with the people, in the gallery with him, he made a long harangue. He implored them to consider the vast power of the Romans, and not, for the sake of a quarrel with one governor, to bring upon themselves the ruin of themselves, their families, and their nation. He pointed out that if they would have patience the state of their country should be fairly placed before the emperor's consideration, and he pledged himself that it would receive his best care. "Have pity," he concluded, with a burst of tears,—" have pity on your children and your wives, have pity upon this your city and its holy walls, and spare the Temple; preserve the holy house for yourselves."

The Jews, ever an impressionable race, yielded to the entreaties of Agrippa and the tears of Berenice, and making up the tribute money, paid it into the treasury. Then they began to repair the damage they had done to Antonia. All looked well; but there was one thing yet wanting to complete their submission, they were to obey Florus till he should be removed. This condition they refused to comply with, and when Agrippa urged it upon them, they threw stones at him and reproached him with the uttermost bitterness. Then Agrippa went away in despair, taking with him Berenice, and leaving the city to its fate.

The insurrection began, as it ended, with the taking of the stormy fortress of Masada near the Dead Sea. Here the Roman garrison were all slaughtered. Eleazar the son of Ananias the high priest began the insurrection in Jerusalem, by passing a law that the sacrifices of strangers were henceforth to be forbidden, and no imperial gifts to be offered. The moderate party used all their influence, but in vain, to prevent this. Agrippa sent a small army of three thousand men to help the moderates. The insurgents seized the Temple: the moderates, who included all the wealthy classes, occupied the upper city, and hostilities commenced. A great accession of strength to the insurgents was caused by the burning of the public archives, where all debts were incurred, and consequently the power of the rich was taken from them at one blow.

Then appeared on the scene another leader, for a very brief interval, Manahem, the youngest son of Judas the Galilæan. He came dressed in royal robes and surrounded with guards, no doubt eager to play the part of another Maccabæus. The insurgents took Antonia and the royal palace, and drove the Roman garrison to the three strong towns of Hippicus, Phasaelus, and Marianme. Ananias, found hidden in an aqueduct, was killed at once; and Manahem became so puffed up with his success that he became intolerable. It was easy to get rid of this mushroom king, who was deposed without any trouble by Eleazar and tortured to death. And then the Roman garrison yielded, Metilius, their commander, stipulating only for the lives of his soldiers. This was granted; but no sooner had they laid down their arms than the Jews fell upon them, vainly calling on the faith of a treaty, and murdered them all except Metilius. Him they spared on condition of his becoming a proselyte.

On that very day and hour, while the Jews were plunging their daggers in the hearts of the Romans, a great and terrible slaughter of their own people was going on in Cæsarea, where the Syrians and Greeks had risen upon the Jews, and massacred twenty thousand of them in a single day. And in every Syrian city the same madness and hatred seized the people, and the Jews were ruthlessly slaughtered in all. No more provocation was needed; no more was possible. In spite of all their turbulence, their ungovernable obstinacy, their fanaticism and pride, which made the war inevitable, and in the then state of mankind these very massacres inevitable,—one feels a profound sympathy with the people who dared to fight and die, seeing that it was hopeless to look for better things. The heads of the people began the war with gloomy forebodings; the common masses with the wildest enthusiasm, which became the mere intoxication of success when they drove back Cestius from the walls of the city, on the very eve of his anticipated victory—for Cestius hastened southwards with an army of twenty thousand men, and besieged the city. The people, divided amongst themselves, were on the point of opening the gates to the Romans, when, to the surprise of everybody, Cestius suddenly broke up his camp and began to retreat. Why he did so, no one ever knew;

possessed by a divine madness, Josephus thinks, because God would take no pity on the city and the Sanctuary. As the heavy armed Romans plodded on their way in serried ranks, they were followed by a countless multitude, gathering in numbers every hour, who assailed them with darts, with stones, and with insults. The retreat became a flight, and Cestius brought back his army with a quarter of its numbers killed, having allowed the Roman arms to receive the most terrible disgrace they had ever endured in the East.

Vespasian was sent hastily with a force of three legions, besides the cohorts of auxiliaries. A finer army had never been put into the field, nor did any army have ever harder work before them. Of the first campaign, that in Galilee, our limits will not allow us to write. In the graphic pages of Josephus, himself the hero of Jotapata, or in the still more graphic pages of Milman, may be read how the Jews fought, step by step, bringing to their defence not only the most dogged courage, but also the most ingenious devices; how the blue waves of the Lake of Galilee were reddened with the blood of those whom the Romans killed in their boats; how Vespasian broke his word and sold as slaves those he had promised to pardon; how Gamala fought and Gischala fell, and how for the sins of the people, John was permitted by Heaven to escape and become the tyrant of Jerusalem.

The months passed on, and yet the Romans appeared not before the walls of the city. This meantime was a prey to internal evils, which when read appear almost incredible. The bold rough country folk who followed John, who had fought in Galilee, and escaped the slaughter of Vespasian, came up to the city filled with one idea, that of resistance. In their eyes a Moderate, a Romanizer, was an enemy worse than a Roman, for he was a traitor to the country. They found themselves in a rich and luxurious town, filled with things of which in their distant homes they had had no idea. And these things all belonged to the Romanizers. They needed little permission to pillage, less, to murder the men who had everything to lose, and nothing to gain, by continuing the war. And then ensued a civil war, the scenes of which surpass in horror those of any other page in history. Through the streets ran the zealots dressed in fantastic garb, which they had pillaged, some of them attired as women, murdering all the rich and those who were obnoxious to their party. It is vain to follow their course of plunder, murder, and sedition. They invited the Idumæans to come to their assistance—a fierce and warlike race, who had been all Judaized since the time of Hyrcanus. These gladly came. By night, while a dreadful tempest raged overhead, a sign of God's wrath, and amid the shrieks of wounded men and despairing women, the Idumæans attacked and gained possession of the Temple, and when the day dawned eight thousand bodies lay piled within the sacred area. Among them were those of Ananus, and Jesus the son of Gamala, the high priests. Stripped naked, their corpses were thrown out to the dogs, and it was forbidden even to bury them. Simon Ben Gioras, who had first signalized himself in the defeat of Cestius, came to the city to add one more to the factions. The moderate party were stamped out and exterminated, and the city divided between John and Simon, who fought incessantly till Titus's legions appeared before the walls.

NOTE.—The materials for this chapter were chiefly found in Josephus and Milman's 'History of the Jews.' In the chapters which follow, it has not been thought necessary to name the authorities for each chapter. References will be found occasionally, among other books, to Williams's 'Holy City,' and Lewin's 'Siege of Jerusalem.'

CHAPTER II.

THE SIEGE OF JERUSALEM.

> Bella, sublimis, inclyta divitiis,
> Olim fuisti celsa ædificiis,
> Mœnibus clara, sed magis innumerum
> Civium turmis.

THE events at Rome which elevated Vespasian to the throne were the principal reasons that the siege of Jerusalem was not actually commenced till the early summer of the year 70, when, in April. Titus began his march from Cæsarea. His army consisted of four legions: the 5th, under Sextus Cerealis; the 10th, under Lartius Lepidus; the 12th, that which had suffered defeat under Cestius, and was still in disgrace, and the 15th. Besides this formidable force of regulars, he had a very large number of auxiliaries. The exact number of his troops is not easy to estimate. We may at once put aside, as clearly below the mark, the estimate which puts Titus's army at thirty thousand; for if we agree in accepting Josephus's statement* with

---

* Let us take the opportunity of stating our opinion that Josephus's testimony may generally be relied upon. It was for a long time the fashion to hold up his exaggerations to ridicule. Thus, when he spoke of the height of the wall as being such as to make the head reel, travellers remembered the fifty feet of wall or so at the present day and laughed. But Captain Warren has found that the wall was in parts as much as 200 feet high. Surely a man may

regard to Vespasian's army in the year 67, it consisted of sixty thousand, including the auxiliaries. The campaign in Galilee cost him a few, but not many, killed in the sieges. We may deduct a small number, too, but not many, for garrison work, for the conquest of the country had been, after the usual Roman fashion, thorough and complete. Not only were the people defeated, but they were slaughtered. Not only was their spirit crushed, but their powers of making even the feeblest resistance were taken away from them ;* and all those who were yet desirous of carrying on the war, those of the fanatics who escaped the sword of Vespasian, had fled to Jerusalem to fall by the sword of Titus. A very small garrison would be required for Galilee and Samaria, and we may be very sure that the large army which was with Vespasian in 67 nearly all followed Titus in 70. The legions had been filled up, and new auxiliaries had arrived.† Besides these, Josephus expressly says that the army of Vespasian, and therefore that of Titus, was accompanied by servants‡ "in vast numbers, who, because they had been trained up in war with the rest, ought not to be distinguished from the fight-

---

be excused for feeling giddy at looking down a depth of 200 feet. Whenever Josephus speaks from personal knowledge, he appears to us to be accurate and trustworthy. There is nothing on which he could speak with greater authority, which would sooner have been discovered, than a misstatement as regards the Roman army.

* Milman gives a list of the losses of the Jews in this war compiled from the numbers given by Josephus. It amounts to more than three millions. Deductions must, of course, be made.

† No argument ought to be founded on the supposed numbers of the legions. The number *generally* composing a legion in the time of the Empire was 6000, and before the Empire, was 4000. But at Pharsalia Cæsar's legions were only 2000 each, while Pompey's were 7000.

‡ It is very curious that these "servants" are not mentioned either by Mr. Lewin or Mr. Fergusson. Mr. Williams puts down the number of the legions at 10,000 each, perhaps including the servants.

ing men; for, as they were in their masters' service in times of peace, so did they undergo the like danger with them in time of war, insomuch that they were inferior to none either in skill or in strength, only they were subject to their masters."

It is not easy to make any kind of estimate of the number of these servants. Perhaps, however, we shall be within the mark if we put down the whole number of forces under Titus's command at something like eighty thousand—an army which was greatly superior in numbers to that of the besieged. It was also fully provided and equipped with military engines, provisions and material of all kinds. It marched, without meeting any enemy, from Cæsarea to Jerusalem, where it arrived on the 11th of April.*

The city, meanwhile, had been continuing those civil dissensions which hastened its ruin. John, Simon Bar Gioras, and Eleazar, each at the head of his own faction, made the streets run with blood. John, whose followers numbered six thousand, held the Lower, New, and Middle City; Simon, at the head of ten thousand Jews and five thousand Idumeans, had the strong post of the Upper City, with a portion of the third wall; Eleazar, with two thousand zealots, more fanatic than the rest, had barricaded himself within the Temple itself. There they admitted, it is true, unarmed worshippers, but kept out the rest. The stores of the Temple provided them with abundance of provisions, and while the rest of the soldiers were starving, those who were within the Temple walls † were well fed and in good case. This was, however, the only advantage which Eleazar possessed over the rest. Their position, cooped up in a narrow fortress—for such the Temple was—and exposed to a constant shower of darts,

* The dates of the siege are all taken from Professor Willis's 'Journal,' given in Williams's 'Holy City,' vol. i. p. 478.

† After Eleazar had succumbed to John.

stones, and missiles of all sorts, from John's men, was miserable enough. John and Simon fought with each other in the lower ground, the valley of the Tyropœon, which lay between the Temple and Mount Zion. Here were stored up supplies of corn sufficient, it is said, for many years' supply. But in the sallies which John and Simon made upon each other all the buildings in this part of the town were destroyed or set on fire, and all their corn burned; so that famine had actually begun before the commencement of the siege.

"And now," to quote the words of the historian, "the people of the city were like a great body torn in pieces. The aged men and the women were in such distress by their internal calamities that they wished for the Romans, and earnestly hoped for an external war, in order to deliver them from their domestic miseries. The citizens themselves were under a terrible consternation and fear; nor had they any opportunity of taking counsel and of changing their conduct; nor were there any hopes of coming to an agreement with their enemies; nor could such as wished to do so flee away, for guards were set at all places, and the chiefs of the robbers agreed in killing those who were for peace with the Romans."

Day and night, he goes on to tell us, the wretched inhabitants were harassed with the shouts of those who fought, and the lamentation of those who mourned, until through the overwhelming fear, every one for himself, relations ceased to care for each other, the living ceased to mourn for the dead, and those who were not among the defenders of the walls ceased to care for anything or to look for anything except for speedy destruction; and this even before the siege began.

And yet, with the city in this miserable and wretched condition, with the certain knowledge that the Romans were coming, the usual crowds of Jews and Idumeans flocked to the city to keep the feast of the Passover.

Their profound faith was proof against every disaster.
That the Temple should actually fall, actually be destroyed,
seems never even to have entered into their heads; and
there can be little doubt that the rude, rough, country
people, coming to keep the Passover with their wives and
children, were filled with a wild hope that the God of
Joshua was about to work some signal deliverance for
them. The population thus crowded into the city is estimated by Tacitus at six hundred thousand; by Josephus
at more than double that number. There are reasons
for believing the number at least as great as that stated by
Tacitus. A register of the buried had been kept in the
city, and the registrar of one gate, out of which the dead
were thrown, gave Josephus a note of his numbers. The
historian conversed with those who escaped. A list of the
captives would be, no doubt, made—the Romans were not
in the habit of doing things carelessly, even after a great
victory—and they would be accessible to Josephus. So far
as these go we ought to allow Josephus's right to the
consideration due to an eye-witness; and it seems to
us absolutely unwarranted by any historical or other
arguments, to put down, as has been done, the population of this city during the siege at sixty or seventy
thousand.* This was doubtless something like the ordinary population; but it was swelled tenfold and twenty-
fold by the crowds of those who came yearly to keep the
feast. Again, the argument based by Mr. Fergusson on
the area of the city fails for the simple reason that it
is founded on wrong calculations† as to the number of

* Fergusson's Art. 'Jerusalem,' Biblical Dictionary.

† Taking the shape of the city to be circular and 33 stadia in
circumference (it was more nearly circular than square), we find
its area to have been rather more than 3,500,000 square yards.
This, at 30 square yards to one person, gives about 120,000 for the
ordinary population. And there were extensive gardens and numerous villas to the north and east which contained another popu-

square yards. Moreover, it seems to assume the besieged to have been all comfortably lodged; it ignores altogether the estimate taken by Cestius; while, if the numbers adopted by Mr. Fergusson be correct, the horrors of the siege must have been grossly exaggerated, and the stories told by Josephus cannot be accepted; and, for a last objection, it appears to be assumed, what is manifestly incorrect, that every able-bodied man fought. For this vast mass of poor helpless people were like a *brutum pecus;* they took no part whatever in the fighting. Nothing is clearer than the statement made by Josephus of the fighting men. They were twenty-three thousand in all at the beginning: they did not invite help, and probably would not allow it, from the population within the walls. These, who very speedily found relief, in the thinning of death, for their first lack of accommodation, sat crouching and cowering in the houses, desperately hoping against hope, starving from the very commencement, beginning to die in heaps almost before the camp of the 10th Legion was pitched upon the Mount of Olives. The numbers given by Josephus may not be correct within a great many thousands; there is reason enough, however, to believe that, within limits very much narrower than some of his readers are disposed to believe, his numbers may be fairly depended on. After all, it matters little enough what the numbers really were; and even if we let them be what any one chooses to call them, there

---

lation altogether quite impossible to estimate. And it must not be forgotten that Cestius (Joseph. 'Bell. Jud.' vi. ix. 3) caused an estimate to be made, a very few years before the siege, of the numbers actually present at the Passover, and that the *official* return was 2,560,500 persons. The whole question is clearly stated by Mr. Williams ('Holy City,' vol. i. p. 481). And, as he points out very justly, it is not a question how many would be comfortably accommodated in Jerusalem, but how many were actually *crammed* into it.

yet remains no doubt that the sufferings of the people were very cruel, and that, of all wretched and bloody sieges in the world's history, few, if any, have been more wretched or more bloody than the siege of Jerusalem by Titus.

The people knew full well, of course, that the Romans were coming. Fear was upon all, and expectation of things great and terrible. As in all times of general excitement, signs were reported to have been seen in the heavens, and portents, which, however, might be read both ways, were observed. A star shaped like a sword, and a comet, stood over the city for a whole year. A great light had shone on the altar at the ninth hour of the night. A heifer, led up to be sacrificed, brought forth a lamb in the midst of the Temple. The eastern gate of the inner court, so heavy that it required twenty men to move it, flew open of its own accord in the night. Chariots and troops of soldiers in armour were seen running about in the clouds, and surrounding cities. When the priests were one night busy in their sacred offices, they felt the earth quaking beneath them, and heard a cry, as of a great multitude, "Let us remove hence!" And always up and down the city wandered Jesus, the son of Ananus, crying, "Woe, woe to Jerusalem!" until the siege began in earnest, when he ceased; for being on the wall, he cried, "Woe, woe to the city again! and to the people, and to the holy House!" and then, as he added, "Woe, woe to myself also!" a stone from one of the engines smote him and he died.

Titus posted the 10th Legion on the Mount of Olives, and the 12th and 15th on Mount Scopus, the 5th remaining some little distance behind. As the 10th were engaged in pitching their camp, the Jews, whose leaders had hastily patched up a kind of peace, suddenly sallied forth from the eastern gate, and marching across the valley of the Kedron, charged the Romans before they had time to form in battle. Titus himself brought a

<small>April 11.</small>

chosen body to their relief, and the Jews were, with great difficulty, driven back.

The next four days were spent in clearing the ground to the north of the city, the only part where an attack could be made. "They* threw down the hedges and walls which the people had made about their gardens and groves of trees, and cut down the fruit-trees which lay between them and the wall of the city."

The Jews, furious at sight of this destruction, made a sally, pretending at first to be outcasts from the city, and hiding their weapons until they were close upon the enemy. On this occasion the Romans were utterly routed, and fled, pursued by the Jews "as far as Helen's monument." It was a gleam of sunshine, and nearly the only gleam that fell to the lot of the besieged. Titus removed his camp to the north side of the city, and, leaving the 10th still on the Mount of Olives, placed the 5th on the west of the city, over against the towers of Hippicus and Pharsaelus, and the 12th and 15th on the north. A cordon of men, seven deep, was drawn round the north and west of the city. This must have taken some twenty-five thousand men to effect.

April 23. On the morning of the Passover, John contrived —taking advantage of the permission freely granted to all who chose to enter the Temple unarmed—to send in his own men, choosing those whose features were not known to Eleazar's followers, with concealed weapons. Directly they got into the Inner Temple, they made an attack on the men of the opposite faction. A good many were slaughtered, and the rest, finding it best to yield, made terms with their conquerors, Eleazar's life being spared. There now remained only two factions in the city, Simon holding the strongest place—the Palace of Herod, which commanded the Upper Town—and John the Temple

---

* Joseph. 'Bell. Jud.' v. iii. 2.

Fortress, without which the Lower Town could not be taken.

It was determined to begin the assault with the north-western part of the wall, that part of it where the valley turns in a north-westerly direction and leaves a level space between the wall and its own course. The engines used by the Romans were those always employed in the conduct of a siege—the ballistæ, the towers, and the battering rams. Then banks were constructed, on each of which was a tower and a ram. In the construction of these last all the trees round Jerusalem were cut down. Nor have they ever been replanted, and a thousand years later on the siege of the city by the Crusaders, only inferior in horror to that of Titus, nearly miscarried for want of timber to construct the towers of assault.

As soon as the banks were sufficiently advanced the battering rams were mounted and the assault commenced. The Jews, terrified by the thunder of the rams against the city, annoyed, too, by the stones which came into the city from the ballistæ, joined their forces and tried a sortie from a secret gate near Hippicus. Their object was to destroy the machines by fire; and in this they well-nigh succeeded, fighting with a desperation and courage which no Roman troops had ever before experienced. Titus himself was in the conflict; he killed twelve Jews with his own hands; but the Romans would have given way had it not been for the reinforcement of some Alexandrian troops who came up at the right moment and drove back the Jews.

On the fifteenth day of the siege the biggest battering ram, "Nikon," the Conqueror, effected a breach in the outer wall. The Jews, panic-stricken, forgot their wonted courage and took refuge within the second wall. Titus became therefore master of Bezetha, in the New Town; forming about a third of the city.

As nothing is said about the population of this, which was probably only a suburb and never actually filled with people till the siege began, we may suppose that very early in the assault they hastened out of reach of the ballistæ and arrows by fleeing to the inner city. And by this time a fortnight of the siege had passed away and already their numbers were grievously thinned by starvation.

Between the palace of Herod and the Temple area there stretched the second wall across the Tyropœon valley, which was filled, before the faction fights of Simon and John, with houses of the lower sort of people. This was the most densely populated part of the city. The wall which defended it was not so strong as the rest of the fortifications, and in five days, including an unsuccessful attempt to storm the palace of Herod, a breach was effected and the Romans poured into the town, Titus at their head.

In hopes of detaching the people from the soldiers, Titus ordered that no houses should be destroyed, no property pillaged, and the lives of the people spared. It was an act of mercy which the fierce passions of the Jews interpreted as a sign of weakness, and renewing their contest, fighting hand to hand in the streets, from the houses, from the walls, they beat the Romans back, and recaptured their wall, filling the breach with their own bodies. The battle lasted for four days more when Titus, entering again, threw down the whole northern part of the wall and became master of the whole Lower Town.

Partly to give his troops rest, partly to exhibit his power before the Jews, Titus gave orders that the paying of the troops should be made the opportunity for a review of the whole army almost under the walls of the city, and in full view of the besieged. The pageant lasted four days, during which there was a grand march-past of the splendid Roman troops, with burnished armour and weapons, and in full uniform.

"So the soldiers, according to custom, opened the cases where their arms before lay covered, and marched with their breastplates on; as did the horsemen lead the horses in their fine trappings. . . . The whole of the old wall and the north side of the Temple were full of spectators, and one might see the houses full of such as looked at them; nor was there any part of the city which was not covered over with their multitudes; nay, a great consternation seized upon the hardiest of the Jews themselves, when they saw all the army in the same place, together with the success of their arms and the good order of the men."*

The Jews saw and trembled. But they did not submit. There could be no longer any hope. The multitude, pent up in limits too narrow for one-tenth of their number, daily obtained more room by death, for they died by thousands. The bodies were thrown out into the valleys, where they lay rotting, a loathsome mass. Roaming bands of soldiers went up and down the city looking for food. When they came upon a man who looked fat and well-fed they tortured him till he told the secret of his store: to be starving or to appear to be starving was the only safety: and "now," says Josephus, "all hope of escaping was cut off from the Jews, together with their liberty of going out of the city. Then did the famine widen its progress, and devoured the people by whole houses and families; the upper rooms were full of women and children that were dying by famine; and the lanes of the city were full of the dead bodies of the aged; the children also and the young men wandered about the market-places like shadows, all swelled with the famine, and fell down dead wheresoever their misery seized them. As for burying them, those that were sick themselves were not able to do it; and those that were hearty and well, were deterred from doing it by the great multitude of those dead bodies, and by the uncertainty there was how

* Joseph. 'Bell. Jud.' y. ix. 1.

soon they should die themselves; for many died as they were burying others, and many went to their coffins before that fatal hour was come! Nor was there any lamentation made under these calamities, nor were heard any mournful complaints; but the famine confounded all natural passions; for those who were just going to die, looked upon those that were gone to their rest before them with dry eyes and open mouths. A deep silence also, and a kind of deadly night, had seized upon the city; while yet the robbers were still more terrible than these miseries were themselves; for they brake open those houses which were no other than graves of dead bodies, and plundered them of what they had; and carrying off the coverings of their bodies, went out laughing, and tried the points of their swords on their dead bodies; and, in order to prove what mettle they were made of, they thrust some of those through that still lay alive upon the ground; but for those that entreated them to lend them their right hand, and their sword to despatch them, they were too proud to grant their requests, and left them to be consumed by the famine. Now every one of these died with their eyes fixed upon the Temple. Children pulled the very morsels that their fathers were eating out of their very mouths, and what was still more to be pitied, so did the mothers do as to their infants; and when those that were most dear were perishing under their hands, they were not ashamed to take from them the very last drops that might preserve their lives; and while they ate after this manner, yet were they not concealed in so doing; but the seditious everywhere came upon them immediately, and snatched away from them what they had gotten from others; for when they saw any house shut up, this was to them a signal that the people within had gotten some food; whereupon they broke open the doors, and ran in, and took pieces of what they were eating, almost up out of their very throats, and this by force: the old men, who held their food fast, were beaten; and if the women hid what they had within their hands, their hair was torn for so doing; nor was there any commiseration shown either to the aged or to infants, but they lifted up children from the ground as they hung upon the morsels they had gotten, and shook them down upon the floor; but still were they more barbarously cruel to those that had prevented their coming in, and had actually swallowed down what they were going to seize upon, as if they had been unjustly defrauded of their right. They also invented terrible methods of torment to discover where any food was, and a man was forced to bear what it is terrible even to hear, in order to make him confess that he had but one loaf of bread, or that he might discover a handful of barley-meal that was concealed; this was done when these tormentors were not themselves hungry; for the thing had been less barbarous had necessity forced them to it; but it was done to keep their madness in exercise, and as making preparation of provisions for themselves for the following days."

At night the miserable wretches would steal into the ravines, those valleys where the dead bodies of their children, their wives, and kin, were lying in putrefying masses, to gather roots which might serve for food. The lot of these was pitiable indeed. If they remained outside they were captured by the Romans, and crucified, sometimes five hundred in a morning, in full view of the battlements: if they went back laden with a few poor roots of the earth, they were robbed by the soldiers at the gate, and sent home again to their starving children, starving themselves, and unable to help them.

The cruelty of Titus, designed to terrify the Jews, only stimulated them to fresh courage. Why, indeed, should they surrender? Death was certain for all; it was better to die fighting, to kill one of the enemy at least, than to die amid the jeers of the triumphant soldiers. Besides, we must remember that they were defending their sacred mountain, their Temple, the place to which every Jew's heart looked with pride and fondness, whither turned the eyes of those who died with a sort of sad reproach. Simon and John were united in this feeling alone—that it was the highest duty of a Jew to fight for his country. The portraits of these two commanders have been drawn by an enemy's hand. We must remember that the prolonged resistance of the Jews was a standing reproof to Josephus, who had been defeated, captured, and taken into favour. No epithets, on his part, can be too strong to hurl at John and Simon. It is impossible now to know what were the real characters of these men, whether they were religious patriots, or whether they were filled with the basest and most selfish motives. One thing is quite certain and may be said of both: if John hated Simon much, he loved the city more. Neither, at the worst moment, hinted at a surrender of the town; neither tried to curry favour for himself by compassing the fall of his adversary.

And the Jews, though emaciated by hunger, reeling and fainting for weakness, were yet full of courage and resource. While Titus was spending seventeen days of arduous labour in getting ready his new banks against the Temple, the Jews were busy burrowing beneath his feet; and when the rams had been mounted and already were beginning to play, a subterranean rumbling was heard, and the works of weeks fell suddenly to the ground.

"The Romans had much ado to finish their banks after labouring hard for seventeen days continually. There were now four great banks raised, one of which was at the tower of Antonia; this was raised by the 5th Legion, over against the middle of that pool which was called Struthius. Another was cast up by the 12th Legion, at the distance of about twenty cubits from the other. But the labours of the 10th legion, which lay a great way off these, were on the north quarter, and at the pool called Amygdalon; as was that of the 15th legion, about thirty cubits from it, and at the high priest's monument. And now, when the engines were brought, John had from within undermined the space that was over-against the tower of Antonia, as far as the banks themselves, and had supported the ground over the mine with beams laid across one another, whereby the Roman works stood upon an uncertain foundation. Then did he order such materials to be brought in as were daubed over with pitch and bitumen, and set them on fire; and as the cross beams that supported the banks were burning, the ditch yielded on the sudden, and the banks were shaken down, and fell into the ditch with a prodigious noise. Now at the first there arose a very thick smoke and dust, as the fire was choked with the fall of the bank; but as the suffocated materials were now gradually consumed, a flame brake out; on which sudden appearance of the flame a consternation fell upon the Romans, and the shrewdness of the contrivance discouraged them; and indeed, this accident coming upon them at a time when they thought they had already gained their point, cooled their hopes for the time to come. They also thought it would be to no purpose to take the pains to extinguish the fire, since, if it were extinguished, the banks were swallowed up already [and become useless] to them."

The other banks against the west wall were not more fortunate. For Simon's soldiers, with torches in their hands, rushed out suddenly when the engines were beginning to shake the walls. They seized the iron of the engines, which was red hot, and despite this held them till the wood was consumed. The Romans retreated: the guards, who would not desert their post, fell in numbers, and Titus found his whole army wavering under the attacks of a half-starved and haggard mob, whose courage arose from despair. And the engines had all been burned, the labour of three weeks gone. Titus held a council to decide what should next be done. It was resolved, on his own suggestion, that a wall of circumvallation should be raised round the city, and that a strict blockade, cutting off all communication with the country, should be established, until starvation should force a surrender.

The wall, which was probably little more than a breastwork, though strong and solid, was completed, together with thirteen external redoubts, in three days,* every soldier giving his labour. No attempt seems to have been made by the Jews to prevent or hinder the work. Probably they were too weak to attempt any more sorties. A strict watch was set by the Romans—up to this time the blockade does not seem to have been complete—and no one was allowed to approach the wall. And now the last feeble resource of the Jews, the furtive gathering of roots under the city walls, was denied them; and the sufferings of the besieged became too great for any historian to relate. Titus himself, stoic though he was, and resolute to succeed in spite of any suffering, called God to witness, with tears in his eyes, that this was not his doing.

Even the obstinacy of the Jews gave way under these sufferings, and more than one attempt was made to introduce the Romans. Matthias opened a communication with the enemy. He was detected, and, with three sons, was executed. One Judas, the son of Judas, who was in command of a tower in the Upper City, concerted with ten of his men, and invited the Romans to come up and take the tower. Had Titus at once ordered a troop to mount, the Upper City might have been easily taken. But he had been too often deceived by feints, and hesitated.

---

* This alone is sufficient to prove the extent of Titus's army. An army of thirty thousand would be utterly unable to accomplish such a work in three days.

The plot was discovered, and Judas, with his ten fellows, was hurled over the ramparts at the feet of the Romans.

It was then that Josephus, whom of all men the besieged hated, was wounded in the head, but not seriously, by a stone. The Jews made a tremendous acclamation at seeing this, and sallied forth for a sortie, in the excess of their joy. Josephus, senseless, was taken up and conveyed away, but the next day reappeared and once more offered the clemency of Titus to those who would come out. The hatred which his countrymen bore to Josephus, as to an apostate, natural enough, shows remarkably the love of justice which in all times has distinguished the Jew. His father and mother were in the city. They were not, till late in the siege, interfered with in any way: and his father was set in prison at last, more, apparently, to vex his son than with any idea of doing him an injury.*

The miserable state of the city drove hundreds to desert. They came down from the walls, or they made a pretended sortie and passed over to the Romans; but here a worse fate accompanied them, in spite of Josephus's promises, for Josephus had not reckoned on the expectation that the Jews, famishing and mad for food, would, as proved the case, cause their own death by over-eating at first. And a more terrible danger awaited them. It was rumoured about that the deserters swallowed their gold before leaving the city, and the auxiliaries in the Roman camp, Arabians and Syrians, seized the suppliants, and fairly cut them open to find the gold. And though Titus was incensed when he heard of it, and prohibited it strictly, he could not wholly stop the practice, and the knowledge of this cruelty getting into the city stopped many who would otherwise have escaped: they remained to die.

---

* Josephus narrates how his mother wept at the false report of his death, and quotes with complacency her lamentation that she had brought so distinguished a man into the world for so early a death.

One of those who kept the register of burials and paid the bearers of the dead, told Josephus that out of his gate alone 115,880 bodies had been thrown since the siege began, and many citizens, whose word could be depended on, estimated the number who had died at 600,000.

Banks, meanwhile, were gradually rising against the fortress of Antonia. The Romans had swept the country clear of trees for ninety furlongs round to find timber for their construction: they took twenty-one days to complete, and were four in number. The besieged no longer made the same resistance. Their courage, says Josephus, was no longer Jewish, "for they failed in what is peculiar to our nation, in boldness, violence of assault, and running upon the enemy all together . . . but they now went out in a more languid manner than before . . . and they reproached one another for cowardice, and so retired without doing anything." The attacks of the enemy were, however, courageously defended. For a whole day the Romans endeavoured with rams to shake the wall, and with crows and picks to undermine its foundations. Darkness made them withdraw, and during the night the wall, which had been grievously shaken, fell of its own accord.

But even this calamity had been foreseen by the defenders, and, to the astonishment and even dismay of Titus, a new wall was found built up behind the old, and the Jews upon it, ready to defend it with their old spirit. Titus exhorted his soldiers, who were getting dejected at the renewal of the enemy's obstinacy, and offered the highest rewards to him who would first mount the wall. His exhortation, like the rest of the speeches in Josephus, is written after the grand historic style, and embodies all those sentiments which a general ought to feel under the circumstances, together with a verbosity and length quite sufficient to deprive it of all hortatory effect.

One Sabinus, with only eleven others, made the attempt. He alone reached the top of the wall, and after a gallant fight was killed by the Jews. His followers were also either killed or wounded. Two days afterwards "twelve of the men who were in the front," to give the story in Josephus's own words, "got together, and calling to them the standard-bearer of the fifth legion and two others of a troop of horse, and one trumpeter, went out noiselessly about the ninth hour of the night through the ruins to the tower of Antonia. They found the guards of the place asleep, cut their throats, got possession of the wall, and ordered the trumpeter to sound his trumpet. Upon this the rest of the guard got up suddenly and ran away before anybody could see how many they were who had got into the tower." Titus heard the signal and came to the place. The Jews, in their haste to escape, fell themselves into the mine which John had dug under the banks; they rallied again, however, at the entrance of the Temple, and the most determined fight, in a narrow and confined space, took place there. The Temple was not to fall quite yet, and after a whole day's battle the Romans had to fall back, masters, however, of Antonia.

July 17. But on that very day the daily sacrifice failed for the first time, and with it the spirit of the starving besieged.

The end, now, was not far off. In seven days nearly the whole of Antonia, excepting the south-east tower, was pulled down and a broad way opened for the Roman army to march to the attack of the Temple. Cloisters, as we have seen, united the fortress with the Temple, and along these either on the flat roofs or along the galleries.*

And now many of the priests and higher classes deserted the falling city and threw themselves upon the clemency of Titus. They were received with kindness and sent to Gophna. John's last resource was to pretend they

---

* Mr. Lewin makes this very clear. It seems to us to be made still clearer by taking his graphic description and applying it to any plan which follows the old traditions.

had all been murdered, and Titus was obliged to parade them before the walls to satisfy the suspicions thus raised.

An attempt was made to take the Temple by a night attack. This, however, failed, and Titus foresaw the necessity of raising new banks. Fighting went on daily in the cloisters, until the Jews set fire to them, and occasional sorties were made by the besieged in hopes to catch the enemy at unguarded moments.

The banks were finished on the 1st of August. Titus ordered that they should be brought and set over against the western wall of the inner Temple. For six days the battering rams played against the masonry of the inner Temple, for by this time the beautiful cloisters which surrounded it, and ran from east to west, were all destroyed, and the inner Temple, a fortress in itself, stood naked and alone, the last refuge of John and his men. Had they yielded this at least would have been spared. But it was not to be. With a pertinacity which had no longer any hope in it the obstinate zealots held out. On the north side the Romans undermined the gate, but could not bring it down; they brought ladders and endeavoured to tunnel the wall. The Jews allowed them to mount, and then killed every one and captured their ensigns. And thus it was that Titus, fearing perhaps that the spirit of his own troops would give way, ordered the northern gate to be set on fire. This was done, and the cloisters, not those of the outer court, but of the inner, were soon destroyed. But Titus resolved still to save the Holy of Holies.

Aug. 9. It was the day on which Nebuchadnezzar had burned the Temple of Solomon. The Jews made another sortie, their last but one. They could effect nothing, and retired after five hours' fighting into their stronghold, the desecrated Temple, on whose altar no more sacrifices were now made, or ever would be made again.

Titus retired to Antonia, resolving to take the place the next day; but the Jews would not wait so long. They made a last sortie, which was ineffectual. "The Romans put the Jews to flight, and proceeded as far as the holy House itself. At which time one of the soldiers, without staying for any orders, and without any concern or dread upon him at so great an undertaking, and being hurried on by a certain divine fury, snatched somewhat out of the materials that were on fire, and being lifted up by another soldier, set fire to a golden window, through which there was a passage to the rooms that were round about the holy House, on the north side of it. As the flames went upward the Jews made a great clamour, such as so mighty an affliction required, and ran together to prevent it; and now they spared not their lives any longer, nor suffered anything to restrain their force, since that holy House was perishing, for whose sake it was that they kept such a guard about it."*

Titus, with all his staff, hastened to save what he could. He exhorted the soldiers to spare the building. He stood in the Holy of Holies itself, and beat back the soldiers who were pressing to the work of destruction. But in vain: one of the soldiers threw a torch upon the gateway of the sanctuary, and in a moment the fate of the building was sealed. And while the flames mounted higher the carnage of the poor wretches within went on. None was spared; ten thousand were killed that were found there—children, old men, priests and profane persons, all alike; six thousand fled to the roof of the royal cloister, that glorious building which crowned the Temple wall to the south, stretching from "Robinson's Arch" to the valley of the Kedron. The Romans fired that too, and the whole of the multitude perished together.

"One would have thought that the hill itself, on which the Temple stood, was seething hot, full of fire in every part; that the blood was larger in quantity than the fire;

---

* Joseph. vi. iv. 5.

and those that were slain more in number than those that slew them, for the ground nowhere appeared visible for the dead bodies that lay on it; but the soldiers went over heaps of these bodies as they ran from such as fled from them."*

The really guilty among the Jews, the fighting men, had cut their way through the Romans and fled to the upper city. A few priests either hid themselves in secret chambers or crouched upon the top of the wall. On the fifth day they surrendered, being starving. Titus ordered them to execution.

And so the Temple of Herod fell.

The Roman army flocked into the ruins of the Temple which it had cost them so many lives to take; sacrifices were offered, and Titus was saluted as Imperator. An immense spoil was found there, not only from the sacred vessels of gold, but from the treasury, in which vast sums had been accumulated. The upper town, Zion, still held out. Titus demanded a parley. Standing on that bridge, the ruined stones of which were found by Captain Warren lying eighty feet below the surface of the ground, he for the last time offered terms to the insurgents. He explained that they could no longer entertain any hope, even the slightest, of safety, and renewed his offers of clemency to those who should yield.

But the offers of Titus were supposed to be the effect of weakness. Again the insurgents, now indeed possessed with a divine madness, declined them. They demanded that they might be allowed to march out with all their arms, and what would now be called the honours of war. This proposition from a handful of starved soldiers surrounded by the ruins of all that they held dear, with a triumphant army on all sides, was too monstrous to be accepted even by the most clement of conquerors, and Titus resolved with reluctance on the destruction of the

---

* Joseph. vi. v. 1.

whole people. The royal family of Adiabene, descendants of Queen Helena, had not left Jerusalem during the siege; on the contrary, they had lent every aid in their power to the Jews. Now, however, seeing that no hope was to be got from any but Titus, they went over in a body to the Romans and prayed for mercy. Out of consideration for their royal blood this was granted. But the Jews revenged the fainthearted conduct of these royal proselytes by an incursion into the lower New Town (on the Hill of Ophel), burning their palace and sacking the rest of the town. The last part of the siege, which Mr. Lewin finely calls the fifth act of a bloody tragedy, was commenced by the usual methods of raising banks, all attempts to carry the Upper City by assault being hopeless. These were raised over against the Palace of Herod on the west, and at a point probably opposite Robinson's Arch in the east.. And now, at the last moment, no longer sustained by any hopes of miraculous interference,—for if their God had allowed his Temple to fall, why should he be expected to spare the citadel?—the Jews lost all courage and began to desert in vast numbers. The Idumeans, finding that Simon and John remained firm in their resolution of defence to the last, sent five of their chiefs to open negotiations on their own account. Simon and John discovered the plot; the five commissioners were executed; care was taken to entrust the walls to trusty guards, but thousands of the people managed to escape. The Romans began by slaying the fugitives, but, tired of slaughter, reserved them as prisoners to be sold for slaves. Those who were too old or too worn out by suffering to be of any use they sent away to wander about the mountains, and live or die. One priest obtained his life by giving up to Titus the sacred vessels of the Temple, and another by showing where the treasures were—the vestments of the priests, and the vast stores of spices which had been used for burning incense daily.

Sept. 8. It took eighteen days to complete the siege-works. At last the banks were ready to receive the battering-rams, and these were placed in position. But little defence was made. Panic-stricken and cowering, the hapless Jews awaited the breach in the wall, and the incoming of the enemy. Simon and John, with what force they could collect, abandoned the towers, and rushed to attempt an escape over Titus's wall of circumvallation at the south. It was hopeless. They were beaten back; the leaders hid themselves in the subterranean chambers with which Jerusalem was honeycombed, and the rest stood still to be killed. The Romans, pouring into the town, began by slaying all indiscriminately. Tiring of butchery they turned their thoughts to plunder; but the houses were filled with dead and putrefying corpses, so that they stood in horror at the sight, and went out without touching anything. "But although they had this commiseration for such as were destroyed in this manner, yet had they not the same for those that were still alive; and they ran every one through whom they met with, and obstructed the streets with dead bodies, and made the whole city run with blood to such a degree, indeed, that the fire of many of the houses was quenched with their men's blood."

And then they set fire to the houses, and all was over.

As for the prisoners who remained alive, they were destined to the usual fate of slaves. To fight as gladiators; to afford sport among the wild beasts in the theatres; and to work for life in the mines, was their miserable lot. Woe, indeed, to the conquered in those old wars, where defeat meant death, whose least cruel form was the stroke of the headsman, or, worse than death, life, whose least miserable portion was perpetual slavery in the mines. It would have been well had Josephus, after narrating the scenes which he tells so well, gone to visit these his miserable fellow-countrymen in slavery, and described for us, if he could, the wretchedness of their after-life, the unspeakable degradation and misery which the Jew, more than any other man, would feel, in his condition of slavery. Their history began with the slavery in Egypt: to these unfortunate captives it would seem as if it was to end with slavery in Egypt.

The Romans, knowing that Jerusalem had a sort of subterranean city of excavated chambers beneath it, proceeded to search for hiding insurgents and for hidden wealth. The chambers were, like the houses, often full of dead bodies. They found fugitives in some of them; these they put to death. In others they found treasure; in others they found corpses.

Simon and John were not among the prisoners, nor were they among the killed. John, several days after the capture of the city, came out voluntarily from his hiding-place, and gave himself up to Titus. He was reserved for the triumph. And then came the grand day of rejoicing for the conquerors. Titus made a long and laudatory oration to the army, adjudged promotions, coronets, necklaces, and other prizes of valour, and with lavish hand distributed the spoils among his soldiers. For three days the troops banqueted and rejoiced. Then Titus broke up his camp, and departed for Cæsarea with the 5th and 15th Legions, leaving the 10th, under Terentius Rufus, to guard the city, and sending the 12th to the banks of the Euphrates.*

It was not till October that Simon gave himself up. To prevent being killed at once, he emerged by night from his hiding-place dressed in a long white robe, so that the astonished soldiers took him for a ghost. "I am Simon, son of Gioras," he cried. "Call hither your general." Terentius received him as a prisoner, and sent him to Titus.

One of the most important things in the conduct of a

* Joseph. vii. v. 3.

triumph at Rome was the execution of the general of the vanquished army. Titus had both generals to grace his procession. He assigned to Simon the post of honour. At the foot of the Capitoline Hill the intrepid Jew was led to the block, with a halter round his neck, and scourged cruelly. He met his death with the same undaunted courage as he had defended his city. John of Giscala remained a prisoner for life.

No historian, except perhaps Milman, whose sympathies are ever with the fallen cause, seems to us to have done justice, not only to the bravery and heroism of the Jews, but also to the heroism of their leaders. Their leaders have been described by an enemy and a rival—that Josephus, son of Matthias, who, after making an heroic resistance at Jotapata, obtained his life by pretending to be a prophet, and continued in favour with the conquerors by exhorting his fellow-countrymen to submission. That Simon and John were men stained with blood, violent, headstrong, we know well; but it does not seem to us that they were so bad and worthless as Josephus would have us to believe. After the siege fairly began they united their forces: we hear no more of the faction-fights. If their soldiers committed excesses and cruelties, they were chiefly for food; and everything was to give way to the preservation of the defenders. Moreover, discipline was not thought of among the Jews, whose notion of fighting was chiefly a blind and headlong rush. But we must again recall the religious side of the defence. To the Jew his Temple was more, far more, than Mecca can ever be to a Mohammedan. It had traditions far higher and more divine. The awful presence of Jehovah had filled the sanctuary as with a cloud. His angels had been seen on the sacred hill. There, for generation after generation, the sacrifice had been offered, the feast kept, the unsullied faith maintained. The Temple was a standing monument to remind them by whose aid they had escaped captivity;

it taught them perpetually that freedom was the noblest thing a man can have; it was the glorious memorial of a glorious history; it was a reminder that theirs was a nation set apart from the rest of the world. To defend the Temple from outrage and pollution was indeed the bounden duty of every Jew. And these Romans, what would they do with it? Had they not the keys of the treasury where the vestments of the priests were laid up? Had not one of their emperors ordered a statue of himself to be set up, an impious idol, in the very Holy of Holies?

A handful of men, they offered war to the mistress of the world. True, the insurgents were rude and unlettered, who knew nothing of Rome and her power. Even if they had known all that Rome could do, it would have mattered nothing, for they were fighting for the defence of all that made life sweet to them; and they were sustained by false prophets, poor brainstruck visionaries, who saw the things they wished to see, and foretold what they wished to happen. God might interfere; the mighty arm which had protected them of old might protect them again. The camp of the Romans might be destroyed like the camp of the Assyrians; and because these things might happen, it was a natural step, to an excited and imaginative people, to prophesy that they would happen. But when the time passed by, when none of these things came to pass, and the deluded multitude hoped that submission would bring safety at least, the tenacity of their leaders held them chained to a hopeless defence. Whether Simon and John fought on with a stronger faith, and still in hope that the arm of the Lord would be stretched out, or whether they fought on with the desperate courage of soldiers who preferred death by battle to death by execution, it is impossible now to say.

It has been suggested by Josephus, as well as by modern writers, that the courage of the Jews was shaken by predictions, omens, and rumours; but if there were predictions of disaster, there were also predictions of triumph. If Jesus, whom a few called Christ, had prophesied the coming fall of the city, there were others who had announced the fall of the enemy. Omens could be read either way. If a sword-shaped comet hung in the sky, who could deny that the sword impended over the heads of the Romans? And when the gate of the Temple flew open, did it not announce the opening of the gates for the triumph of the faithful? In that wild, unsettled time, when there was nothing certain, nothing stable, the very faith of the people would be intensified by these prophecies of disaster; their courage would be strengthened by the gloomy foretellers of defeat; and, as the Trojans fought none the worse because Cassandra was with them, so the Jews fought none the worse because voices were whispering among them about the prophecies of him whom some recognised as the Messiah.

Let us, at least, award them the meed of praise for a courage which has never been equalled. Let us acknowledge that, in all the history of the world, if there has been no siege more bloody and tragic, so there has been no city more fiercely contested, more obstinately defended; and though we may believe that the fall of Jerusalem had been distinctly prophesied by our Lord, we must not therefore look on the Jews as the blind and fated victims of prophecy. The city fell, not in order to fulfil prophecy, but because the Jews were, as they ever had been, a turbulent, self-willed race; because they were undisciplined, because they loved freedom above everything else in the world except their religion; and their religion was the ritual and the Temple.

CHAPTER III.

FROM TITUS TO OMAR.

> "Wild Hours, that fly with hope and fear,
>   If all your office had to do
>   With old results that look like new,
> If this were all your mission here,
>
> "To draw, to sheathe a useless sword,
>   To fool the crowd with glorious lies,
>   To cleave a creed in sects and cries,
> To change the bearing of a word.
>
> * * * *
>
> "Why then my scorn might well descend
>   On you and yours. I see in part
>   That all, as in some piece of art,
> Is toil co-operant to an end."
>
> *In Memoriam.*

Its Temple destroyed, its people killed, led captive, or dispersed, Jerusalem must have presented, for the next fifty years, at least, a dreary and desolate appearance. At first its only inhabitants were the Roman garrison, but gradually the Jews came dropping in, at first, we may suppose, on sufferance and good behaviour. When the Christians returned is not certain. Eusebius says that directly after the destruction of Jerusalem, they assembled together and chose Simeon as their bishop; but he does not say that they gathered together in Jerusalem. All the traditions represent them as returning very soon after the siege. As for the Jews, the destruction of the Temple—that symbol of the law—only made them more scrupulous in their obedience to the Law. The great school of Gamaliel was set up at Jabneh, where lectures were delivered on all the minutiæ of Rabbinical teaching, and the Jews were instructed how to win the favour of Jehovah by carrying out to its last letter the smallest details of the Law. And because this, minute as it was, did not comprehend all the details of life, there arose a caste, recruited from all tribes and families alike, which became more holy than that of the priests and Levites—the caste of the Rabbis, the students and interpreters of the Law. The Rabbi had, besides the written law, the Tradition, *Masora*, or *Cabala*, which was pretended to have been also given to Moses on Mount Sinai, and to have been handed down in an unbroken line through the heads of the Sanhedrim. The growth of the Rabbinical power does not date from the destruction of the Temple; it had been slowly developing itself for many centuries before that event. In the synagogues which were scattered all over Palestine, and wherever the Jews could be got together, the learned Rabbi, with his profound knowledge of the Law, written and oral, had already, before the destruction of Jerusalem, taken the place of the priests and their sacrifices; so that, in spite of the fall of the Temple, the spiritual life of the Jews was by no means crushed out of them. Rather was it deepened and intensified, and their religious observances more and more invaded the material life. The Rabbinical tribunals usurped entire rule over the Jews. Like the Scotch elders, they had power to summon before them persons accused of immorality, persons who neglected their children, persons who violated details of the Law. They could also impose on offenders punishment by scourging, by censure, by interdict, by the *cherem*, or excommunication, which inflicted civil death, but for which pardon might be obtained on repentance and submission, and, lastly, by the fatal *shammata*, the final curse, after which there was no pardon possible: "Let nothing good come out of him; let his end be sudden; let all creatures become his enemies; let the whirlwind crush him; let fever and every other malady, and the edge of the sword, smite him; let his death be unforeseen, and drive him into outer darkness."* With this machinery of internal government, the Jews were not only united together and separated from the rest of the world, in each particular town, not only did they maintain their nationality and their religion, but, which was of much more importance to their conquerors, they were able to act in concert with each other, to demand redress together, to give help to each other, to rise in revolt together.

As for their treatment by the Romans, it is not certain that they were at first persecuted at all. A tax of two drachms was levied by Vespasian on every Jew for the rebuilding of the Temple of Jupiter Capitolinus, and was exacted with the greatest rigour. He also searched everywhere for descendants of the House of David, in order to extinguish the royal line altogether; otherwise there is no evidence to show that the Jews were ill-treated by the conquerors, but rather the contrary, because the policy of the Romans was always to treat the conquered nations with consideration and humanity, and to extend to them the privilege of citizenship. But whether they were persecuted or not, and whatever the cause, the whole of the Jews in Egypt, Cyrene, Babylonia, and Judæa, rose in universal revolt in the time of Trajan. Perhaps they had experienced some affront to their religion; perhaps they had been persecuted with the Christians; perhaps they expected the Messiah; perhaps their fanatical and turbulent spirit was the cause of the rising; perhaps the stories

---

* Milman, 'Hist. of the Jews,' iii. 146.

told in the Rabbinical accounts contain some truth. In these it is related how the birthday of an Imperial Prince fell on the 9th of August, the anniversary of the taking of Jerusalem, and the Jews in Rome were wailing and lamenting while the rest of the world was rejoicing. Also, on another occasion, while the Imperial family were lamenting the death of a daughter, the Jews were celebrating, with the customary semblance of joy, their Feast of Lamps. Heavy persecution followed these unfortunate coincidences.

The hostility of the Jews was manifested against the Greeks rather than against the Romans. In Alexandria the Greeks massacred all the Jews. In return the Jews, under Lucuas and Andrew, spread themselves over the whole of Lower Egypt, and perpetrated ghastly atrocities. The Roman Governor, meantime, could do nothing for want of troops. In Cyprus the Jews are said to have killed two hundred and forty thousand of their fellow-citizens. Hadrian came to their rescue, and fairly swept the insurgents out of the island, where in memory of these troubles no Jew has ever since been allowed to reside. Martius Turbo quieted the insurrection in Cyrene, and then marched into Egypt, where he found Lucuas at the head of an enormous army. Mindful, as all Jewish insurgents, of his people's traditions, and no doubt hoping for another miracle, Lucuas tried to pass by way of Suez into Palestine; but, no miracle being interposed, he and his men were all cut to pieces. Then the Jews of Mesopotamia rose in their turn, impatient of a change of masters which gave them the cold and stern Roman, in place of their friends, and sometimes coreligionists, the Parthians. The revolt was quelled by Lucius Quietus, who was appointed to the government of Judæa; and when Trajan died, and Hadrian ascended the throne, all the conquests in the East beyond the Euphrates were abandoned: the Jews across that river settled peacefully down with their old masters again; and henceforward the tranquillity of these trans-Euphrates Jews wonderfully contrasts with the turbulence and ferocity of their Syrian brethren. But Hadrian resolved to suppress this troublesome and turbulent Judaism altogether. He forbade circumcision, the reading of the Law, the observance of the Sabbaths; and he resolved to convert Jerusalem into a Roman colony. And then, because the Jews could no longer endure their indignities, and because before the dawn they ever looked for the darkest hour, the most cruel wrong, there arose Barcochebas, the "Son of the Star," and led away their hearts, in the belief that he was indeed the Messiah. This, the last, was the wildest and the most bloodthirsty of all the Jewish revolts.

The Messiah, the rumour ran forth among all Jews in all lands, had come at last, and the prophecy of Balaam was fulfilled. The mission of the pretender was recognised by no less a person than Akiba, the greatest of living doctors, perhaps the greatest of all Jewish doctors. He, when he saw Barcochebas, exclaimed loudly, "Behold the Messiah!" "Akiba," replied Rabbi Johannan Ben Torta, whose faith was perhaps as strong, but whose imagination was not so active as his learned brother's, " the grass will be growing through your jaws before the Messiah comes." But Akiba's authority prevailed.

Rabbi Akiba, according to the story of the Rabbis, traced his descent from Sisera, through a Jewish mother. He was originally a poor shepherd boy, employed to tend the sheep belonging to a rich Jew named Calva Sheva. He fell in love with his master's daughter, and was refused her hand on the ground of his poverty and lowness of condition. He married her secretly, went away and studied the Law. In course of time he came back to his master, followed, we are told, like Abelard, by twelve thousand disciples: he was a second time refused as a son-in-law. He went away again, but returned once more, this time with twenty-four thousand disciples, upon which Calva Sheva gave him his daughter and took him into favour. He is said to have been one hundred and twenty years of age when Barcochebas appeared. Probably he was at least well advanced in years. The adherence of Akiba to the rebel leader was doubtless the main cause of the hold which he obtained over his countrymen, for the authority of Akiba was greater than that of any other living Jew. Other pretenders had obtained followers, but not among the doctors learned in the law, not among such Rabbis as Akiba. When the mischief was done and, by the influence of Akiba, Barcochebas found himself at the head of two hundred thousand warriors, mad with religious zeal, Turnus Rufus, the new governor, seized and imprisoned the aged rabbi.* He was brought out to trial. In the midst of the questioning Akiba remembered that it was the time for prayer, and with his usual calmness, in the presence of his judges, disregarding and heedless of their questions, he proceeded with his devotions. He was condemned to be flayed with iron hooks.

No one knows the origin and previous history of Barcochebas, nor how the insurrection first began. All kinds of legends were related of his prowess and personal strength. He was so strong that he would catch the stones thrown from the catapults with his feet, and hurl them back upon the enemy with force equal to that of the machines which cast them; he could breathe flames; he would, at first, admit into his ranks only those men who, to show their courage, endured to have a finger cut off, but was dissuaded from this, and ordered instead, and as a proof of strength, that no one should join his ranks who could not himself tear up a cedar of Lebanon with his own hands.

The first policy of the Jews was to hide their strength, for the insurrection was long in being prepared. They knew, and they alone, all the secrets of the caves, subterranean passages, and hidden communications with which their city and whole country were honeycombed. They

* Other accounts say that he was taken prisoner in the taking of Jerusalem.

knew, too, where were the places best fitted for strongholds, and secretly fortified them; so that when they appeared suddenly and unexpectedly as the aggressors, they became masters almost at one stroke of fifty strong places and nearly a thousand villages. The first thing they did was to take Jerusalem, which probably offered only the small resistance of a feeble garrison. Here, no doubt, they set up an altar again, and, after a fashion, rebuilt the Temple. Turnus Rufus, the Roman governor, whose troops were few, slaughtered the unoffending people all over Judæa, but was not strong enough to make head against the rebellion, which grew daily stronger. Then Julius Severus, sent for by Hadrian in haste, came with an overwhelming force, and, following the same plan as had been adopted by Vespasian, attacked their strong places in detail. Jerusalem was taken, the spirits of the insurgents being crushed by the falling in of the vaults on Mount Zion, and Barcochebas himself was slain. The rebels, in despair, changed his name to Bar Koziba, the "Son of a Lie," and fled to Bether, their last stronghold, where they held out, under Rufus, the son of Barcochebas, for two years more. A story is told of its defence which shows at least how the hearts of the Jews were filled with the spirit of their old histories.* Seeing the desperate state of things, Eliezer, the Rabbi, enjoined the besieged to seek their last resource in prayer to God. All day long he prayed, and all day long, while he prayed, the battle went in favour of the Jews. Then a treacherous Samaritan stole up to the Rabbi and whispered in his ear. The leader of the insurgents† asked what he whispered. The Samaritan refused at first to tell, and then, with assumed reluctance, pretended that it was the answer to a secret message which

---

* Milman, iii. p. 122. See also Derenbourg, Hist. de la Palestine, chap. xxiv.

† Milman says Barcochebas, but though all is uncertainty, it appears probable, as stated above, that he was dead already.

Eliezer had sent to the Romans proposing capitulation. The Jewish leader, infuriated with this act of treason, ordered the Rabbi to be instantly executed. This was done, and then, there being no longer any one to pray, the tide of battle turned, and on the fatal 9th of August the fortress of Bether was taken and the slaughter of the insurgents accomplished. The horses of the Romans, we are told, were up to their girths in blood. An immense number fell in this war; Dio Cassius says five hundred and eighty thousand by the sword alone, not including those who fell by famine, disease, and fire. The fortress itself, when the last stand was made, whose position was long unknown, has been identified beyond a doubt by Mr. George Williams.* It appeared as if Hadrian's purpose was achieved and Judaism at last suppressed for ever. He turned Jerusalem into a Roman colony, calling it Ælia Capitolina, forbade any Jew on pain of death to appear even within sight of the city, and built a temple of Jupiter on the site of the Temple. On the site of the sepulchre of Christ, if indeed it was the site, was a temple to Venus, placed there, Eusebius would have us believe, in mockery of the Christian religion, and with a design to destroy the memory of the sepulchre. Meantime the Christians, who had suffered greatly during the revolt of Barcochebas, being tortured by the Jews and confounded with them by the Romans, hastened to separate themselves as much as possible from further possibility of confusion by electing a Gentile convert, Marcus, to the bishopric of Jerusalem. To this period may be referred the first springing up of that hatred of the Jews which afterwards led to such great and terrible persecutions.†

---

* 'Holy City,' vol. i. p. 210.

† An account of the Christian bishops, and of the controversies and discussion which harassed the church, will be found in Williams's 'Holy City.' It may be as well to mention that throughout this work we have studiously refrained from touching, except where it was impossible to avoid doing so, on things ecclesiastical.

The history of the next hundred years presents nothing remarkable. The persecution of Diocletian raged throughout the East; the usual stories of miracles are recorded; a library was founded in Jerusalem by Bishop Alexander; and meantime the old name of the city was forgotten entirely out of its own country. So much was this the case, that a story is related of an Egyptian martyr who, on being asked the name of his city, replied that it was Jerusalem, meaning the heavenly Jerusalem. The judge had never heard of such a city, and ordered him to be tortured in order to ascertain the truth.

And now grew up the spirit of pilgrimage, and the superstition of sacred places began, or rather was grafted into the new religion from the old. Of the pilgrims of these early times we have to speak in another place. At present they interest us only that they brought about two events of the greatest importance to the history of the world and the future of the Christian Church—the building of Constantine's church and the Invention of the Cross by Helena. Well would it have been in the interest of humanity if the cave of Christ's sepulchre had never been discovered, and if the wood of the Cross had still remained buried in the earth.

The historians quarrel as much over the birthplace of Helena as that of Homer. She was the daughter of a Breton king named Coël; she was born in York; she was the daughter of an innkeeper at Drepanium, near Nicomedia; she was a native of Dalmatia, of Dacia, of Tarsus, of Edessa, of Treves. Whether she was ever married to Constantius does not appear. If she was, he deserted her for Theodora, the daughter-in-law of Maximian. But Constantius made his son, Constantine, by Helena, his legal heir, and presented him to the troops as his successor, and Constantine regarded his mother with the greatest affection, surrounded her with every outward sign of respect and dignity, granted her the title of *Augusta*, stamped her name on coins, and gave her name to divers towns. Helena was at this period a Christian, whether born in the new religion or a convert does not appear; nor is it clear that she had anything to do with the conversion of her son. This illustrious and Imperial convert, stained with the blood of his father-in-law, whom he strangled with his own hands, of his son, whom he sacrificed at the lying representations of his wife, and of that wife herself, whom he executed in revenge for the death of his son, was converted, we are informed by some historians, through a perception of the beauty and holiness of the teaching of Christ. Probably he saw in the Cross a magical power by which he could defeat his enemies. It was after the death of Crispus the Cæsar, Constantine's son, that Helena, whose heart was broken by the murder of her grandson, went to Jerusalem to visit the sacred spots and witness the fulfilment of prophecy. On her way she delivered captives, relieved the oppressed, rewarded old soldiers, adorned Christian churches, and arrived in the Holy City laden with the blessings of a grateful people. And here she discovered the Cross in the following manner. Led by divine intimation, she instructed her people where to dig for it, and after removing the earth which the heathen had heaped round the spot, she found the Sepulchre itself, and close beside it the three crosses still lying together, and the tablet bearing the inscription which Pilate ordered to be written. The true Cross was picked out from the three by the method commonly pursued at this period, and always attended with satisfactory results. A noble lady lay sick with an incurable disease; all the crosses were brought to her bedside, and at the application of one, that on which our Lord suffered, she was immediately restored to perfect health. This is the account given by the writers of the following century; but not one of the contemporary writers relates the story, though Cyril, who was Bishop of Jerusalem from the year 748, alludes to the finding of the Cross. Eusebius preserves a total silence about it, a silence which to us is conclusive. The following is his account of the discovery of the Holy Sepulchre. ('Life of Constantine,' iii. 25.)

"After these things the pious emperor . . . judged it incumbent on him to render the blessed locality of our Saviour's resurrection an object of attraction and veneration to all. He issued immediate injunctions, therefore, for the erection in that spot of a house of prayer.

"It had been in time past the endeavour of impious men to consign to the darkness of oblivion that divine monument of immortality to which the radiant angel had descended from heaven and rolled away the stone for those who still had stony hearts. . . . This sacred cave certain impious and godless persons had thought to remove entirely from the eyes of men. Accordingly they brought a quantity of earth from a distance with much labour, and covered the entire spot; then, having raised this to a moderate height, they paved it with stone, concealing the holy cave beneath this massive mound. Then . . . . . they prepare on the foundation a truly dreadful sepulchre of souls, by building a gloomy shrine of lifeless idols to the impure spirit whom they call Venus. . . . These devices of impious men against the truth had prevailed for a long time, nor had any one of the governors, or military commanders, or even of the emperors themselves, ever yet appeared with ability to destroy those daring impieties save only our prince . . . as soon as his commands were issued these engines of deceit were cast down from their proud eminence to the very ground, and the dwelling-place of error was overthrown and utterly destroyed.

"Nor did the emperor's zeal stop here; but he gave further orders that the materials of what was thus destroyed should be removed and thrown from the spot as far as possible; and this command was speedily executed. The emperor, however, was not satisfied with having proceeded thus far: once more, fired with holy ardour, he directed that the ground should be dug up to a considerable depth, and the soil which had been polluted by the foul impurities of demon worship transported to a far distant place. . . . But as soon as the original surface of the ground, beneath the covering of earth, appeared, immediately, and contrary to all expectation, the venerable and hallowed monument of our Saviour's resurrection was discovered. Then, indeed, did this most holy cave present a faithful similitude of return to life, in that, after lying buried in darkness, it again emerged to light, and afforded to all who came to witness the sight a clear and visible proof of the wonders of which that spot had once been the scene."

In other words; in the time of Constantine a report existed that the spot then occupied by a temple of Venus was the site of our Lord's burial-place: Constantine took down the temple, meaning to build the church upon it: then, in removing the earth, supposed to be defiled by the idol worship which had taken place upon it, they found to their extreme astonishment the cave or tomb which is shown to this day. Then came the building of the Basilica.

"First of all,* he adorned the sacred cave itself, as the chief part of the whole work, and the hallowed monument at which the angel, radiant with light, had once declared to all that regeneration which was first manifested in the Saviour's person. This monument, therefore. as the chief part of the whole, the emperor's zealous magnificence beautified with rare columns, and profusely enriched with the most splendid decorations of every kind.

"The next object of his attention was a space of ground of great extent, and open to the pure air of heaven. This he adorned with a pavement of finely polished stone, and

---

* Euseb. 'Life of Constantine,' iii. ch. xxxiii. *et seq.*

enclosed it on three sides with porticoes of great length. At the side opposite to the sepulchres, which was the eastern side, the church itself was erected; a noble work, rising to a vast height, and of great extent, both in length and breadth. The interior of this structure was floored with marble slabs of various colours; while the external surface of the walls, which shone with polished stone exactly fitted together, exhibited a degree of splendour in no respect inferior to that of marble. With regard to the roof, it was covered on the outside with lead, as a protection against the rains of winter. But the inner part of the roof, which was finished with sculptured fretwork, extended in a series of connected compartments, like a vast sea, over the whole church; and, being overlaid throughout with the purest gold, caused the entire building to glitter, as it were, with rays of light. Besides this were two porticoes on each side, with upper and lower ranges of pillars, corresponding in length with the church itself; and these had, also, their roofs ornamented with gold. Of these porticoes, those which were exterior to the church were supported by columns of great size, while those within these rested on piles of stone beautifully adorned on the surface. Three gates placed exactly east, were intended to receive those who entered the church.

"Opposite these gates the crowning part of the whole was the hemisphere, which rose to the very summit of the church. This was encircled by twelve columns (according to the number of the apostles of our Saviour), having their capitals embellished with silver bowls of great size, which the emperor himself presented as a splendid offering to his god.

"In the next place, he enclosed the atrium, which occupied the space leading to the entrance in front of the church. This comprehended, first, the court, then. the porticoes on each side, and lastly the gates of the court. After these, in the midst of the open market-place, the entrance gates of the whole work, which were of exquisite workmanship, afforded to passers-by on the outside a view of the interior, which could not fail to excite astonishment."

According, therefore, to the account of Eusebius, Constantine built *one* church, and only one. This was not over the sepulchre at all, but to the east of it, and separated from it by a space open to the heavens, the sepulchre itself being set about with pillars.

In the transport of enthusiasm which followed the conversion of Constantine, the Jews probably found it convenient to keep as quiet as possible. They held at this time exclusive possession of four large towns in Galilee where they governed themselves, or rather submitted to the government of the Rabbis. Attempts were made to convert them. Sylvester succeeded, it is related, in converting a number of them by a miracle. For a conference was held between the Christians and Jews in the presence of the Emperor himself. One of the Rabbis asked permission that an ox should be brought in. He whispered in the ear of the animal the ineffable name of God, and the beast fell dead. "Will you believe," asked the Pope, "if I raise him to life again?" They agreed. Sylvester adjured the ox, in the name of Christ, and if Jesus was veritably the Messiah, to come to life again. The beast rose and quietly went on feeding. Whereupon the Jews all went out and were baptized.

Stories of this kind were invented whenever it seemed well to stimulate zeal or to promote conversions. The Jews were probably only saved from a cruel persecution by the death of the zealous convert. Already severe decrees had been issued. Constantine's laws enact that any Jew who endangers the life of a Christian convert shall be buried alive; that no Christian shall be permitted to become a Jew; that no Jew shall possess Christian slaves. But the laws were little lightened in their favour by the successor of Constantine, and the Jews made one or two local and feeble attempts to rise in Judæa and in Alexandria. Here they had an opportunity of plundering and slaying the Christians by joining the side of Arius.

And then there came a joyful day, too short, indeed, for the Jews, when Julian the Apostate mounted the throne. Julian addressed a letter to the Patriarch, annulling the aggressive laws, and promising great things for them on his return from the East. At the same time he issued his celebrated edict ordering the rebuilding of the Temple of Jerusalem; the care of the work being intrusted to his favourite, Alypius. And now, it seemed, the restoration of the Jews was to be accomplished in an unexpected manner, not foretold by prophecy. The wealth of the people was showered upon the projected work; Jews of all ages and both sexes streamed along the roads which led to Jerusalem; and, amid hopes more eager than any the hapless people had yet experienced, the work was begun. Hardly were the foundations uncovered, the joyful Jews crowding round the workmen, when flames of fire burst forth from underground accompanied by loud explosions. The workmen fled in wild affright, and the labours were at once suspended. Nor were they ever renewed. The anger of heaven was manifested in the mysterious flames: not yet was to be the rebuilding of the Temple. And then Julian died, cut off in early manhood, and whatever hopes remained among the Jews were crushed by this untimely event.

As for the miracle of the flames, it has been accounted for by supposing the foul gas in the subterranean passages to have caught fire. Perhaps, it has been maliciously suggested, the flames were designed by the Christians themselves, eager to prevent the rebuilding of the Temple. In any case there seems no reason to doubt the fact.

And now for three hundred years the history of Jerusalem is purely ecclesiastical. The disputes of the Christians, the quarrels among the bishops over the supremacy of their sees, the bitter animosities engendered by Arius, Pelagius, and other heretics, and leaders of heterodox thought, made Palestine a battlefield of angry words, which the disputants would gladly have turned into a battlefield of swords. The history of their controversies does not belong to us, and may be read in the pages of Dean Milman and the Rev. George Williams.

The Samaritans gave a good deal of trouble in the time of Justinian by revolting and slaughtering the Christians in their quarter. They were, however, quieted in the usual way, "by punishment," and peace reigned over all the country. Justinian built a magnificent church, of which the Mosque El Aksa perhaps preserves some of the walls, at least. It was so magnificent that in the delight of his heart, the Emperor exclaimed, "I have surpassed thee, O Solomon!" All Syria became a nest of monasteries, nunneries, and hermitages. In the north Simeon Stylites and his followers perched themselves on pillars, and soothed their sufferings with the adorations of those who came to look at them. In Palestine were hundreds of monasteries, while in every cave was a hermit, on every mountain-side the desolate dwelling of some recluse, and the air was heavy with the groans of those who tortured the flesh in order to save the soul. Moreover, the country was a great storehouse of relics. To manufacture them, or rather to find them, was a labour of love and of profit for the people. It was not difficult, because bones of saints were known always to emit a sweet and spice-like odour. They were thus readily distinguished. No doubt the aid of history was resorted to in order to determine whose bones they were. Nor was it at all a matter to disturb the faith of the holder if another man possessed the same relic of the same saint. Meantime, the wood of the Cross was discovered to have a marvellous property. It multiplied itself. If you cut a piece off to sell to a distinguished pilgrim, or to send to a powerful prince for a consideration, this invaluable relic, by a certain inherent *vis viva*, repaired itself and became whole again, as it had been before. So that, if the owners had chosen, a piece might have been cut off for every man in the world, and yet the wood have been no smaller. But the holders of the Cross were not so minded. So the time went on, and pleasant days, with leisure for theological quarrelling, were enjoyed in the Holy Land. The litanies of the Church were heard and said night and day, and no part of the country but resounded with the psalms and hymns of Christ, the intervals of the services being occupied by the monks in the finding and sale of relics, and in bitter dissensions between those who held views contrary to themselves. It was a land given over to monks, with a corrupt and narrow-minded Church, daily growing more corrupt and more narrow; and, when its fall took place, the cup of its corruptions appears to have been full. King Chosroes, the Persian conqueror, advanced into Syria, and the Jews, eager for some revenge for all their miseries, gladly joined his victorious arms. With him would be, without doubt, many of their own countrymen, the brethren of the Captivity, and the Mesopotamian Jews. Those in Tyre sent messengers to their countrymen in Damascus and other places, urging them to rise and massacre the Christians. The messengers were intercepted. The Christians in Tyre put the leading Jews in prison and barred the gates. Then the insurgents appeared outside and began to burn and waste the suburbs. For every Christian church burned, the Christians beheaded a hundred prisoners, and threw their heads over the wall. The Jews burned twenty churches, and two thousand heads were thrown over.* Then came the news that Chosroes

* Milman, iii. 238.

was marching on Jerusalem, and all the Jews flocked with eager anticipations to follow him. The city, feebly defended, if at all, by its priestly inhabitants, was taken at once: ninety thousand Christians are reported as having been slaughtered; it matters little now whether the number is correct or not—so large a number means nothing more definite than the indication of a great massacre —the Church of the Holy Sepulchre, *i.e.*, what Eusebius calls, speaking of it as a whole, the Temple, the Basilica with its porticoes and pillars, and the decorations of the Sepulchre, were all destroyed: the churches built by Helena on the Mount of Olives shared the same fate: the sacred vessels were carried off by the conquerors: the wood of the true Cross was part of the booty, and the Patriarch Zacharias was made prisoner, and carried away with it. But the wife of Chosroes was a Christian. By her intercession, Zacharias was well treated and the wood of the Cross preserved. And immediately after the retreat of the Persians, one Modestus, aided by gifts from John Eleemon of Alexandria, began to repair and rebuild, as best he might, the ruined churches. Fifteen years later Heraclius reconquered the provinces of Syria and Egypt, regained the wood of the Cross, and in great triumph, though clad in mean and humble dress, and as a pilgrim, entered Jerusalem (Sept. 14, A.D. 629) bearing the wood upon his shoulder. The restoration of the Cross was accompanied also by revenge taken upon the Jews. Henceforth in the annals of Christendom every revival of religious zeal is to be marked by the murdering and massacring of Jews.

What little we have to say on the *vexata quæstio* of the topography of Jerusalem will be found further on (see Appendix); but on leaving this, the second period of our history, one remark must be made, which may help to explain the uncertainty which rests upon the sites of the city. The destruction of the buildings, first under Titus, and next under Chosroes, appears to have been thorough and complete. Pillars may have remained standing with portions of walls; foundations, of course, remained, these being covered up and buried in the *débris* of roofs, walls, and decorations. On these foundations the Christians would rebuild, imitating, as far as possible, the structures that had been destroyed; in many cases they would have the very pillars to set up again, in all cases they would have the same foundations. But there was no time between the conquest by Heraclius and that by Omar to repair and restore the whole, and perhaps nothing was actually built except a church over the site of the Holy Sepulchre, formed of the materials which remained of the Basilica of the Martyrium. This theory would partly account for the silence about Justinian's Basilica, and for the apparent discrepancy between the statement made by Eusebius of decorations only having been set round the Sepulchre itself, contrasted with his admiration of the splendid Church of the Martyrium.

However all this may be, Jerusalem presents in history three totally distinct and utterly unlike appearances. It has one under Herod; one under Justinian; and one under Saladin. Under the first it possesses one building splendid enough to excite the admiration of the whole world; under the second it has its clustered churches as splendid as the art of the time would admit; under the third it has its two great buildings, the Dome of the Rock, and the Church of the Sepulchre, standing over against each other, two enemies bound by mutual expediency to peace.

Only one of these buildings is ancient; but somewhere in the ruins and rubbish in which the whole city is buried lie the foundations of those which have been destroyed.

F

CHAPTER IV.

THE MOHAMMEDAN CONQUEST. A.D. 632—1104.

Πάψετε τὸ Χερουβικό, κί ἃς χαμηλώσουν τ' Ἅγια!
Παπάδες πάρτε τὰ ἱερά, καὶ σ̓εῖς κεριὰ σβυστῆτε,
Γιατὶ εἶναι θέλημα Θεοῦ ἡ Πόλι νὰ τουρκέψῃ.

To the Arab wanderer on the barren and sun-stricken plains of the Hejjáz the well-watered, fertile land of Syria had always been an object of admiration and envy. As Mohammed the camel-driver sat on the hill which overlooks Damascus, and gazed upon the rich verdure of that garden of the East, his religious phrenzy, his visionary schemes for the unity and regeneration of his race had well-nigh yielded to the voluptuous fascination of the scene. But enthusiasm and ambition triumphed: his eyes filled with tears, and exclaiming, "Man can enter Paradise but once," he turned sorrowfully back, and in that moment changed the fortunes of the world.

When Abu Bekr, Mohammed's first successor, had quelled the disturbances which threatened the Muslim power, and found himself the acknowledged head of an immense confederation of restless and enthusiastic warriors, thoughts of conquest naturally presented themselves to his mind, and Syria was, as naturally, the first quarter to which he turned.

His resolution once taken, he addressed a circular-letter to the petty chieftains of Arabia, in which, appealing to their national prejudices and newly-awakened religious zeal, he exhorted them to wrest the long-coveted Syria out of the infidels' hands. His proposal was hailed with satisfaction by all those to whom it was addressed, and in a short space of time a considerable army was assembled around Medinah, waiting for the caliph's orders. Yezid ibn Abi Sufiyán was appointed commander-in-chief of the forces, and received immediate orders to march. Nothing could have been more moderate than the instructions which Abu Bekr delivered to his general for the conduct of the war. He was to respect the lives of women, children, and aged persons; to permit no wanton mischief or destruction of property, and to adhere religiously to any covenant or treaty which they might make with the opposite side.

The Emperor Heraclius made immediate preparations for averting the threatened invasion, but his hastily-collected and ill-organised forces were defeated in the very first engagement, while the Arabs scarcely suffered any loss. Encouraged by the success of their countrymen the inhabitants of Mecca and of the Hejjáz flocked to Abu Bekr's standard, and another division, under 'Amer ibn el 'As, the future conqueror of Egypt, was despatched into Palestine. Abu 'Obeidah ibn el Jerráh, of whom we shall hear more anon, was at the same time sent to take the command in Syria; but, meeting with some reverses, he was in turn superseded by Khálid ibn el Walíd, who was recalled from Irák for that purpose. This warrior's achievements against "the Infidels" had, during Mohammed's lifetime, earned for him the title of "The drawn Sword of God," and his name had already become a terror to the Greeks.

The important town of Bostra was the first to yield, being betrayed by its governor Romanus, and the Saracens thus obtained a footing in Syria, of which they were not slow to take advantage.

The forces now marched upon Damascus, when a change took place in the relative position of the generals. Abu Bekr shortly before his decease, which happened in 634 A.D., had appointed 'Omar ibn el Khattáb his successor. The first act of the new caliph on assuming the reins of government was to depose Khálid from the command of the army in Syria, and to appoint Abu 'Obeidah generalissimo in his stead. 'Omar's letter containing these commands reached them outside Damascus, and Abu 'Obeidah, immediately upon receiving it, posted himself with his division at the Báb el Jábieh; Khálid occupied the eastern gate, and the two remaining chiefs Yezíd ibn Abi Sufiyán, and "Amer ibn el "As, having disposed their forces on the north and south sides respectively, a strict blockade was commenced.

For seventy days Damascus held out; when Khálid having forced his position, the inhabitants retreated to the opposite side of the city, and, finding further resistance impossible, admitted Abu 'Obeidah peaceably within the walls; the two generals thus met in the centre of the city.

The conquest of Damascus was followed by the taking of Homs, after a protracted siege; Hamath and Ma'arrah surrendered without a blow; Laodicea, Jebeleh, Tarsus, Aleppo, Antioch, Cæsarea, Sebastiyeh, Nablús, Lydda, and Jaffah, one after another fell into the hands of the invaders. But it was at the battle of Yarmúk (A.D. 636) that the Christian power in Syria experienced the most fatal blow.

The Emperor Heraclius, driven to desperation by the continued successes of the enemy, had determined upon making a great and final effort for the preservation of his empire in the East. He had accordingly raised an immense army from all parts of his dominions, and despatched the main body to give battle to the Saracens; while the remaining portion, which was still very considerable in point of numbers, received instructions to defend the seaboard of Syria.

On the approach of the Greek army the Arab generals,

who were at Homs (the ancient Emessa), retreated toward Yarmúk, where they would be in a better position for receiving reinforcements from home, and Mahan (or Manuel), the Greek general, followed them in hot pursuit. At first their progress was opposed by the Christian Arabs, under Jebaleh ibn Aihám; but this chief was defeated with little loss to the Muslims, although some men of note, and amongst them Yezíd ibn Abi Sufiyán were taken prisoners. Abu 'Obeidah now sent a message to the caliph, urging him to send them immediate reinforcements, and another army of eight hundred men was quickly levied in Arabia, and sent to the relief of the Syrian generals. When Mahan's army reached Yarmúk some negotiations were opened between the Greeks and Christians. Khálid, who acted as *parlementaire* on the occasion, succeeded in obtaining the release of the prisoners; but, as they were unable to come to terms, both sides began to prepare for the battle which was to determine the fate of Syria.

For several days the fighting continued with fluctuating fortune, but at last an incident happened which decided the contest in favour of the Mohammedans. A native of Homs who happened to be staying in the neighbourhood of Yarmúk, had hospitably entertained some of the Grecian officers; this kindness they requited by the violation of his wife and the murder of his infant son. Maddened by his wrongs, and unable to obtain redress from the Greek general, he went over to the Mohammedans, and, having betrayed the Christians into an ambuscade near the ford of the river, they were attacked and completely routed by their enemies; more than forty thousand men perishing by the sword or being whirled away by the resistless stream and drowned. Thus the same licentious barbarity and corruption which, more than Arab prowess, had contributed to the success of the Muslim arms at the outset of the war, ultimately resulted in the entire overthrow of the Christian power in the East.

Nothing now remained to complete the triumph of the invaders but the capture of Jerusalem itself; accordingly a little time after the decisive battle of Yarmúk (A.D. 636), Abu 'Obeidah prepared to march upon the Holy City. Yezíd ibn abi Sufiyán was sent forward with a detachment of five thousand men; Abu 'Obeidah himself brought up the main body a few days later, and was joined shortly after by the division under "Amer ibn el "As. Desiring to afford the inhabitants every opportunity of coming to terms without further bloodshed, the general, before actually commencing hostilities, halted at the ford of the Jordan, and indited a letter to the Christian Patriarch and people of Ælia, demanding their immediate submission, and requiring them either to embrace the Mohammedan faith, or to pay the usual tribute exacted from unbelievers. " If you refuse," said he, " you will have to contend with people who love the taste of death more than you love wine and swine's flesh, and rest assured that I will come up against you, and will not depart until I have slain all the able-bodied men among you, and carried off your women and children captive."

To this message a decisive refusal was returned, and Abu 'Obeidah, in accordance with his threat, marched upon Jerusalem and besieged the town. The Christians, after several unsuccessful sallies, finding themselves reduced to great straits by the protracted siege, made overtures for capitulation, but refused to treat with any but the caliph himself. Having exacted a solemn oath from them that they would hold to the proposed conditions in case of his sovereign's arrival, the general sent a message to 'Omar, inviting him to leave Medína, and receive in person the capitulation of the town. The messengers from Abu 'Obeidah's camp were accompanied by some representatives of the Christian community, and the latter were much astonished at the stern simplicity and comparative retirement in which the caliph was living, which but ill accorded with their previously conceived ideas of the great monarch who had conquered the whole of Arabia and Syria, and made even the Emperors of Greece and Persia to tremble on their thrones. The meeting between the caliph and his victorious general was still further calculated to impress them. 'Omar was mounted on a camel, and attired in simple Bedawí costume—a sheepskin cloak, and coarse cotton shirt; Abu 'Obeidah was mounted on a small she-camel, an 'abba' or mantle of haircloth, folded over the saddle, and a rude halter of twisted hair forming her only trappings; he wore his armour, and carried his bow slung across his shoulder. Abu 'Obeidah, dismounting from his beast, approached the caliph in a respectful attitude; but the latter dismounting almost at the same moment, stooped to kiss his general's feet, whereupon there ensued a contest of humility, which was only put an end to by the two great men mutually consenting to embrace after the usual fashion of Arab sheikhs when meeting upon equal terms. A story of 'Omar's compensating a man for some grapes which his followers had heedlessly plucked as they came in from their thirsty ride, and several other instances of his great integrity and unassuming manners, are related by the Arab historians. No doubt these incidents were, to some extent, the offspring of "the pride that apes humility;" yet the Muslim sovereign really seems to have possessed some good and amiable qualities.

'Omar pitched his camp upon the Mount of Olives, where he was immediately visited by a messenger from the Patriarch of Jerusalem, who sent to welcome him and renew the offers of capitulation. This patriarch was named Sophronius, and was a native of Damascus. He was as remarkable for his zeal and erudition as for the purity of his life, which presented a striking contrast to the prevailing immorality of the age. The patriarch's observation, upon first setting eyes on 'Omar, was anything but complimentary, though, perhaps, justified by the meanness of the caliph's attire: "Verily," said he, "this is the abomination of Desolation, spoken of by Daniel the Prophet, standing in the Holy Place." The commander of the faithful was rather flattered by the remark, which the Arab historians have construed into an admission on the part of Sophronius that the conquest of 'Omar was foretold in Holy Writ. The armistice previously granted having been confirmed, and the personal safety of the patriarch and his immediate followers being guaranteed, that dignitary set out with a large company of attendants for the caliph's tent, and proceeded to confer with him personally and to draw up the articles of peace. These terms, exacted from Jerusalem in common with the other conquered cities, were, in spite of 'Omar's boasted generosity and equity, extremely hard and humiliating for the Christians. They ran as follows:—

The Christians shall enjoy security both of person and property, the safety of their churches shall be, moreover, guaranteed, and no interference is to be permitted on the part of the Mohammedans with any of their religious exercises, houses, or institutions; provided only that such churches, or religious institutions, shall be open night and day to the inspection of the Muslim authorities. All strangers and others are to be permitted to leave the town if they think fit, but any one electing to remain shall be subject to the herein-mentioned stipulations. No payment shall be exacted from any one until after the gathering in of his harvest. Mohammedans are to be treated everywhere with the greatest respect; the Christians must extend to them the rights of hospitality, rise to receive them, and accord them the first place of honour in their assemblies. The Christians are to build no new churches, convents, or other religious edifices, either within or without the city, or in any other part of the Muslim territory;

they shall not teach their children the Cor'án, but, on the other hand, no one shall be prevented from embracing the Mohammedan religion. No public exhibition of any kind of the Christian religion is to be permitted. They shall not in any way imitate the Muslims, either in dress or behaviour, nor make use of their language in writing or engraving, nor adopt Muslim names or appellations. They shall not carry arms, nor ride astride their animals, nor wear or publicly exhibit the sign of the cross. They shall not make use of bells; nor strike the *nákús* (wooden gong) except with a suppressed sound; nor shall they place their lamps in public places, nor raise their voices in lamentation for the dead. They shall shave the front part of the head and gird up their dress, and lastly, they shall never intrude into any Muslim's house on any pretext whatever. To these conditions 'Omar added the following clause to be accepted by the Christians: That no Christian should strike a Muslim, and that if they failed to comply with any single one of the previous stipulations, they should confess that their lives were justly forfeit, and that they were deserving of the punishment inflicted upon rebellious subjects.

When these terms had been agreed upon by both sides and the treaty signed and sealed, 'Omar requested the patriarch to lead him to the Mosque (*Masjid*, or "place of adoration,") of David. The patriarch acceding to this request, 'Omar, accompanied by four thousand attendants, was conducted by him into the Holy City. They first proceeded to the church of the Holy Sepulchre,* which the patriarch pointed out as the site of David's temple. "Thou liest," said 'Omar, curtly, and was proceeding to

* In the original *El Camámah*, "dung;" which is explained a little further on to be a designed corruption of the word *Caiyámah*, "Anastasis." These words are at the present day applied by the Muslim and Christian population respectively to the church of the Holy Sepulchre.

leave the spot when the hour of prayer arrived, and the caliph declared his intention of retiring to perform his religious duties. The patriarch invited him to pray where he stood, in the church itself. This 'Omar refused to do, and was next led to the church of Constantine, where a *sejjádeh*, or prayer mat, was spread for him. Declining this accommodation also, the caliph went outside the church, and prayed alone upon the door-steps. When asked the reason for his objection to pray within the church, he told the patriarch that he had expressly avoided doing so, lest his countrymen should afterwards make his act a precedent and an excuse for confiscating the property. So anxious was he not to give the least occasion for the exercise of injustice, that he called for pen and paper, and then and there wrote a document, which he delivered to the patriarch, forbidding Moslems to pray even upon the steps of the church, except it were one at a time, and strictly prohibiting them from calling the people to prayer at the spot, or in any way using it as one of their own mosques.

This honourable observance of the stipulations contained in the treaty, and careful provision against future aggression on the part of his followers, cannot but excite our admiration for the man. In spite of the great accession to our knowledge of the literature of this period which has been made during the last century, we doubt if the popular notions respecting the Saracen conquerors of Jerusalem have been much modified, and many people still regard them as a fierce and inhuman horde of barbarous savages, while the Crusaders are judged only by the saintly figures that lie cross-legged upon some old cathedral brasses, and are looked upon as the beau-ideals of chivalry and gentle Christian virtue. But we shall have occasion to recur to this subject further on.

Leaving the church of Constantine they next visited that called Sion, which the patriarch again pointed out as the Mosque of David, and again 'Omar gave him the lie. After this they proceeded to the *Masjid of Jerusalem*, and halted at the gate called Bâb Mohammed. Now the dung in the mosque had settled on the steps of the door in such quantities that it came out into the street in which the door is situated, and nearly clung to the roofed archway of the street.* Hereupon the patriarch said, "We shall never be able to enter unless we crawl upon our hands and knees." "Well," replied the caliph, "on our hands and knees be it." So the patriarch led the way, followed by 'Omar and the rest of the party, and they crawled along until they came out upon the courtyard of the Temple, where they could stand upright. Then 'Omar, having surveyed the place attentively for some time, suddenly exclaimed: "By Him in whose hands my

* This important passage has been but imperfectly understood; Reynolds, in his translation of "Jelâl ed dín," makes absolute nonsense of it, rendering the words:—
 "So he went with him to the *Mosques of* the Holy City, until he came at last near unto a gate, called the gate of Mohammed; and *he drew down* all the filth that was on the declivity of the steps of the gate, until he came to a narrow passage, and he went down a number of steps until *he almost hung upon the top of the interior or upper surface*. . . . So 'Omar went upon his hands, and we went upon our hands and knees after him until we came to the *central sewer*. And we stood here upright."
 The word here rendered *mosques* is in the singular, not in the plural, and plainly refers to a spot well known as "the Temple (Masjid) of Jerusalem." The word rendered "he drew down" is passive, and implies that the dirt had collected in such quantities upon the raised platform as to run down the steps into the street, where it had made a heap high enough to reach the arched roof of the public way. Not to mention the difficulty of four thousand men standing upright in a sewer, I may remark that the word rendered "*central sewer*" is *sahn*, "an open court," the name applied at the present day to the platform upon which the Cubbet es Sakhrah stands. Reynolds's translation would imply that the site of the Sakhrah was in a sewer below the level of the rest of the city as it then stood!

soul is, this is the mosque of David, from which the prophet told us that he ascended into heaven. He (upon whom be peace) gave us a circumstantial account thereof, and especially mentioned the fact that we had found upon the Sakhrah a quantity of dung which the Christians had thrown there out of spite to the children of Israel."* With these words he stooped down and began to brush off the dung with his sleeve, and his example being followed by the other Mussulmans of the party, they soon cleared all the dung away, and brought the Sakhrah to light. Having done so he forbade them to pray there until three showers of rain had fallen upon it.

Another account relates that, on conquering the city, 'Omar sent for Ka'ab, a Jew who had been converted to Mohammedanism during the prophet's lifetime, and said to him, " Oh, Abu Ishak, dost thou know the site of the Sakhrah?" "Yes," replied Ka'ab, "it is distant such and such a number of cubits† from the wall which runs parallel to the Wády Jehennum; it is at the present time used for a dunghill." Digging at the spot indicated, they found the Sakhrah as Ka'ab had described. Then 'Omar asked Ka'ab where he would advise him to place the mosque? Ka'ab answered, " I should place it behind the

---

* It needed no prophetic inspiration to acquaint Mohammed with this fact. The site of the Temple was not only well known to the Christians, but was systematically defiled by them out of abhorrence for the Jews. Eutychius expressly tells us that—" when Helena, the mother of Constantine, had built churches at Jerusalem, the site of the rock and its neighbourhood had been laid waste, and so left. But the Christians heaped dirt on the rock so that there was a large dunghill over it. And so the Romans had neglected it, nor given it that honour which the Israelites had been wont to pay it, and had not built a church above it, because it had been said by our Lord Jesus Christ in the Holy Gospel, ' Behold, your house shall be left unto you desolate.' "

† Reynolds, again misunderstanding the Arabic, renders this " one cubit."

Sakhrah, so that the two Kiblahs,* namely, that of Moses and that of Mohammed, may be made identical." " Ah," said 'Omar, " thou leanest still to Jewish notions, I see; the best place for the mosque is in front of it," and he built it in front accordingly.

Another version of this conversation is, that when Ka'ab proposed to set the praying-place behind the Sakhrah, 'Omar reproved him, as has just been stated, for his Jewish proclivities, and added, " Nay, but we will place it in the *sudr* ('breast or forepart'), for the prophet ordained that the Kiblah of our mosques should be in the forepart. I am not ordered," said he, " to turn to the Sakhrah, but to the Ka'abah." Afterwards, when 'Omar had completed the conquest of Jerusalem, and cleared away the dirt from the Sakhrah, and the Christians had entered into their engagements to pay tribute, the Muslims changed the name of the great Christian church from *Caiyámah* (Anastasis), to *Camámah* (dung), to remind them of their indecent treatment of the holy place, and to further glorify the Sakhrah itself.

The mosque erected by 'Omar is described by an early pilgrim who saw it as a simple square building of timber, capable of holding three thousand people, and constructed over the ruins of some more ancient edifice.

The annals of the Mohammedan Empire during the next forty-eight years, although fraught with stirring events, bear but little on the history of Jerusalem itself; and although the visit of 'Omar had impressed the followers of the Cor'án with the idea that they possessed an equal interest in the Holy City with the adherents of the Law and of the Gospel, still their devotion to the Temple of Mecca and their prophet's tomb at Medína was too deeply rooted to leave them much reverence for the Masjid

* The *Kiblah* is a "point of adoration," that is, the direction in which Mecca lies. In the Mohammedan mosques it is indicated by a small niche called a *mihráb*.

el Aksa. But political exigencies did what religious enthusiasm had failed to accomplish, and in 684 A.D., in the reign of 'Abd el Melik, the ninth successor of Mohammed, and the fifth caliph of the House of Omawíyah, events happened which once more turned people's attention to the City of David.

For eight years the Mussulman empire had been distracted by factions and party quarrels. The inhabitants of the two holy cities, Mecca and Medína, had risen against the authority of the legitimate caliphs, and had proclaimed 'Abdallah ibn Zobeir their spiritual and temporal head. Yezíd and Mo'áwíyeh had in vain attempted to suppress the insurrection; the usurper had contrived to make his authority acknowledged throughout Arabia and the African provinces, and had established the seat of his government at Mecca itself. 'Abd el Melik trembled for his own rule; year after year crowds of pilgrims would visit the Ka'abah, and Ibn Zobeir's religious and political influence would thus become disseminated throughout the whole of Islam. In order to avoid these consequences, and at the same time to weaken his rival's prestige, 'Abd el Melik conceived the plan of diverting men's minds from the pilgrimage to Mecca, and inducing them to make the pilgrimage to Jerusalem instead. This was an easier task than might have been at first supposed.

The frequent mention of Jerusalem in the Cor'án, its intimate connection with those Scriptural events which Mohammed taught as part and parcel of his own faith, and, lastly, the prophet's pretended night journey to Heaven from the Holy Rock of Jerusalem—these were points which appealed directly to the Mohammedan mind, and to all these considerations was added the charm of novelty—novelty, too, with the sanction of antiquity—and we need not, therefore, wonder that the caliph's appeal to his subjects met with a ready and enthusiastic response.

Having determined upon this course he sent circular letters to every part of his dominions, couched in the following terms:—

"'Abd el Melik desiring to build a dome over the Holy Rock of Jerusalem, in order to shelter the Muslims from the inclemency of the weather, and, moreover, wishing to restore the Masjid, requests his subjects to acquaint him with their wishes on the matter, as he would be sorry to undertake so important a matter without consulting their opinion."

Letters of approval and congratulation flowed in upon the caliph from all quarters, and he accordingly assembled a number of the most skilled artisans, and set apart for the proposed work a sum of money equivalent in amount to the whole revenue of Egypt for seven years. For the safe custody of this immense treasure he built a small dome, the same which exists at the present day to the east of the Cubbet es Sakhrah, and is called Cubbet es Silsilah. This little dome he himself designed, and personally gave the architect instructions as to its minutest details. When finished, he was so pleased with the general effect that he ordered the Cubbet es Sakhrah itself to be built on precisely the same model.

Having completed his treasure-house and filled it with wealth, he appointed Rija ibn Haiyáh el Kendi controller thereof, with Yezíd ibn Sallám, a native of Jerusalem, as his coadjutor. These two persons were to make all disbursements necessary for the works, and were enjoined to expend the entire amount upon them, regulating the outlay as occasion might require. They commenced with the erection of the Cubbeh, beginning on the east side and finishing at the west, until the whole was so perfect that no one was able to suggest an addition or an improvement. Similarly in the buildings in the fore part of the Masjid,* that is, on the south side, they worked from

* See p. 83.

east to west, commencing with the wall by which is the Mehd 'Aisa (cradle of Jesus), and carrying it on to the spot now known as the Jam'i el Magháribeh.

On the completion of the work, Rijá and Yezíd addressed the following letter to 'Abd el Melik, who was then at Damascus:—

"In accordance with the orders given by the Commander of the Faithful, the building of the Dome of the Rock of Jerusalem and the Masjid el Aksa is now so complete that nothing more can be desired. After paying all the expenses of the building there still remains in hand a hundred thousand dinárs of the sum originally deposited with us; this amount the Commander of the Faithful will expend in such manner as may seem good to him."

The caliph replied that they were at liberty to appropriate the sum to themselves in consideration of their services in superintending the financial department of the works. The two commissioners, however, declined this proposition, and again offered to place it at the caliph's disposal, with the addition of the ornaments belonging to their women and the surplus of their own private property. 'Abd el Melik, on receipt of their answer, bade them melt up the money in question, and apply it to the ornamentation of the Cubbeh. This they accordingly did, and the effect is said to have been so magnificent that it was impossible for any to keep his eyes fixed on the dome, owing to the quantity of gold with which it was ornamented. They then prepared a covering of felt and leather, which they put upon it in winter time to protect it from the wind and rain and snow. Rijá and Yezíd also surrounded the Sakhrah itself with a latticed screen of ebony, and hung brocaded curtains behind the screen between the columns. It is said that in the days of 'Abd el Melik a precious pearl, the horn of Abraham's ram, and the crown of the Khosroes, were attached to the chain which is suspended in the centre of the dome, but when the caliphate passed into the hands of the Beni Háshem they removed these relics to the Ka'abah.

When the Masjid was quite completed and thrown open for public service, no expense or trouble was spared to make it as attractive as possible to the worshippers. Every morning a number of attendants were employed in pounding saffron, and in making perfumed water with which to sprinkle the mosque, as well as in preparing and burning incense. Servants were also sent into the Hammám Suleimán ("Solomon's bath") to cleanse it out thoroughly. Having done this they used to go into the store-room in which the *Khalúk** was kept, and changing their clothes for fresh ones of various costly stuffs, and putting jewelled girdles round their waists, and taking the *Khalúk* in their hands, they proceeded to dab it all over the Sakhrah as far as they could reach; and when they could not reach with their hands they washed their feet and stepped upon the Sakhrah itself until they had dabbed it all over, and emptied the pots of *Khalúk*. Then they brought censers of gold and silver filled with *'ud* (perfumed aloes wood) and other costly kinds of incense, with which they perfumed the entire place, first letting down the curtains round all the pillars, and walking round them until the incense filled the place between them and the dome, and then fastening them up again so that the incense escaped and filled the entire building, even penetrating into the neighbouring bazaar, so that any one who passed that way could smell it. After this, proclamation was made in the public market, "The Sakhrah is now open for public worship," and people would run in such crowds to pray there, that two *reka'as* was as much as most men could accomplish, and it was only a very few who could succeed in performing four.

So strongly was the building perfumed with the incense,

---

* A species of aromatic plant rather larger than saffron.

that one who had been into it could at once be detected by the odour, and people used to say as they sniffed it, "Ah! So and so has been in the Sakhrah." So great, too, was the throng that people could not perform their ablutions in the orthodox manner, but were obliged to content themselves with washing the soles of their feet with water, wiping them with green sprigs of myrtle, and drying them with their pocket-handkerchiefs. The doors were all locked, ten chamberlains were posted at each door, and the mosque was only opened twice a week—namely, on Mondays and Fridays; on other days none but the attendants were allowed access to the buildings.

Ibn 'Asákir, who visited Jerusalem early in the twelfth century of the Christian era, tells us that there were 6000 planks of wood in the Masjid used for roofing and flooring, exclusive of wooden pillars. It also contained fifty doors, amongst which were:—Báb el Cortobi (the gate of the Cordovan), Báb Dáud (the gate of David), Báb Suleimán (the gate of Solomon), Báb Mohammed (the gate of Mohammed), Báb Hettah (the gate of Remission*), Báb el Taubah (the gate of Reconciliation), where God was reconciled to David after his sin with Bathsheba, Báb er Rahmeh (the gate of Mercy), six gates called Abwáb al Asbát (the gates of the tribes), Báb el Walíd (the gate of Walíd), Báb el Háshimí (the gate of the Háshem Family), Báb el Khidhir (the gate of St. George or Elias), and Báb es Sekínah (the gate of the Shekina). There were also 600 marble pillars; seven mihrábs (or prayer niches); 385 chains for lamps, of which 230 were in the Masjid el Aksa, and the rest in the Cubbet es Sakhrah; the accumulative length of the chains was 4000 cubits, and their weight 43,000 *ratals* (Syrian measure). There were also 5000 lamps, in addition to which they used to light 1000 wax candles every Friday,

---

* Cf. Cor'án, cap. ii. v. 55, "Enter the gate with adoration, and say 'Remission.'"

and on the night of the middle of the months Rejeb, Sha'ban, and Ramadhán, as well as on the nights of the two great festivals. There were fifteen domes, or oratories, exclusive of the Cubbet es Sakhrah; and on the roof of the mosque itself were 7700 strips of lead, and the weight of each strip was 70 Syrian ratals. This was exclusive of the lead which was upon the Cubbet es Sakhrah. There were four-and-twenty large cisterns in the Masjid, and four minarets—three in a line on the west side of the Masjid, and one over the Babel Esbát.

All the above work was done in the days of 'Abd el Melik ibn Merwán. The same prince appointed three hundred perpetual attendants to the mosque, slaves purchased with a fifth of the revenue; and whenever one of these died, there was appointed in his stead either his son, grandson, or some one of the family, and the office was made hereditary so long as the generation lasted. There were also Jewish servants employed in the Masjid, and these were exempted, on account of their services, from payment of the capitation-tax; originally they were ten in number, but, as their families sprung up, they increased to twenty. Their business was to sweep out the Masjid all the year round, and to clean out the lavatories round about it. Besides these, there were ten Christian servants also attached to the place in perpetuity, and transmitting the office to their children; their business was to brush the mats, and to sweep out the conduits and cisterns. A number of Jewish servants were also employed in making glass lamps, candelabras, &c. (These and their families were also exempted in perpetuity from tax, and the same privilege was accorded to those who made the lamp-wicks.)

Ibn 'Asákir informs us that the length of the Masjid el Aksa was 755 cubits, and the breadth 465 cubits, the standard employed being the royal cubit. The author of the 'Muthír el Gharám' declares that he found on the inner surface of the north wall of the Haram, over the door, which is behind the Báb ed Dowaidáríyeh, a stone tablet, on which the length of the Masjid was recorded as 784 cubits, and its breadth as 455; it did not, however, state whether or no the standard employed was the royal cubit. The same author informs us that he himself measured the Masjid with a rope, and found that in length it was 683 cubits on the east side, and 650 on the west; and in breadth it was 438 cubits, exclusive of the breadth of the wall.

'Abdallah Yácút el Hamawí, a Christian Arab writer of the twelfth century, tells us that the substructure of the Jewish Temple served for the foundations of 'Abd el Melik's edifice, and that that monarch built a wall of smaller stones upon the more massive ancient blocks. The great substructures at the south-west angle are said to be the work of 'Abd el Melik, who is reported to have made them in order to obtain a platform on which to erect the el Aksa.*

In order to understand the native accounts of the sacred area at Jerusalem, it is essentially necessary to keep in mind the proper application of the various names by which it is spoken of. When the Masjid el Aksa is mentioned, that name is usually supposed to refer to the well-known mosque on the south side of the Haram, but such is not really the case. The latter building is called El Jámi el Aksa, or simply El Aksa, and the substructures are called El Aksa el Kadímeh (the ancient Aksa), while the title El Masjid el Aksa is applied to the whole sanctuary. The word *jámi·* is exactly equivalent in sense to the Greek συναγωγὴ, and is applied only to the church or building in which the worshippers congregate. *Masjid*, on the other hand, is a much more general term; it is derived from the verb *sejada*, "to adore," and is applied to

---

* *Vide* M. de Vogüé, p. 76.

any spot, the sacred character of which would especially incite the visitor to an act of devotion. Our word *mosque* is a corruption of *masjid*, but it is usually misapplied, as the building is never so designated, although the whole area on which it stands may be so spoken of.

The Jám'i el Aksa, Jám'i el Maghâribeh, &c., are *mosques* in our sense of the word, but the entire Haram is a *masjid*. This will explain what is meant by saying that 'Omar, after visiting the churches of the Anastasis, Sion, &c., was taken to the "Masjid" of Jerusalem; and will account for the statement of Ibn el 'Asa'kir and others, that the Masjid el Aksa measured over six hundred cubits in length—that is, the length of the whole Haram area. The name Masjid el Aksa is borrowed from the passage in the Cor'án (xvii. 1), where allusion is made to the pretended ascent of Mohammed into heaven from the Temple of Jerusalem: "Praise be unto Him who transported His servant by night from El Masjid el Harâm (*i. e.*, 'the Sacred place of Adoration,' at Mecca) to El Masjid el Aksa (*i. e.*, 'the Remote place of Adoration' at Jerusalem), the precincts of which we have blessed," &c. The title *El Aksa*, "the Remote," according to the Mohammedan doctors, is applied to the Temple of Jerusalem, "either because of its distance from Mecca, or because it is in the centre of the earth." The title Haram, or "sanctuary," it enjoys in common with those of Mecca, Medina, and Hebron.

As M. de Vogüé has pointed out, the Cubbet es Sakhrah, notwithstanding its imposing proportions, is not, properly speaking, a mosque, and is not constructed with a view to the celebration of public prayers and services. It is only an oratory, one of the numerous *cubbehs* with which the Haram es Sherîf abounds—domed edifices that mark the various spots to which traditions cling. The form is, in fact, almost identical with that of an ordinary Muslim *weli*, or saint's tomb. El Jám'i el Aksa is, on the other hand, a mosque designed expressly for the accommodation of a large congregation, assembled for public worship, and resembling in its architectural details the celebrated mosques of Constantinople or elsewhere.

The erection of the Cubbet es Sakhrah, Jám'i el Aksa, and the restoration of the temple area by 'Abd el Melik, are recorded in a magnificent Cufic inscription in mosaic, running round the colonnade of the first-mentioned building. The name of 'Abd el Melik has been purposely erased, and that of 'Abdallah el Mamún fraudulently substituted; but the shortsighted forger has omitted to erase the date, as well as the name of the original founder, and the inscription still remains a contemporary record of the munificence of 'Abd el Melik. The translation is as follows:—

"In the name of God, the Merciful, the Compassionate! There is no god but God alone; He hath no partner; His is the kingdom, His the praise. He giveth life and death, for He is the Almighty. In the name of God, the Merciful, the Compassionate! There is no god but God alone; He hath no partner; Mohammed is the Apostle of God; pray God for him. The servant of God 'Abdallah, the Imám al Mamún [*read* 'Abd el Melik], Commander of the Faithful, built this dome in the year 72 (A.D. 691). May God accept it at his hands, and be content with him, Amen! The restoration is complete, and to God be the praise. In the name of God, the Merciful, the Compassionate! There is no god but God alone; He hath no partner. Say He is the one God, the Eternal; He neither begetteth nor is begotten, and there is no one like Him. Mohammed is the Apostle of God; pray God for him. In the name of God, the Merciful, the Compassionate! There is no god but God, and Mohammed is the Apostle of God; pray God for him. Verily, God and His angels pray for the Prophet. Oh ye who believe, pray for him, and salute ye him with salutations of peace. In the name of God, the Merciful, the Compassionate! There is no god but God alone; to Him be praise, who taketh not unto Himself a son, and to whom none can be a partner in His kingdom, and whose patron no lower creature can be; magnify ye Him. Mohammed is the Apostle of God; God, and His angels, and apostles pray for him; and peace be upon him, and the mercy of God. In the name of God, the Merciful, the Compassionate! There is no god but God alone; He hath no partner; His is the kingdom, and His the praise; He giveth life and death, for He is Almighty. Verily, God and His angels pray for the Prophet. Oh ye who believe, pray for him, and salute him with salutations of peace. Oh! ye who have received the Scriptures, exceed not the bounds in your religion, and speak not aught but truth concerning God. Verily, Jesus Christ, the son of Mary, is the Apostle of God, and His word which He cast over Mary, and a spirit from Him. Then believe in God and His apostles, and do not say there are three gods; forbear, and it will be better for you. God is but One. Far be it from Him that He should have a son. To Him belongeth whatsoever is in the heaven and in the earth, and God is a sufficient protector. Christ doth not disdain to be a servant of God, nor do the angels who are near the throne. Whosoever then disdains His service, and is puffed up with pride, God shall gather them all at the last day. O God, pray for Thy apostle Jesus, the son of Mary; peace be upon me the day I am born, and the day I die, and the day I am raised to life again. That is Jesus, the son of Mary, concerning whom ye doubt. It is not for God to take unto Himself a son; far be it from Him. If He decree a thing, He doth but say unto it, Be, and it is. God is my Lord and yours. Serve Him, this is the right way. God hath testified that there is no god but He, and the angels, and beings endowed with knowledge (testify it), He executeth righteousness. There is no God but He, the Mighty, the

Wise. Verily, the true religion in the sight of God is Islám. Say praise be to God, who taketh not unto Himself a son; whose partner in the kingdom none can be; whose patron no lowly creature can be. Magnify ye Him!"*

'Abd el Melik died on the 8th of September, 705 A.D., and was succeeded by his son Walíd. During that prince's reign the eastern portion of the Masjid fell into ruins; and as there were no funds in the treasury available for the purpose of restoring it, Walíd ordered the requisite amount to be levied from his subjects.

On the death of Walíd, the caliphate passed into the hands of his brother Suleimán, who was at Jerusalem when the messengers came to him to announce his accession to the throne.

He received them in the Masjid itself, sitting in one of the domes in the open court—probably in that now called Cubbet Suleimán, which is behind the Cubbet es Sakhrah, near the Báb ed Duweidáríyel. He died at Jerusalem, after a short reign of three years, and was succeeded (A.D. 717) by 'Omar ibn Abd el 'Azíz, surnamed El Mehdí. It is related that this prince dismissed the Jews who had been hitherto employed in lighting up the sanctuary, and put in their places some of the slaves before-mentioned as having been purchased by 'Abd el Melik, at the price of a fifth of the treasury (El Khums).

---

* This inscription, which is composed chiefly of Coranic texts, is interesting both from a historical point of view, and as showing the spirit in which Christianity was regarded by the Muslims of these early times. It has never before been published in its entirety. Its preservation during the subsequent Christian occupation of the city may occasion some surprise, as the Latins (by whom the Cubbet es Sakhrah was turned into a church) could not but have been offended at quotations which so decidedly deny the Divinity of Christ and the doctrine of the Trinity. It is probable, however, that the Cúfic character, in which it is written, was as unintelligible to the Christian natives of that time, as it is now, even to most of the learned Muslims of the present day.

One of these last came to the caliph, and begged him to emancipate him.

"I have no power to do so," replied 'Omar. "But look you, if you choose to go of your own accord, I claim no right over a single hair of your head."*

In the reign of the second 'Abbasside caliph, Abu Ja'afer Mansúr (A.D. 755), a severe earthquake shook Jerusalem; and the southern portion of the Haram es Sherif, standing as it did upon an artificially-raised platform, suffered most severely from the shock. In order to meet the expense of repairing the breaches thus made, the caliph ordered the gold and silver plates, with which the munificence of 'Abd el Melik had covered the doors of the Masjid, to be stripped off, converted into coin, and applied to the restoration of the edifice. The part restored was not, however, destined to last long; for during the reign of El Mehdí, his son and successor, the mosque had again fallen into ruins, and was rebuilt by the caliph upon a different plan, the width being increased at the expense of the length.

The foundation, by the Caliph Mansúr, of the imperial city of Baghdád, upon the banks of the Tigris, and the removal of the government from Damascus thither, was very prejudicial to the interests of the Christian population of Syria, who were now treated with great harsh-

---

* The following extract from Reynolds's 'Temple of Jerusalem,' purporting to be a translation of this passage, will, I hope, excuse me from again quoting or referring to that *valuable work*:—"The Jews purveyed the furniture (necessaries) for the temple, but when Omar-Rudh-Ullah-anhu-ibn—Abdul Azíz—ascended the throne, he dismissed them, and placed therein some of the tribe of Khims (of Arabia Felix). And then came to him a man of the family of Khims, and said unto him, 'Give me some present.' But he said, 'How can I give thee? for if thou shouldst strain thine eyes in staring, I have not a single one of thy dog's hairs (to give).'"

And this astounding display of ignorance was "published under the auspices of the Oriental Translation Fund of Great Britain and Ireland!"—E. H. P.

ness, deprived of the privileges granted them by former monarchs, and subjected to every form of extortion and persecution.

In 786 the celebrated Harún er Rashíd, familiar to us as the hero of the 'Arabian Nights,' succeeded his father, El Hádí, in the caliphate.

This prince was illustrious alike for his military successes, and his munificent patronage of learning and science; and although his glory is sullied by one act of barbarity and jealous meanness—the murder of his friend and minister, Ja'afer el Barmaki, and the whole of the Barmecide family—he seems to have well merited his title of Er Rashíd, "the Orthodox," or "Upright."

The cordial relations between the East and West, brought about by his alliance with the Emperor Charlemagne, were productive of much good to the Christian community in Syria and Palestine, and more especially in Jerusalem, where churches were restored, and hospices and other charitable institutions founded, by the munificence of the Frank emperor.

In the year 796 new and unexpected troubles came upon Palestine. A civil war broke out between two of the border-tribes—the Beni Yoktán and the Ismaelíyeh,—and the country was devastated by hordes of savage Bedawín. The towns and villages of the west were either sacked or destroyed, the roads were rendered impassable by hostile bands, and those places which had not suffered from the incursions of the barbarians were reduced to a state of protracted siege. Even Jerusalem itself was threatened, and, but for the bravery of its garrison, would have again been pillaged and destroyed. The monasteries in the Jordan valley experienced the brunt of the Arabs' attack, and one after another was sacked; and, last of all, that of Már Saba—which, from its position, had hitherto been deemed impregnable—succumbed to a blockade, and many of the inmates perished.

On the death of Harún, his three sons contended fiercely for the throne; the Mussulman empire was again involved in civil dissensions, and Palestine, as usual, suffered most severely in the wars. The churches and monasteries in and around Jerusalem were again laid waste, and the great mass of the Christian population was obliged to seek safety in flight.

El Mamún having at last triumphed over his brothers, and established himself firmly in the caliphate, applied his mind with great ardour to the cultivation of literature, art, and science. It was at his expense, and by his orders, that the works of the Greek philosophers were translated into the Arabic language by 'Abd el Messiah el Kendí, who, although a Christian by birth and profession, enjoyed a great reputation at the Court of Baghdád, where he was honoured with the title of Feilsúf el Islam—"The Philosopher of Mohammedanism."

Since their establishment on the banks of the Tigris, the Abbasside caliphs had departed widely from the ancient traditions of their race; and the warlike ardour and stern simplicity, which had won so vast an empire for 'Omar and his contemporaries, presently gave way to effeminate luxury and useless extravagance. But although this change was gradually undermining their power, and tending to the physical degeneracy of the race, it was not unproductive of good; and the immense riches and careless liberality of the caliphs attracted to the Court of Baghdád the learned men of the Eastern world. The Arabs were not an inventive, but they were eminently an acquisitive people, and,

"Græcia capta ferum victorem cepit,"

the nations conquered by their arms were made to yield up intellectual as well as material spoils. They had neither art, literature, nor science of themselves, and yet we are indebted to them for all three; for what others produced and neglected, they seized upon and made their own. Born in the black shapeless "tents of Shem," and nursed amidst monotonous scenery, the Arabs could conceive no grander structure than the massive tetragonal Ka'abah; but Persia was made to supply them with the graceful forms and harmonious colours suggested by the flower-gardens of Iran.* The art of painting, cultivated with so much success in Persia even at the present day, found but little favour with the iconoclast followers of Mohammed; but its influence is seen in the perfection to which mural decoration, writing, and illumination have been brought by the professors of Islam. Caligraphy has been cultivated in the East to an extent which can be scarcely conceived in this country; and the rules which govern that science are, though more precise, founded on æsthetic principles as correct as those of fine art-criticism here.

A people whose hereditary occupation was war and plunder, and who looked upon commerce as a degrading and slavish pursuit, were not likely to make much progress, even in simple arithmetic; yet, when it was no longer a mere question of dividing the spoils of a caravan, but of administering the revenues and regulating the frontiers of conquered countries, then the Saracens both appreciated and employed the exact mathematical sciences of India.

"The Arabs' registers are the verses of their bards," was the motto of their Bedawín forefathers, but the rude lays of border-warfare and pastoral life were soon found unsuited to their more refined ideas; while even the cultivation of their own rich and complex language was insufficient to satisfy their literary taste and craving for intellectual exercise. Persia therefore was again called

---

* Nearly all the technical terms used in Arab architecture are Persian—an additional proof that the so-called Saracenic style is of foreign and not native origin.

in to their aid, and the rich treasures of historical and legendary lore were ransacked and laid bare, while later on the philosophy and speculative science of the Greeks were eagerly sought after and studied.

Jerusalem also profited by Mamún's peaceful rule and æsthetic tastes, and the Haram buildings were thoroughly restored. So completely was this done that the Masjid may be almost said to owe its present existence to El Mamún; for had it not been for his care and munificence, it must have fallen into irreparable decay. I have already mentioned the substitution of El Mamún's name for that of the original founder, 'Abd el Melik, in the mosaic inscription upon the colonnade of the Cubbetes Sakhrah; inscriptions, implying the same wilful misstatement of facts, are found upon large copperplates fastened over the doors of the last-named building. Upon these we read, after the usual pious invocations and texts, the following words: "Constructed by order of the servant of God, 'Abdallah el Mamún, Commander of the Faithful, whose life may God prolong! during the government of the brother of the Commander of the Faithful, Er Rashíd, whom God preserve! Executed by Sáleh ibn Yahyah, one of the slaves of the Commander of the Faithful, in the month Rabí' el Ákhir, in the year 216." (May, A.D. 831.) It is inconceivable that so liberal and intellectual a prince should have sanctioned such an arrogant and transparent fiction; and we can only attribute the misstatement to the servile adulation of the officials entrusted with the carrying-out of the restorations.

The Christian patriarch Thomas now sought for an opportunity to restore the ruined Church of the Holy Sepulchre, and the occasion was not long wanting. One of those great plagues of locusts, which from time to time devastate Jerusalem, had just visited the city; the crops entirely failed in consequence of their depredations, and as a famine appeared imminent, every Mohammedan who could afford to do so quitted the city, with his family and household effects, until a more convenient season. Thus secured from interruption, the patriarch proceeded to put his plan into execution, and, aided by the contributions of a wealthy Egyptian named Bocam, set about rebuilding the church. The Muslims, on their return, were astonished and annoyed to find that the Christian temple had risen again from its ruins with such magnificent proportions that the newly-restored glories of their own Masjid were quite thrown into the shade. The Patriarch Thomas and other ecclesiastical dignitaries were accused of a contravention of the treaty under which they enjoyed their immunities and privileges, and were thrown into prison pending the inquiry. The principal charge against them, and one which embodied the whole cause of complaint, was that the dome of the Church of the Holy Sepulchre overtopped that of the Cubbet es Sakhrah. By a miserable subterfuge, to which we have already referred, the patriarch threw the onus of proof upon his accusers, and declared that his dome had been restored exactly upon the original plan, and that the dimensions of the former one had been rigidly observed. This deliberate falsehood the Mohammedans were unable to disprove, notwithstanding the direct evidence of their senses to the contrary, and the prisoners were perforce set at liberty, and the charge abandoned. Equity, either in its technical or ordinary sense, is not a distinguishing characteristic of Muslim law-courts, but in this case no one suffered by the omission but themselves.

Mamún's brother, El Mo'tasim Billah, succeeded him upon the throne. In the year 842 a fanatical chieftain, named Temím Abu Háreb, headed a large army of desperadoes, and, after some temporary successes in Syria, made himself master of Jerusalem. The churches and other Christian edifices were only saved from destruction on the payment of a large ransom by the patriarch;

on receiving this, the insurgents vacated the city, and were shortly afterwards entirely defeated by the caliph's forces.

A wonderful story is told of the great earthquake which took place in the year 846 A.D.: namely, that in the night, the guards of the Cubbet es Sakhrah were suddenly astonished to find the dome itself displaced, so that they could see the stars and feel the rain splashing upon their faces. Then they heard a low voice saying gently, "Put it straight again," and gradually it settled down into its ordinary state.

The power of the caliphs was now upon the wane: the disorders consequent upon the introduction of Turkish guards at Baghdád by El Mo'tassem first weakened their authority; but the revolt of the Carmathians in 877, during the reign of El Mo'tammed Billah, struck the first fatal blow against the House of Abbas. The sect of the Carmathians was founded by a certain Hamdán, surnamed Carmat. His doctrines consisted in allegorising the text of the Cor'án and the precepts of Islamism, and in substituting for their exterior observance other and fanciful duties. Carmat was an inhabitant of the neighbourhood of Basora, and his sect took its origin in that place, and soon spread over the whole of Irak and Syria. Under a chief, named Abu Táher, these fanatics defeated the Caliph el Moktader Billah, and held possession of the whole of the Syrian desert. With a force of more than a hundred and seven thousand men, Abu Táher took Rakka, Baalbekk, Basra, and Cufa, and even threatened the imperial city of Baghdád itself. The caliph made strenuous exertions to suppress the rebellion, but his soldiers were defeated, and his general taken captive and treated with the utmost indignities. A strange story is told of this struggle, which illustrates the fierce fanaticism and blind devotion of Abu Táher's followers. A subordinate officer from the Mussulman army penetrated to the rebel camp, and warned the chief to betake himself to instant flight. "Tell your master," was the reply, "that in all his thirty thousand troops he cannot boast three men like these." As he spoke, he bade three of his followers to put themselves to death; and without a murmur, one stabbed himself to the heart, another drowned himself in the waters of the Tigris, and a third flung himself from a precipice and was dashed to pieces. Against such savages as these, the luxurious squadrons of Baghdád could do nothing—they were ignominiously defeated; and the Carmathians roamed whithersoever they pleased, and devastated the country with fire and sword. In 929 Mecca itself was pillaged, thirty thousand pilgrims slain. and the black stone, the special object of adoration to the true believer, was carried off. This circumstance caused another diversion in favour of Jerusalem; the Ka'abah was again deserted, and crowds of devotees flocked from all parts of the Mohammedan world, to prostrate themselves before the Holy Rock of David. For the Christian inhabitants of Jerusalem the change was an unfortunate one: Mussulman bigotry was again in the ascendant in the Holy City, and we learn that in 937 the church of Constantine was destroyed, and the churches of Calvary and the Resurrection once more ruined and despoiled.

A few years later the "black stone" was restored and the Ka'abah and Mecca were once more opened for the Mohammedan pilgrims. The Carmathians themselves were suppressed, and their legions dispersed; but the seeds of religious and political heresy were sown broadcast throughout Islam, and were destined speedily to bring forth most disastrous fruit.

Since the conquests of 'Omar and his generals, no successful attempt had been made to recover the eastern provinces for the Grecian Empire; but in the reign of the Caliph El Motí' al Illah, a movement was made, which threatened to wrest the sceptre from the hands of the Muslim princes, and restore the pristine glory of the

Byzantine arms. Nicephorus Phocas and his murderer, John Zimisces, having successively married Theophania, the widow of Romanus, emperor of Constantinople, though nominally regents, really held the supreme command, and during a period of twelve years (A.D. 963-975) gained a series of brilliant victories over the Saracens. The whole of Syria was conquered, and Baghdád itself would have fallen, but for the prompt measures and stern resolution of the Bowide lieutenant, who compelled his imperial master to provide for the defence of the capital. Satisfied, however, with the rich plunder they had already obtained, the Greeks retired without attacking the town, and returned in triumph to Constantinople, leaving Syria to bear the brunt of the Muslim's anger and revenge.

A bloody persecution of the Christians was the result, and the churches of the East were once more exposed to the assaults of iconoclastic fanaticism. Jerusalem suffered severely in the reaction; the Church of the Holy Sepulchre was destroyed; and the patriarch, suspected of treasonous intercourse with the Greeks, was taken prisoner and burnt alive.

The establishment of independent dynasties in various parts of the empire, by the revolts of the provincial governors, had been for some time a source of danger to the Abbasside power, and ultimately accomplished the downfall of the dynasty.

The Aglabites in Africa, the Taherites in Khorassan, the house of Bowíyeh in Persia, had, one by one, fallen off from their allegiance, and the authority of the caliphs extended scarcely beyond the walls of Baghdád; and even in the capital itself they lingered on with fluctuating fortune, alternately the tools or victims of rival factions.

The alienation of Egypt—involving, as it nearly always did, that of Syria as well—more immediately affected the fortunes of Jerusalem, and therefore merits a rather more circumstantial account.

In the year 868 Ahmed ibn Túlún, the son of a Turkish slave, who had been appointed viceroy of Egypt by the Caliph el M'otazz Billah, rebelled against his master's authority, and assumed the style and title of Sultán, or independent sovereign. The kingdom remained in his family about thirty years, when it was retaken by Mohammed ibn Suleimán, general of the Caliph el Moktadhí Billah, and the authority of the Abbassides was again established in Egypt. This state of things, however, continued but for a short time, and in 936 the government of Egypt was again usurped by a Turk named Ikhshíd, who, after some opposition from the troops of the Er Rádhí Billah (the last of the caliphs who enjoyed the authority or deserved the name), obtained undisputed possession of Syria. He was nominally succeeded by his sons, but the government remained in the hands of his black slave, Káfúr, who ultimately contrived to seat himself upon the throne. At his death the kingdom passed to 'Alí el Ikshíd, a nephew of the founder of the family; but, after a short reign of one year, he was deposed (A.D. 970) by Jauher, the general of El Mo'ezz li dín Allah, fourth of the Fatemite caliphs.

This dynasty (the Fatemite, or Ismáïlí) was the most formidable of all who had resisted the authority of the caliphs of Baghdád; for it was not as the insurgent possessors of a province that they asserted their independence, but, as legitimate heirs, they disputed their master's title to the caliphate itself.

The family traced its origin to Mohammed, through Fatimah, wife of 'Alí ibn Abi Táleb, and daughter of the prophet; and on the strength of this illustrious pedigree, they claimed to be the true successors of the prophet, and rightful heirs to the supreme authority. Their pretensions were combated with great obstinacy by the Abbasside princes, but there seems good reason for believing that their claims were well-grounded. The founder of the house was one 'Obeid Allah, who, at the head of a number of political and religious fanatics, had succeeded in establishing himself in Irák and Yemen. After a series of romantic adventures, he made himself master of Africa (A.D. 910), where he assumed the title and authority of Caliph, and gave himself out to be the Mehdí, or last of the Imáms, foretold by Mohammed. At his death, which happened in A.D. 934, he was succeeded by his son, Al Cáïm bi Amr Illah, who reigned until A.D. 946. His son, El Mansúr Ismael, then came to the throne, and dying in 952, the caliphate passed into the hands of El Mo'ezz li dín Allah Abu Temím Ma'ad. It was this prince who conquered Egypt and founded the city of Cairo, which then became the seat of empire. He died in 969, and was succeeded by his son El 'Azíz billah Abu Mansúr Nizár. His death happened in October, A.D. 996; and the caliphate then passed to El Hakem bi Amr Illah, about whom it will be necessary to speak more in detail.

Hakem was born at Cairo on the 23rd of August, 985 A.D., and was consequently only eleven years and five months old when he ascended the throne. His father had assigned the guardianship of the young prince, during his minority, to a white eunuch named Barjewán; but the real power was vested in a certain Ibn 'Ammár, who had previously exercised the functions of Cádhi ul Codhát, or chief magistrate, and whom Hakem had been obliged to appoint as his prime minister. About the year 996, Hakem, or rather Ibn Ammár, had sent Suleimán ibn Ja'afer (better known as Abu Temím Ketámí) to be governor-general of Syria. Manjutakín, the governor who had been thus superseded, marched against Suleimán; but he was defeated near Ascalon, and sent a prisoner to Cairo. Abu Temím was now invested with the governor-generalship of Syria, and proceeded to Tiberias, where he fixed his residence, and appointed his brother 'Alí to replace him at Damascus. At first the inhabitants of that city refused to recognise his authority; but Abu Temím having written them a threatening letter, they proffered their submission, and asked pardon for having resisted. 'Alí refused to listen to their excuses, attacked the city, and put a number of the inhabitants to death; but, on the arrival of Abu Temím himself, order was at last restored. The governor-general then proceeded to occupy himself with the reduction of the maritime ports of Syria, and dismissing Jaish ibn Samsamah from the government of Tripoli, gave the post to his own brother 'Alí. Jaish at once returned to Egypt, where he made common cause with Barjewán against Ibn 'Ammár. The latter was not idle, and in the meantime had laid a deep plot against the life of his rival and his associates. Barjewán, however, obtained information of the plot; open hostilities were commenced, and Ibn 'Ammár was defeated, and compelled to seek safety in concealment. Barjewán now succeeded to the duties and responsibilities of his office, and appointed as his secretary one Fahd ibn Ibrahím, a Christian, to whom he gave the title of Reis. At the same time he wrote privately to the principal officers and inhabitants of Damascus, inciting them to rise and attack Abu Temím. Abu Temím thus found himself assailed at a moment when he least expected it; his treasures were pillaged, all his immediate followers were killed, and he himself was but too glad to escape by flight. While Damascus was thus suddenly exposed to all the horrors of civil war, the other provinces of Syria were agitated by diverse insurrections. In the same year (A.D. 997) the Tyrians had revolted, and placed at their head a fellah named Olaka; while Mofarrij ibn Daghfal ibn Jerráh had also headed a party of insurgents, and was making raids in the neighbourhood of Ramleh. The Greeks, under a general named Ducas, were also, at the same time, laying siege to the castle of Apameus. Meanwhile, Barjewán had committed the government of Syria to Jaish ibn Samsamah, who at once repaired to Ramleh, where he found his deposed predecessor Abu Temím, and sent him a prisoner to Egypt. After this he despatched Husein—a great-grandson of Hamdan, the founder of the Carmathian sect—to quell the insurrection at Tyre. Olaka, being besieged both by land and sea, sought the aid of the Greek emperor, who sent several vessels filled with troops to the relief of the city. The Mussulman vessels encountered this squadron before their arrival at Tyre; the Greeks were defeated, and put to flight with considerable loss. Tyre, thus deprived of its last hope of resistance, fell into the hands of Husein, who sacked the city, and put the inhabitants to the sword. Olaka himself fled to Egypt, where he was arrested and crucified. The new governor-general (Jaish) marched against Mofarrij ibn Jerráh, put the latter to flight, and shortly afterwards entered Damascus, where he was received with every mark of submission and obedience. The complete rout of the Grecian army followed shortly afterwards, and Jaish having, by a *coup d'état*, massacred all the powerful chiefs at Damascus whom he suspected of disaffection to his rule, established himself firmly in the government of Syria.

Barjewán now wielded the sovereign authority, Hakem remaining more of a puppet in his hands than ever he had been in those of Ibn 'Ammár. But the eunuch's triumph was shortlived. Barjewán had frequently applied to Hakem, during the infancy of the latter, the contemptuous name of "The Lizard," and this indignity rankled in the young caliph's breast. One morning (on the 15th of April, 999 A.D.) he sent a message to his guardian, couched in the following words: "The little lizard has become a huge dragon, and calls for thee!" Barjewán hastened, all trembling, into the presence of Hakem, who then and there ordered him to be beheaded.

About the year 1000 Hakem began to exhibit those eccentricities of character which ultimately betrayed him into such preposterous fancies and pretensions. He began to promenade the city on horseback every night, and on these occasions the inhabitants of Cairo vied with each other in illuminations, banquets, and other festive displays. As no limit was observed in these amusements, and a great deal of licentiousness was the natural result, the caliph forbade any woman to leave her house after nightfall, and prohibited the men from keeping their shops open after dusk. During the next two years, Hakem displayed an unbounded zeal for the Shiah sect, inflicting indignities upon "the enemies of 'Ali," and even putting many distinguished Sunnís to death. At the same time he commenced a rigorous persecution of the Jews and Christians: the more eminent persons of both religions were compelled either to embrace the Mohammedan creed, or to submit to an entire confiscation of their property—and, in many cases, to undergo a violent death; while the common people were robbed and illtreated on all sides, and obliged to wear a ridiculous uniform, to distinguish them from their Muslim neighbours.

Between the years 1004 and 1005, he became more extravagant and ridiculous in his behaviour than before. He prohibited the sale of certain vegetables, ordered that no one should enter the public baths without drawers upon pain of death, and caused anathemas to be written up, over the doors of all the mosques, against the first three caliphs, and all those persons whom history mentions as having been inimical to the family and succession of 'Ali. About this time he began to hold public assemblies, in which the peculiar doctrines of the Fatemite or Batení sect were taught, and Muslims of all classes and both sexes presented themselves in crowds for initiation.

The most ridiculous laws and ordinances were now promulgated: all persons were forbidden to show themselves in the streets after sunset; strict search was made for vessels containing wine, and wherever found they were broken to pieces, and their contents poured into the road; all the dogs in Cairo were slaughtered, because a cur had barked at the caliph's horse.

In the year 1007—probably inspired by a revolt which had, at one time, threatened the total extinction of his power—he began to display some slight signs of moderation, and, amongst other things, caused the anathemas against the enemies of 'Alí to be defaced from the mosques, and otherwise sought to conciliate his Sunní subjects. The Christians, however, in no way profited by the change, and a more rigorous persecution than ever was instituted against them. Three years later, Hakem gave the order for the destruction of the Church of the Holy Sepulchre at Jerusalem. The excuse alleged by the Mohammedan authorities for this outrage was the caliph's pious horror at the disgraceful orgies and juggling imposture attending the so-called descent of the Holy Fire at the Easter celebration: "on which occasion," as the Arab historian naïvely remarks, "the most frightful and blasphemous enormities are committed before the very eyes of the faithful. The Christians positively make a parade of their misbelief, reading and reciting their books aloud, in a manner too horrible to speak of, while they raise their crucifixes over their heads till one's hair absolutely stands on end!"

The real cause, however, appears to have been the machinations of a certain monk named John. This man had in vain endeavoured to induce his patriarch (Zacharias) to consecrate him to the office of bishop, but his superior had persistently refused to accede to his repeated request. Impelled by ambition and revenge, John came to Egypt, presented himself before Hakem at Jebel Mokattem (where the caliph was in the habit of resorting to practise his superstitious and profane ceremonies), and addressed to him a petition filled with the grossest calumnies against the patriarch. "Thou art the king of the country," so the document ran; " but the Christians have a king more powerful than thee, owing to the immense riches which he has amassed,—one who sells bishoprics for gold, and conducts himself in a manner highly displeasing to God." Hakem, on reading these words, at once commanded that all the churches throughout the kingdom should be closed, and the patriarch himself arrested, and wrote to the governor of Jerusalem in the following terms: " The Imam, the Commander of the Faithful, orders you so to destroy the Church of El Camámah,* that its earth shall become its heaven, and its length its breadth." The order was immediately put into execution; the church was razed to the ground, and an attempt made—though fortunately without success—to destroy the rock-hewn tomb itself, which had been for so many years the special object of devotion to myriads of Christian pilgrims.

In 1012 Hakem renewed the greater part of his absurd police regulations. He forbade women to take any part in funeral ceremonies, or to visit the tombs of their deceased relatives; the edicts against wine and forbidden fruits were more rigidly enforced; all the vines were destroyed, and their cultivation for the future prohibited; immense quantities of raisins were burnt, and the merchants forbidden to expose the fruit for sale; the same course was taken with regard to honey and dates, and no compensation whatever was allowed to the owners.

In 1014 he ordered all the women of Cairo to confine themselves rigorously to their houses, and forbade them even to appear at the doors or windows, and shoemakers were forbidden to make shoes for them. This state of constraint they were compelled to endure until his death,—that is, for more than seven years and a half.

It is related that, passing one day by certain baths, he heard a noise inside, and on being informed that some

* See p. 71.

women were there, in contravention of his law, he ordered the doors and other approaches to be walled up, and the entire number perished of starvation.

But it would be tedious to detail the numerous acts of fanaticism and folly of which he was guilty. Suffice it to say, that he committed every extravagance which could shock the prejudices or offend the scruples of his subjects.

At last his folly reached its height, and he gave himself out to be the Deity incarnate, and called upon all men to render him divine honours. In these preposterous pretensions he was supported (perhaps instigated in the first place) by certain Persian *Da'is*, or emissaries of the Bateni sect, of whom the principal were Mohammed ibn Ismail ed Darazí and Hamza ibn Alí ibn Ahmed el Hadí. These persons endeavoured to spread their doctrines in Cairo itself; but although a certain number of persons, impelled either by fear or love of gain, did acknowledge the divinity of the caliph and abjure the Mussulman religion—yet the greater part of the populace shrank from the profession of such impiety, and Hamza and Ed Darazí were compelled to seek safety in flight. They chose Syria for the next scene of their operations, and found ready believers in the mountaineers of Lebanon and Hermon—men who still clung in secret to the idolatrous sun-worship of their forefathers.

Thus was the sect of the Druzes established in Syria: they take their name from Ed Darazí, but they regard Hamza as the true founder of their religion. And for eight hundred years a hardy and intelligent race have acknowledged for their god one of the maddest monsters that the world has ever produced!

As for Hakem himself, his extravagant conduct could not long go unpunished. In the year 1021 he was assassinated, by the orders of his own sister, while engaged in one of his nocturnal ceremonies in Jebel Mokattem, where he was in the habit of retiring "to worship the planet Saturn, and hold converse with the devil."

It will not be out of place here to give some account of the tenets of the Druzes.* This remarkable sect profess to recognise but one God, without seeking to penetrate into the nature of His being and attributes; to confess that He can neither be comprehended by the senses, nor defined by language; to believe that the Deity has manifested itself to mankind at different epochs under a human form, without participating in any of the weaknesses and imperfections of human nature; that the last of these avatars descended upon earth in the person of El Hakem bi Amr Illah, in whom they ceased for all time; that Hakem disappeared in the year 411 of the Hijrah (A.D. 1021), in order to put the faith of his worshippers to the test; and that he will one day appear again, clothed in majesty and glory, to extend his empire over the whole face of the globe, and to consummate the happiness of those who faithfully believe in him. They believe, moreover, that the Universal Intelligence is the first of God's creatures, and the immediate production of His omnipotence, and that this intelligence was incarnate in the person of Hamza ibn Ahmed during Hakem's reign; that it is by his ministry that all other creatures have been produced; that Hamza alone possesses the knowledge of truth and of true religion, and that he communicates, directly or indirectly, but in different proportions, to the other ministers, and to the faithful themselves, that knowledge and grace which he receives from the Deity, and of which he is the sole channel; that he alone has immediate access to the presence of God, and serves as the mediator to all other worshippers of the Supreme Being; and that he will be, at the second advent,

* The following account of the Druzes, as well as that of the life of Hakem, is abridged from the 'Exposé de la Religion des Druzes,' by the celebrated Orientalist, Sylvestre de Sacy.

the instrument by which all rewards and punishments are to be distributed, and the kingdom of Hakem to be established upon earth. They hold that all souls are created by this Universal Intelligence; that the number of human beings is always the same, and that souls pass successively into different bodies; that their condition during this transmigration is progressive or the reverse, according to their adherence in the previous state to the dogmas and precepts of their religion, and their strict performance of the duties enjoined by the seven commandments of Hamza. These are—Veracity; Charity; the renunciation of their ancient faith; submission to the will of God; to believe that all preceding religions are but types of the true faith; that all their precepts and ceremonies are allegories; and that their own religion abrogates all other creeds which have gone before. Such are the doctrines taught in the religious works of the Druzes themselves; the followers of the sect are known amongst themselves by the name of Unitarians. The Druzes are accused of worshipping a small idol in the form of a calf, and it is a well-ascertained fact that they do make use of some such figure in their religious ceremonies. It is, however, the symbol of Iblis, the rival or enemy of Hakem, the calf ('*ejl*') being opposed to the Universal Intelligence ('*akl*') just mentioned.

Before his death, Hakem appears to have somewhat relaxed in his persecutions of the Jews and Christians; the latter were allowed to rebuild their churches, and many who had become apostates openly renounced Mohammedanism, and were rebaptized into the Christian community.

The Church of the Holy Sepulchre thus destroyed must have been (see p. 133) very speedily repaired, for we find, during the reign of El Mostanser Billah, Hakem's grandson, that the fabric was completely restored, the permission of the caliph having been obtained by the release of five thousand Muslim prisoners on the part of the Greek emperor.

In the year 1016 a fresh earthquake occurred, and the great cupola over the Sakhrah fell down, though without much injury happening to the foundations of the building. The walls at the south-west angle of the Haram es Sheríf also suffered by the shock, and a Cufic inscription tells us that the damage done in that quarter was repaired by Ed Dháher li 'Ezaz dín Alláh. The same prince also restored the cupola itself, as we learn from another inscription, engraved upon the wooden framework of the cupola, and repeated at each of the four points of the compass. It runs as follows: "In the name of God the Merciful, the Compassionate! 'None repair the mosques of God but such as believe in Him' (Cor. c. v.) The Imám Abu el Hasan ed Dháher li 'Ezaz dín Allah, son of El Hakem bi Amr Illah, Prince of the Faithful (the blessing of God be upon his noble ancestry!), ordered the restoration of this blessed cupola. The work was executed by the servant of God, the Emír, the confidant of the Imáms, the prop of the empire, 'Alí ibn Ahmed Ináhet Allah, in the year 413 (A.D. 1022). May God perpetuate the glory and stability of our lord the Commander of the Faithful, and make him to possess the east and west of the earth! We praise God at the beginning and end of all our works."

In 1034 fresh earthquakes devastated Syria and Egypt; some of the walls of Jerusalem were destroyed, and a large portion of the Mihráb Dá'úd (that is, the building now called the Cala'at Jálút) fell to the ground.

Again, in the year 1060, an accident happened in the Cubbet es Sakhrah: the great candelabra suspended from the dome, and containing five hundred candles, suddenly gave way, and fell with an awful crash upon the Sakhrah, greatly to the consternation of the worshippers assembled in the mosque, who looked upon it as foreboding some great calamity to Islám. Their fears were not unfounded, for the conquest of the Holy City by the Crusaders followed not many years this incident. This period seems to have been especially fertile in volcanic disturbances, for again, in the year 1068, a fearful earthquake convulsed all Palestine. On this occasion, the Sakhrah is said to have been rent asunder by the shock, and the cleft miraculously reclosed.

Another event of evil omen, but of doubtful authenticity, is related by the Arab historians as having happened about the same period. The sea, they declare, suddenly receded for the distance of a day's journey; but on the inhabitants of the neighbourhood taking possession of the reclaimed land, it suddenly returned and overwhelmed them, so that an immense destruction of life ensued.

The conflict between the Abbasside and Fatimite caliphs had been from time to time renewed; but fortune seemed at length to have decided the struggle in favour of the latter family, and the name of El Mostanser Billah was formally introduced into the Khotbah (or Friday "bidding prayer"), in the sacred mosques of Mecca and Jerusalem—a proceeding which was tantamount to recognising the Fatimite monarch as the legitimate successor of the Prophet, and sovereign of the whole Mussulman empire. But scarcely had they attained the summit of their ambition when the fall came, and events happened which resulted in the total overthrow of the Fatemite dynasty, and the restoration, in name at least, of the authority of the Abbasside caliphs.

The nomad tribe of Turkomans had made themselves masters of Khorassan, and determined upon the election of a king. Toghrul Beg, a grandson of a noble chief named Seljuk, was chosen by lot for the office, and in a short time extended his conquests over the whole of Persia; and, being a rigid Mohammedan of the orthodox sect, compelled the revolted lieutenants of the Abbasside caliphs to return to their allegiance. For this service he was named Emír el Omará ("Chief of chiefs"), and appointed the vicegerent and protector of the caliph. His nephew, Alp Arslán, succeeded him, and, after a brilliant career of conquest, left the sceptre to his son Melik Shah (A.D. 1072). This prince, a worthy scion of the Seljukian line, resolved upon the extension of the Fatemite dynasty, and the establishment of his own authority in Syria and Egypt. His lieutenant, Atsiz, a native of Kh'árezm, invaded the former country, and took possession of Ramleh and Jerusalem—the latter after a protracted siege. The names of the Abbasside caliph, and of the Sultán Melik Shah, were now formally substituted for that of the Egyptian caliph, El Mostanser Billah, in the Friday Khotba, at the Masjid el Aksa. Five years later he besieged Damascus, and the capital of Syria also fell before his troops: the inhabitants, already reduced to the last extremities by famine, were punished for their resistance by the resentful Emír, and the city being given up to pillage, the most frightful scenes of carnage ensued. Emboldened by this victory, he marched upon Egypt at the head of a large army of Turkomans, Kurds, and Arabs, and laid siege to Cairo. Here, however, he was repulsed with considerable loss, and compelled to return to Syria, which he found already in a state of insurrection against his authority. Those of his troops who had escaped slaughter in Egypt were butchered by the insurgents as they passed Palestine; and Atsiz, accompanied only by a small band of adherents, escaped with difficulty to Damascus, where his brother had been left at the head of affairs during his absence. Jerusalem had, in the meantime, risen against the Turkish chief; but the insurrection was soon quelled, and the Cadhí and other municipal officers, together with three thousand of the inhabitants, were put to death. Atsiz was shortly afterwards besieged in Damascus by the Egyptian forces, and called in to his aid the Emír Tutush, a son of Alp

Arslan. The Egyptians fled without attempting to oppose the advancing army, and Emír Tutush was welcomed by Atsiz at the city-gate. Jealous, doubtless, of his subordinate's previous victories and growing influence, the prince commanded him to be seized and executed upon the spot, —alleging, as an excuse for the barbarous act, that the general had been wanting in respect, and had not awarded him the reception to which his rank entitled him. The Emír Tutush now assumed the post of governor-general of Syria, and assigned that of Jerusalem and Palestine to a Turkish chief, named Urtuk ibn Eksek, who remained in authority until A.D. 1091. Urtuk was succeeded by his two sons, Elghází and Sukmán, who ruled Jerusalem until the assassination of Tutush, at Damascus, in A.D. 1095. Taking advantage of the disturbances which followed upon this event, the Fatimite caliph of Egypt, El Most'aíla Billah, sent his general, Afdhal el Jemálí, with a large force, into Syria. Damascus yielded without a blow in the month of July 1096, and Syria and Palestine remained for some time afterwards in the hands of the Egyptian government.

CHAPTER V.

THE CHRISTIAN PILGRIMS.

> Dulce mihi cruciari ;
> Parva vis doloris est :
> Malo mori quam fædari :
> Major vis amoris est.
> *Hymn attributed to St. Augustine.*

AT what period in the history of Christianity began the practice of going on pilgrimage it is difficult to decide. Probably the first places held sacred were those of local martyrs and confessors to the faith. Every part of the civilised world had these in abundance; there was not a village where some saint had not fallen a victim to persecution, not a town which could not boast of its roll of martyrs. When the day of persecution was over, and stories of miracles and wonderful cures at holy shrines began to grow, it was natural that the minds of a credulous age should turn to the holiest place of all, the city of Jerusalem. It had so turned even before the Invention of the Holy Cross; for Helena herself was on a pilgrimage when she made her discovery. But the story, noised abroad, the building by Constantine of the church of the Martyrdom, and the immediate fixing, without any hesitation, of all the sacred sites recorded in the New Testament, were the causes of a vast increase in the number of pilgrims who every year flocked to Jerusalem. And then flames which burst from the foundations of the Temple when Julian made his vain attempt to rebuild it were reported throughout Christendom, and added to the general enthusiasm. For the feeble faith of the nations had to be supported by miracles ever new. Moreover, the dangers of the way were diminished; more countries day by day became Christian; the Pagans, who had formerly intercepted and killed the pilgrims on the road, were now themselves in hiding; the Christians destroyed the old shrines and temples wherever they found them; and all the roads were open to the pious worshipper who only desired to pray at the sacred places.

But the passion for pilgrimages grew to so great an extent, and was accompanied by so many dangers to virtue and good manners, that attempts were made from time to time to check it. Augustine teaches that God is approached better by love than by long travel. Gregory of Nyssa points out that pilgrimage of itself avails nothing; and Jerome declares that heaven may be reached as easily from Britain as from Jerusalem, that an innumerable throng of saints never saw the city, and that the sacred places themselves have been polluted by the images of idols.

But this teaching was in vain. Going on pilgrimage served too many ends, and gratified too many desires. Piety, no doubt, in greater or less degree, had always something to do with a resolve to undertake a long and painful journey. But there were other motives. The curious man, by becoming a pilgrim, was enabled to see the world; the lazy man to escape work; the adventurous man to find adventures; the credulous and imaginative man to fill his mind with stories; the vain man to gratify his vanity, and procure life-long honour at the cost of some peril and fatigue; the sincere to wipe off his sins; and all alike believed that they were doing an act meritorious in itself and pleasing in the sight of heaven.

The doctors of the Church protested, but in vain.

Indeed, they often went themselves. St. Porphyry, afterwards Bishop of Gaza, was one of those who went. He had betaken himself to the Thebaid at the age of twenty, to become a hermit. There, after five years of austerities, he became seized with an irresistible desire to see Jerusalem. Afflicted with a painful disorder, and hardly able to hold himself upright, he managed to crawl across the deserts to the city; as soon as he arrived there, he sent his companion back to Thessalonica, his native place, with injunctions to sell all that he had and distribute the proceeds among the faithful. And then he laid himself down to die. Mark departed; what was his astonishment, on returning, his mission accomplished, to find his friend restored to health? Porphyry went no more to the Thebaid, probably but a dull place at best, even for a hermit, and betaking himself to a handicraft, he preached the Gospel and became a bishop. St. Jerome himself, in spite of his protests, went to Palestine, accompanied by Eusebius of Cremona. The voice of calumny had attacked Jerome in revenge for his exposure of the sins and follies of the day, and he was pleased to leave Rome. The two future saints landed at Antioch, and after seeing Jerusalem went on to Bethlehem, and thence to the Thebaid, where they solaced themselves with admiring the austerities of the self-tormentors, the hermits there. Returning thence to Bethlehem, they resolved on selling their property and forming a monastery in that town. This they accomplished by the assistance of Paula and Eudoxia, two noble ladies, mother and daughter, who followed them to Palestine, and passed their lives like Jerome himself, under a rigid rule of prayer and labour. Paula died in Bethlehem. Her daughter and Jerome, less happy, were turned out of their peaceful retreat by a band of Arabs, bribed, we are told, by the heretics in Jerusalem, who burned and pillaged the monastic houses, dispersed the monks and nuns, and drove the venerable Jerome, then past the age of seventy years, to a bed from which he never rose again.

The story of the pilgrimage of Paula is useful because it shows that the multiplication of the sacred sites was not due entirely to the invention of later times. At Cæsarea she saw the house of Cornelius the centurion, turned into a church; and here, also, was the house of Saint Philip, and the chambers of his four virgin daughters, prophetesses; on Mount Zion she saw the column where our Lord was scourged, still stained with His blood, and supporting the gallery of a church; she saw, too, the place where the Holy Spirit descended on the apostles; at Bethphage they showed her the sepulchre of Lazarus, and the house of Mary and Martha; on Mount Ephraim she saw the tombs of Joshua and Eleazar; at Shechem the well of Jacob, and the tombs of the twelve patriarchs, and at Samaria the tombs of Elisha and John the Baptist. Hither were brought those possessed with devils, that they might be exorcised, and Paula herself was an eye-witness of the miraculous cure effected. With regard to miracles, indeed, Antoninus Martyr, to whose testimony on the site of the church of the Holy Sepulchre we have referred in another place,* relates many which he himself pretends to have seen. If you bring oil near the true cross, he says, it will boil of its own accord, and must be quickly removed, or it will all escape; at certain times a star from heaven rests on the cross. He tells us, too, that there is on Sinai an idol, fixed there by the infidels, in white marble, which on days of ceremony changes colour and becomes quite black.

The impending fall of the empire, and the invasion of the hordes of barbarians, proved but a slight check to the swarms of pilgrims. For the barbarians, finding that these unarmed men and women were completely harmless, respected their helplessness and allowed them to pass

* See Appendix.

unmolested. When, as happened shortly after their settlement in Italy and the West, they were gradually themselves brought within the pale of the Christian faith, they made laws which enforced the protection and privileges of pilgrims. These laws were not, it is true, always obeyed.

The route was carefully laid down for the pilgrims by numerous Itineraries, the most important of which is that called the Itinerary of the Bordeaux Pilgrim. The author starts from Bordeaux, perhaps because it is his own city, perhaps because it was then the most considerable town in the West of Europe. He passes through France by Auch, Toulouse, Narbonne, thence to Beziers, Nîmes, and Arles. At Arles he turns northwards, and passes through Avignon, Orange, and Valence, when he again turns eastwards to Diez, Embrun and Briançon; thence he crosses the Alps and stops at Susa. In Italy he passes through the towns of Turin, Pavia, Milan (not because Milan was on his way, but because it would be a pity to lose the opportunity of seeing this splendid city), to Brescia, Verona, and Aquileia, a town subsequently destroyed by Attila, at the head of the Gulf of Trieste. Crossing the Italian Alps he arrives at the frontiers of the empire of the East. His course lies next through Illyria, Styria, and along the northern banks of the river Drave, which he leaves after a time and follows the course of the Save, to its confluence with the Danube at Belgrade. He now follows the Danube until he comes to the great Roman road, which leads him to Nissa. Thence, still by the road, to Philippopolis, Heraclia, and Constantinople. Across Asia Minor he passes through Nicomedia, Nicæa, across what is now Anatolia to Ancyra, thence to Tyana and Tarsus. From Tarsus he goes to Iskanderoon, thence to Antioch, Tortosa, Tripoli (along the Roman road which lay by the Syrian sea-board), Beyrout, Sidon, Tyre, Acre, and Cæsarea. Here he leaves the direct and shortest way to Jerusalem in order first to visit the Jordan and other places.

It is instructive to follow the route of the pilgrim, because this was doubtless the road taken by the hundreds who every year flocked to Jerusalem, and because, as we shall see, nearly the same road was subsequently taken by the Crusaders.

Palestine, during some centuries, enjoyed a period of profound peace, during which the sword was sheathed, and no voice of war, save that of a foray of Arabs, was heard in the land. Thither retreated all those who, like Saint Jerome, were indisposed altogether to quit the world, like the hermits of Egypt, but yet sought to find some quiet spot where they could study and worship undisturbed. Thither came the monks turned out of Africa by Genseric; and when Belisarius in his turn overcame the barbarians, thither were brought back the spoils of the Temple which Titus had taken from Jerusalem. Nor was the repose of the country seriously disturbed during the long interval between the revolt of Barcochebas and the invasion of the Persians under Chosroes. But after Heraclius had restored their city to the Christians, a worse enemy even than Chosroes was at hand, and when Caliph Omar became the master of Jerusalem, the quiet old days were gone for ever.

The Mohammedans were better masters than the Persians; they reverenced the name of Jesus, they spared the Church of the Sepulchre, they even promised to protect the Christians. But promises made by the caliph were not always observed by his fanatic soldiers. The Christians were pillaged and robbed; they were insulted and abused; they were forced to pay a heavy tribute; forbidden to appear on horseback, or to wear arms; obliged to wear a leathern girdle to denote their nation; nor were they even permitted to elect their own bishops and clergy.

The pilgrims did not, in consequence of these persecutions, become fewer. To the other excitements which called them to the Holy Land was now added the chance of martyrdom, and the records of the next two centuries are filled with stories of their sufferings, which appear to have been grossly exaggerated, at the hands of the Muslim masters of the city. If the pilgrim returned safely to his home, there was some comfort for his relations, deprived of the glory of having a martyr in the family, in being able to relate how he had been buffeted and spat upon. To this period belong the pilgrimages of Arnulphus and Antoninus. That of the former is valuable, inasmuch as not only his own account has been preserved, but even the map which he drew up from memory. Bede made use of his narrative, which was taken down by the abbot Adamnanus, who gave Arnulphus hospitality when he was shipwrecked in the Hebrides on his return.

So extensive was the desire to "pilgrimize," so many people deserted their towns and villages, leaving their work undone and their families neglected, while disorders multiplied on the road, and virtue was subjected to so many more temptations on the way to the Holy Land than were encountered at home, that the Church, about the ninth century, interfered, and assumed the power to grant or to withhold the privilege of pilgrimage. The candidate had first to satisfy the bishop of his diocese of his moral character, that he went away with the full consent of his friends and relations, and that he was actuated by no motives of curiosity, indolence, or a desire to obtain in other lands a greater licence and freedom of action. If these points were not answered satisfactorily, permission was withheld; and if the applicant belonged to one of the monastic orders he found it far more difficult to obtain the required authority. For it had been only too well proved that in assuming the pilgrim's robe the monks were often only embracing an opportunity to return to the world again. But when all was satisfactory, and the bishop satisfied as to the personal piety of the applicant, the Church dismissed him on his journey with a service and a benediction. He was solemnly invested with the scrip and staff, he put on the long woollen robe which formed the chief part of his dress, the clergy and his own friends accompanied him to the boundaries of his parish, and there, after giving him a letter or a passport which ensured him hospitality so long as he was in Christian countries, they sent him on his way.

"In the name of God," ran the commendatory letter, "we would have your highness or holiness to know that the bearer of the present letters, our brother, has asked our permission to go peaceably on pilgrimage to Jerusalem, either for his own sins, or to pray for our preservation. Thereupon, we have given him these present letters, in which we salute you, and pray you, for the love of God and Saint Peter, to receive him as your guest, to be useful to him in going and coming back, so that he may return in safety to his house; and as is your good custom, make him pass happy days. May God the Eternal King protect you, and keep you in his kingdom!"

Thus provided, the pilgrim found hostels open for him, and every castle and monastery ready to receive him. Long and weary his journey may have been, but it could not have been tedious to him with eyes to see and observe, when every city was a sort of new world, when a new country lay beyond every hill, and new manners and customs were marked on every day. The perils and dangers of the way were not until the Mohammedan conquest—nor indeed after it, until the time of Hakem—very great. True, the woods harboured wild beasts, but the pilgrims travelled in bands; and there were robbers, but these did not rob those who had nothing. The principal dangers were those of which they knew nothing, the diseases due to malaria, exposure, sun-stroke, fatigue, and change of climate. These, and not the Turks, were the chief enemies of pilgrims. And in spite of these, known and unknown, dangers, there cannot be a doubt that the pilgrimage to Syria was a long series of new and continually changing wonders and surprises. The church which blessed the pilgrim, also celebrated the act of pilgrimage, and a service has been preserved which was performed on the Second Sunday after Easter, in the cathedral of Rouen. Of this the following is an abridgment:—In the nave of the church was erected a fort, "castellum," representing that house at Emmaus where the two travellers entered and broke bread with Christ. At the appointed time two priests, "of the second seats," appointed for the day, came forth from the vestry, singing the hymn which begins "Jesu, nostra redemptio." They were to be dressed in tunics, "et desuper cappis transversum," were to have long flowing hair and beards, and were each to carry a staff and scrip. Singing this hymn, and slowly marching down the right aisle, they came to the western porch, when they put themselves at the head of the procession of choristers waiting for them, and all began together to sing, "Nos tuo vultu saties." Then the priest for the day, robed in alb and surplice, barefooted, carrying a cross on his right shoulder, advanced to meet them, and "suddenly standing before them," asked, "What manner of communications are these that ye have one to another as ye walk, and are sad?"* To which the two pilgrims replied, "Art thou only a stranger in Jerusalem, and hast not known the things which are come to pass there in these days?"

"What things?" asked the priest.

"Concerning Jesus of Nazareth," they replied, with the words which follow.

"Oh, fools!" said the priest, "and slow of heart, to believe all that the prophets have spoken."

And then, feigning to retire, the priest would there have

* We take the words of the authorized version.

left them, but they held him back, and pointing to the "castellum," entreated him to enter, singing, "Abide with us, for it is towards evening, and the day is far spent." Then singing another hymn, they led him to the "Fort of Emmaus," when they entered and sat down at a table already spread for supper. Here the priest brake bread sitting between them, and being recognised by this act for the Lord, "suddenly vanished out of their sight." The pilgrims pretending to be stupefied, arose and sung sorrowfully (*lamentabiliter*), "Alleluia," with the verse, "Did not our hearts burn within us, while he talked with us by the way, and while he opened to us the Scriptures?"

Singing this twice they walked to the pulpit, where they sang the verse, "Dic nobis Maria." After this, another priest, dressed in a dalmatic and surplice, with head muffled up like a woman, came to them and sang, "Sepulcrum Christi Angelicos testes."

He then took up a cloth from one place, and a second from another place, and threw them before the great door of the choir. "And then let him sing, 'Christ has risen,' and let the choir chaunt the two other verses which follow, and let the women and the pilgrims retire within; and the memory of this act being thus recalled, let the procession return to the choir, and the vespers be finished."

These ceremonies were not, of course, designed to meet the case of pilgrimages undertaken by way of penance. These were of two kinds, *minores peregrationes*, which were pilgrimages on foot to local shrines, such as, later on, that of St. Thomas-à-Becket, for instance; or *majores*, to Rome or Jerusalem. The latter, of which Frotmond's pilgrimage—which will be described further on—is an example, were for murder, sacrilege, or for any other great crime. One of the rules as regards a murderer was as follows:—"Let a chain be made of the very sword with which the crime was committed, and let the neck, arms, and body of the criminal be bound round with this chain;

thus let him be driven from his native country, and wander whither the Pope shall direct him, till by long prayer he obtain the Divine mercy."

The roads were crowded with these miserable wretches, limping along to their shrines. Only the more distinguished, either in rank or enormity of offence, were ordered to go to Palestine. The custom was carried on to comparatively late times, and it was not till the fourteenth century that a law was passed restraining the practice— "better is it that these criminals should remain all together in one place, and there work out the sentence imposed upon them by the Church,"—so long was it before justice was taken out of the hands of the Church.

It could not have added greatly to the delights of travelling in these days occasionally to meet bands of these wretches, toiling painfully along, half naked, and dragging the weight of their chains, while they implored the prayers and alms of the passers-by.

But the triumph of the pilgrim (not the criminal) was in coming home again. Bearing a palm branch in his hands, as a sign that he had seen the sacred places, he narrated his adventures, and gathered—those at least that were poor—alms in plenty. Arrived at his native village, the palm branch was solemnly offered at the altar, and the pilgrim returned to his home to spend the rest of his life in telling of the miracles he had seen wrought.

Not all, however, came home. So long as the pilgrim passed the rough lands where his passport was recognised, all was easy enough. He got food to eat, and a bed to sleep in. But he sometimes came to places, if he went by way of Constantinople, where there were no monasteries, and where his passport proved useless. The ferocious Bulgarians, or the treacherous Croats, in theory friendly, and by profession Christian, sometimes proved cut-throats and robbers. The Mohammedans, though they acknowledged the harmlessness of the crowds that flocked about the gates, could not avoid showing the contempt they naturally felt for those who refused to think as they thought themselves; when the pilgrims arrived at the city, they could not enter without payment, and often they had no money to pay. And if they were able to pay for admission, they were not exempt from the insults of the Saracens, who sometimes pleased themselves with interrupting the sacred office, trampling on the vessels of the Eucharist, and even scourging the priests.

But these persecutions belong to a somewhat later time than we have yet arrived at.

About the same time as the pilgrimage of Arnulf took place that of Willibald. Willibald, afterwards Bishop of Eichstädt, was an Englishman by birth. He was dedicated at an early age by his father to the monastic life, and received a pious and careful education. Arrived at the period of manhood, he persuaded his father, his sister Walpurga, and his brother Wunebald, accompanied by a large party of servants and followers, to undertake a pilgrimage to Palestine. In Italy his father died, and his brother and sister left him and returned to England. Willibald, with a few companions, went on eastward. At Emessa they were detained, but not harmed, by the Emir, but, released through the intercession of a Spanish merchant, they proceeded to Jerusalem. Willibald visited the city no less than four times. He was once, we are told, miraculously cured of blindness by praying at the church where the Cross had been found. Probably he had contracted an ophthalmia, of which he recovered in Jerusalem.

About the year 800, Charlemagne conceived the idea of sending a special embassy to the Caliph Harûn er Raschíd. He sent three ambassadors, two of whom died on the way. The third, Isaac the Jew, returned after five years' absence, bearing the presents of the great Caliph, and accompanied by his envoys. The presents consisted of an elephant, which caused huge surprise to the people, carved ivory, incense, a clock, and the keys of the Church of the Holy Sepulchre. Charlemagne sent, in return, white and green robes, and a pack of his best hounds. He also astonished the caliph's envoys by the magnificence of his church ceremonials. Charlemagne established a hostel at Jerusalem for the use of pilgrims, and continued to cultivate friendly relations with Haroun. The latter, for his part, inculcated a toleration far enough indeed from the spirit of his creed, and ordered that the Christians should not be molested in the exercise of their worship.

One of the most singular histories of the time is that, already alluded to, of the pilgrimage of Frotmond. At the death of their father, Frotmond and his brothers proceeded to divide the property which he left behind. A great-uncle, an ecclesiastic, in some way interfered with the partition of the estates, and roused them to so great a fury that they killed him. But immediately afterwards, struck with horror at the crime they had committed, they betook themselves to the court of King Lothaire, and professed their penitence and resolution to perform any penance. In the midst of an assembly of prelates the guilty brothers were bound with chains, clothed with hair shirts, and with their bodies and hair covered with ashes, were enjoined thus to visit the sacred places. They went first to Rome, where Benedict III. received them and gave them letters of recommendation. Thence they went by sea to Palestine, and spent four years in Jerusalem, practising every kind of austerity and mortification. Thence, because their penance was not hard enough, they went to the Thebaïd in Egypt, where they remained two years more among hermits the most rigid, and self-tormentors the most cruel. They then wandered along the shores of the Mediterranean to Carthage, where was the tomb of Saint Cyprian. After seven years of suffering they returned to Rome, and begged for the pardon of the Church. It was in vain. They had murdered a churchman; they were of noble birth; and the example must be striking. And once more they set off for a renewal of their weary travels in lands already familiar to them. This time, after revisiting Jerusalem, they went north to Galilee, and thence south to Sinai, where they remained for three years. Again they returned to Rome, and again implored the pardon of the Pope, again to be refused. And then, tired, we may suppose, of sufferings which seemed useless, and fatigues without an object, they bent their steps homewards. At Rennes the eldest brother died, unforgiven. Frotmond turned his steps once more towards Rome. But on the way he was met by an aged man. "Return," said he, "to the sanctuary which thou hast quitted. I order thee, in the name of the Lord! It is there that absolution waits thee by the mercy of God."

He turned back: the weight of his chains had bent him double, he could not stand upright, the sores which the iron had caused were putrefying, and the time of his deliverance from the earth seemed to draw nigh. In the night the same old man appeared again, accompanied by two fair youths. "Master," said one, "it is time to restore health to this pilgrim." "Not yet," replied the old man, "but when the monks shall rise to chant the vigils." At the hour of vigils Frotmond crawled with the rest into the church. There he fell asleep, and while he slept, the old man appeared again and tore off the chains, which fell to the ground, and by the noise of their falling awakened Frotmond. They placed him in a bed, and in three days he was well and sound again, miraculously cured of his festering sores; but he was not yet satisfied, and was preparing for a third pilgrimage when he fell ill and died. The old man and the dream, were they his disguise for a resolution to endure no more the tyranny of the Church? or were they the invention of a later time, and of some bolder spirit than the rest, who would not allow that to Rome alone belonged the power of binding and of loosing?

With the passion for pilgrimages grew up the desire to find and to possess relics. These, towards the end of the tenth century, when a general feeling that the end of the world was approaching caused the building of new churches everywhere and the reconstruction of old ones, were found in great abundance. "Thanks to certain revelations and some signs," says Raoul the Bald, "we succeeded in finding holy relics, long hidden from human eyes. The saints themselves, by word of God, appeared to the faithful and reclaimed an earthly resurrection." The revelations began at Sens-sur-Yonne, in Burgundy, where they still show a goodly collection of holy bones, including the finger with which Luke wrote his Gospel, and the chair in which he sat while he was writing it. Archbishop Leuteric was so fortunate as to find a piece of Moses' rod; with this many miracles were wrought. Almost every returning pilgrim had something which he had either picked up, or bought, or been instructed in a vision of the night to bring home with him. This treasure he deposited in the parish church: pious people set it with pearls and precious stones, or enclosed it in a golden casket: stories grew up about it, sick people resorted to the place to be cured, and one more legend was added to the innumerable fables of relics. It is useful to remember, as regards the pilgrimages, the finding of relics, and the strange heresies of the time, that it was a period of great religious excitement, as well as of profound ignorance: nothing was too wonderful to be believed; no one so wise as not to be credulous. No one had actually seen a miracle with his own eyes, but everybody knew of countless miracles seen by his neighbour's eyes. Meantime, the toleration granted to the Christians through the wisdom of Harûn er Rashíd continued pretty well undisturbed for many years, and life at least was tolerably safe, though insult might be probable and even certain.

Commerce, the great civiliser, had its own part, too, in keeping the peace between Christian and infidel.

On the fifteenth of every September there was held a kind of fair in Jerusalem. Thither flocked merchants from Pisa, Venice, Genoa, and Marseilles, eager to satisfy at once their desire for gain, and their desire to obtain a reputation for piety. And for a short time Jerusalem seems to have served as the chief emporium, whither the East sent her treasures, to sell them to the West.

The objects in demand at this fair were those which were luxuries to the West; cloves, nutmegs, and mace from India; pepper, ginger, and frankincense by way of Aden; silks from India and China; sugar from Syria;* dates, cassia, and flax from Egypt; and from the same country quicksilver, coral, and metals; glass from Tyre; almonds, saffron, and mastic, with rich stuffs and weapons from Damascus; and dyed stuffs from Jerusalem itself, when the Jews had a monopoly, for which they paid a heavy tax, for dying.†

Gold in the West was scarce, and the trade was carried on either by exchange, or by means of silver. The chief traders were the Italians, but the French, especially through the port of Marseilles, were great merchants, and we find Guy de Lusignan, King of Jerusalem, according to French traders singular privileges and immunities, solely in reward for their assistance at Saint Jean d'Acre.

There can be no doubt that this trade had a great deal

---

* Albert of Aix speaks of the Crusaders first coming upon the sugar-cane: "The people sucked sweet reeds which were found in abundance in the meadows, called *zucra*. . . . . . This reed is grown with the greatest care every year; at the time of harvest the natives crush it in mortars, and collect the juice in vessels, when they leave it till it hardens, and becomes white like snow or salt."

† See Mémoires de l'Académie des Inscriptions. M. de Guignes sur l'état du commerce des François dans le Levant avant les Croisades.

to do with pilgrimages. The two motives which most of all persuade men cheerfully to incur danger are religion and gain. When were the two more closely allied than in those comparatively peaceful times when Jerusalem was open both to worshippers and traders? With his money bags tied to his girdle, the merchant could at once perform the sacred rites which, as most believed, made him secure of heaven, and could purchase those Eastern luxuries for which the princes of the West were ready to pay so dearly. A state of things, however, so favourable to the general welfare of the world could not be expected to last very long. Luxury and sensuality destroyed the Abassides, and their great kingdom fell to pieces. Then Nicephorus Phocas, Emperor of Constantinople, saw in the weakness of the Mohammedans the opportunity of the Christians. With wisdom worthy of Mohammed he resolved on giving his invasion a religious character, and endeavoured to persuade the clergy to proclaim a holy war. These, however, refused to help him; religion and the slaughter of the enemy were not to be confounded, and the great army of Nicephorus, which might have been made irresistible, was disheartened for want of that spirit which makes every soldier believe himself a possible martyr. The Greek Emperor took Antioch, but was prevented by death from following up his success, while the Patriarch of Jerusalem was condemned to the flames on suspicion of having corresponded with the Greeks. But before the taking of Antioch troubles had befallen the Christians. The Church of the Holy Sepulchre was greatly injured by the fanatics, who took every opportunity of troubling their victims. When it had been restored, the Patriarch was cast into prison on a charge of having built his church higher than the Mosque of Omar. He got off by a singular artifice. An old Mohammedan offered, for a consideration, to show him a way of escape. His offer being accepted, he simply told the Patriarch to deny the fact, and call on them to prove it. The plan succeeded; the charge, though perfectly true, could not be proved, and the Patriarch escaped.*

At this period the massacre of an immense number of Mohammedan pilgrims on their way to Mecca led to the substitution for thirty years of Jerusalem for Mecca.†

The city thus had two streams of pilgrims, one to the Holy Rock, the Mosque of Omar, and the other to the Holy Cave, the Sepulchre of Christ. Nicephorus being murdered, John Zimisces, his successor and murderer, followed up his victories. He easily gained possession of Damascus and Syria, and reduced to submission all the cities of Palestine. He did not, however, enter Jerusalem, to which he sent a garrison. Death‡ interrupted his victorious career, and Islam once more began to recover its forces. The Fatemite Caliphs, who had succeeded in establishing themselves in Egypt, made themselves masters of Jerusalem, and though for a short time the Christians were treated rather as allies and friends than as a conquered people, the accession of Hakem was an event which renewed all former troubles with more than their former weight.

He ordered that Jews should wear blue robes and Christians black, and in order to mark them yet more distinctively, that both should wear black turbans. Christians, moreover, were at first ordered to wear wooden stirrups, with crosses round their necks, while the Jews were compelled to carry round pieces of wood, to signify the head of the golden calf which they had worshipped in the desert. The destruction of the Church of the Holy Sepulchre by this madman has been already alluded to.§

---

* Williams's 'Holy City,' vol. i. pp. 338, 339.   † See Chap. V.

‡ After having murdered Nicephorus, he was himself poisoned by Basil, his grand chamberlain, who succeeded him. In the Greek empire murder seems to have formed the strongest title to the crown.

§ If there is any one fact in history which seems absolutely clear and certain, it is this, that *the Church of the Holy Sepulchre was destroyed by command of Hakem.* William of Tyre expressly

For another account of the same transaction and of the causes which led to it we are indebted to Raoul the Bald (Glaber), who describes the excitement produced in Europe by this act. "In the year 1009," he says, though his date appears to be wrong by one year, "the Church of the Sepulchre was entirely destroyed by order of the prince of Babylon. . . . The devil put it into the heads of the Jews to whisper calumnies about the servants of the true religion. There were a considerable number of Jews in Orleans, prouder, more envious, and more audacious than the rest of their nation. They suborned a vagabond monk named Robert, and sent him with secret letters, written in the Hebrew character, and for better preservation enclosed in a stick, to the prince of Babylon. Therein they told how, if the prince did not make haste to destroy the shrine at which the Christians worshipped, they would speedily take possession of his kingdom and deprive him of his honours. On reading the letter, the prince fell into fury, and sent to Jerusalem soldiers charged with the order to destroy the church from roof to foundation. This order was but too well executed; and his satellites even tried to break the interior of the Sacred Sepulchre with their iron hammers, but all their efforts were useless. . . . A short time after, it was known beyond a doubt that the calamity must be imputed to the Jews, and when their secret was divulged, all Christendom resolved with one accord to drive out the Jews from their territory to the very last. They became thus the object of universal execration. Some were driven out, some massacred by the sword, some thrown into the sea, or given up to different kinds of punishment. Others devoted themselves to voluntary deaths: so that, after the just vengeance executed

---

describes the reconstruction of the church. Raoul, as shown above, tells how the news of the destruction was received. All the Arabic historians record the event.

upon them, very few could be seen in the Roman world.
. . . These examples of justice were not calculated to inspire a feeling of security in the mind of Robert when he came back. He began by looking for his accomplices, of whom there were still a small number in Orleans; with them he lived familiarly. But he was denounced by a stranger, who had made the journey with him, and knew perfectly well the object of his mission. He is seized, scourged, and confesses his crime. The ministers of the king take him without the city, and there, in the sight of all the people, commit him to the flames. Nevertheless, the fugitive Jews began to reappear in the cities, and there is no doubt that, because some must always exist as a living testimony to their shame, and the crime by which they shed the blood of Christ, God permitted the animosity of the Christians to subside. However that may be by the divine will, Maria, mother of the Emir, prince of Babylon, a very Christian princess, ordered the church to be rebuilt with square and polished stones the same year.
. . . . . And there might have been seen an innumerable crowd of Christians running in triumph to Jerusalem from all parts of the world, and contending with one another in their offerings for the restoration of the house of God."

It was an unlucky day for the Jews when Robert went on his embassy, whatever that was, to the East. But a renewal of the religious spirit in the West was always attended by a persecution of the Jews. No story was too incredible to be believed of them, no violence and cruelty too much for them. When the Crusades began, almost the first to suffer were the hapless Jews, and we know how miserable was their situation so long as the Crusading spirit lasted. Even when this was dying out, when the Christians and the Saracens were often firm friends, the Jews alone shared none of the benefits of toleration. To be a descendant of that race by whom Christ was crucified, was to be subjected to the very wantonness of cruelty and persecution.

One of the principal sights in Jerusalem then, as now, though the Latins have long since given it up, was the yearly appearance of the holy fire. Odolric was witness, not only of this, but of another and a more unusual miracle. For while the people were all waiting for the fire to appear, a Saracen began to chant in mockery the *Kyrie Eleison*, and snatching a taper from one of the pilgrims, he ran away with it. "But immediately," says Raoul, "he was seized by the devil, and began to suffer unimaginable torments. The Christian who had been robbed regained his taper, and the Saracen died immediately after in the arms of his friends." This example inspired a just terror into the hearts of the infidels, and was for the Christians a great subject of rejoicing. And at that very moment the holy fire burst out from one of the same lamps, and ran from one to the other. Bishop Odolric bought the lamp which was first lit for a pound of gold, and hung it up in his church at Orleans, "where it cured an infinite number of sick."

One can easily understand the growth of stories, such as that of the stricken Saracen. An age like the tenth was little disposed to question the truth of a miracle which proved their faith. Nor was it likely to set against the one Saracen who died in torture after insulting the Cross the tens of thousands who insulted it with impunity. The series of miracles related by Raoul and others are told in perfect good faith, and believed by those to whom they were related as simply as they were believed by those who told them. And we can very well understand how they helped, in a time when hardly any other thing would have so helped, to maintain the faith of a people, coarse, rough, unlettered, and imaginative.

The destruction of the Church of the Holy Sepulchre, the stories spread abroad about the miraculous preservation of the cave, and its rebuilding in 1010, all served to increase the ardour of pilgrims. And there had been another cause already mentioned. Throughout western Christendom a whisper ran that the end of the world was approaching. A thousand years had nearly elapsed since the Church of Christ was founded. The second advent of the founder was to happen when this period was accomplished: the advent was to take place in Palestine; happy those who could be present to welcome their Lord. Therefore, of all conditions and ranks in life, from the lowest to the highest, an innumerable multitude of pilgrims thronged to Jerusalem. And so deep was the feeling that the end of all things was at hand, that legal documents were drawn up beginning with the words, "Appropinquante etenim mundi termino et ruinis crebrescentibus jam certa signa manifestantur, pertimescens tremendi judicii diem." Among the best known pilgrims of the last century before the Crusades is Fulke the Black, Count of Anjou. He was accused, and justly, of numerous acts of violence. But he had also violated the sanctity of a church, and for this pardon was difficult to obtain. Troubled with phantoms which appeared to him by night, the offspring of his own disordered conscience, Fulke resolved to expiate his sins by a pilgrimage. After being nearly shipwrecked on his voyage to Syria—the tempest appeared to him a special mark of God's displeasure—he arrived safely in Jerusalem, and caused himself to be scourged through the streets, crying aloud, "Lord, have mercy on a faithless and perjured Christian; on a sinner wandering far from his own country." By a pious fraud he obtained admission to the Church of the Holy Sepulchre: and we are told that, while praying at the tomb, the stone miraculously became soft to his teeth, and he bit off a portion of it and brought it triumphantly away. Returned to his own country, Fulke built a church at Loches in imitation of that at Jerusalem. Tormented still by his conscience, he went a second time as a pilgrim to Palestine, and returning safely again, he occupied himself for many years in building monasteries and churches. But he could not rest in quiet, and resolved for the good of his soul to make a third pilgrimage. This he did, but died on his way home at Metz. A very different pilgrim was Raymond of Plaisance. Born of poor parents, and himself apprenticed to a shoemaker, Raymond's mind was distracted from the earliest age by the desire to see Palestine. He disguised his anxiety for a time, but it became too strong for him, and he fell ill and confessed his thoughts to his mother. She, a widow, resolved to accompany him, and they set off together. They arrived safely at Jerusalem, and wept before the sepulchre, conceiving, we are told, a lively desire to end their days there and then. This was not to be, however. They went on to Bethlehem, thence to Jerusalem again, and thence homewards. On board the ship Raymond was seized with an illness, and the sailors wanted to throw him overboard, thinking, according to the usual sailors' superstition, that a sick man would bring disaster. His mother, however, dissuaded them, and he quickly recovered. But the mother died herself shortly after landing in Italy, and Raymond went on alone. He was met at Plaisance by a procession of clergy and choristers, and led to the cathedral, where he deposited his palm branch, sign of successful pilgrimage, and then returned to his shoemaking, married, and lived to a good old age—doubtless telling over and over again the stories of his travels.

And now began those vast pilgrimages when thousands went together, "the armies of the Lord," the real precursors of the Crusades. Robert of Normandy (A.D. 1034), like Fulke the Black, anxious to wipe out his sins, went accompanied by a great number of barons and knights, all barefooted, all clothed with the penitential sackcloth, all bearing the staff and purse. They went by Constantinople and through Asia Minor. There Robert was seized with an illness, and being unable to walk, was borne in a litter by Saracens. "Tell my people," said the duke, "that you have seen me borne to Paradise by devils;" a speech which shows how far toleration had spread in those days. Robert found a large number of pilgrims outside the city unable to pay the entrance money. He paid for all, and after signalizing himself by numerous acts of charity he returned, dying on the way in Bithynia, regretting only that he had not died sooner, at the sacred shrine itself.

To die there, indeed, was, as we have seen in the case of Raymond, a common prayer. The form of words is preserved: "Thou who hast died for us, and art buried in this sacred place, take pity on our misery, and withdraw us from this vale of tears." And the Christians preserved the story of one Lethbald, whose prayer was actually answered, for he died suddenly in the sight of his companions, after crying out three times aloud, "Glory to thee, O God!"

Sometimes, but seldom, a sort of missionary spirit would seize a pilgrim, and he would try to convert the infidels. Thus Saint Macarius of Armenia, bishop of Antioch, learned Arabic and Hebrew, and going to Jerusalem began to preach to the Jews and Saracens. Of course he was beaten and thrown into prison. And we need not record the miracles that happened to him therein.

Richard, Abbot of Saint Vitou, left Normandy at the head of seven hundred pilgrims, with whom was Saint Gervinus. There are accounts preserved of this pilgrimage, which offers little of interest except the miracles which were wrought for Richard.

Lietbert, in 1054, bishop of Cambray, headed a band of no fewer than three thousand. They followed the road which the Crusaders were afterwards to take, through Hungary and Bulgaria. Here many of his men were disheartened and wished to return, but he persuaded them to go on. They passed into Asia Minor, but only got as far as Laodicea, where they heard that the Church of the Sepulchre was finally closed to Christians. Most of the pilgrims set off on their way home. Lietbert persevered, and embarked with a few for Jaffa. They were shipwrecked on the isle of Cyprus. Again they took ship for Jaffa, and again they failed, being landed again at Laodicea. After so many disappointments, Lietbert lost courage, and went home again without accomplishing his pilgrimage.

The most important of all the pilgrimages, however, was that of the Archbishop of Mayence, accompanied by the bishops of Utrecht, Ramberg, and Ratisbon, and by seven thousand pilgrims of every rank. They were not dressed, as was the wont of pilgrims, in sackcloth, but wore their more costly robes; the bishops in dress of state and cloth of gold, the knights with burnished arms and costly trappings.

The army, for an army it was, too well equipped to escape without attack, too small to ensure victory in case of attack, followed the usual route across Asia Minor from Constantinople. It was not, however, till they were near Ramleh, almost within sight of Jerusalem, that the pilgrims were actually attacked, and then not by the Saracens, but by a large troop of Arabs, whom they attempted at first to repel by blows with their fists. Many were wounded, including the Bishop of Utrecht. They drove off the enemy for the moment with stones, and retired to a ruined fort, which was fortunately near the spot, where they cowered behind the falling walls. The Arabs came on with shrill cries; the Christians, nearly unarmed, rushed out and tore their swords and bucklers from them. But they were obliged to fall back, and the Arabs getting reinforced, encamped round the fort to the number of twelve thousand, and resolved to starve out the enemy.

The Christians held a hasty council. "Let us," urged a priest, "sacrifice our gold, which is all that the infidels want; having that, they will let us go free." This advice was adopted, and on a parley being held, the chief of the Arabs, with a small body of seventeen men, consented to enter the fort and come to terms. The Bishop of Mayence, who was the stateliest and handsomest man among the Christians, was chosen to speak with him. He proposed, in return for freedom and safety, to hand over to the Arabs all the treasure in the hands of the Christians. "It is not for you," replied the Arab, "to make terms with your conquerors!" And taking off his turban, as we are told, as a modern Bedawí would do with his head-dress under similar circumstances, he threw it, like a halter, round the neck of the bishop. The Christian prelate was not prepared for a reception so rude, and fairly knocked him down with a blow from his fist, upon which the knights set upon the whole eighteen Arabs, and bound them tightly. The news of the detention of their chief quickly spreading outside, the Arab army commenced a furious attack, which would have been fatal to the Christians but for a stratagem which procured them some little delay. For the Christians, holding swords to the throats of their prisoners, promised to fight with their heads if the attack was continued; and the chieftain's son, in alarm for his father, hastened from rank to rank, imploring the men to desist. And at this juncture arrived the Emir of Ramleh with troops, at sight of whom the Arabs turned and fled. The Arab chieftain remained a prisoner. "You have delivered us," said the emir, "from our greatest enemies." And so, with congratulations and in friendship, they marched to Jerusalem, which they entered in a kind of triumph by torchlight, with the sound of cymbals and trumpets. They were received by the Patriarch Sophronimus, and made the round, next day, of the sacred places, still bearing the marks of the destruction wrought by Hakem fifty years before.

And now approached the period of the first Crusade.

All these pilgrimages were like preparatory and tentative expeditions; the final provocations were yet to come which should rouse the Christians to unanimous action.

In the year 1077 the city had been taken, after holding out till the defenders were in danger of starvation, by Atsiz the Kharesmian, and transferred from the Fatemite Caliph of Egypt to the Abbaside Khalif. After the defeat of Atsiz at Gaza, a rebellion was attempted in Jerusalem, which resulted in the massacre of three thousand of the people. Atsiz called in Tutush, brother of Melek Shah, to his assistance. Tutush came, but instead of helping Afsis, he arrested and executed him, and proceeded to make himself master of Syria. A Turk, named Ostok, was made Governor of Jerusalem, and fresh persecutions began for the Christians. The Turks had now conquered the whole of Asia Minor. Too few in numbers to occupy the whole country, they held the towns by garrison, the effeminate Greeks having fallen an easy prey to them. But before this event, the Emperor Michael Ducas, foreseeing the conquest of his country unless the Mohammedans were driven back, had written to Pope Gregory VIII., imploring the assistance of the Western Christians, and offering to throw down the barriers which separated the two Churches. Gregory quickly matured a complete plan of united action on the part of all the Christians. The price of the assistance of Western Europe was to be the submission of the Eastern Church. The conquest of Palestine was to be the triumph of Rome. Gerbert had entertained a similar dream; but Gregory did more than dream. He exhorted the Christians to unite in the Holy War, and obtained fifty thousand promises: he was himself to head the Crusade. But other schemes intervened, and Gregory died without doing anything.

Victor III. did more than Gregory: he not only exhorted, but persuaded. The Tuscans, Venetians, and Genoese fitted out a fleet, fully manned and equipped, and sent it against the Mohammedans, who were now impeding the navigation of the Mediterranean. A signal triumph was obtained, and the conquerors returned laden with spoils from the towns they had captured and burned. This was the first united effort of the Christians against the Saracens, and perhaps the most successful of any.

All, then, was ripe for the Crusade. The sword had been already drawn; the idea was not a new one; letters, imploring help, had been received from the Emperor of the Greeks; three popes had preached a holy war; the sufferings of the Christians went on increasing. Moreover, the wickedness of the Western Church was very great. William of Tyre declares that virtue and piety were obliged to hide themselves; there was no longer any charity, any reverence for rank, any hesitation at plunging whole countries in war; there was no longer any security for property; the monasteries themselves were not safe against robbers; the very churches were pillaged and the sacred vessels stolen; the right of sanctuary was violated; the highways were covered with armed brigands; chastity, economy, temperance, were regarded as things "stupid and worthless;" the bishops were as dumb dogs who could not bark; and the priests were no better than the people.

The description of William of Tyre is vague, though heavily charged; but there can be no doubt that the times were exceptionally evil. Crimes common enough in an age distinguished above all by absence of self-restraint and abandonment to unbridled rage, would be naturally magnified by a historian who saw in them a reason for the infidel's persecution of pilgrims, and an argument for the taking of the Cross. Yet, making allowance for every kind of exaggeration, it is clear enough that Gregory had great mischiefs to contend with, and that the awakening of the world's conscience by any means whatever could not but produce a salutary effect. The immediate effect of the Crusades was the substitution of higher for lower motives, the sudden cessation of war, the shaming of the clergy into something like purity of life, the absorption into the armies of the Cross of the "men of violence," and some temporary alleviation to the sufferings of the poor.

The hour and the man were both at hand.

CHAPTER VI.

THE FIRST CRUSADE.

> " The sound
> As of the assault of an imperial city,
> The shock of crags shot from strange engin'ry,
> The clash of wheels, and clang of armed hoofs,
>   *   *   *   and now more loud
> The mingled battle cry. Ha! hear I not
> 'Εν τούτῳ νίκη. Allah-illah-Allah!"
>
> *Shelley.*

PETER the Hermit, the preacher and main cause of the first Crusade, was born about the year 1050, of a noble family of Picardy. He was at first, like all men of gentle birth of his time, a soldier, and fought in some at least of the wars that were going on around him. For some cause —no one knows why—perhaps disgusted with the world, perhaps struck with repentance for a criminal or dissolute life —he withdrew from his fellow-men, and became a hermit. But it would seem that his turbulent and unquiet spirit could not stand the monotony, though it might support the austerities, of a hermit's life, and he resolved about the year 1093 to go as a pilgrim to Palestine. He found the pilgrims miserable indeed. As most of them had been robbed or exorbitantly charged on the road, there was not one in a hundred who, on arriving before Jerusalem, found himself able to pay the fee demanded for admittance within the gates. The hapless Christians, starving and helpless, lay outside the walls, dependent on the small supplies which their brethren within could send them.

Many of them died; many more turned away without having been able to enter the city; famine, thirst, nakedness, and the sword of the infidel, constantly thinned their ranks, which were as constantly renewed. Even if they got within the walls, they were not much safer: the monasteries could do little for them, though they did what they could; in the streets they were insulted, mocked, spat upon, and sometimes beaten. And in the very churches, and during the celebration of services, they were liable, as we have seen, to the attacks of a fanatic crowd, who would sometimes break in upon them, and outrage the most sacred ceremonies.

Among all the indignant and pious crowd of worshippers none was more indignant or more devout than Peter. He paid a visit to Simeon, the aged patriarch, and wept with him over the misfortunes of the Christians. "When," said Simeon, "the cup of our sufferings is full, God will send the Christians of the West to the help of the Holy City." Peter pressed him to write urgent letters to the sovereign powers of Europe: he himself promised to exhort the people to arm for the recovery of Jerusalem and to testify to the statements of Simeon.

And then, to the fiery imagination of the Hermit, strange voices began to whisper, and strange forms began to be seen. "Arise, Peter," cried our Lord Himself to him, when he was worshipping at the Holy Sepulchre, "Arise, Peter. Hasten to announce the tribulations of my people. It is time that my servants were succoured and my sacred places delivered." Peter arose and departed to obey what he believed to be a divine command. The pope Urban, who certainly saw in this an opportunity for strengthening himself against the anti-pope, received him with ardour, real or assumed, and authorized him to preach the Crusade over the whole of Europe. He crossed the Alps, and began first to preach in France. His appearance was mean and unprepossessing, his stature low; he rode on a mule, bare-headed and bare-footed, dressed in a gown of the coarsest stuff and with a long rope for a girdle. The fame of his austerity, the purity of his life, the great purpose he had on hand, went before him. The irresistible eloquence of his words moved to their deepest depths the hearts of the people. He preached in country and in town; on the public roads and in the pulpits of churches; he reminded his hearers of the profanation of the holy places; he spoke of the pilgrims, and narrated his own sufferings; he read the letters of the venerable Simeon; and finally he told them how from the very recesses of the Holy Sepulchre the voice of Jesus Himself had called aloud to him, bidding him go forth and summon the people to the recovery of Jerusalem. And as he spoke, the souls of those that heard were moved. With tears, with repentant sobs, with loud cries of anger and sorrow, they vowed to lead better lives, and dedicated themselves for the future to the service of God; women who had sinned, men who had led women astray, robbers who lived by plunder, murderers rich with the rewards of crime, priests burdened with the heavy guilt of long years of hypocrisy—all came alike to confess their sins, to vow amendment, to promise penance by taking the Cross. Peter was reverenced as a saint: such homage as never man had before was his; they tried to get the smallest rag of his garment; they crowded to look upon him, or, if it might be, to touch him. Never in the history of the world has eloquent man had such an audience, or has oratory produced such an effect. And in the midst of this agitation, confined as yet, be it observed, to France, whose soil has ever been favourable to the birth of new ideas, came letters from the emperor Alexis Comnenus, urging on the princes of the West the duty of coming to his help. The leader of the infidels was at his very gates. Were Constantinople to fall, Christendom itself might fall. He might survive the loss of his empire: he could never survive the shame of seeing it pass under the laws of Mohammed. And if more were wanted to urge on the enthusiasm of the people, Constantinople was rich beyond all other cities of the world; her riches should be freely lavished upon her defenders; her daughters were fairer than the daughters of the West; their love should be the reward of those who fought against the Infidels.

The pope received the letters, and held a council, first at Plaisance, then at Clermont (1094). His speech at the latter council has been variously given; four or five reports of it remain, all evidently written long after the real speech had been delivered; all meant to contain what the pope ought to have said; and all, as appears to us, singularly cold and artificial. The council began by renewing the Peace of God; by placing under the protection of the Church all widows, orphans, merchants, and labourers; by proclaiming the inviolability of the sanctuary; and by decreeing that crosses erected by the wayside should be a refuge against violence. And at its tenth sitting, the council passed to what was its real business, the consideration of Peter's exhortations and the reading of the letters of the patriarch Simeon and the emperor Alexis. Peter spoke first, narrating, as usual, the sufferings of the pilgrims. Urban followed him. And when he had finished, with one accord the voices of the assembled council shouted, "Dieu le veut! Dieu le veut!" "Yes," answered the pontiff, "God wills it, indeed! Behold how our Lord fulfils his own words, that where two or three are gathered together in his name He will be in the midst. He it is who has inspired these words. Let them be for you your only war-cry." Adhémar, Bishop of Puy, begged to be the first to take the vow of the Crusade. Other bishops followed. Raymond, Count of Toulouse, first of the laity, swore to conduct his men to Palestine, and then the knights and barons followed in rapid succession. Urban declined himself to lead the host, but appointed Bishop Adhémar as his deputy. Meantime he promised all Crusaders a full and complete remission of their sins. He promised their goods and their families the protection of Saint Peter and the Church; he placed under anathema all who should do violence to the soldiers of the Cross; and he threatened with excommunication all who should fail to perform their oaths. As if the madness of enthusiasm was not sufficiently kindled already, the pope himself went to Rouen, to Angers, to Tours, and to Nismes, called councils, harangued the people, and enjoined on the bishops the duty of proclaiming the Crusade; and the next year was spent in preaching, exhorting, in maintaining the enthusiasm already kindled, and in preparing for the war. The kings of Europe, for their part, had good reasons for holding aloof, and so took no part in the Crusade: the king of France, because he was under excommunication; the emperor of Germany, because he was also under excommunication; William Rufus, because he was an unbeliever and a scoffer. But for the rank and file, the First Crusade, which was instigated by a Frenchman, was mainly recruited from France.

Here, indeed, the delirium of enthusiasm grew daily in intensity. During the winter of 1095-96 nothing but the sound of preparation was heard throughout the length and breadth of the land. It was not enough that knights and men-at-arms should take upon them the vows of the Cross; it behoved every man who could carry a pike or wield a sword to join the army of deliverance. Artisans left their work, merchants their shops, labourers their tools, and the very robbers and brigands came out from their hiding-places, with the intention of atoning for their past sins by fighting in the army of the Lord. All industry, save that of the forging of weapons, ceased; for six whole months there was no crime; for six months an uninterrupted Peace of God, concluded by tacit consent, while the *croisés* crowded the churches to implore the divine protection and blessing, to consecrate their arms, and to renew their vows. In order to procure horses, armour, and arms, the price of which went up enormously, the knights sold their lands at prices far below their real value; the lands were in many cases bought up by far-seeing abbots and attached to monasteries, so that the Church, at least, might be enriched, whatever happened. No sacrifice, however, appeared too great in the enthusiasm of departure; no loss too heavy to weigh for one moment against the obligation of the sacred oath. And strange signs and wonders began to appear in the heavens. Stars were seen to fall upon the earth: these were the kings and chiefs of the Saracens; unearthly flames were visible at night: these betokened the conflagration of the Mohammedan strong places; blood-red clouds, stained with the blood of the Infidel, hovered over the east; a sword-shaped comet, denoting the sword of the Lord, was in the south; and in the sky were seen, not once, but many times, the towers of a mighty city and the legions of a mighty host.

With the first warm days of early spring the impatience of the people was no longer to be restrained. Refusing to wait while the chiefs of the Crusade organised their forces, laid down the line of their march, and matured their plans, they flocked in thousands to the banks of the Meuse and the Moselle, clamouring for immediate departure. Most of them were on foot, but those who by any means could raise the price of a horse came mounted. Some travelled in carts drawn by oxen. Their arms were such as they could afford to buy. Every one, however, brandished a weapon of some kind; it was either a spear, or an axe, or sword, or even a heavy hammer. Wives, daughters, children, old men, dragged themselves along with the exultant host, nothing doubting that they too would be permitted to share the triumph, to witness the victory. From the far corners of France, from Brittany, from the islands, from the Pyrenees, came troops of men whose language could not be understood, and who had but one sign, that of the Cross, to signify their brotherhood. Whole villages came *en masse*, accompanied by their priests, bringing with them their children, their cattle, their stores of provision, their household utensils, their all; while the poorest came with nothing at all, trusting that miracles, similar to those which protected the Israelites in the Desert, would protect them also—that manna would drop from heaven, and the rocks would open to supply them with water. And such was their ignorance, that as the walls of town after town became visible on their march, they pressed forward, eagerly demanding if that was Jerusalem.

Who should be the leader of the horde of peasants, robbers, and workmen who came together in the spring of 1096 on the banks of the Meuse? Among all this vast host there were found but nine knights: Gaultier Sans Avoir—Walter the Penniless—and eight others. But there was with them, better than an army of knights, the great preacher of the Crusade, the holy hermit and worker of miracles, Peter. To him was due the glory of the movement: to him should be given the honour of leading the first, and, it was believed, the successful army. By common acclamation they elected Peter their leader. He, no less credulous than his followers, accepted the charge; confident of victory, and mounted on his mule—the mule which had borne him from town to town to preach the war—clothed in his monastic garb, with sandals on his feet and a cross in his hand, he led the way.

Under his command were a hundred thousand men, bearing arms, such as they were, and an innumerable throng of women, old men, and children. He divided this enormous host into two parts, keeping the larger under his own orders, and sending on the smaller as an advance-guard, under the knight Walter.

Walter started first. Marching down the banks of the Rhine, he experienced no difficulties with the Germans. These, slow to follow the example of the fiery French, and, moreover, not yet stimulated by the preaching of a Peter, still sympathised with the object of the army, which they doubtless thought was but a larger and a fiercer band of pilgrims, like many that had gone before, and assisted those who were too poor to buy provisions, to the best of their power. Passing, therefore, safely through Germany, the disorderly host, among whom all sorts of iniquities were already rife, entered Hungary. The Hungarians, by this time christianised, had yet no kind of enthusiasm for the objects of the Crusaders or desire to aid them; but their King, Coloman, gave them guides through his vast marshes and across his rivers, and permitted them to purchase what they wanted at the public market-places; and by great fortune no accident happened to them, save the beating of a few laggards after the crossing of the river Maros. Judging it idle to avenge an insult which it cost little to endure, Walter pushed on till he reached Belgrade, the frontier town of the Bulgarians. These were even a ruder people than the Hungarian Christians; they refused to recognise the Crusaders as their brethren: subjects of the Greek crown, they refused any submission but that which was extorted by arms, and living in the midst of inaccessible forests, they preserved a wild and savage independence which made them the terror of the pilgrims, whom they maltreated, and the Greeks, who tried to reduce them to submission.

Here the first troubles began. The Governor of Belgrade refusing them permission to buy provisions, the army found themselves reduced to the greatest straits for want of food; and seeing no other way for help, they left the camp and dispersed about the country, driving in the cattle, and laying hands on everything they could find. The Bulgarians armed in haste, and slaughtered vast numbers of the marauders, burning alive a hundred and forty who had taken refuge in a chapel. Walter broke up his camp in haste, and pressing on, left those to their own fate who refused to obey his order to follow. What that fate was may easily be surmised. With diminished forces, starving and dejected, he pushed on through the forests till he found himself before Nissa, when the governor, taking pity on the destitute condition of the pilgrims, gave them food, clothes, and arms. These misfortunes fell upon them, it will be observed, in Christian lands, and long before they saw the Saracens. Thence the humbled Crusaders, seeing in these disasters a just punishment for their sins—they were at least always ready to repent—proceeded, with no other enemy than famine, through Philippopolis and Adrianople to Constantinople itself. Here the emperor, Alexis Comnenus, gave them permission to encamp outside the town, to buy and sell, and to wait for the arrival of Peter and the second army.

But if the first expedition was disastrous the second was far worse. Peter seems to have followed at first a somewhat different route to that of his advanced guard. He went through Lorraine, Franconia, Bavaria, and Austria, and entered Hungary, some months after Walter, with an army of forty thousand men. Permission was readily granted to march through the country, on the condition of the maintenance of order and the purchase of provisions; nor was it till they arrived at Semlin, the place where their comrades had been beaten, that any disturbance arose. Here they unfortunately saw suspended the arms and armour which had been stripped from the stragglers of Walter's army. The soldiers, incensed beyond control, rushed upon the little town, and, with the loss of a hundred men, massacred every Hungarian in the place. Then they sat down to enjoy themselves for five days. The people of Belgrade, panic-stricken on hearing of the fate of Semlin, fled all with one accord, headed by their governor, and hurriedly carrying away everything portable; and Peter, before the King of Hungary had time to collect an army to avenge the taking of his city, managed to transport everything to the other side of the Danube, and pitched his camp under the deserted walls of Belgrade. There the army, laden with spoils of all kinds, waited to collect their treasures, which they carried with them on their march to Nissa. They stopped here one night, obtaining, as Walter had done, permission to buy and sell, and giving hostages for good conduct. All went well; the camp was raised, the hostages returned, and the army on its march again, when an unhappy quarrel arose between some of the stragglers, consisting of about a hundred Germans, and the townspeople. The Germans set fire to seven mills and certain buildings outside the town. Having done this mischief they rejoined their comrades; but the indignant Bulgarians, furious at this return for their hospitality, rushed after them, arms in hand. They attacked the rear-guard, killed those who resisted, and returned to the town, driving before them the women and children, and loaded with the spoil which remained from the sacking of Semlin. Peter and the main body hastened back on receiving news of the disaster, and tried once more to accommodate matters. But in the midst of his interview with the governor, and when all seemed to promise well, a fresh outbreak took place, and a second battle began, far worse than the first. The Crusaders were wholly routed and fled in all directions, while the carnage was indiscriminate and fearful. In the evening the unhappy Peter found himself on an adjoining height with five hundred men. The scattered fugitives gradually rallied, but one-fourth of his fighting men were killed on this disastrous day, and the army lost all their baggage, their treasures, and their stores; while of the women and children by far the greater number were either killed or taken captive. Starving and destitute, they straggled on through the forests, dreading the further vengeance of the Bulgarians, until they entered Thrace. Here deputies from the emperor met them, with reproaches for their disorderly conduct, and promises that, should they conduct themselves with order, his clemency would not be wanting.

Arrived at Constantinople, and having rejoined Walter, Peter lost no time in obtaining an audience from the emperor. Alexis heard him patiently, and was even moved by his eloquence; but he advised him, above all things, to wait for the arrival of the princes who were to follow. Advice was the last thing these wild hordes would listen to; and, eager to be in the country of the Infidels—to get for themselves the glory of the conquest—they crossed the Dardanelles, and pitched their camp at a place called Gemlik or Ghio.

The first effervescence of zeal in Europe had not yet, however, worked off its violence. A monk named Gotschalk, emulating the honours of Peter, had raised, by dint of preaching, an army of twenty thousand Germans, sworn to the capture of the Holy Land. Setting out as leader of this band, he followed the same road as his predecessors and met with the same disasters. It was in early autumn that they passed through Hungary. The harvest was beginning, and the Germans pillaged and murdered wherever they went. King Coloman attacked them, but with little success. He then tried deceit, and, persuading the Germans to lay down their arms and to join the Hungarians as brothers, he fell on them, and massacred every one. Of all this vast host only one or two escaped through the forests to their own country to tell the tale.

One more turbulent band followed, to meet the same fate; but this was the worst—the most undisciplined of all. Headed by a priest named Volkmar, and a Count Emicon, they straggled without order or discipline, filled with the wildest superstitions. Before their army was led sometimes a she-goat, sometimes a goose, which they imagined to be filled with the Holy Spirit; and as all sins were to be expiated by the recovery of the Holy Land, there was a growing feeling that there was no longer any need of avoiding sin. Consequently, the wildest licence was indulged in, and this, which called itself "the army of the Lord," was a horde of the most abandoned criminals. Their greatest crime was the slaughter of the Jews along the banks of the Rhine and Moselle. "Why," they asked, "should we, who march against the Infidels, leave behind us the enemies of our Lord?" The bishops of the sees through which they passed vainly interposed their entreaties. In Cologne and Mayence every Jew was murdered; some of the miserable people tied stones round their own necks, and leaped into the river; some killed their wives and children, and set fire to their houses, perishing in the flames; the mothers killed the infants at their breasts, and the Christians themselves fled in all directions at the approach of an army as terrible to its friends as to its foes.

But their course was of short duration. At the town of Altenburg, on the confines of Hungary, which they attempted to storm, they were seized with a sudden panic and fled in all directions, being slaughtered like sheep. Emicon got together a small band, whom he led home again; a few others were led by their chiefs southwards, and joined the princes of the Crusade in Italy. None of them, according to William of Tyre, found their way to Peter the Hermit. Once across the Dardanelles, Peter's troops, who amounted, it is said, in spite of all their losses, to no fewer than a hundred thousand fighting men, fixed a camp on the shores of the Gulf of Nicomedia, and began to ravage the country in all directions. The division of the booty soon caused quarrels, and a number of Italians and Germans, deserting the camp, went up the country in a body, and took possession of a small fortress in the neighbourhood of Nicæa, whose garrison they massacred. Then they were in their turn besieged, and, with the exception of their leader, Renaud, or Rinaldo, who embraced the Mahometan faith, were slaughtered to a man. The news of this disaster roused the Christians, not to a sense of their danger (which they could not yet comprehend), but to a vehement desire for revenge. They made the luckless Walter lead them against Nicæa, and issued forth from their camp *en masse*, a disordered, shouting multitude, crying for vengeance against the Turks. But their end was at hand. The Sultan of Nicæa placed half his army in ambuscade in the forest, keeping the other half in the plain; the Christians were attacked in the front and in the rear, and, cooped up together in confusion, badly armed, offered very slight resistance. Walter himself fell, one of the first; the carnage was terrific, and of all the hundred thousand whom Peter and Walter had brought across the Dardanelles, but three thousand escaped. These fled to a fortress by the sea-shore. The bones of their comrades, whitened by the eastern sun, long stood as a monument of the disaster, pointing skeleton fingers on the road to Jerusalem—the road of death and defeat.

Only three thousand, out of all these hordes, certainly a quarter of a million in number, which flocked after Peter on his mule! We can hardly believe that all were killed. Some of the women and children at least might be spared, and without doubt their blood yet flows in the veins of many Hungarian and Bulgarian families. But this was only the first instalment of slaughter. There remained the mighty armies which were even then upon the road. As for Peter, whose courage was as easily daunted as his enthusiasm was easily roused, he fled in dismay and misery back to Constantinople, having lost all authority, even over the few men who remained with him.

He inveighed against their disorders and their crimes, and he declared that these were the causes of their defeat. He might have added that his own weakness, the vanity which led him to accept the *rôle*, offered him by an ignorant crowd, of general as well as preacher, was no less a cause of disaster than the disorder which it was his business to check and combat day by day. His disappointment was such as would be enough to kill a really proud and strong man; but Peter was not a strong man; in the hour of danger he bent like the reed to the storm; the violence of the tempest once past, however, like the reed, he lifted up his head again. He could preach endurance, but he could not himself endure; his faith required constant stimulants, his courage the fresh fire of continual success. Peter lifted up his head again when he saw the splendid array of Godfrey and Raymond; but his old authority with the chiefs was gone. Like a worn-out tool, he had served his purpose and was cast aside. He had no more voice in their councils—no more power over their enthusiasm. He lapsed into utter insignificance, save once, when we find him actually trying to desert the army at Antioch and endeavouring to run away; and once, later on, when he received the brief ovation from the native Christians in the hour of final triumph at Jerusalem. He returned, it may be added, in safety to France when the war was over, and spent sixteen years more in honourable obscurity, the head of a monastery. Never in the world's history, with the exception of Mohammed alone, has one man produced an effect so great and so immediate; and seldom has one man wielded an instrument so potent as Peter, when he set forth at the head of an army which wanted only discipline to make it invincible.

But now *vexilla regis prodeunt:* armies of a different character are assembling in the west. Foremost among them is that headed by Godfrey de Bouillon, Duke of

Lorraine. Of him, and of his brother Baldwin, who accompanied him, we shall have to speak again. A word on the other chiefs of the First Crusade.

With the army of Godfrey were joined the troops of Robert Duke of Normandy and Count Robert of Flanders.

Robert, who had pledged his duchy for five years to his brother for ten thousands marks, we all know. He was strong, brave, and generous. But he had no other good quality. Had his prudence, his wisdom in council, been equal to his courage, or had his character for temperance and self-restraint been better, he would probably have obtained the crown of Jerusalem before Godfrey. As it was, he went out for the purpose of fighting; he fought well; and came home again, no richer than when he went. He was joined in Syria by the Saxon prince, Edgar Atheling, the lawful heir to the English crown; but the chroniclers are silent as to the prowess of the English contingent.

The other leaders who followed separately were Hugh Vermandois, Hugh le Grand, the brother to the king of France, and Stephen, Count of Blois, a scholar and a poet. He it was who married Adela, daughter of William the Conqueror, and was the father of our King Stephen. Both of these chiefs left the Crusade at Antioch and went home disgusted at their sufferings and ill-success; but, after the taking of the city, popular opinion forced them to go out again.

Count Raymond, of Toulouse, who led his own army by an independent route, is perhaps the most difficult character to understand. He was not pious; he was cold and calculating; he was old and rich; he had already gained distinction by fighting against the Moors; he loved money. Why did he go? It is impossible to say, except that he had vague ambitions of kingdoms in the East more splendid than any in the West. He alienated a great part of his territory to get treasure for the war, and he was by far the richest of the princes. The men he led, the Provençaux, were much less ignorant, less superstitious, and less smitten with the divine fury of the rest. Provence, which in two more centuries was to be itself the scene of a crusade as bloody as any in Palestine, was already touched with the heresy which was destined to break out in full violence before very many years. The Provençaux loved music, dancing, good cheer; but they were indifferent to the Church. They could plunder better than they could pray, and they were more often gathered round the provisions than the pulpits. It is singular, therefore, that the most signal miracle which attended the progress of the Christian arms should have been wrought among the Provençaux. It was so, however: Peter Bartholomeus, who found the Holy Lance, was a priest of Provence. Adhémar, Bishop of Puy, himself a Provençal, the most clear-headed, most prudent, and most thoughtful of the army, treated the story of Peter, it is true, with disdain; nor did Raymond believe it; as was evident when, on there appearing, shortly afterwards, symptoms that another miracle, of which he saw no use, was about to happen, he suppressed it with a strong hand. At the same time, he did not disdain to make use of the Holy Lance, and the "miracle" most certainly contributed very largely, as we shall see, to the success of the Christians.

The two remaining great chiefs were Bohemond and Tancred. Bohemond, who was a whole cubit taller than the tallest man in the army, was the son of that Norman, Robert Guiscard, who, with a band of some thirty knights, managed to wrest the whole of Calabria, Apulia, and Sicily from the Greeks. On his father's death he had quarrelled with his brother Roger over the inheritance, and was actually besieging him in the town of Amalfi, when the news of the Crusades reached him. The number of those engaged, the rank of the leaders, the large share taken by the Normans, inspired him with the hope that here, at last, was the chance of humiliating, and even conquering, his enemy the Emperor of Constantinople. Perhaps, too, some noble impulse actuated him.

However that may be, he began himself to preach a crusade to his own army, and with so much success—for he preached of glory and plunder, as well as of religion—that he found himself in a few days at the head of ten thousand horse and twenty thousand foot. With these he joined the other chiefs at Constantinople. His life was a long series of battles. He was crafty and sagacious; hence his name of Guiscard—the wise one; quite indifferent to the main object of the Crusaders—in fact, he did not go on with them to Jerusalem itself—and anxious only to do the Greeks a mischief and himself some good.

With him went his cousin Tancred, the hero of the "Jerusalem Delivered." The history of the First Crusade contains all his history. After the conquest of Jerusalem, and after displaying extraordinary activity and bravery, he was made Prince of Galilee, and his cousin was Prince of Antioch. Tancred is a hero of romance. Apart from his fighting he has no character; in every battle he is foremost, but when the battle is over we hear nothing about him. He appears however to have had a great deal of his cousin's prudence, and united with the bravery of the lion some, at least, of the cunning of the fox. He died about the year 1113.

Hugh, Count of Vermandois, who was one of the chiefs of the army brought by Robert of Normandy, was the third son of Henry I. of France. He was called Le Grand, not on account of any mental or physical superiority, but because by marriage he was the head of the Vermandois house. He was one of the first to desert the Crusade, terrified by the misfortunes which overtook the expedition; but, like Stephen of Blois, he was obliged by the force of popular opinion to go back again as a Crusader. The second time he was wounded by the Turks near Nicæa, and only got as far as Tarsus in Cilicia, where he died. Like Robert of Normandy, he joined to great bravery and an extreme generosity a certain weakness of character, which marred all his finer qualities.

Robert of Flanders seems to have been a fighting man pure and simple—by the Saracens called "St. George," and by his own side the "Sword and Lance of the Christians." He, no more fighting remaining to be done, returned quietly to his own states, with the comfortable conviction that he had atoned for his former sins by his conduct in the Holy War. He enjoyed ten years more fighting at home, and then got drowned in the River Marne; an honest single-minded knight, who found himself in perfect accord with the spirit of his age.

With these principal barons and chiefs were a crowd of poorer princes, each with his train of knights and men-at-arms. The money for the necessary equipments had been raised in various ways: some had sold their lands, others their seigneurial rights; some had pawned their states; while one or two, despising these direct and obvious means of raising funds, had found a royal road to money by pillaging the villages and towns around them.

It was not till eight months after the Council of Clermont* that Godfrey's army, consisting of ten thousand knights and eighty thousand foot, was able to begin its march. Fortunately, a good harvest had just been gathered in, and food of all kinds was abundant and cheap. The army, moreover, was well-disciplined, and no excesses were committed on its way through Germany. It followed pretty nearly the same line as that taken by Walter and Peter, and must have been troubled along the whole route by news of the extravagances and disasters of those who had preceded them. Arriving on the frontiers of Hungary, Godfrey sent deputies to King Coloman, asking permission to march peaceably, buying whatever he had need of, through his dominions. Hostages, consisting of his brother Baldwin and his family, were given for the

* August, 1096.

good behaviour of the troops, and permission was granted; the King of Hungary following close on the track of the army, in case any breach of faith should be attempted. But none took place, and at Semlin, when the last Crusader had crossed the river into Bulgarian territory, King Coloman personally, and with many expressions of friendship and goodwill, delivered over the hostages, and parted. Getting through the land of the Bulgarians as quickly as might be, Godfrey pushed on as far as Philippopolis. There he learned that Count Hugh, who had been shipwrecked, sailing in advance of his army, on the shores of Epirus, was held a prisoner by Alexis Comnenus, very probably as a sort of hostage for the good behaviour of the very host whose help he had implored. Godfrey sent imperatively to demand the release of the Count, and being put off with an evasive reply, gave his troops liberty to ravage and plunder along the road—a privilege which they fully appreciated. This practical kind of reply convinced Alexis that the barbarians were not, at least, awed by the greatness of his fame. He hastened to give way, and assured Godfrey that his prisoner should be released directly the army arrived at Constantinople.

Meantime, the other armies were all on their way, converging to Constantinople. The route followed by them is not at all times clear. Some appear to have marched through Italy, Dalmatia, and across Thessaly, while a few went by sea; and though the first armies of Peter and Walter carried off a vast number of pilgrims, there can be no doubt that these armies were followed by a great number of priests, monks, women, and persons unable to fight.

Alexis, on hearing of Bohemond's speedy arrival, was greatly alarmed—as, indeed, he had reason to be. With his usual duplicity, he sent ambassadors to flatter his formidable visitor, while he ordered his frontier troops to harass him on his march; and Bohemond had alternately to receive the assurances of the Emperor's friendship, and to fight his troops. No wonder that he wrote to Godfrey at Constantinople to be on his guard, as he had to do " with the most ferocious wild beast and the most wicked man alive." But, in spite of his hatred, the fierce Norman found himself constrained to put off his resentment in the presence of Greek politeness; and the rich gifts with which Alexis loaded him, if they did not quiet his suspicions, at least allayed his wrath. Alexis got rid of his unwelcome visitors as speedily as he could. After going through the ceremony of adopting Godfrey as his son, and putting the empire under his protection, he received the homage of the princes, one after the other, with the exception alone of Tancred. And then he sent them all across the straits, to meet whatever fortune awaited them on the other side.

The story of the First Crusade is an oft-told tale. But it is a tale which bears telling often. There is nothing in history which may be compared with this extraordinary rising of whole peoples. The numbers which came from Western Europe cannot, of course, be even approximately stated. Probably, counting the women, children, and camp-followers, their number would not be less than a million. Of these, far more than a half, probably two-thirds, came from the provinces of France. The Germans were but slightly affected by the universal enthusiasm—the English not at all. Edgar Atheling brought a band of his countrymen to join Robert of Normandy; but these were probably those who had compromised themselves in former attempts to raise Northumbria and other parts of England. The Italians came from the south, but not from the north; and nearly the whole of Spain was occupied by the caliphat of Cordova. That all these soldiers were fired with the same ardour, were led by the same disinterested hope, is not to be supposed; but it is certain from every account, whether Christian or Arabic, that the main object of their enterprise was a motive power strong enough, of itself, to enable them to endure hardships and privations almost incredible, and to combat with forces numerically, at least, ten times their superior.

The way to the Holy Land lay through a hostile country. Asia Minor, overrun by the Mohammedans since twenty years, was garrisoned rather than settled. Numerous as were the followers of the Crescent, they had not been able to do more, in their rapid march of conquest, than to take strongholds and towns, and keep them. There were even some towns which had never surrendered, while of those which belonged to them, many were held by insufficient forces, and contained an element of weakness in the large number of Christian inhabitants. And the first of these towns which came in their way was the town of Nicæa.

The miserable remnant of Peter's army, on the arrival of their friends, made haste to show them the places of their own disasters. These fugitives had lived hidden in the forest, and now, on seeing the *brassard* of the Cross, emerged—barefooted, ragged, unarmed, cowed—to tell the story of their sufferings. They took the soldiers to see the plain where their great army had been massacred—there were the piles of bones, the plain white with them; they took them to the camp where the women and children had been left. These were gone, but the remains were left of the old men and those who had tried to defend them. Their bodies lay in the moat which had been cut round the camp. In the centre, like a pillar of reproach, stood the white stones which had served for the altar of the camp.

Filled with wrath at the sight of these melancholy objects, the soldiers cried out to be led against their enemy; and the whole army, preceded by four thousand pioneers to clear the way, was marched in good order towards Nicæa, where the enemy awaited them. The Crusaders—they spoke nineteen different languages—were accoutred with some attempt at similarity. The barons and knights wore a coat of chain-armour, while a helmet, set with silver for the princes, of steel for knights, and of iron for the rest, protected their heads. Round bucklers were carried by the knights, long shields by the foot-soldiers; besides the lance, the sword, the arrow, they carried the mace and battleaxe, the sling, and the terrible crossbow; while, for a rallying-point for the soldiers, every prince bore painted on his standard those birds, animals, and towns, which subsequently became coats-of-arms, and gave birth to the science of Heraldry.

The total number of the gigantic host amounted, it is said, to one hundred thousand knights and five hundred thousand foot-soldiers. But this is evidently an exaggeration. If it is not, the losses by battle, famine, and disease were proportionately greater than those of any wars recorded in history.

The first operation was the siege of Nicæa—Nicæa, the city of the great Council—and the avenging of the slaughtered army of Peter. Nicæa stood on the low shores of a lake. It was provided with vessels of all kinds, by which it could receive men and provisions, and was therefore practically impregnable. But the Mohammedans, fully advertised of the approach of their enemies, had made preparations to receive them; and with an immense army, all mounted, charged the array of the Christians on the moment of their arrival in the plains, and while they were occupied in putting up their tents. Victory, such as it was, remained with the Crusaders, but cost them the lives of more than two thousand of their men. The siege of Nicæa, undertaken after this battle, made slow progress. While the Christians wasted their strength in vain efforts to demolish the walls and cross the moats, the garrison, constantly reinforced during the night by means of the lake, held out unshaken for some weeks. Finding out the means by which their strength was recruited, Godfrey, by immense exertions, transported overland from the neighbouring sea a number of light craft, which he launched on the lake, and succeeded in accomplishing a perfect blockade of the town. The Nicæans, terrified at the success of this manœuvre, and by the fate of their most important town, were ready to surrender at discretion, when the cunning of Alexis Comnenus—who had despatched a small force, nominally for the assistance of the Crusaders, but really for the purpose of watching after his own interests—succeeded in inducing the town to surrender to him alone; and the Christians, after all their labour, had the mortification of seeing the Greek flag flying over the citadel, instead of their own. From his own point of view, the Emperor was evidently right. The Crusaders had sworn to protect his empire; he claimed sovereignty over all these lands; his object was neither to revenge the death of a horde of invaders, nor to devastate the towns, nor to destroy the country—but to recover and preserve. Nicæa, at least, was almost within his reach; and though he could not expect that his authority would be recognised in the south of Asia Minor, or in Syria, he had reason to hope that here at any rate, so near to Constantinople, and so recently after the oaths of the princes, it would be recognised.

So, certainly, thought the princes; for, in spite of the unrepressed indignation of the army, they refrained from pillaging the town and murdering the infidels, and gave the word to march.

It was now early summer; the soldiers had not yet experienced the power of an Asiatic sun; no provision was made against the dangers of famine and thirst, and their way led through a land parched with heat, devastated by wars, over rocky passes, across pathless plains. The Crusaders neither knew the country, nor made any preparations, beyond carrying provisions for two or three days. They were, moreover, encumbered with their camp-followers, their baggage, and the weight of their arms.

They were divided, principally for convenience of forage,

into two *corps d'armée*, of which one was commanded by Godfrey, Raymond, Robert of Flanders, and the Count of Vermandois, while the other was led by the three Norman chiefs, Robert, Tancred, and Bohemond. For seven days all went well, the armies having completely lost sight of each other, but confident, after their recent successes, that there would be no more enemies at hand to combat. They were mistaken. Tancred's division, on the evening of the 30th of June, pitched their camp in a valley called by William of Tyre the valley of Gorgona. It was protected on one side by a river, on the other by a marsh filled with reeds. The night was passed in perfect security, but at daybreak the enemy was upon them. Bohemond took the command. Placing the women and the sick in the midst, he divided the cavalry into three brigades, and prepared to dispute the passage of the river. The Saracens discharged their arrows into the thick ranks of the Crusaders, whose wounded horses confused and disordered them. Unable to endure these attacks with patience, the Christians crossed the river and charged their enemies; but the Saracens, mounted on lighter horses, made way for them to pass, and renewed the discharge of their arrows. Another band, taking advantage of the knights having crossed the river, forded it at a higher point, and attacked the camp itself. Then the slaughter of the sick and wounded, and even of the women, save those whose beauty was sufficient to ransom their lives, began. On the other side of the stream the knights fought every one for himself. Tancred, nearly killed in the *mêlée*, was saved by Bohemond; Robert of Normandy performed prodigies; the camp was retaken, and the women rescued. But the day was not won. Nor would it have been won, but for the arrival of Godfrey, to whom Bohemond, early in the day, had sent a messenger. He brought up the whole of his army, and the Saracens, retreating to the hills, found themselves attacked on all sides. They fled in utter disorder, leaving twenty-three thousand dead on the field, and the whole of their camp and baggage in the hands of the Christians. These had lost four thousand, besides the number of followers killed in the camp. The booty was immense, and the soldiers pleased themselves by dressing in the long silk robes of the Mussulmans, while they refurnished themselves with arms from those they found upon the dead. Conscious, however, of the danger they had escaped, they were careful to acknowledge that they would not have carried the day, had it not been for St. George and St. Demetrius, who had been plainly visible to many fighting on their side; and the respect which they conceived for the Saracens' prowess taught them, at least, a salutary lesson of caution.

While they were rejoicing, the enemy was acting. The defeated Turks, retreating southwards, by the way which the Christians must follow, devastated and destroyed every thing as they traversed the country, procuring one auxiliary at least in the shape of famine. They had two more—thirst and heat.

The Crusaders, once more on the march, resolved not to separate again, and formed henceforth but one army. But they journeyed through a desert and desolate country; there was no food but the roots of plants; their horses died for want of water and forage; the knights had to walk on foot, or to ride oxen and asses; every beast was converted into a beast of burden, until the time came when the beasts themselves perished by the way, and all the baggage was abandoned. Their path led through Phrygia, a wild and sterile country, with no fountains or rivers; the road was strewn as they went along by the bodies of those who died of sunstroke or of thirst; women, overcome by fatigue and want of water, lay down and were delivered of children, and there died, mothers and infants; in one terrible day five hundred died on the march; the falcons and hawks, which the knights had been unable to leave behind, fell dead from their perches; the hounds deserted their masters, and went away to seek for water; the horses themselves, in which the hope of the soldier was placed, lay down and died. At last they came to a river; even this timely relief was fatal, for three hundred killed themselves by drinking too much. They rested, after this disastrous march, at Antiocheia, the former capital of Pisidia. Here Raymond fell ill, but happily recovered, and Godfrey was dangerously wounded in a conflict with a bear. To account for the discomfiture of the prince, it is recorded that the bear was the biggest and most ferocious bear ever seen.

During their stay at Antiocheia, Tancred and Baldwin—the former with a detachment of Italians, the latter with one of Flemings—were sent to explore the country, to bring help to the Christians, and report on the means of obtaining provisions. They went first to Iconium; finding no enemies, they went southwards, and Tancred, leading the way, made an easy conquest of Tarsus, promising to spare the lives of the garrison. Baldwin arrived the next day, and on perceiving the flag of Tancred on the towers, insisted, on the ground that his own force was superior in numbers, on taking it down and replacing it by his own. A violent quarrel arose, the first of the many which were to disgrace the history of the Crusades. Neither would give way. They agreed at last to refer the dispute to the inhabitants. These, at first, gave the preference to Tancred; but at last, yielding to the threats of Baldwin, transferred their allegiance to him, and threw Tancred's flag over the ramparts. Tancred withdrew, indignant, and marched with all his men to Adana, an important place some twenty miles from Tarsus. This he found in the possession of a Burgundian adventurer, who had got a company of pilgrims to follow him, and seized the place. History does not deign, unfortunately, to notice the exploits of the *viri obscuri*, but it is clear enough, that while the great princes were seizing states and cities, bands of armed soldiers, separated from the great army, were overrunning the country, taking possession of small forts and towns, where they lived at their own will and pleasure, till the Turks came and killed them all. The Burgundian was courteous to Tancred, and helped him with provisions on his way to Malmistra, a large and important place, before which he pitched his camp.

But a terrible calamity had happened at Tarsus. Baldwin got into the town, and, jealous of his newly-acquired possession, ordered the gates to be carefully closed and guarded. In the evening, a troop of three hundred Crusaders, sent by Bohemond to reinforce Tancred, arrived at the town, and asked for admission. Baldwin refused. They pleaded the extremity of fatigue and hunger, to which a long march had reduced them. Baldwin still refused. His own men urged him to admit them. Baldwin refused again. In the morning they were all found dead, killed in the night by the Turks, who took advantage of their sleep and exhaustion. At this spectacle the grief and rage of the soldiers were turned against the cause of their comrades' death. Baldwin took refuge in a tower, but presently came out, and, lamenting the disaster of which he alone was the cause, pointed his soldiers to the towers where the garrison of the Turks (prisoners, but under promise of safety) were shut up. The Christians massacred every one.

Here they were joined by a fleet of pirates, who, after having been for ten years the terror of the Mediterranean, were desirous of expiating their crimes by taking part in the Crusade. Their leader, Guymer, was a Boulogne man, and readily brought his men as a reinforcement to the troops of Baldwin, his seigneur. Baldwin left a garrison in Tarsus, and set out to rejoin Tancred. But the death of the three hundred could not so easily be forgotten. Tancred and his army, maddened at the intelligence of Baldwin's approach, clamoured for revenge, and Tancred, without much reluctance, gave the order to attack Baldwin's camp. A sanguinary battle followed, in which Tancred's forces, inferior in numbers, were worsted, and obliged to withdraw. The night brought reflection, and the next morning was occupied in reconciliation and promises of friendship. Malmistra was taken, and all the Mohammedans slaughtered, and after a few more exploits, Tancred returned to the army. Baldwin, however, whose ardour for the recovery of Jerusalem had yielded by this time to his ambition, only saw, in the disordered state of the country, the splendid opportunities which it presented to one who had the courage to seize them. Perhaps the sight of the successful Burgundian of Adana helped him to form projects of his own; perhaps the remarks of an Armenian named Pancrates, who was always whispering in his ear of the triumphs to be won by an independent line of action. He returned to Godfrey, indeed, but only to try his powers of seduction among the soldiers, whom he incited to follow him by magnificent promises. The princes were alarmed at the first news of his intended defection; at a council hastily assembled, it was resolved to prohibit any Crusader, whatever his rank, from leaving the army. Baldwin, however, the very night on which this resolution was carried, secretly marched out of the camp, at the head of some twelve hundred foot-soldiers and two hundred knights, accompanied by his Armenian friend. His exploits, until he was summoned back to Jerusalem, hardly concern us here. After taking one or two small towns, and quarrelling with Pancrates, whom he left behind, he pushed on to Edessa, which, by a series of lucky escapes, he entered with only a hundred knights, to become its king. Here he must for the present be left.

Meantime, the great army of the Crusaders was pressing on. For the moment it was unmolested. Both Christian and Saracen had begun to conceive a respect for each other's prowess. The latter found that his innumerable troops of light cavalry were of little use against the heavily-armed and disciplined masses of the Crusaders: while these, harassed by the perpetual renewal of armies which seemed only destroyed to spring again from the earth, and convinced now that the recovery of the Holy City would be no holiday ramble in a sunny land, marched with better discipline and more circumspection. But the Saracens, unable to raise another army in time, fled before them, leaving towns and villages unoccupied. The Christians burnt the mosques, and plundered the country. Even the passes of Mount Taurus were left unguarded, and the Christian army passed through defiles and valleys, where a very small force might have barred the passage for the whole army. They suffered, however, from their constant enemies, heat and thirst. On one mountain, called the "Mountain of the Devil," the army had to pass along a path so narrow that the horses were led, and the men could not walk two abreast. Here, wearied with the ascent, faint with thirst, hundreds sank, unable to proceed, or fell over the precipices. It was the last of the cruel trials through which they were to pass before they reached the land of their pilgrimage. From the summit of the last pass, they beheld, stretched out at their feet, the fair land of Syria. Covered with ruins, as it was—those ruins which exist to the present day—and devastated by so many successive wars, nothing had been able to ruin the fertility of the soil; and after the arid plains through which they had passed, no wonder the worn and weary soldiers rejoiced and thanked God aloud, when they saw at last the very country to which they were journeying. The ordeal of thirst and heat had been passed through, and their numbers were yet strong. Nothing now remained, as they fondly thought, but to press on, and fight the enemy before the very walls of Jerusalem.

The successes of Tancred cleared the way for the advance of the main army. Nothing interposed to stop them; provisions were plentiful, and their march was unimpeded by any enemy. Count Robert of Flanders led the advance corps. At Artasia, a town about a day's march from Antioch, the gates were thrown open to them; and though the garrison of Antioch threw out flying squadrons of cavalry, they were not able to check the advance of the army, which swarmed along the roads, in numbers reduced, indeed, by one half, from the six hundred thousand who gathered before Nicæa, but still irresistible. The old bridge of stone which crossed the Orontes was stormed, and the Crusaders were fairly in Syria, and before Antioch.

The present governor of this great and important town was Baghi Seyan, one of the Seljukian princes. He had with him a force of about twenty-five thousand, foot and horse; he was defended by a double wall of stone, strengthened by towers; he was plentifully supplied with provisions; he had sent messengers for assistance to all quarters, and might reasonably hope to be relieved; and he had expelled from the town all useless mouths, including the native Christians. Moreover, it was next to impossible for the Crusaders to establish a complete line round the city, and cut him off from supplies and reinforcements.

It was late in the autumn when the Christian army sat down before the first place. For the first two or three weeks the country was scoured for provisions, and the soldiers, improvident and reckless, lived in a luxury and abundance which they had never before experienced. But even Syria, fertile and rich, could not long suffice for the daily wants of a wasteful army of three hundred thousand men. Food began to grow scarce; foraging parties brought in little or nothing, though they scoured the whole country; bands of Turks, mounted on fleet and hardy horses, intercepted straggling parties, and robbed them of their cattle; the fleet brought them very small supplies; Baldwin had as yet sent nothing from Edessa, and famine once more made its appearance in the camp. The rains of winter fell, and their tents were destroyed. The poor lived on what they could find, bark and roots; the rich had to spend all their money in buying food; and all the horses died. Worse still, there was defection among the very leaders; Robert of Normandy went to Laodicea, and was persuaded with great difficulty to come back. Peter the Hermit fairly ran away, and was brought back a prisoner to the army which his own voice had raised. And when Bohemond and Tancred went out, with as large a force as could be spared, to procure provisions, they were attacked by superior numbers, and obliged to return empty-handed. Bishop Adhémar, seeing in the sins of the camp a just cause for the punishments that were falling upon it, enjoined a three days' fast, and public prayers. The former was superfluous, inasmuch as the whole camp was fasting. But he did more. He caused all women to be sent away, and all games of chance to be entirely prohibited. The distress continued, but hope and confidence were revived; and when, early in the year 1098, supplies were brought in, the army regained most of its old *bravoure*. A victory gained over a reinforcement of twenty-five thousand Turks aided in reviving the spirit of the soldiers: it was in this action that Godfrey is reported to have cut a Turk completely through the body, so that his horse galloped off with the legs and lower part of the trunk still in the saddle. The camp of the enemy was taken, and for a time there was once more abundance. But the siege was not yet over. For eight months it lingered on, defended with the obstinacy that the Turks always displayed when brought to bay within stone walls. It was not till June that the town, not the citadel, was taken, by the treachery of one Pyrrhus, an Armenian renegade. He offered secretly to put the town, which was in his charge, into the hands of Bohemond. The Norman chief, always anxious to promote his own interests, proposed, at the council of the Crusaders, to take the town on condition that it should be given to him. Raymond of Toulouse alone objected— his objection was overruled; and on the night of the 2nd of June, Pyrrhus admitted the Christians. They made themselves masters, under cover of the darkness, of ten of the towers round the walls; and opening the gates to their own men, made an easy conquest of the town in the morning, slaughtering every Mussulman they could find. Baghi Seyan fled, and, being abandoned by his guards, was murdered by some Syrian woodcutters, who brought his head to the camp. And then, once more, untaught by their previous sufferings, the Crusaders for a few days gave themselves up to the enjoyment of their booty. But the citadel was not taken, and the host of Kerboga was within a short march of the town. He came with the largest army that the Christians had yet encountered. Robert of Flanders defended the bridge for a whole day with five hundred men, but was obliged to retire, and the Christians were in their turn the besieged.

And then, again, famine set in. The seashore was guarded by the Turks, and supplies could not be procured from the fleet; the horses, and all the beasts of burden, were slaughtered and eaten; some of the knights who were fainthearted managed to let themselves down by ropes from the walls, and made their way to Stephen of Blois, who had long since separated from the main army, and was now lying at Alexandretta. They brought such accounts of the misery of the army, that Stephen abandoned the cause as hopeless, and set sail with his men for Cilicia. Here he found Alexis himself, with a large army, consisting chiefly of those who had arrived too late to join the army of Godfrey. The newcomers heard with dismay the accounts given by Stephen; they gave themselves up to lamentation and despair; they blasphemed the God who had permitted His soldiers to be destroyed, and for some days would actually permit no prayers to be offered up in their camp. Alexis broke up his camp, and returned to Constantinople. And when the news arrived in Antioch, the Crusaders, too wretched to fight or to hope, shut themselves up in the houses, and refused to come out. Bohemond set fire to the town, and so compelled them to show themselves, but could not make them fight.

Where human eloquence failed, one of those miracles, common enough in the ages of credulity, the result of overheated imaginations and excited brains, succeeded. A vision of the night came to one Peter Bartholomæus, a monk, of two men in shining raiment. One of them, St. Andrew himself, took the monk into the air, and brought him to the Church of St. Peter, and set him at the south side of the altar. He then showed him the head of a lance. "This," he said, "was the lance which opened the side of Our Lord. See where I bury it. Get twelve men to dig in the spot till they find it." But in the morning Peter was afraid to tell his vision. This was before the taking of Antioch. But after the town was taken, the vision came again, and in his dream Peter saw once more the apostle, and received his reproaches for neglect of his commands. Peter remonstrated that he was poor and of no account; and then he saw that the apostle's companion was none other than the Blessed Lord himself, and the humble monk was privileged to fall and kiss His feet.

We are not of those who believe that men are found so base as to contrive a story of this kind. There is little doubt in our minds that this poor Peter, starving as he was, full of fervour and enthusiasm, dreamed his dream, not once but twice, and went at last, brimful of pious gratitude, to Adhémar with his tale. Adhémar heard him with incredulity and coldness. But Raymond saw in this incident a means which might be turned to good account. He sent twelve men to the church, and from morning till night they dug in vain. But at length Peter himself, leaping into the hole they had made, called aloud on God to redeem his promise, and produced a rusty spear-head. Adhémar acquiesced with the best grace in his power; the lance was exhibited to the people the next morning, and the enthusiasm of the army, famished, and ragged, and dismounted, once more beat as high as when they sewed the red Cross badge upon their shoulders, and shouted " Dieu le veut."

They had been besieged three weeks; all their horses, except three hundred, were killed. Their ranks were grievously thinned, but they went out to meet the enemy with such confidence that the only orders given related to the distribution of the plunder. As they took their places in the plain, Adhémar raised their spirits by the announcement of another miracle. Saint George, Saint Maurice, and Saint Demetrius, had themselves been distinctly seen to join the army, and were in their midst. The Christians fought as only religious enthusiasts can fight—as the Mohammedans fought when the Caliph Omar led his conquering bands northwards, with the delights of heaven for those who fell, and the joys of earth for those who survived. The Turks were routed with enormous slaughter. Their camp, rich and luxurious, fell into the hands of the conquerors;* plenty took the place of starvation; the common soldiers amused themselves with decking their persons with the silken robes they found in the huts; the cattle were driven to the town in long processions; and once

---

* Among the spoils taken by the Christians one of the chroniclers reports a mass of manuscripts, " on which were traced the sacrilegious rites of the Mahometans in execrable characters," doubtless Arabic. Probably among these manuscripts were many of the greatest importance. Nothing is said about their fate, but of course they were all destroyed.

more, forgetful of all but the present, the Christians revelled and feasted.

The rejoicings had hardly ceased when it was found that another enemy had to be encountered. Battle was to be expected: famine had already twice been experienced: this time it was pestilence, caused, no doubt, by the crowding together of so large an army and the absence of sanitary measures. The first to fall was the wise and good Adhémar, most sensible of all the chiefs. His was a dire loss to the Crusaders. Better could they have spared even the fiery Tancred, or the crafty Bohemond. The Crusaders, terrified and awe-stricken, clamoured to be led to Jerusalem, but needs must that they remained till the heats of summer passed, and health came again with the early winter breezes, in their camp at Antioch.

It was not till November that they set out on their march to Jerusalem. The time had been consumed in small expeditions, the capture of unimportant places, and the quarrels of the princes over the destination of Antioch, which Bohemond claimed for himself. Their rival claims were still unsettled, when the voice of the people made itself heard, and very shame made them, for a time at least, act in concert. and the advance corps, led by Bohemond, Robert of Normandy, and Raymond of Toulouse, began their southward march with the siege of Marra, an important place, which they took, after three or four weeks, by assault. Fresh disputes arose about the newly-acquired town, but the common soldiers, furious at these never-ending delays, ended them by the simple expedient of pulling down the walls. It was the middle of January, however, before they resumed their march. From Marah to Capharda, thence along the Orontes, when the small towns were placed in their hands, to Hums, when they turned westward to the sea, and sat down before the castle of Arca till they should be joined by the main body, which was still at Antioch. It came up in April, and the army of the Crusaders, united again, were ready to resume their march when they were interrupted by more disputes. In an ill-timed hour, Bohemond, the incredulous Norman, accused Raymond of conniving with Peter to deceive the army by palming off upon them an old rusty lance-head as the sacred spear which had pierced the side of the Lord. Arnold, chaplain to Duke Robert of Normandy, was brought forward to support the charge. He rested his argument chiefly on the fact that Adhémar had disbelieved the miracle: but he contended as well that the spear-head could not possibly be in Antioch. He was confuted in the manner customary to the time. One bold monk swore that Adhémar, after death, for his contumacy in refusing to believe in the miracle, had been punished by having one side of his beard burned in the flames of hell, and was not permitted a full enjoyment of heaven till the beard should grow again. Another quoted a prophecy of Saint Peter, alleged to be in a Syrian gospel, that the invention of the lance was to be a sign of the deliverance of the Christians; a third had spoken personally with Saint Mark himself; while the Virgin Mary had appeared by night to a fourth to corroborate the story. Arnold pretended to give way before testimony so overwhelming, and was ready to retract his opinion publicly, when Peter, crazed with enthusiasm, offered to submit his case to the ordeal of fire. This method was too congenial to the fierce and eager spirits of the Crusaders to be refused. Raymond d'Agiles, who was a witness, thus tells the story.

"Peter's proposition appeared to us reasonable, and after enjoining a fast on Peter, we agreed to kindle the fire on Good Friday itself.

"On the day appointed, the pile was prepared after noon; the princes and the people assembled to the number of forty thousand; the priests coming barefooted and dressed in their sacerdotal robes. The pile was made with dry branches of olive-trees, fourteen feet long, and four feet high, divided into two heaps, with a narrow path, a foot wide, between each. As soon as the wood began to burn, I myself, Raymond,* pronounced these words, 'If the Lord himself has spoken to this man face to face, and if Saint Andrew has shown him the lance of the Lord, let him pass through the fire without receiving any hurt: or, if not, let him be burnt with the lance which he carries in his hand.' And all bending the knee, replied, 'Amen.'

"Then Peter, dressed in a single robe, kneeling before the bishop of Albaric, called God to witness that he had seen Jesus on the cross face to face, and that he had heard from the mouth of the Saviour, and that of the apostles, Peter and Andrew, the words reported to the princes: he added that nothing of what he had said in the name of the saints and in the name of the Lord had been invented by himself, and declared that if there was found any falsehood in his story, he consented to suffer from the flames. And for the other sins that he had committed against God and his neighbours, he prayed that God would pardon him, and that the bishop, all the other priests, and the people would implore the mercy of God for him. This said, the bishop gave him the lance.

"Peter knelt again, and making the sign of the cross he reached the flames without appearing afraid. He remained one moment in the midst of the fire, and then came out by the grace of God. . . . After Peter had gone through the fire, and although the flames were still raging, the people gathered up the brands, the ashes, and the charcoal, with such ardour that in a few moments nothing was left. The Lord in the end performed great miracles by means of these sacred relics. Peter came out of the flames without even his gown being burned, and the light veil which covered the lance-head escaped uninjured. He made immediately the sign of the cross, and cried with a loud voice, 'God help!' to the crowd, who pressed upon him to be certain

* He was chaplain to Count Raymond of Toulouse.

that it was really he. Then, in their eagerness, and because everybody wanted to touch him, and to have even some little piece of his dress, they trampled him under their feet, cut off pieces of his flesh, broke his back-bone, and broke his ribs. He was only saved from being killed there and then by Raymond Pelot, a knight, who hastily called a number of soldiers and rescued him.

"When he was brought into our tent, we dressed his wounds, and asked him why he had stopped so long in the fire. 'Because,' he said, 'the Lord appeared to me in the midst of the flames, and taking me by the hand, said, 'Since thou hast doubted of the holy lance, which the blessed Andrew showed to thee, thou shalt not go out from this sound and safe. Nevertheless, thou shalt not see hell.' After these words He sent me on. 'See now the marks of fire on my body.' And, in fact, there were certain burnings in the legs, small in number, though the wounds were great."

Peter Bartholomew died the day after—of the fire, said Bohemond, the doubter, who continued in his disbelief, in spite of the ordeal; of the injuries he had received in the crowd, said Raymond of Toulouse. But the authority of the lance was established, and it was to do good service in the battles to come. The faith of the Crusaders was kept up by many other visions and miracles. One that had the greatest effect was a vision seen by Anselm. To him appeared by night Angelram, the young son of the Count of Saint Paul, who had been killed at Marra. "Know," said the phantom, "that those who fight for Christ die not." "And whence this glory that surrounds you?" Then Angelram showed in the heavens a palace of crystal and diamonds. "It is there," he said, "that I have borrowed my splendour. There is my dwelling-place. One finer still is preparing for you, into which you will soon enter." The next day Anselm, after telling of this apparition, confessed and received the sacraments, though full of health, and going into battle, was struck by a stone in the forehead, and died immediately.

On their way to Tripoli,* where they first saw the sugar-cane, the impatience of the soldiers manifested itself so strongly that the chiefs could not venture to sit down before the place, but pushed on, after making a sort of treaty with its governor. Here messengers arrived from Alexis, entreating them to wait for him, and promising to bring an army in July. But the time was gone for negotiation and delay, and taking the sea-shore route, by which they ensured the protection of the fleet, they marched southwards to Beirout. Sidon, and Tyre, and Acre, were passed without much opposition, and the Crusaders arrived at Cæsarea, which is within sixty miles of Jerusalem. By marches quick rather than forced, for the enthusiasm of the army was once more at its height, they reached Lydda, where the church of Saint George lay in ruins, having recently been destroyed by the Turks, and thence to Ramleh. Here an embassy from Bethlehem waited for them with prayers to protect their town. Tancred, with a hundred knights only, rode off with them. The people received them with

---

* While they were considering which road was the easiest for their march to Jerusalem, the Crusaders received a deputation from a Christian people, said to be sixty thousand in number, living in the mountains of Lebanus. They offered their services as guides, and pointed out that there were three roads: the first by way of Damascus, level and plain, and always abounding in provisions; the second over Mount Lebanon, safe from any enemy, and also full of provisions, but difficult for beasts of burden; and the third by the sea-shore, abounding in defiles, where "fifty Mussulmans would be able, if they pleased, to stop the whole of mankind." "But," said these Christians, "if you are of a verity that nation which is to overcome Jerusalem, you must pass along the sea-shore, however difficult that road may appear, *according to the Gospel of St. Peter.* Your way, such as you have made it, and such as you must make it, is all laid down in that Gospel which we possess."

What was this Gospel? or is it only one of the credulous stories of Raymond d'Agiles?

psalms of joy, and took them to see the Church of the Nativity. But they would not stay. Bethlehem is but four miles from Jerusalem, and Tancred rode on in advance, eager to be the first to see the city. He ascended the mount of Olives unmolested, and there found a hermit who pointed out to him the sacred sites. The little troop rode back in triumph to tell the Crusaders that the city was almost within their grasp. The soldiers, rough and rude as they were, and stained with every vice, were yet open to the influences of this, the very goal of their hopes. From a rising ground they beheld at last the walls of the Holy City. "And when they heard the name of Jerusalem, the Christians could not prevent themselves, in the fervour of their devotion, from shedding tears; they fell on their faces to the ground, glorifying and adoring God, who, in His goodness, had heard the prayers of His people and had granted them, according to their desires, to arrive at this most sacred place, the object of all their hopes."

The army which sat down before Jerusalem numbered about twenty thousand fighting men, and an equal number of camp followers, old men, women, and children. This was the miserable remnant of that magnificent army of six hundred thousand, with which Godfrey had taken Nicæa and punished the massacre of Walter and his rabble. Where were all the rest? The road was strewn with their bones. Across the thirsty deserts of Asia Minor, on the plain of Dorylæum, and on the slopes and passes of Taurus, the Crusaders' bodies lay unburied, while before and within Antioch, the city of disasters, thousands upon thousands were thrown into the river or lay in unhallowed soil. But they were not all killed. Many had returned home, among whom were Hugh le Grand and Stephen of Blois; many had left the main body and gone off in free-handed expeditions of their own, to join Baldwin and others. Thus we have heard of Wolf, the Burgundian conqueror of Adana. Presently we find that Guymer the pirate of Boulogne, who joined Baldwin at Tarsus, must have left him again, and returned to his piratical ways, for we find him in prison at Tripoli; he was delivered up by the governor of Tripoli to the Christians, after which he appears no more. Then some had been taken prisoners, and purchased their lives by apostacy, like Rinaldo the Italian. And those of the captive women who were yet young were dragging out their lives in the Turkish harems. Probably the boys, too, were spared, and those who were young enough to forget their Christian blood brought up to be soldiers of the Crescent.

The neighbourhood of Jerusalem was covered with light brushwood, but there were no trees; there had been grass in plenty, but it was dried up by the summer sun; there were wells and cisterns, but they had all been closed,— "the fountains were sealed." Only the pool of Siloam was accessible to the Crusaders; this was intermittent and irregular, and its supply, when it did flow, was miserably inadequate for a host of forty thousand. Moreover, its waters were brackish and disagreeable. And the camp was full of sick, wounded, and helpless.

On the west, east, and south sides of the city no attack was possible, on account of the valleys by which it was naturally protected. The Crusaders pitched their camp in the north. First in the post of danger, as usual, was the camp of Godfrey, Duke of Lorraine. His position extended westwards from the valley of Jehoshaphat, along the north wall. Next to him came the Count of Flanders; next, Robert of Normandy, near whom was Edgar Atheling with his English; at the north-west angle was Tancred; and lastly, the camp of the Count of Toulouse extended along the west as far as the Jaffa Gate. Later on, however, Raymond moved a portion of his camp to that part of Mount Sion stretching south of the modern wall. But the only place where an attacking party could hope for success was on the north. Bohemond was not with the army. He cared less about taking the city than wreaking his vengeance upon the Greek emperor. Meantime, within the city was an army of forty thousand men. Provisions for a long siege had been conveyed into the town; the zeal of the defenders had been raised by the exhortations of the Imams; the walls were strengthened and the moats deepened. Communication and relief were possible from the east, where only scattered bands of the Christians barred the way.

Immediately before the arrival of the Crusaders, the Mohammedans deliberated whether they should slaughter all the Christians in cold blood, or only fine them and expel them from the city. It was decided to adopt the latter plan; and the Crusaders were greeted on their arrival not only by the flying squadrons of the enemy's cavalry, but also by exiled Christians telling their piteous tales. Their houses had been pillaged, their wives kept as hostages; immense sums were required for their ransom; the churches were desecrated; and, even worse still, the Infidels were contemplating the entire destruction of the Church of the Holy Sepulchre. This last charge, at least, was not true. But it added fuel to a fire which was already beyond any control, and the chiefs gave a ready permission to their men to carry the town, if they could, by assault. They had neither ladders nor machines, but, covering themselves with their bucklers, rushed against the walls and tried to tear them down with pikes and hammers. Boiling oil and pitch, the best weapons for the besieged, were poured upon their heads, with huge stones and enormous beams. In spite of heavy losses, they managed to tear down and carry a portion of the outer wall, and the besieged retired to their inner works, which were impregnable, at least to hammers and pikes. One ladder, and only one, was found. Tancred, with his usual hardihood, was the first to place his foot on the ladder, but he was forcibly held back by his knights, who would not allow him to rush upon certain death. Two or three gained the wall, and were thrown from it dead. Night put an end to the fight, and the Christians, dejected and beaten back, retired to their camp. Heaven would work no miracles for them, and it was clear that the city must be taken according to the ordinary methods of warfare. Machines were necessary, but there was no wood. Chance threw into their possession a cavern, forgotten by the Saracens, filled with a store of timber, which went some way. There were still some beams in the houses and churches round Jerusalem not yet burned. All these were brought into the camp, but still there was not enough. Then a Syrian Christian bethought him of a wood six miles off, on the road to Samaria, whither he led the Crusaders. The trees were small, and not of the best kind, but such as they were they had to suffice, and all hands were employed in the construction of towers and engines of assault. They worked with the energy of men who have but one hope. For, in the midst of a Syrian summer, with a burning sun over their heads, they had no water. The nearest wells, except the intermittent spring of Siloam, were six or seven miles away. To bring the water into the camp, strong detachments were daily sent out; the country was scoured for miles in every direction for water; hundreds perished in casual encounters with the enemy, while wandering in search of wells; and the water, when it was procured, was often so muddy and impure that the very horses refused to drink it. As for those who worked in the camp, they dug up the ground and sucked the moist earth; they cut pieces of turf and laid them at their hearts to appease the devouring heat; in the morning they licked the dew from the grass; they abstained from eating till they were compelled by faintness; they drank the blood of their beasts. Never, not even in Antioch, not even in Phrygia, had their sufferings been so terrible, or so protracted.

And, as the days went on, as the sun grew fiercer, the dews more scanty—as the miracle, still expected, delayed to come—some lay despairing in their tents, some worked on in a despairing energy, and some threw themselves down at the foot of the walls to die, or to be killed by the besieged, crying, "Fall, oh walls of Jerusalem, upon us! Sacred dust of the city, at least cover our bones!"

These trials were to have an end. In the midst of their greatest distress, the news came that a Genoese fleet had arrived off Joppa, loaded with munitions and provisions. A detachment of three hundred men was sent off at once to receive them. They fought their way to Joppa. Here they found that the Christian ships had been abandoned to a superior Egyptian fleet, but not till after all the stores and provisions had been landed. With the fleet was a large number of Genoese artificers and carpenters, whose arrival in the camp was almost as timely as that of the wine and food.

The hopes of the Crusaders, always as sanguine as they were easily dejected, revived again. This unexpected reinforcement—was it not a miracle? and might there not be others yet to follow? Gaston of Béarn superintended the construction of the machines. In the carriage of their timber, as they had no carts or wheels, they employed their Saracen prisoners. Putting fifty or sixty of them in line, they made them carry beams "which four oxen could not drag." Raymond of Toulouse, who alone had not spent all he had brought with him, found the money to pay those few who were exempted from gratuitous service. A regular service for the carriage of water was organised, and some alleviation thus afforded to the sufferings caused by thirst.

Three great towers were made, higher than the walls. Each of these was divided into three stages; the lowest for the workmen, and the two higher for the soldiers. The front and sides exposed to the enemy were cased with plates of iron, or defended by wet hides; the back part was of wood. On the top was a sort of drawbridge, which could be lowered so as to afford a passage to the wall.

All being ready, it was determined to preface the attack by a processional march round the city. After a fast of three days and solemn services, the Crusaders solemnly went in procession, barefooted and bareheaded, round the city. They were preceded by their priests in white surplices, carrying the images of saints, and chanting psalms; their banners were displayed, the clarions blew. As the Israelites marched round Jericho, the Crusaders marched round Jerusalem, and doubtless many longing eyes, though more in doubt than in hope, were turned upon the walls to see if they, too, would fall. They did not. The besieged crowded upon them, holding crosses, which they insulted, and discharging their arrows at the procession. But the hearts of the rough soldiers were moved to the utmost, not by the taunts of their enemies, but by the sight of the sacred spots, and the memory of the things which had taken place there: there was Calvary; here Gethsemane, where Christ prayed and wept; here the place where He ascended; here the spot on which He stood while He wept over the city. They, too, could see it lying at their feet, with the Church of the Holy Sepulchre, and the Great Mosque in the midst of the place where had been the Temple of the Lord. These places cried aloud to them for deliverance. Or, if they looked behind them, to the east, they saw the banks of the river across which Joshua had passed, and the Dead Sea which lay above the Cities of the Plain.

Arnold, chaplain to Duke Robert of Normandy—an eloquent man, but of dissolute morals—harangued them. His discourse had been preserved after the manner of historians; that is, we are told what he ought to have said; very likely, in substance, what he did say. God, he told them, would pardon them all sins in recompense for their recovery of the holy places. And he made the chiefs themselves, who had sinned by quarrelling and dissension, embrace in presence of the whole army, and thereby set the example of perfect union. Then they renewed, for the last time, their oaths of fidelity to the Cross. Peter the Hermit, who was with them, harangued them also. And in the evening the soldiers returned to the camp to confess their sins, to receive the Eucharist, and to spend the night in prayer.

Godfrey alone was active. He perceived that the Saracens had constructed on the wall opposite to the position of his great tower, works which would perhaps render it useless. He therefore took it down, and transported it, with very great labour, and in a single night, to a spot which he considered the weakest in the north wall. Here it was re-erected to the dismay of the besieged.

At break of day on Thursday, July 14th, 1099, the attack began. The towers were moved against the walls, the mangonels hurled their stones into the city, and the battering-rams were brought into play. All day long the attack was carried on, but to little effect, and at nightfall, when the Crusaders returned to their camp, the tower of Raymond was in ruins; those of Tancred and Godfrey were so damaged that they could not be moved; and the princes were seen beating their hands in despair, and crying that God had abandoned them. "Miserable men that we are!" cried Robert of Normandy; "God judges us unworthy to enter into the Holy City, and worship at the tomb of His Son."

The next day was Friday, the day of the Crucifixion. At daybreak the battle began again. It went well for the Crusaders; the wall was broken in many places, and the besieged with all their endeavours could not set fire to the towers. In the middle of the day they brought out two magicians—witches, it is said, though one hardly believes it. They made their incantations on the walls, attended by their maidens.* These were all destroyed at once by stones from the mangonels. But the day went on, and the final assault could not be delivered for the courage and ferocity of the Saracens. And then, the usual miracle happened. Godfrey and Raymond, shouting that heaven had come to their rescue, pointed to the Mount of Olives, where stood a man, "miles splendidus et refulgens," one clothed in bright and glittering armour, waving his shield as a signal for the advance. Who could it be but Saint George himself? In the midst of a shower of arrows, Greek fire, and stones, the tower of Godfrey was pushed against the wall; the drawbridge fell; Godfrey himself was among the first to leap upon the wall. And then the rumour ran, that not only Saint George, but Bishop Adhémar—dead Bishop Adhémar himself—was in the ranks, and fighting against the Infidel. The supreme moment was arrived! A whisper went through the troops that it was now three o'clock; the time, as well as the day, when our Lord died, on the very spot where they were fighting. Even the women and children joined in the attack, and mingled their cries with the shouts of the soldiers. The Saracens gave way, and Jerusalem was taken.

The city was taken, and the massacre of its defenders began. The Christians ran through the streets, slaughtering as they went. At first they spared none, neither man, woman, nor child, putting all alike to the sword; but when resistance had ceased, and rage was partly appeased, they began to bethink them of pillage, and tortured those who remained alive to make them discover their gold. As for the Jews within the city, they had fled to their synagogue, which the Christians set on fire, and so burned them all. The chroniclers relate with savage joy, how

* Robert of Normandy might have remembered that a similar plan had been adopted by his father against Hereward in Ely.

the streets were encumbered with heads and mangled bodies, and how in the Haram Area, the sacred enclosure of the Temple, the knights rode in blood up to the knees of their horses. Here upwards of ten thousand were slaughtered, while the whole number of killed amounted, according to various estimates, to forty, seventy, and even a hundred thousand. An Arabic historian, not to be outdone in miracles by the Christians, reports that at the moment when the city fell, a sudden eclipse took place,. and the stars appeared in the day. Fugitives brought the news to Damascus and Baghdad. It was then the month of Ramadan, but the general trouble was such that the very fast was neglected. No greater misfortune, except, perhaps, the loss of Mecca, could have happened to Islamism. The people went in masses to the mosques; the poets made their verses of lamentation: "We have mingled our blood with our tears. No refuge remains against the woes that overpower us. . . . How can ye close your eyes, children of Islam, in the midst of troubles which would rouse the deepest sleeper? Will the chiefs of the Arabs resign themselves to such evils? and will the warriors of Persia submit to such disgrace? Would to God, since they will not fight for their religion, that they would fight for the safety of their neighbours! And if they give up the rewards of heaven, will they not be induced to fight by the hope of booty?"*

Evening fell, and the clamour ceased, for there were no more enemies to kill, save a few whose lives had been promised by Tancred. Then from their hiding-places in the city came out the Christians who still remained in it. They had but one thought, to seek out and welcome Peter the Hermit, whom they proclaimed as their liberator. At the sight of these Christians, a sudden revulsion of feeling seized the soldiers. They remembered that the

* From a poem by Mozaffer el Abiwardí.

city they had taken was the city of the Lord, and this impulsive soldiery, sheathing swords reeking with blood, followed Godfrey to the Church of the Holy Sepulchre, where they passed the night in tears, and prayers, and services.

In the morning the carnage began again. Those who had escaped the first fury were the women and children. It was now resolved to spare none. Even the three hundred to whom Tancred had promised life were slaughtered in spite of him. Raymond alone managed to save the lives of those who capitulated to him from the tower of David. It took a week to kill the Saracens, and to take away their dead bodies. Every Crusader had a right to the first house he took possession of, and the city found itself absolutely cleared of its old inhabitants, and in the hands of a new population. The true Cross, which had been hidden by the Christians during the siege, was brought forth again, and carried in joyful procession round the city, and for ten days the soldiers gave themselves up to murder, plunder—and prayers!

And the First Crusade was finished.

CHAPTER VII.

THE CHRISTIAN KINGDOM. KING GODFREY.

A.D. 1099—1100.

Signor, ceste cité vous l'avez conquesté;
Or faut élire un roi dont elle soit gardée,
Et la terre environ des païens recensée.
Romans de Godefroi.

FOR seven days after the conquest of the city and the massacre of the inhabitants the Crusaders, very naturally, abandoned themselves to rest, feasting, and services of thanksgiving. On the eighth day a council was held to determine the future mode of holding and governing their newly-acquired possessions. At the outset a remonstrance was presented by the priests, jealous as usual of their supremacy, against secular matters being permitted to take the lead of things ecclesiastical, and demanding that, before aught else was done, a Patriarch should be first elected. But the Christians were a long way from Rome. The conduct of their priests on the journey had not been such as to inspire the laity with respect for their valour, prudence, or morality, and the chiefs dismissed the remonstrance with contempt.

Robert of Flanders, in this important council, was the first to speak. He called upon his peers, setting aside all jealousies and ambitions, to elect from their own body one who might be found to unite the best valour of a knight with the best virtue of a Christian. And in a noble speech which has been preserved—if, indeed, it was not written long after the time—he disclaimed, for his own part, any desire to canvass their votes, or to become the king of Jerusalem. "I entreat you to receive my counsel as I give it you, with affection, frankness, and loyalty; and to elect for king him who, by his own worth, will best be able to preserve and extend this kingdom, to which are attached the honour of your arms, and the cause of Jesus Christ."

Many had begun to think of offering the crown to Robert himself. But this was not his wish; and among the rest their choice clearly lay between Godfrey, Robert of Normandy, Raymond of Toulouse, and Tancred. Of these, Tancred and Robert were men ambitious of glory rather than of honours. The latter had thrown away the crown of England once, and was going to throw it away again. With equal readiness he threw away the crown of Jerusalem. Raymond, who had sworn never to return to Europe, was old and unpopular, probably from the absence of the princely munificence and affability that distinguished Godfrey, perhaps also from lack of those personal charms which his rival possessed. To be handsome as well as brave was given to Godfrey, but if it had ever been given to Raymond, his day of comeliness was past. A sort of committee of ten was appointed, whose business it was to examine closely into the private character of the chiefs, as well as into their prowess. History is prudently silent as to the reports made on the characters of the rest, but we know what was said about Godfrey. Though the Provençal party invented calumnies against him, his own servants were explicit and clear in their evidence. Nothing whatever could be set down against him. Pure and unsullied in his private life, he came out of this ordeal with no other accusation against him, by those who were with him at all hours of the day and night, but one, and that the most singular complaint ever brought against a prince by his servants. They stated that in all the private acts of the duke, the one which they found most vexatious (*absonum*) was that when he went into a church he could not be got out of it, even after the celebration of service; but he was used to stay behind and inquire of the priests and those who seemed to have any knowledge of the matter, about the meaning and history of each picture and image: his companions, being otherwise minded, were affected with continual tedium and even disgust at this conduct, which was certainly thoughtless, because the meals, cooked, of course, in readiness for a certain hour, were often, owing to this exasperating delay, served up cold and tasteless. There is a touch of humour in the grave way in which this charge is brought forward by the historian, who evidently enjoys the picture of Godfrey's followers standing by and waiting, while their faces grow longer as they think of the roast, which is certain to be either cold or overdone.

No one was astonished, and most men rejoiced, when the electors declared that their choice had fallen upon Godfrey. They conducted him in solemn procession to the Church of the Sepulchre with hymns and psalms. Here he took an oath to respect the laws of justice, but when the coronation should have taken place, Godfrey put away the crown. He would not wear a crown of gold when his Lord had worn a crown of thorns. Nor would he take the title of king. Of this, he said he was not worthy. Let them call him the Baron of the Holy Sepulchre. He never wore the crown, but the voice of posterity has always given him the name of king.

Godfrey of Lorraine, born at Boulogne in the year 1058, or thereabouts, was the son of Count Eustace, and the nephew of the Duke of Lorraine. His brother Baldwin, who came with him as far as Asia Minor, but separated then from the Crusaders and gained the principality of Edessa, was the second son. Eustace, who afterwards became Count of Boulogne, was the third. And his sister, Matilda, was the wife of our king Stephen.

The story of Godfrey, who is the real hero of the First Crusade, is made up of facts, visions, and legends. Let us tell them altogether.

At an early age he was once playing with his two brothers, when his father entered the room. At that moment the children were all hiding in the folds of their mother's dress. Count Eustace, seeing the dress shaken, asked who was behind it, "There," replied the Lady Ida, in the spirit of prophecy, "are three great princes. The first shall be a duke, the second a king, and the third a count," a prediction which was afterwards exactly fulfilled. Unfortunately, no record exists of this prophecy till nearly a hundred years after it was made. Godfrey was adopted by his uncle, the Duke of Lorraine, and, at the age of sixteen, joined the fortunes of the emperor Henry IV. He fought in all the campaigns of that unquiet sovereign; he it was who, at the battle of Malsen, carried the Imperial banner, and signalized himself by killing Rudolph of Swabia with his own hand. He was present when, after three years' siege, Henry succeeded in wresting Rome from Hildebrand in 1083, and in reward for his bravery on that occasion, he received the duchy of Lorraine when it was forfeited by the defection of Conrad. An illness, some time after, caused him to vow a pilgrimage to the Holy Land, and until the Crusade started Godfrey had no rest or peace.

During this period of expectation, a vision, related by Albert of Aix, came to one of his servants. He saw, like Jacob, a ladder which was all pure gold, ascending from earth to heaven. Godfrey, followed by his servant Rothard, was mounting this ladder. Rothard had a lamp in his hand; in the middle of the ascent the lamp went out suddenly. Dismayed at this accident, Rothard came down the ladder, and declined to relight his lamp or to climb up again. Godfrey, however, undaunted, went on. Then the seer of the vision himself took the lamp and followed his master; both arrived safely at the top, and there, which was no other place than Heaven itself, they enjoyed the favours of God. The ladder was of pure gold, to signify that pilgrims must have pure hearts, and the gate to which it led was Jerusalem, the gate of heaven. Rothard, whose light went out half way, who came down in despair, was an image of those pilgrims who take the Cross but come back again in despair; and he who saw the vision and went up with Godfrey typified those Crusaders, a faithful few, who endured unto the end.

Stories are told to illustrate the prowess of this great and strong man. On one occasion, when he was compelled to defend his rights to some land by the ordeal of battle, his sword broke off short upon the buckler of his adversary, leaving him not more than six inches of steel. The knights present at the duel interposed in order to stop a combat so unequal, but Godfrey himself insisted on going on. His adversary pressed him with all his skill and strength, but Godfrey, collecting all his force, sprang upon and literally felled him to the ground. Then taking his sword from him, he broke it across his knee, and called upon the president of the duel to make such terms as would spare his enemy's life.

Again, a noble Arab, desirous of seeing so great a warrior, paid him a visit, and asked him, as a special favour, to strike a camel with his sword. Godfrey, at a single blow, struck off the head of the beast. The Arab begged to speak apart with him, thinking it was the effect of magic, and asked him if he would do the same thing with another sword. "Lend me your own," said Godfrey, and repeated the feat with his guest's own sword.

At the time of his election, Godfrey was in the fulness of his strength and vigour, about forty years of age. He was tall, but not above the stature of ordinarily tall men;

his countenance was handsome and attractive; and his beard and hair were a reddish brown. In manners he was courteous, and in living, simple and unostentatious. The first king of Christian Jerusalem, the only one of all the Crusaders whose life was pure, whose motives were disinterested, whose end and aim was the glory of God, was also the only king who came near the standard set up by Robert of Flanders, as one who should be foremost in virtue as well as in arms. The kingdom over which he ruled was a kingdom without frontiers, save those which the sword had made. · Right and left of the path of the Crusaders, between Cæsarea and Jerusalem, the Saracens had fallen back in terror of the advancing army. The space left free was all that Godfrey could call his own. To the north, Bohemond held Antioch, Baldwin, Edessa, and Tancred was soon to occupy Galilee. Egypt threatened in the south, wild Bedawín in the east, and on the north and north-west were gathering, disorganized as yet, but soon to assume the form of armies, the fanatic Mohammedans, maddened by their loss. It must be remembered that during the whole eighty years of its existence the kingdom of Jerusalem was never for one single moment free from war and war's alarms.

At this time the joy of the soldiers was increased by the announcement made by a Christian inhabitant of Jerusalem that he had buried in the city, before the Crusaders came, a cross which contained a piece of the True Cross. This relic was dug up after a solemn procession, and borne in state to the Church of the Holy Sepulchre, where it was intrusted to the care of Arnold, who had been appointed to act in the place of the patriarch. The appetite for relics had grown *en mangeant*. Besides the holy lance, and this piece of the True Cross, every knight, almost every common soldier, had been enabled to enrich himself with something precious—a bone or a piece of cloth, which had once belonged to a saint, a nail which had helped to crucify him, or the axe which had beheaded him. And there can be no doubt that the possession of these relics most materially helped to inspire them with courage.

While the princes were still deliberating over the choice of a king, came the news that the Egyptian Caliph had assembled together a vast army, which was even then marching across the desert under the command of a renegade Armenian named Afdhal. He it was who had taken Jerusalem from the Turks only eleven months before the siege by the Crusaders. The army contained not only the flower of the Egyptian troops, but also many thousands of Mohammedan warriors from Damascus and Bagdad, eager to wipe out the disgrace of their defeats.

Tancred, Count Eustace of Boulogne, and Robert of Flanders, sent forward to reconnoitre, despatched a messenger to Jerusalem with the news that this innumerable army was on its way, and would be, within a few days, at the very gates of the city. The intelligence was proclaimed by heralds through the city, and at daybreak the princes went bare-footed to the Church of the Sepulchre, where they received the Eucharist before setting out on their way to Ascalon. Peter the Hermit remained in charge of the women and children, whom he led round in solemn procession to the sacred sites, there to pray for the triumph of the Christian arms. Even at this solemn moment, when the fate of the newly-born kingdom trembled on the decision of a single battle, the chiefs could not abstain from dissensions. At the last moment, Robert of Normandy and Count Raymond declared that they would not go with the army; the former because his vow was accomplished, the latter because he was still sullen over the decision of the electors. But by the entreaties of their soldiers they were persuaded to yield. The Christian army collected in its full force at Ramleh, attended by Arnold with the True Cross, whence they came to the Wady Sorek.

The battle took place on the plain of Philistia, that lovely and fertile plain which was to be reddened with blood in a hundred fights between the Christians and their foes.

The Christian army had been followed into the plain by thousands of the cattle which were grazing harmlessly over the country. The dust raised by the march of the men and beasts hung in clouds over these flocks and made the Egyptian army take them for countless squadrons of cavalry. Hasty arrangements were made. Godfrey took two thousand horse and three thousand foot to prevent a sortie of the inhabitants of Ascalon; Raymond placed himself near the seashore, between the fleet and the enemy; Tancred and the two Roberts directed the attack on the centre and right wings. In the first rank of the enemy were lines of African bowmen, black Ethiopians, terrible of visage, uttering unearthly cries, and wielding, besides their bows, strange and unnatural weapons, such as flails loaded with iron balls, with which they beat upon the armour of the knights and strove to kill the horses. The Christians charged into the thickest of these black warriors, taking them probably for real devils, whom it was a duty as well as a pleasure to destroy. A panic seized the Mohammedans; Robert Courthose, always foremost in the *mêlée*, found himself in the presence of Afdhal himself, and seized the grand standard. And then the Egyptians all fled. Those who got to the seashore fell into the hands of Raymond, who killed all, except some who tried to swim, and were drowned in their endeavours to reach their fleet; some rushed in the direction of Ascalon and climbed up into the trees, where the Christians picked them off with arrows at their leisure; and some, laying down their arms in despair, sat still and offered no resistance, while the Christians came up and cut their throats. Afdhal, who lost his sword in the rout, fled into Ascalon, and two thousand of his men, crowding after him, were trampled under foot at the gates. From the towers of Ascalon he beheld the total rout and massacre of his splendid army and the sack of his camp. "Oh, Mohammed," cried the despairing renegade, "can it be true that the power of the Crucified One is greater than thine?" Afdhal embarked on board the Egyptian fleet and returned alone. No one has told what was the loss sustained by the Mohammedans in this battle. They were mown down, it is said, like the wheat in the field; and those who escaped the sword perished in the desert.

It is well observed by Michault, that this is the first battle won by the Christians in which the saints took no part. Henceforth Saint George appears no more. The enthusiasm of the soldiers was kindled by religious zeal, but it is kept alive henceforth by success. When success began to fail, religion could do nothing more for them.

Raymond and Godfrey quarrelled immediately after the battle about the right of conquest over Ascalon, which Raymond wished to take for himself, and Godfrey claimed as his own. Raymond, in high dudgeon, withdrew, and took off all his troops, like Achilles. Godfrey was obliged to raise the siege of Ascalon, and followed him. On the way Raymond attacked the town of Arsûf, but meeting with a more determined resistance than he anticipated, he continued his march, maliciously informing the garrison that they had no reason to be afraid of King Godfrey. Consequently, when Godfrey arrived, they were not afraid of him, and gave him so warm a reception that he was obliged to give up the siege, and learning the trick that Raymond had played him, flew into so mighty a passion, that he resolved to terminate the quarrel according to European fashion. Tancred and the two Roberts used all their efforts to appease the two princes, and a reconciliation was effected between them. What is more important is, that the reconciliation was loyal and sincere. Raymond gave up all his schemes of ambition in Jerusalem; ceded all pretensions to the tower of David, over which he had claimed rights of conquest, and so long as he lived was a loyal supporter of the kingdom which he had so nearly obtained for himself. But Ascalon remained untaken, a thorn in the sides of the conquerors for many years to follow, and a standing reminder of the necessity of concord.

The army returned to Jerusalem singing hymns of triumph, and entered the city with sound of clarion and display of their victorious banners. The grand standard and the sword of Afdhal were deposited in the Church of the Sepulchre; and a great service of thanksgiving was held for their deliverance from the Egyptians.

And then the princes began to think of going home again. They had now been four years away. Their vow was fulfilled. Jerusalem was freed from the yoke of the Mussulman, and they could no longer be restrained. Three hundred knights and two thousand foot-soldiers alone resolved to stay with Godfrey and share his fortunes. Among them was Tancred, almost as great a Christian hero as Godfrey himself. "Forget not," those who remained cried with tears—these knights were not ashamed to show their emotion—to those who went away, "forget not your brethren whom you leave in exile; when you get back to Europe, fill all Christians with the desire of visiting those sacred places which we have delivered; exhort the warriors to come and fight the infidels by our side."

So went back the Crusaders, bearing each a palm-branch from Jericho, in proof of the accomplishment of their pilgrimage. It was but a small and miserable remnant which returned of those mighty hosts which, four years before, had left the West. There was not a noble family of France but had lost its sons in the great war; there was not a woman who had not some one near and dear to her lying dead upon the plains of Syria; not even a monk who had not to mourn a brother in the flesh or a brother of the convent. Great, then, must have been the rejoicing over those who had been through all the dangers of the campaign, and now returned bringing their sheaves with them; —not of gold, for they had none; nor of rich raiment, for they were in rags—but of glory, and honour, and of precious relics, better in their simple eyes than any gold, and more priceless than any jewels. With these and their palm-branches they enriched and decorated their native churches, and the sight of them kept alive the crusading ardour even when the first soldiers were all dead.

Raymond of Toulouse went first to Constantinople, where Alexis received him with honour, and gave him the principality of Laodicea. Eustace of Boulogne went back to his patrimony, leaving his brothers in Palestine. Robert of Flanders went home to be drowned in the Marne. Robert of Normandy, to eat out his heart in Cardiff Castle. Bohemond, Tancred, and Baldwin, with Raymond, remained in the East.

The miserably small army left with King Godfrey would have ill-sufficed to defend the city, had it not been for the continual relays of pilgrims who arrived daily. These could all, at a pinch, be turned into fighting men, and when their pilgrimage was finished there were many who would remain and enter permanently into the service of the king. And this seems to have been the principal way in which the army was recruited. It was nearly always engaged in fighting or making ready for fighting, and without constant reinforcements must speedily have come to an end. A great many Christians settled in the country by degrees, and, marrying either with native Christians or others, produced a race of semi-Asiatics, called *pullani*,* who seem to have united the vices of both sides of their descent, and to have inherited none of the virtues.

As for the people—not the Saracens, who, it must be

---

* Perhaps *fuláni, anybodies.* So in modern Arabic the greatest insult you can offer a man is to call him, *fulán ibn fulán*, so and so, the son of so and so—*i.e.*, a foundling or bastard.

remembered, were always the conquerors, but not always the settlers—we have little information about them. The hand of the Arab was against every man, and every man's against his. When the pilgrims, it will be remembered, killed the sheikh at Ramleh, the Emir expressed his gratitude at being rid of his worst enemy. But, as to the villagers, the people who tilled the ground, the occupants of the soil, we know nothing of what race they were. It was four hundred years since the country had ceased to be Christian—it is hardly to be expected that the villagers were anything but Mohammedan. William of Tyre expressly calls them infidels, or Saracens, and they were certainly hostile. No Christian could travel across the country unless as one of a formidable party; and the labourers refused to cultivate the ground, in hopes of starving the Christians out: even in the towns, the walls were all so ruinous, and the defenders so few, that thieves and murderers entered by night, and no one lay down to sleep in safety. The country had been too quickly overrun, and places which had surrendered in a panic, seeing the paucity of the numbers opposed to them, began now to think how the yoke was to be shaken off.

It was at Christmas, 1099, that Baldwin of Edessa, Bohemond, and Dagobert, or Daimbert, Archbishop of Pisa, came to Jerusalem with upwards of twenty thousand pilgrims. These had suffered from cold and the attacks of Arabs, but had received relief and help from Tancred in Tiberias, and were welcomed by the king at the head of all his people, before the gates of the city. Arrived there, they chose a patriarch, electing Dagobert; and Arnold, who had never been legally elected, was deposed. They stayed during the winter, and gave the king their counsels as to the future constitution of his realm.

Godfrey employed the first six months of the year 1100 in regulating ecclesiastical affairs, the clergy being, as usual, almost incredibly greedy, and in concluding treaties with the governors of Ascalon, Acre, Cæsarea, Damascus, and Aleppo. He was showing himself as skilful in administration as he had been in war, and the Christian kingdom would doubtless have been put upon a solid and permanent footing, but for his sudden and premature death, which took place on July the 18th, 1100. His end was caused by an intermittent fever; finding that there was little hope, he caused himself to be transported from Jaffa to Jerusalem, where he breathed his last. He was buried in the Church of the Holy Sepulchre, where his epitaph might have been read up to the year 1808, when the church was destroyed by fire.

"Hic jacet inclitus dux Godefridus de Bouillon, qui totam istam terram acquisivit cultui Christiano, cujus anima regnet cum Christo." And here, too, were laid up his sword, more trenchant than Excalibur, and the knightly spurs with which he had won more honour than King Arthur.

The *Assises de Jerusalem*, that most curious and instructive code of feudal law, does not belong properly to the reign of Godfrey. As it now exists it was drawn up in the fourteenth century. But it embodies, although it contains many additions and interpolations, the code which Godfrey first began, and the following kings finished. And it is based upon the idea which ruled Godfrey and his peers. It may therefore fairly be considered in this place.

It was highly necessary to have strict and clearly defined laws for this new kingdom. Its subjects were either pious and fanatic pilgrims, or unscrupulous and ambitious adventurers. Bishops and vassals, among whom the conquered lands were freely distributed, were disposed to set their suzerain at defiance, and to exalt themselves into petty kings. The pilgrims were many of them criminals of the worst kind, ready enough, when the old score was wiped out by so many prayers at sacred places, to begin a new one. They were of all countries, and spoke all languages. Their presence, useful enough when the Egyptian army had to be defeated, was a source of the greatest danger in time of peace. It is true that the time of peace was never more than a few months in duration.

The duties and rights of king, baron, and bourgeois were therefore strictly and carefully laid down in Godfrey's *Assises*. Every law was written on parchment, in great letters, the first being illuminated in gold, and all the others in vermilion; on every sheet was the seal of the king; the whole was deposited in a great box in the sacred church, and called the "Letters of the Sepulchre."

The duty of the king was to maintain the laws; to defend the church; to care for widows and orphans; to watch over the safety of the people; and to lead the army to war. The duty of the *seigneur* towards his people was exactly the same as that of the king; towards the king it was to serve him in war and by counsel. The duty of a subject to his lord was to defend and to revenge him; to protect the honour of his wife and daughters; to be a hostage for him in case of need; to give him his horse if he wanted one, or arms if he wanted them; and to keep faith with him. There were three courts of justice; the first presided over by the king, for the regulation of all differences between the great vassals; the second, formed of the principal inhabitants—a kind of jury—to maintain the laws among the *bourgeoisie*; and the third, reserved for the Oriental Christians, presided over by judges born in Syria.

The king, the summit of this feudal pyramid, who was wont to offer his crown at the Holy Sepulchre, "as a woman used to offer her male child at the Temple," had immediately under him his seneschal, who acted as chief justice, chancellor of the exchequer, and prime minister. The constable commanded the army in the name of or in the absence of the king; he presided over the ordeal by battle, and regulated its administration. Under his orders was the marshal, who replaced him on occasion. The chamberlain's duty was about the person of the king.

As regards the power and duties of the barons, it was ruled that they were allowed, if they pleased, to give their fiefs to the church; that the fiefs should always descend to the male heir; that the baron or *seigneur* should succeed to a fief alienated by the failure on the part of the feudatory to perform his duties; that the baron should be the guardian of heirs male and female. These, if male, were to present themselves when the time came, saying, "I am fully fifteen years of age," upon which he was to invest them; while maidens were to claim their fiefs at the age of twelve, on condition that they took a husband to protect it. Nor was any woman who remained without a husband to hold a fief until she was at least sixty years of age.

In the ordeal of battle, the formula of challenge was provided, and only those were excused who had lost limbs, in battle or otherwise, women, children, and men arrived at their sixtieth year. In a criminal case death followed defeat; in a civil case, infamy.

Slaves, peasants, and captives were, like cattle, subject only to laws of buying and selling. A slave was reckoned worth a falcon; two slaves were worth a charger; the master could do exactly as he pleased with his own slaves. They were protected by the natural kindness of humanity alone. In the days of its greatest prosperity the different baronies and cities of the kingdom of Jerusalem could be called upon to furnish in all three thousand seven hundred and twenty-nine knights. But this was after the time of Godfrey, the David of the new kingdom.

Of course the *seigneurs* and barons took their titles from the places they held; thus we hear of the barony of Jaffa, of Galilee, of Acre, and of Nablous; the seigneur of Kerak and of Arsûf. And thus in the soil of Palestine was planted, like some strange exotic, rare and new, the whole of the feudal system, with all its laws, its ideas, and its limitations.

The news of the recovery of Jerusalem, and the return of the triumphant Crusaders, revived the flame of crusading enthusiasm, which in the space of four years had somewhat subsided. Those who had not followed the rest in taking the Cross reproached themselves with apathy; those who had deserted the Cross were the object of contempt and scorn. More signs appeared in heaven; flames of fire in the east—probably at daybreak; passage of insects and birds—emblematic of the swarms of pilgrims which were to follow. Only when the preachers urged on their hearers to take the Cross it was no longer in the minor key of plaint and suffering; they had risen and left the waters of Babylon; they had taken down their harps from the trees and tuned them afresh; they sang, now, a song of triumph; and in place of suffering, sorrow, and humiliation, they proclaimed victory, glory, and riches. . It seemed better to a European knight to be Baron of Samaria than lord of a western state; imagination magnified the splendour of Baldwin and Tancred; things far off assumed such colours as the mind pleased; and letters read from the chiefs in Palestine spoke only of spoils won in battle, of splendid victories, and of conquered lands. Again the cry was raised of *Dieu le veut*, and again the pilgrims, but this time in a very different spirit, poured eastwards in countless thousands.

The way was led by Hugh, Count of Vermandois and the unfortunate Stephen of Blois, whose lives had been a mere burden to them since their desertion of the Cross; the latter, who had little inclination for fighting of any kind, and still less for more hardships in the thirsty East, followed at the instigation of his wife Adela, daughter of William the Conqueror. Neither of them ever returned. William of Poitiers, like Stephen of Blois, a poet and scholar, mortgaged his estates to William Rufus, the scoffer, who, of course, was still lamentably insensible to the voice of the preacher—it must have been just before his death; Humbert of Savoy, William of Nevers, Harpin of Bourges, and Odo, Duke of Burgundy, followed his example. In Italy the Bishop of Milan, armed with a bone of Saint Ambrose, led an army of one hundred thousand pilgrims, while an immense number of Germans followed the Marshal Conrad and Wolf of Bavaria. Most of the knights professed religious zeal; but hoped, their geographical knowledge being small, to win kingdoms and duchies like those of Baldwin and Tancred. Humbert of Savoy, more honest than the others, openly ordered prayers to be put up that he might obtain a happy principality. It does not appear from history that his petition was granted.

The new army was by no means so well conducted as the old. Insolent in their confidence, and ill-disciplined, they plundered and pillaged wherever they came. They menaced Alexis Comnenus, and threatened to take and destroy the city. Alexis, it is said, but it is difficult to believe this, actually turned his wild beasts upon the mob, and his favourite lion got killed in the encounter. After prayers and presents, the Emperor persuaded his unruly guests to depart and go across the straits. *Non defensoribus istis* might have been the constant ejaculation of the much abused and long suffering monarch.

Then they were joined by Conrad with his Germans and Hugh with his French. Their numbers are stated at two hundred and sixty thousand, among whom was a vast number of priests, monks, women, and children. Raymond of Toulouse, who was in Constantinople, undertook reluctantly to guide the army across Asia Minor, and brought with him a few of his Provençaux and a body of five hundred Turcopoles (these were light infantry, so called because they were the children of Christian women by Turkish fathers), the contingent of the Greek Emperor.

But the army was too confident to keep to the old path. They would go eastward and attack the Turks in their strongest place, even in Khorassan itself. Raymond let them have their own way, doubtless with misgiving and anxiety, and went with them. The town of Ancyra, in Paphlagonia, was attacked and taken by assault. All the people were put to death without exception. They went on farther, exulting and jubilant. Presently they found themselves surrounded by the enemy, who appeared suddenly, attacked them in clouds, and from all quarters. They were in a desert where there was little water, what there was being so rigorously watched over by the Turks that few escaped who went to seek it. They were marching over dry brushwood; the Turks set fire to it, and many perished in the flames or the smoke. There was but one thing to do, to fight the enemy. They did so, and though the victory seemed theirs, they had small cause to triumph, for division after division of their army had been forced to fly before the Turks. Still this might have been repaired. But in the night Count Raymond left them, and fled with his soldiers in the direction of Sinope. The news of this defection quickly spread. Bishops, princes, and knights, seized with a sudden panic, left baggage, tents and all, and fled away in hot haste. In the morning the Turks prepared again for battle. There was no enemy. In the camp was nothing but a shrieking, despairing multitude of monks, and women, and children. The Turks killed remorselessly, sparing none but those women who were young and beautiful. In their terror and misery the poor creatures put on hastily their finest dresses, in hopes by their beauty to win life at least, if life shameful, and hopeless, and miserable.

"Alas!" says Albert of Aix, "alas! what grief for these women so tender and so noble, led into captivity by savages so impious and so horrible! For these men had their heads shaven in front, at the sides, and at the nape, the little hair left fell behind in disorder, and in few plaits, upon their necks; their beards were thick and unkempt, and everything, with their garments, gave them the appearance of infernal and unclean spirits. There were no bounds to the cries and lamentations of these delicate women; the camp re-echoed with their groans; one had seen her husband perish, one had been left behind by hers. Some were beheaded after serving to gratify the lust of the Turks; some whose beauty had struck their eyes were reserved for a wretched captivity. After having taken so many women in the tents of the Christians, the Turks set off in pursuit of the foot-soldiers, the knights, the priests, and the monks; they struck them with the sword as a reaper cuts the wheat with his sickle; they respected neither age nor rank, they spared none but those whom they destined to be soldiers. The ground was covered with immense riches abandoned by the fugitives. Here and there were seen splendid dresses of various colours; horses and mules lay about the plain; blood inundated the roads, and the number of dead amounted to more than a hundred and sixty thousand."

As for the arm of St. Ambrose, that was lost too, and it doubtless lies still upon the plain beyond Ancyra, waiting to work more miracles. It is exasperating to find all the chroniclers, with the exception of Albert of Aix, passing over with hardly a word of sympathy the miserable fate of the helpless women, and pouring out their regrets over this trumpery relic.

There was another army still, headed by the Duke of Nevers. They followed in the footsteps of their predecessors as far as Ancyra, where they turned southwards. Their fate was the same as that of the others: all were killed. The leader, who had fled to Germanicopolis, took some Greek soldiers as guides. These stripped him, and left him alone in the forest. He wandered about for some days, and at last found his way to Antioch, as poor and naked as any beggar in his own town.

The third and last army, headed by the Count Hugh of Vermandois, met with a similar end. Thirst, heat, and hunger destroyed their strength, for the Turks had filled the wells, destroyed the crops, and let the water out of the cisterns. On the river Halys they met their end; William of Poitiers, like the Duke of Nevers, arrived naked at Antioch. The luckless Count of Vermandois got as far as Tarsus, where he died of his wounds, and poor Ida of Austria, who came, as she thought, under the protection of the pilgrims, with all her noble ladies, was never heard of any more.

Of these three great hosts, only ten thousand managed to get to Antioch. Every one of the ladies and women who were with them perished; all the children, all the monks and priests. And of the leaders, none went back to Europe except the Count of Blandrat, who with the Bishop of Milan had headed the Lombards, the Duke of Nevers, and William of Poitiers, the troubadour.

These were the last waves of the first great storm. With the last of these three great armies died away the crusading spirit proper—that which Peter the Hermit had aroused. There could be no more any such universal enthusiasm. Once and only once again would all Europe thrill with rage and indignation. It had burned to wrest the city from the infidels; it was to burn once more, but this time with a feebler flame, and ineffectually, to wrest it a second time, when the frail and turbulent kingdom of Jerusalem should be at an end.

We have dwelt perhaps at too great length on the great Crusade which really ended with the death of Godfrey. But the centre of its aims was Jerusalem. The Christian kingdom, one of the most interesting episodes in the history of the city, cannot be understood without knowing some of the events which brought it about.

P

JERUSALEM.

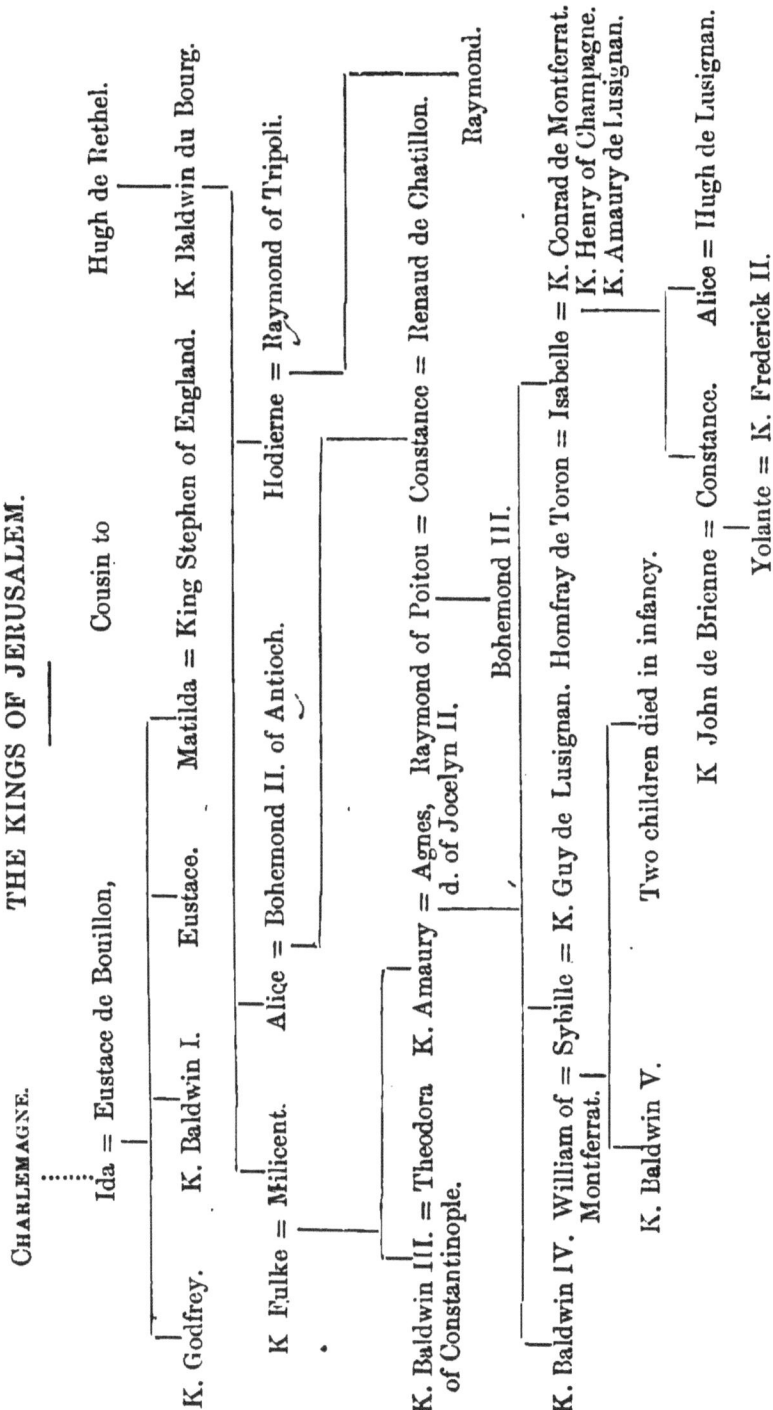

CHAPTER VIII.

KING BALDWIN I.   A.D. 1100—1118.

"Tell me," said Don Quixote, "have you ever seen a more valorous knight than I upon the whole face of the known earth?"

No sooner was the breath out of Godfrey's body, than, according to usual custom, the Christians began to quarrel as to who should succeed him. Count Garnier de Gray, a cousin of Godfrey's, took possession promptly of the Tower of David and other fortified places, and refused to give them up to the patriarch, Dagobert, who claimed them as having been ceded to him by the late king. Unfortunately, Count Garnier died suddenly at this juncture, and his death was of course interpreted by the churchmen as a punishment for his contumacy. Dagobert wrote immediately—the letter is preserved—to Bohemond, urging him to assert his claims. Hardly was the epistle sent off, when the news came that Bohemond was a prisoner. There was, therefore, nothing to prevent Baldwin from stepping quietly into the throne.

Baldwin, the brother of Godfrey, had been originally destined for the Church, and received a liberal education. When he abandoned the robe for the sword is not certain, nor, indeed, do we know anything at all about him until we see him in the Crusade following his brother. He was a man of grave and majestic bearing. Taller by a head than other men, he was also of great strength, extremely active, and well skilled in all the arts of chivalry. His beard and hair were black, his nose aquiline, and the upper lip slightly projecting. He was fond of personal splendour and display. When he rode out in the town of Edessa a golden buckler, with the device of an eagle, was borne before him, and two horsemen rode in front blowing trumpets. Following the Oriental custom, he had allowed his beard to grow, and took his meals seated on carpets. He was not, like his brother, personally pious, nor was he by any means priestridden. His early education had been sufficient to deprive him of any great respect for the cloth, and the facility with which he fell into Oriental customs proves that his Christianity sat lightly enough upon him. As yet, however, there were no declared infidels in the East. His morals were dissolute, but he knew how to prevent scandals arising, and none but those who were immediately about him knew what was the private life of their grave and solemn king. At the same time he does not appear to have been a hypocrite, or to have claimed any merit at all for piety. The figure of Godfrey is clouded with legends and miraculous stories. We hardly seem to see, through the mist of years, the features of the short-lived David of the new kingdom. But that of Baldwin, the new Solomon of Jerusalem, stands out clear and distinct. This king, calm, cold of speech, self-reliant, like Saul, a head taller than anybody else, who will not be seen abroad without a mantle upon his shoulders, who lets his beard grow, and looks out upon the world with those keen bright eyes of his, and that strong projecting upper lip, is indeed a man, and not a shadow of history. He is a clerk, and is not to be terrified, knowing too much of the Church, into giving up his own to the Church, as Godfrey did. His, too, is the sharp, clear-cut, aquiline nose of the general, as well as the strong arm of a soldier, and the Turks will not probably greatly prevail against him. And with Godfrey, as we have said before, vanish for ever those shadowy figures of saints and dead bishops who were wont to fight with the army. King Baldwin believed in no saints' help, either in battle or in the world, and did not look for any. Jerusalem, henceforth, has to get along without many miracles. For the appearance of saints and other ghostly auxiliaries is like the appearance of fairies—they come not, when men believe in them no more:

> "Their lives
> Are based upon the fickle faith of men:
> Not measured out against fate's mortal knives
> Like human gossamers; they perish when
> They fade, and are forgot in worldly ken."

Baldwin did not hesitate one moment to exchange his rich and luxurious principality of Edessa for the greater dignity, with all its thorns and cares, of the crown of Jerusalem. He made over his power to his cousin Baldwin Du Bourg, and himself, with a little army of four hundred knights and one thousand foot, started on his perilous journey, through a country swarming with enemies. He got on very smoothly, despite the paucity of his numbers, until he reached Beyrout. Five miles from that town was a narrow pass, with the sea on one side and rocks on the other, too difficult to force if it were held by even a hundred men. The trouble and anxiety into which the army was thrown are well told by Foulcher, the king's chaplain, who was with him. The worthy chaplain was horribly frightened. "I would much rather," he tells us, "have been at Chartres or Orleans. ... Nowhere was there a place where we could find refuge, no way was open to us to escape death, no passage was left by which we could flee, no hope of safety remained if we stayed where we were. Solomon himself would not have known which way to turn, and even Samson would have been conquered. But God . . . . seeing the peril and distress into which we had fallen for His service, and through love of Him"—rather a daring assertion, considering that Baldwin had deserted the Crusade, and gone off filibustering entirely on his own account, and was now going to receive a crown for which he certainly had not fought—" was touched with pity, and granted in His mercy such an audacity of courage that our men put to flight those who were pursuing them . . . . Some threw themselves from the top of scarped rocks, others rushed to places which seemed to present a little chance of safety, others were caught and perished by the edge of the sword. You ought to have seen their ships flying through the waves, as if we could seize them with our hands; and themselves in their fright scaling the mountains and the rocks." And no doubt it did the excellent chaplain good to see them running away, just after defeat and death appeared so imminent.

In the morning Baldwin rode up to examine the pass, and found the enemy gone. So the little army passed in safety, and went on their way, laden with the spoils of the Turks.

Arrived at Jerusalem, all the people, headed by the clergy, came out to meet the king, singing hymns and bearing tapers. Only the patriarch, Dagobert, chose to be absent and retired to Mount Zion, pretending to be in fear for his personal safety.

Baldwin did not immediately concern himself about the patriarch. Satisfied with the homage of the barons and clergy, and conscious that his crown could only be preserved by establishing respect for his prowess among his own men, and fear among the Mohammedans, he set out with a force of a hundred and fifty knights, and five hundred foot, and appeared before the walls of Ascalon. Here, however, he experienced a check, the garrison having been reinforced. Raising the siege hastily, he

ravaged the country round the town, and then directed
his march in a south-east direction, taking possession of
the cattle everywhere and destroying the crops. At one
place he found a large number of Arabs, robbers, we are
told, who had taken refuge in caverns. Baldwin kindled
fires at the mouth of the cave, hoping to drive them out
by the smoke. Only two came. The king spoke kindly
to them, kept one, dressed up the other in a magnificent
mantle and sent him back. As soon as he was gone
Baldwin killed the one who was left. Presently the
messenger returned with ten more. Baldwin sent back
one, as before, and killed the remaining ten. This one
returned with thirty; one was sent back and the rest
beheaded. The next time two hundred and thirty came
out, and Baldwin beheaded them all. Then more fire
was made, and the miserable wives and children were
forced to come out. Some ransomed their lives, the rest
were beheaded. Baldwin, after this wholesale slaughter,
thence travelled down to the Dead Sea, to the great
delight of his chaplain, who describes the places he saw,
everywhere inspiring terror of his name, and driving the
cattle before him. He returned to Jerusalem laden with
booty, three days before Christmas, having succeeded in
gaining the confidence of his new subjects. Dagobert,
the patriarch, deemed it wisest to cease his opposition to
the king, and the coronation of Baldwin took place at
Bethlehem. Tancred at first refused to recognise his old
enemy as king, but giving way, they were reconciled;
moreover, he was no longer so much in Baldwin's way,
because in his uncle, Bohemond's, captivity he was governing his principality of Antioch. The reconciliation, like
that between Raymond and Godfrey, was sincere and
loyal. By several small expeditions, such as that directed
to the south, Baldwin established a terror for his name
which served him in good stead. For the kingdom was
in an unstable and dangerous condition; there were very

few men with whom to form an army, and had it not been for the pilgrims who flocked to the city in thousands, it might have been lost many times over.

The Easter miracle of the Holy Fire served this year to revive the enthusiasm which was beginning to flag. To the astonishment and horror of the people it did not come as usual. For three days they waited. Tears, prayers, and lamentations were uttered. Then a solemn procession was enjoined, and king, clergy, and people marched barefooted round the church, weeping and praying. Suddenly a bright light filled the church. The flame had lit one of the lamps, it flew from lamp to lamp, and when in the evening Baldwin sat at dinner in the "Temple of Solomon," *i.e.*, the Jamí el Aksa, two lamps were miraculously kindled there also. We can have very little doubt, inasmuch as this impudent imposture is carried on to the present day, avowedly as an imposture, that Baldwin and the clergy devised the scheme as a means to arouse the flagging zeal of the pilgrims, and especially of certain Genoese and Pisans, who had a large fleet with them, the assistance of which he greatly desired.

To bring about this fraud, a reconciliation had been effected between Baldwin and the unworthy patriarch, Dagobert. For it was not long after the return of Baldwin from his first expedition when he discovered how Dagobert had endeavoured, by any means in his power, to prevent his accession. Doubtless he was informed by Arnold,* the late chaplain to the Duke Robert of Normandy. Arnold, a priest of great ambition, was the heir to Bishop Odo of Bayeux, William the Conqueror's half-brother, who had left him great wealth. The object dearest to his heart was the acquisition of the post of patriarch. After the siege he performed the duties temporarily, as a sort of vicar, but had been displaced on Dagobert's appointment. His morals, we are told by William of Tyre, were so

---

* His name is also written Arnoulf and Arnoul.

notoriously bad as to be the theme of rough verses among the soldiers. But William of Tyre, whose favourite name for him is " that first-born of Satan," writes from the side of the Church as represented by Dagobert. The morals of the patriarch himself, too, appear to have been at least doubtful, even before his accession to his new dignity, as he is roundly accused of appropriating to his own purposes moneys and presents destined for the pope. But churchmen, when they talk of morality, always mean chastity and nothing else. As soon as Baldwin was informed of Dagobert's opposition, he wrote a letter to Rome, accusing the patriarch not only of opposing the election of the lawful and hereditary king, but also of trying to procure his death on the road, and of exciting discord among the chiefs of the Crusade. The pope sent his own brother, Cardinal Maurice, to Jerusalem as his legate, with authority to suspend the patriarch until he should be able to purge himself of the charges brought against him. Maurice called a court composed of bishops and abbots directly he arrived in the city, and summoned the king to prove, and the patriarch to disprove, his accusations. Baldwin had, meanwhile, found another charge, no doubt invented by Arnold, as it bears all the marks of private malice, to bring against Dagobert. He had, it was said, purloined and concealed a piece of the wood of the Cross, in addition to his other offences; the king himself must have known well enough that in the eyes of the Church this offence would be far more serious than any of the others. To procure the death of a man would be venial indeed compared with the abstraction of a relic. Dagobert had very little, it would appear, to say, and an adjournment was granted, to give him time to call witnesses in his own defence.

Came, meantime, the season of Easter, and that day, Good Friday, when the Holy Oil was wont to be consecrated for the use of the sick. In place of the patriarch, whom the king assumed to be deposed, but who was really only suspended, the cardinal undertook this duty, and was already on the Mount of Olives, the place assigned to this ceremony, when the patriarch, humiliated beyond all expression by this public degradation from his functions, went to the king and implored him, with tears in his eyes, to reinstate him for that day only. Baldwin refused. Dagobert urged him again not to inflict this punishment upon him in the face of so many pilgrims. But the king remained obdurate. Then the patriarch changed his line. Instead of entreating, he bribed. He offered Baldwin three hundred byzantines. The royal treasury was empty, the knights were clamouring for their pay, and the patriarch obtained his request.

After this some sort of peace was made up between the pope's legate, Cardinal Maurice, and the patriarch; a peace founded, it would seem, on mutual interest, for we are told that they became so friendly that they were accustomed to spend the day and night together in retired places, secretly feasting, and drinking the wine of Gaza, no doubt in happy ignorance that the eye of Arnold— that first-born of Satan—was upon them, and that he was biding his time.

In the spring, at the same time as the memorable miracle of the Holy Fire, and the arrival of the Genoese and Pisan fleet, came emissaries from the Mohammedan towns of Ascalon, Cæsarea, Ptolemais, and Tyre, with presents and money, asking for permission to cultivate their lands in peace. Baldwin took the money and promised security till Pentecost. He also made a little more money by accepting the ransom of certain prisoners whom he had taken at Beyrout. With this capital of ready money he was able to pay his knights, at least, in part, and to ensure their service for the next campaign. He offered the Genoese, on condition of their granting him their assistance with the fleet, to give up to them a third of the booty in every town which he might take with their assistance, and to name one of the principal streets in it, the street of the Genoese. They agreed, and Baldwin made his preparations for an attack on Cæsarea. The patriarch, bearing the wood of the true Cross— all, that is, that he had not stolen—went with the army. When they arrived before the town, the people of Cæsarea, rich merchants, who desired nothing but to be left alone, and were a peaceful folk, sent deputies, who asked the patriarch the following question: " You, who are the doctors of the Christian law, why do you order your men to kill and plunder us, who are made in the image of your God?" The patriarch evaded the point. " We do not desire," said he, softly, " to plunder you. This city does not belong to you, but to Saint Peter. We have no wish to kill you, but the Divine vengeance pursues those who are armed against the law of God." It will be observed that the town was claimed, not for the Christian kingdom, but for the Church. " It belonged to Saint Peter." Dagobert's idea seemed to have been that the king was to be like Godfrey, only the Defender of the Sepulchre. Baldwin, however, thought quite differently. The city was taken with the usual form, and with the usual butchery. As some miserable Saracens had been seen to swallow coins, the Christians cut their prisoners in two to find the money, and burned their bodies to ashes, looking for the gold when the fire was out. And with a view to restoring his own to Saint Peter, they pillaged the whole city and divided the spoils, when they had killed all the inhabitants.* As for the Genoese, they found a relic in their booty, precious indeed. It was no other than the Cup of the Holy Grail, which they bore away in triumph. How its authenticity was established does not appear, nor is there, so far as we know, any subsequent account

* They kept the women, and made them grind corn all day with the handmills.

of its fate. The Christians selected an archbishop. There was a poor and ignorant priest called Baldwin. He had tattooed his forehead with the sign of the cross, and made money by pretending that it was a miraculous sign. Everybody knew that he was an impostor, but probably because the pilgrims insisted on believing in his sanctity, and in order to conciliate this important element of the population, he was chosen to be the archbishop.

The Egyptian Caliph, whose plan of operation seems to have been to send constant reinforcements to Ascalon, and use that strong place as a centre from which to harass the Christians, gave orders to try, with the coming of spring, another incursion. Baldwin met the advanced guard of the Egyptian troops near Ramleh. He had got together three hundred knights and nine hundred foot. The Saracens were ten times as numerous. The king, tying a white banner to his lance, led the way, and performed prodigies of valour. And, as usual, the Mohammedans were seized with a panic and fled.

It was at this time that the wretched remains of the new armies of pilgrims arrived in Palestine. Their numbers were not large, as we have seen, but their arrival was the most opportune thing that could have happened for Baldwin. For, having seen the sacred places, they were preparing for their return home when the news arrived of the coming into Palestine of another vast army of Egyptians. They were, as usual, in the neighbourhood of Ascalon. Baldwin hastened to meet them with a handful of knights, among whom was the unfortunate Count of Blois and the Duke of Burgundy. They were all cut to pieces, Baldwin, himself, escaping with the greatest difficulty, and almost alone, to Ramleh. In the morning he found himself, with his little band, in a place without any means of defence, and surrounded by an enormous army, through which it was hopeless to think of cutting a way. And then occurred one of the most singular instances of gratitude on record. A stranger, a noble Mohammedan, was introduced to the king. "I am," he said, "one to whom you have shown yourself generous. You took my wife prisoner. On the way she was seized with the pains of labour. You made a tent for her on the wayside, laid her in it, and left her provisions, water, and female slaves to help her. So her life was saved. Now, I know the roads which are not guarded. Come with me, but come alone, and I will take you safely through the midst of our army."

Baldwin, who had really been guilty of this humanity to a poor Mohammedan woman, was constrained to accept the generous offer. He went away alone with his benefactor. The emir kept his word and escorted him to a place of safety, where he left him. All his companions at Ramleh were put to death before he had time to help them.

Meantime, the greatest consternation reigned in Jerusalem. The king was reported to be a captive; the great bell tolled; soldiers and knights gathered together; the gates were shut; and the priests and women betook themselves to prayer. The king, however, at Jaffa, collecting all the troops he could raise, prohibited any pilgrim from leaving the country, and went forth once more with all his force. Their war cry was, "Christ conquers, and Christ reigns, Christ commands," in place of the old "Dieu le veut," and "Dieu aide." After a battle, which lasted a whole day—the spirit of the Egyptians had been raised by their temporary success—victory declared for the Christians, and the Mohammedans fled with a loss of four thousand men: the smallness of their loss shows that the victory was not one of the fights like that of Ascalon, where a panic made the Mohammedans absolutely helpless.

The story of this invasion is much confused, and told by the chroniclers in different ways, only one of them relating the gratitude of the Saracen. But we may fairly assume that another of the periodical invasions took place, which was repelled, though with difficulty, by the valour of Baldwin. The arms of the Christians were not, however, always crowned with success, and an ill-omened defeat took place at Harran, where Baldwin du Bourg and Jocelyn were taken prisoners. Bohemond, who had been released, was there with Tancred, and both escaped with great difficulty. It was evident that the Christian strength lay chiefly in the terror inspired by a long series of victories. Once defeated, the prestige of the conquerors was gone. And when the Mohammedans managed to recover their old self-confidence, the kingdom of Jerusalem was as good as lost, and its destruction was only a matter of time.

Baldwin's chief difficulty was not in raising armies, for there were always plenty of men to be got among the pilgrims, but in paying an army when he had raised it. The pilgrims brought daily large sums in offerings to the Church of the Sepulchre, to which the patriarch acted officially as treasurer. To him the king went in his distress, and demanded that some of the money should be put into his hands to pay the soldiers with. Dagobert asked for a day's delay, and then brought the king two hundred marks, with a polite expression of regret that he could do no more. Arnold, who was now Chancellor of the Holy Sepulchre, laughed aloud at the meagreness of this offering, and informed the king that immense treasures had been bestowed upon the church, which were all concealed if not appropriated by the patriarch. Baldwin thereupon urged again on the patriarch the necessity of his contributing towards the support of the army. Dagobert, relying on his friendship with the legate, disdained to take any notice of the king's representation, and continued, with Cardinal Maurice, to use for his own festivals and private luxuries the riches of the Church. One day, when Baldwin was at his wits' end for want of money, some one, probably Arnold, brought him a report of the dissolute and selfish life led by Dagobert. "Even at this moment," he said, "the patriarch is feasting and drinking." The king took some of his officers with him, and forcing his way into the patriarch's private apartments, found him and Maurice at a table spread with all the luxuries of the East. Baldwin flew into a royal rage, and swore a royal oath. "By heavens!" he cried, "you feast while we fast; you spend on your gluttony the offerings of the faithful, and take no notice of our distress. As there is a living God, you shall not touch another single offering, you shall not fill your bellies with dainties even once more, unless you pay my knights. By what right do you take the gifts made to the Sepulchre by the pilgrims, and change them into delicacies, while we, who have purchased the city with our blood, who bear incessantly so many fatigues and combats, are deprived of the fruits of their generosity? Drink with us of the cup that we drink now, and shall continue to drink in these times of bitterness, or prepare yourself to receive no more the goods which belong to the church." Upon which the patriarch, little used to have things set forth in this plain and unmistakeable manner, allowed himself to fall into wrath, and made use of the effective but well-worn text, that those who serve the altar must live by the altar. But he hardly, as yet, knew his man. The king, actually not afraid of a priest, swore again, in the most solemn manner, and in spite of the entreaties of the legate, Cardinal Maurice, that if the patriarch refused to help him he would help himself. There was, indeed, little doubt possible but that he would keep his word. Dagobert, therefore, gave way, and promised to maintain thirty knights. But he soon got into arrears, and, finally, after repeated quarrels with the king, and after being publicly accused of peculation—very possibly he stole right and left for the glory of the Church—he retired to Antioch, hoping that Bohemond would take up his quarrel. In this he was disappointed, for Bohemond had neither the power nor the inclination. Dagobert never returned to the city. Affecting to consider him deposed, the king put in his place a humble and pious monk of great ignorance, named Ebremer. He, however, was speedily displaced, and on the deposition of Dagobert, Arnold was, at last, promoted to the see. He died a year or two afterwards, and in his death William of Tyre sees a plainly marked indication of the Divine displeasure. By others it was read differently.

The career of Bohemond was drawing to an end. Shut up in Antioch, and attacked both by Greeks and Saracens, he could hardly defend himself. But his spirit was as strong as ever. Causing a rumour to be spread that he was dead, he was carried in a coffin on board a ship, and escaped thus through the Greek fleet. Arrived in Italy he went to the pope, and with all his rough and strong eloquence he pleaded his cause, which he represented as that of the Christians against the Greek emperor, the most flagrant of criminals. He went thence to France, with the pope's express authority, to raise men for another Crusade, this time against Alexis. King Philip gave him his daughter, Constance, in marriage; the princes and knights enrolled themselves in his army; he crossed over to Spain, and thence to Italy, finding everywhere the same success, and awakening the same enthusiasm. His army assembled. He led them first to the city of Durazzo, which he attacked, but without success; the city held out; his troops, who discovered that they had enlisted under his banner solely to advance his personal interest and to gratify his blind and unreasoning hatred against the Emperor of Constantinople, deserted him; and the proud Norman had to return to Tarento no richer, except by Antioch, for all his conquests and ambitions. A treaty was concluded with the emperor, which gave him this city. He was preparing to break the conditions of the agreement when a fever seized him, and he died, greatly to the relief of Alexis.

About the same time died gallant old Raymond of Toulouse, still fighting at Tripoli. He was besieging the town with only four hundred men at his back, and with that heroic self-confidence which never deserted the first Crusaders, when either some smoke from Greek fire affected him, or he fell from the roof of a house, and so came to an end.

Tancred, the bravest, if not the best, of all, was to follow within a very few years, and Baldwin found himself for the last six years of his reign without a single one of the old princes, except his cousin, Baldwin du Bourg, to quarrel with, to help, or to look to for help. And, still more to complicate matters, the crusade, which the ambition of Bohemond had directed against the Greek Empire for his own purposes, had alienated the sympathies, such as they were, and the assistance of the Greek Empire, and deprived the Christian Kingdom of every hope from that quarter. Then Tancred and Baldwin du Bourg, as soon as the latter got his release from captivity, began to quarrel, and, turn by turn, called in the assistance of the Saracens. They were persuaded to desist by the exhortations of the king, who told Tancred plainly that unless he ceased to make war against Christians, all the Christians in the East would make common cause against him. The only resources left to the king were those derived from the constant influx of pilgrims, and therefore of fighting men, and the assistance he derived from the annual visit of the Genoese and Pisan fleets; these came, actuated solely by the desire for merchandise and plunder. In return for concessions and the chance of booty, they fought the Egyptian fleets, and co-operated with Baldwin in his operations against sea-side places. Thus, in 1104, after an unsuccessful attempt upon the town, Baldwin took

Q

advantage of the presence of sixty-six Genoese galleys to lay siege to Acre. He invited them to assist him in his enterprise, first, for the love of Christ, and secondly, in the hope of reaping a golden harvest out of victory. The Genoese consented, on the condition of receiving a third of the revenue, and perpetual rights which would be obtained by the capture of the place, and of a street being entirely given up to themselves, where they might exercise their own laws and justice. These conditions, exorbitant as they were, were accepted, and siege was laid in due form, Baldwin investing the place by land and the Genoese by sea. The time was almost gone by for unconditional surrender and capture by assault, and the Christians fought with machines and rams for twenty days before the enemy capitulated. And it was then only on honourable terms. The inhabitants were to take out their wives, families, and whatever they could carry. Those who preferred to remain behind were to be allowed to continue in the peaceful occupation of their homes, on condition of paying an annual tribute to the king. It will be seen that a short space of five years had already materially altered the relative positions of Christians and Mohammedans. The conditions were ill kept, for a large number of the Saracens were massacred by the unruly sailors, and Baldwin seems to have been powerless to interfere. This was, however, a most important position, and threw open a convenient harbour for the Genoese.

Year after year an army came from Egypt and attempted an invasion of Palestine, using Ascalon as the basis of operations and the depôt of supplies. But every year the attack grew more feeble and the rout of the Egyptians more easy.

The next important place attached by the help of the Genoese was Tripoli. After the death of Count Raymond, his affairs in the East were conducted by his nephew, William of Cerdagne, until Bertram, Raymond's son, should arrive. He came in 1109, and immediately began to quarrel with his cousin, who called in the aid of Tancred. Baldwin, however, interfered and substituted a settlement of all the disputed points between them. By his arrangement William kept all the places he had himself conquered, and Bertram had the rest. Moreover, if either died without heirs, Bertram was to have all. A short time after, William was accidentally killed by an arrow in trying to settle a quarrel among his men at arms, and tranquillity among the princes was assured. Operations, meantime, had been going on against the little town of Biblios, which succumbed, after a show of resistance, on the same terms as those obtained by the people of Acre. The strong places which still held out were Tripoli, Tyre, Sidon, Beyrout, and Ascalon. Baldwin's plan was to take them in detail, and always by the aid of the Genoese fleet. He joined his forces to those of Bertram, and the siege of Tripoli was vigorously taken in hand.

It illustrates the untrustworthy character of the materials from which a history of this kingdom has to be drawn that Albert of Aix, one of the most careful of the chroniclers, absolutely passes over the capture of this important place in silence. The inhabitants defended themselves as well as they were able, but seeing no hope of assistance they capitulated on conditions of safety. These were granted, but pending the negotiations, the savage Genoese sailors, getting over the wall by means of ladders and ropes, began to slaughter the people. "Every Saracen," says Foulcher de Chartres, who has a touch of humour, "who fell into their hands, experienced no worse misfortune than to lose his head; and although this was done without the knowledge of the chiefs, the heads thus lost could not be afterwards put on again." All the chronicles but one agree in preserving silence over a barbarism almost worse than the breaking of a treaty. It was this: the Christians found in Tripoli a splendid library. It had been collected in the course of many peaceful years by the family of Ibn-Ammar, who were the hereditary princes, under the Caliph of Cairo, of the place. It consisted of a hundred thousand volumes, and a wretched priest blundering into the place, and finding this enormous mass of books written in "execrable," because unknown characters, called in the assistance of soldiers as ignorant as himself, and destroyed them all. The Tripolitans had, many years before, placed themselves under the protection of the Egyptian Caliph. They looked now for his help. In the midst of the siege a ship managed to put in with a message from the sovereign. He promised them no assistance, and encouraged them to no resistance. Only he recollected that there was in the city a beautiful female slave whom he desired to be sent to him, and asked for some wood of the apricot tree to make him lutes. After this, the people capitulated.

The next place to fall was Beyrout, and through the same assistance. But in this case the place was carried by assault, and a terrible carnage ensued, stayed only by the order of the king. And after the victory and the conquest of Sarepta, the Genoese retired, carrying with them very many of Baldwin's best auxiliaries, and left him with his usually small force, barely enough for purposes of defence. But fortune favoured him again. The fame of the Crusades had taken a long time to travel northwards, but in time it had reached to Norway and kindled the enthusiasm even of the Scandinavians. Hardly had the Genoese left the shores of Palestine, when Sigard, son or brother of King Magnus of Norway, arrived at Jaffa with ten thousand Norwegians, among whom were a large number of English. He was a young man, says Foulcher, of singular beauty, and was welcomed by Baldwin with all the charm of manner which made him the friend of all whom he desired to please. The sturdy

Norsemen, who desired nothing so much as to fight with the Saracens, met the king's wishes half way. They were ready to go wherever he pleased, provided it led to fighting, and without any other pay than their provisions. These were better allies than the greedy Genoese, and Baldwin joyfully led them to Sidon, where for a little while they had fighting enough. The Sidonians seeing no hope of escape, endeavoured, says William of Tyre, to compass their own deliverance by the assassination of the king. Baldwin had a Saracen servant who professed extreme attachment to his person. He had apostatized to the Christian faith, and received the king's own name at the font of baptism. To him the chiefs of Sidon made overtures. They offered him boundless wealth in their city, if he would contrive to assassinate the king. Baldwin the servant agreed to commit the deed, and would have done it, had it not been that certain Christians in the city, getting to know of the plot, conveyed information of it by means of an arrow which they fired into the camp. The king called a council. The unfortunate servant was "examined," which probably meant tortured, confessed his guilty intentions, and was promptly hanged. This appears to be the first mention of an attempted assassination, a method which the Saracens, by means of the celebrated Ismaelite sect, the "Assassins," introduced much later on. The story bears the impress of improbability. Moreover, immediately afterwards, we are told, that Baldwin granted the city easy terms of capitulation, with permission for the inhabitants to stay where they were, provided only they paid tribute. The conditions were faithfully observed, the Norwegians being either less bloodthirsty or more amenable to discipline—probably both—than the Genoese. They went away after this, and Baldwin, having made an unsuccessful attempt on Tyre, which was too strong for his diminished forces, retired to Acre. In the same year died Tancred, who recommended his young wife, Cecilia, to marry Pons, the son of Bertram, who was already dead, as soon as he should be of age. Roger, the son of his sister, was to hold all his states in trust for young Bohemond, and Pons.

During these contests on the seaboard, the Saracens inland had been quietly composing their differences and arranging for a combined assault upon the common enemy. In 1112 they had essayed an expedition against Edessa, but received a check serious enough to make them fall back in disorder. Next year, with a far larger force, they formed a sort of encampment south of the Lake of Tiberias, and overran the country, pillaging and burning as far as they dared. Baldwin hastily sent for Roger of Antioch and the Count of Tripoli, to come to his assistance. Meantime, with a small army, of about five thousand in all, he marched to meet them. With his usual impetuosity he charged into a small advance troop of cavalry which the Turks threw out as a trap. These turned and fled. Baldwin pursued, but fell into an ambuscade, whence he escaped with the greatest difficulty, leaving his banner, that white streamer which he bore at the head of his troops in every battle, behind him. The patriarch, now that same Arnold, "Satan's eldest son," who was with him, had too a narrow escape. In this disastrous day the Christians lost about twelve hundred men. Next morning came the king's auxiliaries, and the Christian army, leaving their camp and baggage, retreated into the mountains, where they waited for reinforcements. This was the most serious check yet given to the victorious career of the Christians. The people of Ascalon, as usual, ready to take advantage of every opportunity, sallied forth and invested Jerusalem, now almost entirely without troops. But they do not seem to have attempted a regular siege, or, at least, were unsuccessful, and, after ravaging the country for miles round, they retreated to their own city. Probably their experience of Baldwin's vigour was greater than their confidence in the success of their coreligionists, and they thought certain plunder was better than the dubious chances of a protracted siege.

Fortunately, it was now late in the summer. With the autumn came the first shiploads of pilgrims, and consequently reinforcements for Baldwin. The Saracens, satisfied with their victory, and fearing reprisals, judged it prudent to retire, and accordingly fell back on Damascus, where their general-in-chief, Maudúd, was murdered. It was well for the Christian kingdom that they went away when they did. For a universal panic had seized on all the cities, and it wanted but an unsuccessful engagement to put an end to the Christian power altogether. More misfortunes fell upon them. There was a terrible famine at Edessa and in Antioch; and an earthquake was felt through the whole of Syria, from north to south. Whole cities of Cilicia were thrown into ruins. Thirteen towns fell in Edessa; and in Antioch many churches were destroyed. In the famine which devastated Edessa, Baldwin du Bourg looked for aid from Count Jocelyn, but was disappointed. Moreover, when he sent deputies to Antioch, these were insulted by Jocelyn's knights, who taunted them with the apathy and indolence of their lord. Baldwin du Bourg determined on revenge. Pretending to be sick he sent for Jocelyn, who came without suspicion, and was received by the other in bed. Then, reproaching him in the bitterest terms for ingratitude, he ordered him to be thrown into prison, loaded with chains, and deprived him of all his possessions. As soon as Jocelyn was free he went to join the king at Jerusalem, and seems, like an honest knight and good fellow, as he was, to have entirely forgiven his ill-treatment. Certainly he deserved it.

The next year saw another defeat of the Saracens. The Emir was accused of complicity in the murder of Maudúd, and a vast army was gathered together, against

Damascus in the first instance, and the Christians in the second. Baldwin entered into alliance with the Emir, and though the Caliph's army avoided a battle, so formidable a coalition sufficed to drive back the invaders. Nevertheless, the Christians looked with horror on an alliance so unnatural. Count Roger of Antioch at the same time dispersed the Turkish army in alliance with Toghtegin, and, for a time at least, Palestine was free from enemies on the north and east.

Baldwin was not, however, disposed to sit down in peace and rest. He employed what little leisure he could get in populating his city of Jerusalem by persuading the Christians across the Jordan to give up their pastures and meadows, and come under his protection. He founded the stronghold of Montreal, in Moab, on the site of the old city of Diban, and he made a second journey to the east and south of his kingdom, with twelve hundred horse and four hundred foot, penetrating as far, we are told, as the Red Sea, probably to Petra—Albert of Aix says Horeb, "where he built in eighteen days a new castle." These affairs being settled, and there being every appearance of tranquillity in all directions, he turned his thoughts to the conquest of Egypt, and actually set off to accomplish this with an army of one hundred and sixteen knights and four hundred foot soldiers. They penetrated as far as Pharamia, near the ancient Pelusium, which the inhabitants abandoned in a panic. They found here food and drink in plenty, and rested for two whole days. On the third, certain of the more prudent came to Baldwin: "We are few in number," they said; "our arrival is known in all the country; it is only three days' march from here to Cairo. Let us therefore take counsel how best to get out of the place."

The king, seeing the wisdom of this advice, ordered the walls to be thrown down, and all the houses of the town to be set on fire. But whether it was the heat of the day, or the effect of over-exertion, he felt in the evening violent pains, which increased hourly. To be sick in the East was then to be on the point of death, and, despairing of recovery, he sent for his chiefs, and acquainted them with the certainty of his end. All burst into tears and lamentations, quite selfishly, it would seem, and on their own accounts, "for no one had any hope, from that moment, of ever seeing Jerusalem again." Then the king raised himself and spoke to them, despite his sufferings. "Why, my brothers and companions in arms, should the death of a single man strike down your hearts and oppress you with feebleness in this land of pilgrimage, and in the midst of our enemies? Remember, in the name of God, that there are many among you whose strength is as great or greater than mine. Quit yourselves, then, like men, and devise the means of returning sword in hand, and maintaining the kingdom of Jerusalem according to your oaths." And then, as if for a last prayer, he implored them not to bury his body in the land of the stranger, but to take it to Jerusalem, and lay it beside his brother Godfrey. His soldiers burst into tears. How could they carry, in the heat of summer, his body so far? But the king sent for Odo, his cook. "Know," he said, "that I am about to die. If you have loved me in health, preserve your fidelity in death. Open my body as soon as the breath is out of it, fill me with salt and spice, and bear me to Jerusalem, to be buried in the forms of the Church."

They bore him along, still living. On the third day of the week the end came, and Baldwin died. With his last breath he named his brother Eustace as his successor, but if he would not take the crown, he gave them liberty to choose any other. Odo the cook executed his wishes; his bowels were buried at Al Arish, and the little army, in sadness and with misgivings of evil, returned to Jerusalem, bringing with them the king who had so often led them to victory.

It was on Palm Sunday when they arrived. They met,

in the valley of Jehoshaphat, the people of the city all dressed in festival garb, and singing psalms of joy, to celebrate the feast. Joy was turned into mourning, and the procession of clergy which was descending the Mount of Olives met, "by express order of God, and an inconceivable chance," the little troop which bore back the remains of the king. They buried him beside his brother: Baldwin du Bourg, the Count of Edessa, being the chief mourner, as he was his nearest relation.*

So died the greatest of the Christian kings, the strongest as well as the wisest. His faults were those of the age; he was, however, before the age; not so cruel, not so ignorant, not so superstitious, not so bigoted. He was among the first to recognise the fact that a man may be an infidel and yet be worthy of friendship; he was also the first to resist the extravagant pretensions of the Church, and the greed of the Latin priests. He was, like his brother, the defender by oath of the Holy Sepulchre, but he would not consent to become a mere servant of the patriarch while he was styled the king of the country. We have stated above that his chief fault was an excessive love of women, and this he was wise enough to conceal. But the charge is brought forward by his priestly biographers, who, which is significant, do not advance against him a single definite case to support it. William of Tyre wanted something, perhaps, to allege against a man who dared beard a bishop at his own table, and swear at his gluttony and luxury. In any case he had very little leisure for indulgence in vice. He married three times, his first wife being an Englishwoman, who died on her way out. His second was the daughter of an Armenian prince, whom he divorced on the charge of adultery. Dagobert maintained

---

* The epitaph on his tomb described him as
>Judæ alter Machabæus
>Spes patriæ, vigor ecclesiæ.

It was obviously not written by the Patriarch Dagobert.

that she was innocent, probably with a view to blacken the character of the king, but the divorced queen, going to Constantinople, justified by her conduct there the worst accusations that could be brought against her. The third time he married the widow of Roger, Count of Sicily, Adelaide by name. She brought whole shiploads of treasure with her; the marriage was celebrated with every demonstration of joy, and the new queen's generosity caused rejoicing through all the land. But the year before he died, and three years after the marriage, Baldwin had an illness which led him to reflect on a marriage contracted while his divorced wife was still living, and he sent her back. It was an unlucky wedding for the country, because the Normans in Sicily could not forgive this treatment of one of their blood, and thus another powerful ally was lost to the kingdom. As for Adelaide, she returned to Sicily filled with shame and rage, and died the same year as her husband.

In that year, too, died Alexis Comnenus, Pascal, the pope, and Arnold, the patriarch. Foulcher of Chartres is careful to tell us that he saw himself that very year a red light in the heavens at dead of night. It certainly portended something, most probably something disastrous. "Quite uncertain as to what the event might prove, we left it in all humility, and unanimously, to the will of the Lord. Some of us, nevertheless, saw in the prodigy a presage of the deaths of those great persons who died that same year." Which doubtless it was.

CHAPTER IX.

KING BALDWIN II. A.D. 1118—1131.

Veramente è costui nato all' impero
Si del regnar del commandar sa l'arti;
E non minor che duce è cavaliere.

As the soldiers bearing the body of King Baldwin entered the city at one gate, his cousin, Baldwin du Bourg, Count of Edessa, came in at another. He was in time to be present at the funeral. Immediately afterwards a council was held to determine on his successor. On the one hand, by the laws of succession, and in accordance with the king's own request, Eustace, his brother, should have been the heir. But Eustace was in France. It would have been many months before he could be brought to Palestine, and the state of affairs brooked no delay. While the minds of the electing council were still uncertain what to do, Jocelyn stood up and spoke: "We have here," he said, "the Count of Edessa, a just man, and one who fears God, the cousin of the late king, valiant in battle, and worthy of praise on all points; no country could furnish us a better king; it were better to choose him at once than wait for chances full of peril."

Jocelyn was the old enemy of Baldwin; he was supposed, but unjustly, to bear him a grudge for the ill-treatment he had received at the count's hands; his advice, therefore, bore the more weight, as it seemed entirely disinterested. Arnold, the patriarch, seconded him, and Baldwin was chosen king unanimously. Whether Jocelyn's advice was altogether disinterested may be doubted. At all events he received from the new king the investiture of the principality of Edessa, as a reward for his services. Baldwin was crowned, like his predecessor, in Bethlehem, on Ascension Day.

The new king, the date of whose birth is uncertain, was the son of Count Hugh of Rethel and his wife Milicent. He was the cousin of Godfrey, with whom he started for Palestine. He had two brothers, one of whom was the Archbishop of Rheims, and the other succeeded his father, but dying without children, the archbishop gave up his episcopate, and married, in order to continue the family. Baldwin himself was above the ordinary stature, wonderfully active, skilful in horsemanship, and of great strength and bravery. His hair, we are told, was thin and fair, and already streaked with grey. He was married to an Armenian princess, by whom he had several daughters, but no sons. He wore a long Oriental beard, but though he conformed in many respects to Eastern habits, he had not forgotten his early piety, and scrupulously obeyed the rules of the church, insomuch that we are told that his knees were covered with callosities, the result of many prayers and penances. He was already well-advanced in years.

Count Eustace, hearing in France of his brother's death, set off at once to take possession of the kingdom which was his by right of succession. But on arriving in Apulia, he heard the news of Baldwin's succession, and immediately turned back, content to spend the rest of his days in obscurity, rather than disturb the peace of Palestine by an unseemly rivalry.

The first year of the king's reign was marked by the customary invasion of the kingdom from Egypt and the dispersion, this time without a battle, of the invaders. The next was a year of calamity. For Count Roger of Aleppo, with his little army, was utterly defeated by the Turks, the Count himself being slain, and a large number of his knights taken prisoner and treated with the greatest cruelty. Nor was this all. Ilgazi, the Prince of Aleppo, who had defeated Roger, died, and was succeeded by his much abler nephew, Balak, who made an incursion into the territory of Edessa, and captured Count Jocelyn with his nephew, Galeran, and sixty knights. Thus the two most important out-lying provinces were deprived of their rulers. Moreover, the whole country was afflicted with countless swarms of locusts and rats, which devoured every green thing, so that the Christians were threatened with famine. Baldwin called together a general council at Nablous, and the patriarch preached to the people on the sinfulness of their lives, pointing out that their afflictions were due to their own crimes and excesses, and calling on them to amend and lead better lives. After confession and protestations of repentance, the king and his army moved northwards to Antioch and defeated the Turks in their turn.

Certain small changes in the internal administration, only of importance as pointing to the decadence of the old ferocity against the Saracens, were introduced by the king in Jerusalem. For, besides remitting the old heavy dues on exportation and importation, so far as the Latins were concerned, Baldwin granted a sort of free trade to all Syrians, Greeks, " and even Saracens," to bring provisions of all kinds into the city for sale without fear of exaction. His wise idea was to increase the population of the city, and therefore its strength, by making it the most privileged town in his realm, and the central market of Palestine.

But in 1124 a misfortune fell upon him which might have been fatal to his kingdom. For, after Jocelyn's capture, he led his forces into Edessa, and there, marching one night in February, without taking proper precautions, his men being allowed to desperse in various directions, he fell into an ambuscade, and was made prisoner himself by Balak, who sent him in irons to the fortress of Khortbert.

And now the country was without a ruler. In this emergency, the barons assembled at Acre and elected as Regent, Eustace Garnier, the Baron of Sidon and Cæsarea, who proved worthy of their confidence. The story of the king's captivity is like a chapter of a romance. For while he was in fetters with Jocelyn at Khortbert, certain Armenians, fifty in number, swore a solemn oath to one another that the king should be released. Disguising themselves as monks,* and hiding daggers under their long robes, they went to the citadel, and putting on a melancholy and injured air, they pretended to have been attacked and robbed on the road, and demanded to be admitted to the governor of the castle, in order to have redress. They were allowed to enter, and directly they got within the walls they drew out their weapons, slaughtered every Saracen, made themselves masters of the place, and released the king from his fetters. But not from his prison, for the Turks, furious at the intelligence, which spread quickly enough, gathered together from all quarters, resolved to bar their escape till Balak could send reinforcements strong enough to retake the place. After a hurried council, it was resolved within the fort that Jocelyn should attempt the perilous task of escaping. Three men were deputed to go with him, two to accompany him on his road, and one to return to the king with the news that he had safely got through the enemy. Jocelyn took a solemn oath that he would lose no time in raising an army of assistance, and swore, besides, that he

* This is William of Tyre's account. He says that, according to others, they were disguised as merchants.

would neither shave his beard, nor drink wine, till the king was released. He then slipped out under cover of the darkness, and the king, resolved to defend the castle till the last, set to work on his fortifications.

That night Balak had a fearful dream. He thought that he met the terrible Jocelyn, alone and unprotected, and that the Christian knight, hurling him to the ground, tore out both his eyes. Awaking with fright, he sent off messengers in hot haste to behead Jocelyn at once. They arrived too late. The castle was taken and the bird was flown. But the flight of the count was full of dangers. He got safely enough to the banks of the Euphrates, but here an unforeseen difficulty met him, for he could not swim. How to cross the river? They had two leathern bottles. These, inflated, they tied round Jocelyn's body, and the other two men, who could swim, steering by the right and left, managed to get him across the water. Then they went on, bare-footed, hungry, and thirsty, till Jocelyn could travel no farther, and, covering himself with branches, in order to conceal himself, he lay down to sleep. One of the attendants, meantime, was sent off to find some inhabitant of the country, and either beg, buy, or rob provisions of some kind. He met an Armenian peasant loaded with grapes and wild figs, whom he brought along to his master. The peasant knew him. "Hail, Lord Jocelyn!" he cried, at sight of the ragged knight. "At these words," says Foulcher, "which the count would fain not have heard, he replied, all in alarm but nevertheless with mildness, 'I am not he whom you name; may the Lord help him wherever he be.'

"'Seek not,' said the peasant, 'to conceal thyself. Fear nothing, and tell me what evil has befallen thee.'

"'Whoever thou art,' said the count, 'have pity on me; do not, I pray, make known my misfortune to my enemies; lead me into some place where I may be in safety. . . . I am a fugitive and a wanderer. . . . Tell me what property thou hast in this place, and what is its value; and I will give thee property of far more worth in my own dominion.'

"'Seigneur, I ask nothing,' replied the other. 'I will lead thee safe and sound where thou wishest to go; once thou didst deprive thyself of bread to make me eat. It is now my turn. I have a wife, an only daughter of tender years, an ass, two brothers, and two oxen. I will go with thee and carry everything away. I have also a pig, which I will bring here immediately.'

"'Nay, my brother,' said the count, 'a whole pig may not be eaten in a single meal, and we must not excite suspicions.'"

The peasant went away, and presently returned with all his family—though, curiously enough, Foulcher says nothing at all about his wife. Perhaps she was left behind, like Creusa. The count mounts the ass, takes the child in his arms, and they start. On the road the child began to cry, and "to torment the count with its wailing." He did not know how to appease it; "for Jocelyn had never learned the art of soothing infants by caresses;" he began at first to think of throwing away the baby, or of leaving it by the wayside, and so getting rid of a travelling companion who might bring them all to grief; but "perceiving that this project did not please the peasant, and fearing to afflict him," he continued, with the greatest consideration, to endure "this new trouble," till they arrived at his castle at Turbessel, where there was great rejoicing. Can there be a quainter figure than this of the count mounted on the ass, carrying the squalling baby, and divided between rage at its screams and gratitude to the peasant, his deliverer?

Meantime, the king was not prospering. Balak, in a rage that one of his enemies had escaped him, hastened himself to the castle of Khortbert with so large an army as to deprive Baldwin of any hope of success. The fort was built on a chalk hill easy to cut into. Balak sent sappers, who made excavations under the principal tower, and then filling the cavern with wood, he set fire to it.

R

When the wood was consumed the chalk was softened and the tower came down with a crash. Then Baldwin, against his will, surrendered unconditionally. Life was granted to him, to Galeran, and to the king's nephew. But the poor faithful Armenians, the cause of Jocelyn's escape and the massacre of the garrison, were treated with the most cruel inhumanity. All were murdered, most by tortures of the most horrid description, of which sawing in halves and roasting alive, being buried alive, and being set up naked as marks for children to fire arrows at, are given as a few specimens. Jocelyn, who had been hastily collecting an army, gave up the design of a rescue in despair, and went to Jerusalem.

And then the Egyptians made a formidable incursion. This time things looked desperate indeed. A rigorous fast was ordered. Even the babes at the breast were denied their mothers' milk, and the very cattle were driven off their pastures, as if the sight of the sufferings of these helpless creatures would incline the Lord to pity. At least, it inclined the Christians to fury. They issued from Jerusalem to the sound of the great bell, under Eustace Garnier, the Regent, to the number of three thousand combatants only. With them was carried the wood of the true Cross, the Holy Lance, and a vase containing some of the milk of the Blessed Virgin. Again the Christians were victorious, and the army of the enemy fled in panic behind the walls of Ascalon. But the Christians could only act on the defensive. There was not only no chance of extending their dominions, but even only a slender one of keeping them. Relief came, in the shape of a great Venetian fleet.

The Venetians had held serious counsel as to whether they should go on with their old traffic with the Mohammedans, by which they had enriched themselves, or should imitate the example of their rivals, the Genoese, and make money out of the Christians in Palestine. They decided on the latter course, and fitted out a strong and well-armed fleet. On the way they fought two victorious battles, one with their rivals, the Genoese, returning laden with the proceeds of the season's trade, whom they stripped, and one with the Egyptian fleet, which they cut to pieces. This accomplished, they arrived off Palestine, and offered to make terms for assistance in the year's campaign. Their terms, like those of the Genoese, were hard. They were to have, if a town was taken, a church, a street, an oven, and a tribunal of their own. Of course these were acceded to. To find money to pay the knights, the Regent had to take all the vessels and ornaments of the churches and melt them down.

Of all the towns on the coast between Antioch and Ascalon, only two remained in the hands of the Mohammedans. But these two were of the greatest importance. For while Tyre remained a Saracen city it could be made the centre of operations against the principality of Antioch on the north and the Kingdom of Palestine on the south; while if Ascalon were taken the Egyptians would be deprived of their means of attack, and would be obliged to invade the country through the desert. Opinions were so much divided on the matter that it was decided to refer the decision to lot, and a child, an orphan, was selected to take from the altar one of two pieces of paper, containing the names of the two towns. The lot fell on Tyre, and Eustace Garnier marched northwards, with all the troops that he could raise.

About this point William of Tyre, who has been gradually passing from the vague hearsay history of events, which happened while he was a child, to a clear and detailed narrative of events of which he was either a spectator or a contemporary, becomes more and more interesting. We cannot afford the space, nor does it fall within the limits of this volume, to give more than the leading incidents in the fortunes of the provinces of the

Christian kingdom. We cannot, therefore, linger over the details of this siege, of the greatest importance to the safety of the Christians. The town belonged to the Caliph of Egypt, who held two-thirds of it, and to the Emir, or King, of Damascus, who owned the rest. The Christian army, demoralized by the absence of the king, and disheartened by the reverses which of late had attended their efforts, began badly. They murmured at the hardships and continual fighting they had to undergo, nor would they have persisted in the siege but for two things, the presence of the Venetians, which stimulated their ardour, and the joyful news that the formidable Balak was dead. He was killed by Jocelyn himself, who ran him through with his sword and then cut off his head without knowing who was his adversary. Thus Balak's dream, says the Christian historian, was in a manner fulfilled, though the Arabs, not having a dream to accomplish, tell the story of his death in another way.

The people of Ascalon, "like unquiet wasps, always occupied with the desire of doing mischief," seeing that the whole army was away at Tyre, and hoping to catch Jerusalem unguarded, appeared suddenly within a few miles of the city, in great force. After ravaging and pillaging for a time, they were seized with a sudden panic, and all fled back to their town, without any enemy in sight.

The siege of Tyre was concluded on the 29th of June, 1124, on the conditions which had now become customary. The Tyrians could go away if they pleased. Those who chose to stay could do so without fear. And the historian tells how, when the treaty of surrender was concluded, Tyrians and Christians visited each other's camp, and admired the siége artillery on the one hand, and the walls and strength of the town on the other. We are therefore approaching the period of what may be called friendly warfare. Godfrey thought an infidel was one with whom no dealings were to be held, to whom no mercy was to be shown. Baldwin, taught by his Armenian wife, and by his experience in Edessa, went so far as to shock the Christians by an alliance with the Damascenes. His successor could not prevent his men, even if he tried, from friendly intercourse with the enemy.

The changes which had been wrought by time are graphically put forth by our friend Foulcher de Chartres: "Consider," he says, "how the West has been turned into the East; how he who was of the West has become of the East; he who was Roman or Frank has become here a Galilæan or an inhabitant of Palestine; he who was a citizen of Rheims or of Chartres is become a citizen of Tyre or of Antioch. We have already forgotten the places of our birth; they are even by this time either unknown to most of us, or at least never spoken of. Some of us hold lands and houses by hereditary right; one has married a woman who is not of his own country—a Syrian, an Armenian, or even a Saracen who has abjured her faith; another has with him his son-in-law, or his father-in-law; this one is surrounded by his nephews and his grandchildren; one cultivates vines, another the fields; they all talk different languages, and yet succeed in understanding one another. . . . The stranger has become the native, the pilgrim the resident; day by day our relations come from the West and stay with us. Those who were poor at home God has made rich here; those who at home had nothing but a farm here have a city. Why should he who finds the East so fortunate return again to the West?" The plenty and sunshine of Palestine, where every Frank was a sort of aristocrat by right of colour, no doubt gave charms to a life which otherwise was one of constant fighting and struggle. Palestine was to France in this century what America was to Europe in the sixteenth, the land of prosperity, plenty, and danger. How the country got peopled is told by another writer, Jacques de Vitry, in too glowing colours.

"The Holy Land flourished like a garden of delight. The deserts were changed into fat and fertile meadows, harvests raised their heads where once had been the dwelling-places of serpents and dragons. Hither the Lord, who had once abandoned this land, gathered together His children. Men of every tribe and every nation came there by the inspiration of heaven, and doubled the population. They came in crowds from beyond the sea, especially from Genoa, Venice, and Pisa. But the greatest force of the realm was from France and Germany. The Italians are more courageous at sea, the French and Germans on land, . . . those of Italy are sober in their meals, polished in their discourse, circumspect in their resolutions, prompt to execute them; full of forethought, submitting with difficulty to others; defending their liberty above all; making their own laws, and trusting for their execution to chiefs whom themselves have elected. They are very necessary for the Holy Land, not only for fighting, but for the transport of pilgrims and provisions. As they are sober, they live longer in the East than other nations of the West. The Germans, the Franks, the Bretons, the English, and others beyond the Alps are less deceitful, less circumspect, but more impetuous; less sober, more prodigal; less discreet, less prudent, more devout, more charitable, more courageous; therefore they are considered more useful for the defence of the Holy Land, especially the Bretons, and more formidable against the Saracens."

But evil came of prosperity. As for the bishops and clergy, they took all, and gave nothing. To them, we are told, it was as if Christ's command had not been "Feed my sheep," but "Shear my sheep." The regular orders, infected with wealth, lost their piety with their poverty, their discipline with their adversity; they fought, quarrelled, and gave occasion for every kind of scandal. As for the laity, they were as bad. A generation dissolute, corrupt, and careless had sprung from the first Crusaders.* Their mothers had been Armenians, Greeks, or Syrians. They succeeded to the possessions, but not to the manners of their fathers; all the world knows, says the historian, how they were lapped in delights, soft, effeminate, more accustomed to baths than to fighting, given over to debauchery and impurity, going dressed as softly as women, cowardly, lazy, and pusillanimous before the enemies of Christ, despised by the Saracens, and preferring rather to have peace at any price than to defend their own possessions. No doubt the climate of Syria rapidly produced a degeneracy in the courage and strength of the Latin race, but the writer's style is too full of adjectives. He screams like an angry woman when he declaims against the age, which was probably no worse than its predecessors, and the heat of his invective deprives it of most of its force.

It was in Baldwin's reign that the Knights Templars were founded, and the Hospitallers became a military order.

From very early times an order, known as that of St. Lazarus, had existed, dedicated to the service of lepers and of pilgrims. They had a hospital, at first, in Acre; they were protected by the late emperors, their brethren accompanied the army of Heraclius as a sort of ambulance corps; they obtained permission to establish themselves in Bethlehem, Jerusalem, and Nazareth, and they had a settlement at Cyprus. After the first Crusade they divided into three classes, the knights, or fighting brothers; the physicians, or medical brothers; and the priests, who administered the last rites of the church to dying men. These establishments spread over France, Italy, and Germany; they became rich. The knights appear to have disappeared gradually; they spent their money in sending pilgrims out in ships, and in paying the ransoms of those who were taken prisoner.

The origin of the Knights Hospitallers, originally only

* They were called Pullani, see p. 200.

the Brothers of St. John, took place just before the first Crusade. The order was founded by a certain citizen of Amalfi, Gerard by name. There are many stories about his life. By some he is confounded with that Gerard d'Avesnes, who, a hostage in the hand of the Emir of Arsûf, was bound by him to a piece of timber in the place against which the machines were chiefly directed, in hopes that the sight might induce Godfrey to desist. But Godfrey persisted, and Gerard, though pierced with arrows, eventually recovered. Probably, however, this was another Gerard. The order began with a monastery near the Church of the Sepulchre, and in 1113 received a charter from the Pope. Their immediate object, like that of the Brothers of St. Lazarus, was to help the wounded; their bread and meat were of the coarsest, they did not disdain the most menial offices; and, in spite of their voluntary hardships, and the repulsive duties of their office, they rapidly grew, and became wealthy. Raymond Dupuy, grand master in 1118, modified the existing statutes of this order, and made every brother take the oath to fight, in addition to his other duties. Henceforth it was a military order, divided into languages, having commandories for every language, and lands in every country. Its habit consisted of a black robe, with a mantle to which was sewn a hood; on the left shoulder was an eight-pointed cross; and later, for the knights, a coat of arms was added. And this habit was so honourable that he who fled was judged unworthy to wear it. Those who entered the order out of Palestine might wear the cross without the mantle. Riches presently corrupted the early discipline, and pope after pope addressed them on the subject of the laxity of their morals. Their history, however, does not belong to us. How they fought at Rhodes, and how they held Malta, belong to another history. It is the only one of the military orders not yet extinct.

It was in the year 1118 that the proud and aristocratic order of Knights Templars was first instituted. Nine knights, nobly born, consecrated themselves, by a solemn vow, to protect pilgrims on the roads, and to labour for the safety and welfare of the Church. Their leaders were Hugh de Payens and Geoffrey de St. Aldemar. They had no church or place of residence, and the king assigned to them the building south of the Dome of the Rock, now called the Jámi‘ el Aksa. It was then called the Palace of Solomon, or the Royal Palace, and William of Tyre is careful to distinguish between it and the Dome of the Rock, which he calls the Temple of the Lord. The canons of the Temple also allowed the knights to make use of their own ground, that is, of the Haram Area. For nine years they wore no distinctive habit, and had no worldly possessions. But at the Council of Troyes, where they were represented by deputies, their cause was taken up by the Church, and they obtained permission to wear a white mantle with a red cross. Then, for some reason or other, they became the most popular of all the orders, and the richest. Their wealth quickly introduced pride and luxury, and William of Tyre complains that even in his time, writing only some fifty years after their foundation, there were 300 knights, without serving brothers, "whose number was infinite," that, though they had kept the rules of their first profession, they had forgotten the duty of humility, had withdrawn themselves from the authority of the Patriarch of Jerusalem, and were already rendering themselves extremely obnoxious to the Church by depriving it of its tithes and first-fruits. Here we see the first appearance of that hostility to the Church which afterwards caused the fall of the Templars. The reception of a new knight was a kind of initiation. The chapter assembled by night with closed doors, the candidate waiting without. Two brothers were sent out, three times in succession, to ask him if he wished to enter the brotherhood. The candidate replied to each interrogatory, and then, to signify the poverty of his condition, and the modest nature of his wants, he was to ask three times for bread and water. After this he was introduced in due form, and after the customary ceremonies and questions, was made to take the oath of poverty, chastity, obedience, and devotion to the defence of Palestine. The following is given as the formula, or part of it:—"I swear to consecrate my speech, my strength, and my life, to defend the belief in the unity of God and the mysteries of the faith; I promise to be submissive and obedient to the grand master of the order; when the Saracens invade the lands of the Christians, I will pass over the seas to deliver my brethren; I will give the succour of my arm to the Church and the kings against the infidel princes; so long as my enemies shall be only three to one against me I will fight them and will never take flight; alone I will combat them if they are unbelievers."

Everything was done by threes, because three signifies the mystery of the Trinity. Three times a year the knights were enumerated; three times a week they heard mass and could eat meat; three times a week they gave alms; while those who failed in their duty were scourged three times in open chapter.

In later times the simple ceremony of admission became complicated by symbolical rites and ceremonies. The candidate was stripped of all his clothes; poor, naked, and helpless, he was to stand without the door and seek admission. This was not all. He yet had his religion. He was required to spit upon the cross and deny his Saviour. And then with nothing to help him, nothing to fall back upon, he was to be rebaptized in the chapter of the order: to owe everything to the Templars, to belong to them by the sacred kiss of brotherhood, by the oaths of secrecy, by the memory of his readmission into Christianity, by the glorious traditions of the order, and lastly, as is more than probable, by that mysterious teaching which put the order above the Church, and gave an inner and a deeper meaning to doctrines which the vulgar accepted in their literal sense. It is impossible now to say whether the Templars were Gnostic or not; probably they may have imbibed in the East not only that contempt for the vulgar Christianity which undoubtedly belonged to them, but also whatever there was left of Gnosticism floating about in the minds and memories of men. In that strange time of doubt and restlessness, the revolt against Rome took many forms. There was the religion of the Troubadour, half a mocking denial, half a jesting question; there was the angry protest of the Provençal, that every man is a priest unto himself; there was the strange and mysterious teaching of the Abbot Joachim; and there was, besides, the secret creed, which owned no bishop and would obey no pope, of these Knights Templars.

But this was to come; we are still in the time when St. Bernard can write of them, "O happy state of life, wherein one may wait for death without fear, even wish for it, and receive it with firmness!" This was when their banner *Beauséant* was borne in the front of every battle, with its humble legend, "Not unto us, O Lord, not unto us, but unto Thy name give the glory."

In the thirteenth century, the Hospitallers had nine thousand manors, and the Templars nineteen thousand. Each of these could maintain a knight in Palestine. And yet they did nothing for the deliverance of the country.

> Li frères, li mestre du Temple,
> Qu'estoient rempli et ample
> D'or, et d'argent, et de richesse,
> Et qui menoient toute noblesse,
> Où sont ils?

After the reconquest of Palestine, and until their final and cruel suppression, they seem to have given up all thoughts of their first vows, and to have become an aristocratic order, admission into which was a privilege, which involved no duties, demanded no sacrifices, and conferred great power and distinction. To be a Templar was for a younger son of a noble house to become a sort of fellow of a college, only a college far more magnificent and splendid than anything which remains to us.

The Teutonic order was founded later, during the Crusade of Frederick Barbarossa. It was at first called the Order of St. George. After a stay of some time at Jerusalem, the knights, who were always Germans, went to Acre. And thence, receiving the provinces of Livonia, Culm, and all they could get of Prussia, they removed to Europe, where they founded Königsberg in honour of Louis IX. of France, and did good service against the pagans of Prussia. The order did not remain a Roman Catholic one, as was decided after the Reformation, and to gain admission into it it was necessary to prove sixteen quarterings of nobility.

History, about this time, occupied chiefly in relating how the Turks on the north, and the Egyptians on the south, made incursion after incursion, to be beaten back, each time with more difficulty, becomes somewhat monotonous. King Baldwin II., when the enemy found that his capture did not affect the success of the Christian arms, and agreed to accept a ransom for him, directly he got out of prison assembled his army and laid siege to Aleppo. Here he was assisted by the Mohammedans themselves, but in spite of his auxiliaries, was compelled to raise the siege, and returned to Jerusalem, where he was welcomed by his people. If he was unfortunate in attack, he was at least fortunate in repelling invasion, and beat back the Turks near Antioch, and again near Damascus. The Turks were only formidable when they were united; when, as often happened, their forces were divided by internal dissensions among the emirs and princes, the

Christians were at rest, and when these discords were appeased an invasion followed. With the Egyptians the invasion was annual, but every year growing weaker. Still, though always beaten back, the Mohammedan troops came again and again, and the crown of Jerusalem was ever a crown of thorns. Among those who came at this time to Palestine was young Bohemond, son of that turbulent Norman who gave Alexis so much trouble. Baldwin gladly resigned into his hands the principality of Antioch, which after the death of Count Roger had been under his own care. Bohemond was young, brave, and handsome. Great things were expected of him. Baldwin gave him his daughter Alice to wife, and for a little while all went well, through the young prince's activity and prudence. But he was killed in Cilicia, leaving no heir but an infant girl. After this a very curious story is told.

The princess Alice, widow of young Bohemond, resolved, if possible, to keep for herself, by any means, the possessions of her late husband. In order to effect this, as she knew very well that her daughter would become the king's ward and heiress of all, she resolved to try for the help of the Christians' greatest enemy, Zanghi. She sent a messenger to the Turk, to open negotiations with him. As a symbol of her good faith, the messenger was provided with a white palfrey, shod with silver, with silver bit, and harness mounted all in silver, and covered with a white cloth. On the way the messenger was arrested and brought to the king, who was travelling in haste to Antioch. He confessed his errand and was executed. But Alice closed the gates of the city, afraid to meet her father. These were opened by some of the inhabitants, who did not choose to participate in this open treason to the Christian cause, and Alice retreated to the citadel. Finally the king was prevailed on to pardon her, and she received the towns which had been already settled on her by the marriage deeds, of Laodicea and Gebail. But she was going to cause more trouble yet.

Another son-in-law of the king was Fulke, who succeeded him. He came to Palestine as a pilgrim, bewailing the death of his wife Ermentrade. Here he maintained in his pay a hundred men-at-arms for a whole year, in the king's service. Baldwin, who had no sons, offered him his daughter Milicent, and the succession to the crown. Fulke, then thirty-eight years of age, gratefully accepted the offer, and consoled himself for his bereavement.

Baldwin the Second died in the year 1131. He had ruled Edessa for eighteen years, and Jerusalem for twelve, during which time he had spent seven years in captivity. He was lamented by his subjects, though his reign had not been fortunate or successful. Still, by dint of sheer courage, the boundaries of the realm had not been contracted. What was really the fatal thing about his reign was that the Mohammedans knew now by repeated trials that the Christians were not invincible. It was a knowledge which every year deepened, and every petty victory strengthened. The prestige of their arms once gone, the power of the Christians was sure to follow.

Religious as Baldwin was, his piety did not prevent him from asserting the rights of the crown over those claimed by every successive patriarch, and many quarrels happened between him and the prelates, who tried perpetually to extend their temporal power. During one of these, the patriarch fell ill. Baldwin went to see him. "I am," said the revengeful priest, "as you would wish to see me, Sir King," implying that Baldwin wished his death, even if he had not compassed it. William of Tyre, a priest to the backbone, relates this incident without a word of comment. It must be remembered that the position of the Latin clergy in Palestine was not by any means so good as that which they enjoyed in Europe. Their lands were not so large in proportion, and their dignity and authority less. On the other hand, they were neither so nobly born, nor so well bred, nor so learned as their clerical brethren of the West. Thus it is reported that a Flemish pilgrim was once raised to the patriarchal seat, simply because, at the imposture of the Holy Fire, his taper was the first to light, and it will be remembered how, after the deposition of Dagobert, Ebremer, a simple and perfectly ignorant monk, was put into his place. And when the pope refused to confirm the appointment, they made him archbishop of another diocese by way of compensation.

We have seen, so far, the growth of this little kingdom, created in a single campaign, sustained by the valour of kings whose crown was an iron helmet, whose throne was seldom anything but a camp-stool in a tent, or the saddle of a horse, whose hands grasped no sceptre but a sword, who lived hardly, and died in harness. We have next to see its decline and fall.

Legends of Baldwin's prowess grew up as the years ran on. As a specimen of the stories which gathered about his name we subjoin the following translation, almost literal, from a French romance of the fourteenth century. It treats of a visit made by Baldwin with two Mohammedan princes, secretly Christian, to the Old Man of the Mountains:

"Now," said the Prince,* "great marvels have I here:"
And summoning from those who waited near
One of his own Assassins, bade him go
Up to the highest tower, and leap below.
Strange was it when the soldier ran
Joyous, and quick, and smiling, as a man
Who looks for great reward, and through the air
Leaped fearless down. And far below him there
King Baldwin noted how his lifeless bones,
Mangled and shattered, lay about the stones.
When leapt the first man marvelled much the king,
More when five others, as 'twere some light thing,

---

* Le Vieux de la Montagne.

At his command leaped down from that tall height.
"Sir," said the Prince, "no man, of all my might,
But blindly hastens where I point the way,
Nor is there one so mad to disobey."
"Now by Mahound," the Caliph cried, "not I:
Far be it from me your power to deny.
For, as it seems, the greatest man on earth,
A very god, a greater far in worth
Than Mahomet himself art thou; for none
Can do, or shall do, what thyself hast done."
"Thou speakest truth," the Prince replied, "and lo!
As yet thou knowest not all, for I can show
The fairest place that ever yet was found."
And so he led, by many a mazy round
And secret passage, to an orchard fair,
Planted with herbs and fruit trees: hidden there,
Deep in a corner, was a golden gate.
This to the Prince flew open wide, and straight
Great brightness shone upon them, and behind
Upwards long flights of silver stairs did wind.
Two hundred steps they mounted: then, behold,
There lay the garden as the Prince had told.
Ah! what a garden! all sweet hues that be,
Azure, and gold, and red, were here to see:
All flowers that God has made were blooming here,
While sparkled three fresh fountains bright and clear—
With claret one; with mead all honey-sweet
The second ran; while at their thirsty feet
The third poured white wine. On a dais high
Was set a golden table, and thereby
Sat Ivorine, the fairest maid of earth.
Round her, each one a jewel of great worth,
Two hundred damsels waited on her word,
Or sang as never Baldwin yet had heard
The maids of Europe sing: and here and there
Minstrels with golden harps made music fair;
Ever they danced and sang: such joy had they,
So light seemed every heart, each maid so gay;
So sweet the songs they sang, so bright their eyes,
That this fair garden seemed like Paradise.
But Lady Ivorine smiled not, and sat
Downcast and sad, though still content to wait
Her knight—the flower of knighthood—who some day
Would surely come and bear her far away.

Baldwin bethought him of the maiden fair,
Whose fame had gone abroad, and everywhere
Looked, till his eyes fell upon one who seemed
Fairer than mind had pictured, brain had dreamed.
She sat upon a golden seat, alone,
In priceless robes; upon her head a crown,
Well worth a county: there, row over row,
Full many a sapphire shone with richest glow,
And many a pearl and many a gem beside
Glittered therein the gold beneath to hide.
Her robe was broidered: three long years and more
Toiled on it he who wrought it; and thrown o'er
A costly mantle lay: from far 'twas brought
In some sweet isle beyond the ocean wrought.
Full seven years a Moslem lady bent
Above her loom, and still her labour spent,
While slowly grew the robe; for buckle light,
A rich carbuncle glowed, which day and night
Shone like the sun of heaven clear and bright.

  * * * * *

And when Lord Baldwin saw this damsel fair,
So mazed he was, he nearly fainted there.
"Baldwin," said Poliban, "look not so pale,
If 'tis for doubt or fear your spirits fail."
"Nay," said Lord Baldwin, "but a sudden pain,
Yet see I what would make me well again."
Then the Prince led them all, these nobles three,
And to his daughter brought them courteously.
"Fair daughter," said he, "is there none of these,
Great princes all and brave, that can you please?"
"Yea, sire," the maid replied, "I see my lord,
The noblest knight is he who wears a sword.
These ten long years I sit, and hope, and wait,
For him, my husband, promised me by fate.
Now leaps my heart: the weary time is past,
My knight, my liege, my lord, is come at last."
When Baldwin heard these words, joy and surprise
Held all his heart; but then, across his eyes,
Fell on him a sudden cloud of doubt, and fear
Ran through his chilled brain lest those praises dear
For a companion, not himself, were told.
And, for he could not silence longer hold,

For all the gold of Europe. "Can it be,"
He asked the maid, "that you have chosen me?"
She smiled upon him. "Baldwin, be my knight."
"By heaven," he cried, "mine is this jewel so bright."
But then the Prince, her sire—who liked not well,
That on the poorest lord her favour fell—
Angry and wrath, cried, "Foolish daughter, know,
Your idle words like running water flow,
And matter nothing, until I have willed."
"Father," cried Ivorine, "I am your child;
And yet, alas! through my words must you die.
Yes; for know well that God who dwells on high
Hates those who own him not: and so hates you.
That lying demon whom you hold for true,
And so teach others, has deceived your heart.
But as for me, ah! let me take my part
With those who trust in Christ, and place my faith
In that sweet pardon won us by his death.
Father, renounce thy superstitions vain;
And leave this place, or die, if you remain."
Fool!" cried the Prince, "I curse thee from this day."
Then to the Caliph: "Slay my daughter, slay.
Strike quickly, lest some evil chance to you.
My daughter kill."
     His sword the Caliph drew,
And struck—but not fair Ivorine. The blade
Smote down the wrathful Prince, and spared the maid.
"Right well," cried Poliban, "hast thou obeyed."

CHAPTER X.

KING FULKE. A.D. 1131—1144.

"I have touched the highest point of all my greatness,
And from that full meridian of my glory,
I haste now to my setting."
King Lear.

FULKE, Count of Anjou, born about the year 1092, was thirty-nine years of age at the time when his father-in-law died, and he became, with his wife Milicent, the successor to the throne. He was a man of affable and generous disposition, patient and prudent rather than impetuous, and of great experience and judgment in military operations. He was of small stature—all the previous kings had been tall men—and had red hair; "in spite of which," says William of Tyre, who regarded red-haired men with suspicion, "the Lord found him, like David, after his own heart." The principal defect in him was that he had no memory. He forgot faces, persons, and promises. He would entertain a man one day in the most friendly spirit possible, making all kinds of offers of assistance, and giving him to understand that he was entirely devoted to his interests. The next day he would meet him and ask people who he was, having meanwhile quite forgotten all about him. This was sometimes extremely embarrassing, and "many men who reckoned on their familiar relations with the king fell into confusion, reflecting that they themselves, who wanted to show as protectors and patrons to other people, required a patron with the king."

The domestic relations of Fulke were somewhat complicated, but they bear a certain special interest for English readers.* His father, Fulke, the Count of Touraine and Anjou, was married three times, and had one child from each marriage. His third wife, Bertrade, the mother of King Fulke, ran away from him, and became the mistress of King Philip of France, by whom she had three children. One of them was that Cæcilia who married Tancred, and, after his death, Count Pons. Fulke, by means of his mother's influence, making a wealthy marriage, was the father of that Geoffrey Plantagenet who married Matilda of England, and produced the Plantagenet line. His daughter Matilda was also betrothed to William, the son of Henry I., and, on the drowning of that prince, she went into a convent, where she remained. Another daughter, Sybille, married Thierry, Count of Flanders. By his second wife, Milicent, Fulke had two sons, Baldwin and Amaury, both of whom became, in turn, Kings of Jerusalem.

In the first year of King Fulke's reign died that stout old warrior, Jocelyn of Edessa. His end was worthy of his life. In the preceding year he had been besieging a fort or castle near Aleppo, and had ordered a certain town to be undermined. While he was personally superintending the works, the tower suddenly fell and buried the old count beneath its ruins. They extricated him, but his legs and limbs were broken, and he never walked again. He retained, however, his power of speech and his lofty courage, and when, next year, the news came that the Sultan of Iconium was besieging in force one of his strong places, he sent for his son and ordered him to collect all the men and knights he could, and march at once to the rescue. But young Jocelyn, who was, like

* See Genealogical Table, p. 268.

most of the Syrian-born Christians, little better than a cur, refused flatly, alleging as an excuse the disproportion of numbers. The old man, sorrowful at heart on account of his son's cowardice, and foreboding the troubles which would surely come after his own death, ordered his litter to be prepared, and was carried at the head of his own army to the relief of the fort. The news reached the Saracens that old Jocelyn was coming himself, and at the very mention of his name they broke up their camp and fled. "And when he heard this, the count ordered those who carried his litter to place it on the ground; then raising his hands to heaven, with tears and sighs, he returned thanks to God, who had visited him in his affliction, and had thus favoured him by suffering him once more, and for the last time, to be formidable to the enemies of Christ. And while he poured out his thanks to heaven, he breathed his last." There was now no one left of the old crusading chiefs, and their spirit was dead.

Most of them had married Armenians, and their sons were degenerate, sensual, and cowardly. Young Jocelyn, for instance, though married to the most beautiful and the best woman in the East, the Lady Beatrice, was so given over to all kinds of licentious excesses and luxuries that he was, says the historian, covered with infamy. His daughter married Fulke's son Amaury, and the evil life of Jocelyn bore its fruits in the leprosy of his grandson, King Baldwin IV.

Directly the Countess Alice of Antioch heard of her father's death, she began to plot and intrigue to break through the settlement made in her daughter's favour, and to get the town and principality for herself. By means of gifts and promises, she drew over to her own interests young Jocelyn of Edessa, and Pons, Count of Tripoli, and the people of Antioch, alarmed for their future, sent hastily to the king for assistance. Fulke went first to Beyrout, whence he intended to proceed through the territories of the Count of Tripoli to Antioch. But Pons, though his wife was the king's own sister, positively refused to allow him to pass. The king went by sea. Then Pons followed him with a small army. Fulke, getting together some troops at Antioch, went out to meet him, and an engagement took place, in which Pons was defeated, and most of his knights taken prisoners. After this the Count of Tripoli made his submission, and was reconciled to the king, who confided the government of Antioch to Renaud de Margat, and returned to his capital. But there was no repose for a King of Jerusalem, and the news came that Zanghi, with a large army, had passed the Euphrates, and was invading the territory of Antioch. Once more the order for preparation was given, and the king marched north. When he arrived at Sidon, he was met by his sister Cæcilia, who told him how her husband was besieged in Montferrand by the Saracens, and implored the king, with all a woman's tears and entreaties, to go first to his assistance. Zanghi thought best to retire, and raising his camp, got back across the Euphrates with all his plunder. But he only retired, "*pour mieux sauter*," and came back in overwhelming force. And then followed one more, almost the last, of those splendid victories which seem to have been won, unless the histories lie, against such fearful odds, and entirely through the personal valour of each individual Christian. The reputation of Fulke rose high by this victory, and he had time to regulate some of his domestic matters. First it became necessary to get a husband for little Constance of Antioch, in order to save himself the trouble of perpetually interfering in the troubles caused by Alice. He could think of no one so suitable as Raymond of Poitiers. But there were difficulties in the way. Raymond was in England at the court of Henry I. If deputies were sent publicly, inviting him to Antioch, Alice would certainly use all her influence with the Norman princes of Sicily, her late husband's cousins, to stop him on the way. A double deceit was therefore practised. Alice was privately informed that Raymond was sent for to marry her, not her daughter. Raymond was written to by a special messenger, a Knight Hospitaller, named Gerard, and ordered to travel to the East in disguise as a simple pilgrim. These precautions proved successful. Alice, rejoiced at the prospect of another gallant husband, ceased her intrigues. Raymond arrived safely in Antioch, where Alice and the Patriarch were both waiting for him. And then he was married without the least delay to Constance, a little girl of eleven or twelve. The Countess Alice, who had been deceived up to the very hour of the wedding, went away to Laodicea, mad with rage and disappointment, and we hear no more of her. Fulke had checkmated her.

His next trouble was on account of her sister, his own wife, Milicent. At a council held in Jerusalem, one Walter, Count of Cæsarea, son-in-law to Hugh, Count of Jaffa, rose and accused his father-in-law of the crime of *lèse-majesté*. The accusation was prompted by the king himself, who had, or thought he had, good reason to be jealous of his wife's relations with Count Hugh. And accordingly he hated Hugh. The barons heard the charge, and summoned Hugh to answer it in person, and to defend his honour, *en champ clos*, against his accuser. On the appointed day Walter of Cæsarea appeared in arms, but Hugh did not come. Whether that he was guilty, or whether that he was unwilling to risk his honour and life on the chance of a single fight, is uncertain. He was accordingly judged guilty in default, and the king marched against him. But Count Hugh was not so easily put down. He hastened to Ascalon, and made an alliance, to the horror of all good Christians, with those hereditary enemies of the faith, the inhabitants of that town. They joyfully joined him, and engaged to harass the country while he defended Jaffa. And then

Hugh drew up his bridges, shut his gates, and sat down, announcing his determination to hold out to the last. There was no one in the kingdom with so great a reputation as he for personal bravery; no one so handsome, no one so strong, and no one of better birth. Moreover, he was the cousin-german to the queen, which gave him a reason, or at least a pretext, for visiting her frequently and privately.

But it could not be endured that civil war should rage so close to the very capital of the realm, and negotiations were entered into between the contending parties. Finally it was agreed that Hugh should put away his unnatural alliance with the Saracens, and should so far acknowledge the sentence of the barons by an exile of three years. Hugh repaired to Jerusalem with the king, where he waited till the preparations for his departure should be completed. One day, while he was playing dice outside a shop in the street, a Breton knight stabbed him with a sword, and Hugh fell apparently dead. He was not dead, however, and was ultimately cured of his wounds, but died in Sicily before the term of his exile was completed. Everybody thought that King Fulke had ordered the assassination, but the murderer stoutly declared, in the midst of the keenest tortures, that he had no accomplices, and that he had acted solely in what he thought obedience to the will of Heaven. Fulke ordered his limbs to be broken and cut off one after the other, all but his tongue, which was left free, in order that full confession might be made. Queen Milicent's resentment pursued those who had compassed the exile of her lover. All who had been concerned in it went in terror and peril, knowing, "furens quid fœmina possit;" and even the king found it prudent to make the peace with his wife, and henceforth, even if he should be jealous, to conceal that passion as much as possible. But the count died in Sicily, and the queen's resentment died with him.

There was not, however, very much more glory awaiting the much troubled Fulke. Pons, Count of Tripoli, was taken prisoner by the Damascenes, and being recognised by certain Syrians, living in Lebanon, was put to death. Evidently the historian is wrong here, as the time was quite gone by for putting illustrious prisoners to death. There must have been some special reason for this barbarity. However, his son Raymond believed the story, and in order to avenge his death, marched a force to the mountains and brought back to Tripoli, loaded with irons, all those whom he could catch, as accessories to the death of his father. There, in presence of all the people, the poor creatures, who appear to have done nothing at all, were put to death with different kinds of tortures, all the most cruel, "in just punishment of their enormous crimes."

And now the misfortunes of the Christian kingdom began fairly to set in. The emperor John Comnenus, son of Alexis, was marching across Asia Minor with the intention of renewing his father's claims on Antioch. Raymond sent hurriedly to the king for assistance. Fulke went northwards again. He arrived in time to hear that Zanghi was again on Christian soil, ravaging and pillaging. He went to meet him, and the Christian army was completely and terribly defeated. Fulke took refuge in the fortress of Montferrand. Raymond of Tripoli was made prisoner. In this juncture an appeal was made to Jocelyn of Edessa and Raymond of Antioch to come to their assistance, and the Patriarch of Jerusalem was ordered to muster every man he could find.

It was the most critical moment in the history of the kingdom. Fortunately John Comnenus was too wise to desire the destruction of the Latin Christians, and he contented himself with the homage of Raymond of Antioch, and came to their assistance. But the Franks quarrelled with the Greeks, and were suspicious of their motives. John retired in disgust with his allies; a year afterwards he came back again; was insulted by the people of Antioch; was actually refused permission to go as a pilgrim to Jerusalem, except in disguise, and was killed by a poisoned arrow, very likely by a Frank. Thus the Latins lost all hope of succour from Constantinople, at a time when succour from some quarter was necessary to their very existence, when the old ardour of crusading which had kept their ranks full was dying out in Europe, and when their chiefs, the children of the old princes, were spending their days in slothful luxury, careless of glory, and anxious only for peace and feasting.

Fulke's own son-in-law, Thierry of Flanders, arriving at this time with a large following, the king made use of his men to go across the Jordan and clear away a nest of brigands which had been established in a cavern on a mountain side. While they were occupied in the regular siege of this place, the Turks took advantage of their absence, and made a predatory incursion into the south of Palestine, taking and plundering the little town of Tekoa. Robert, Grand Master of the Templars, went in hot haste against them. They fled at his approach; but the Christians, instead of keeping together and following up the victory, dispersed all over the plain. The Turks rallied, and forming small detachments, turned upon their pursuers, and slaughtered them nearly all. Among those who were killed was the famous Templar, Odo of Montfaucon. Fulke was sore afflicted by the news of this disaster, but persevered in the siege, and had at least the satisfaction of destroying his robbers.

One more military expedition King Fulke was to make. Allied with the Emir of Damascus, he laid siege to the town of Baucas, which Zanghi had taken. The legate of the pope, Alberic of Ostia, was with the army, and exhorted them to courage and perseverance. After an obstinate resistance, the town capitulated on honourable terms.

The legate had come from Rome to act as judge between the Patriarch of Antioch and the bishops. It is not easy to make out how these quarrels arose, nor is it edifying to relate the progress of squabbles which were chiefly ecclesiastical. Alberic of Ostia had been recalled, and a new legate, Peter, Archbishop of Lyons, sent out in his stead. The charges against the patriarch were chiefly that he refused to submit to Rome. William of Tyre gives the whole story of the trial and consequent deposition of the patriarch. He was taken to a monastery as a prisoner, and kept there for some time, but succeeded in escaping to Rome, where he pleaded his own cause, and was on the point of being reinstated, when he died of poison.

In the last year of King Fulke three important fortresses were built, that of Kerak in Moab, that of Ibelin, and that on Tell es Safiyeh. The fortress of Ibelin, about ten miles from Ascalon, was on the traditional site of Gath. The citadel built on Tell es Safiyeh, about eight miles from Ascalon, and called Blanchegarde, was made the strongest place in Palestine, and played an important part in the subsequent wars.

One day in 1144, Fulke, walking with the queen in the neighbourhood of Acre, put up a hare in the grass. Calling for a horse and a lance, he rode after it; and the horse falling, brought him down with such violence that he fractured his skull. He lingered four days in a state of insensibility, and then died, leaving two sons, of thirteen and seven years respectively, by his wife Milicent.

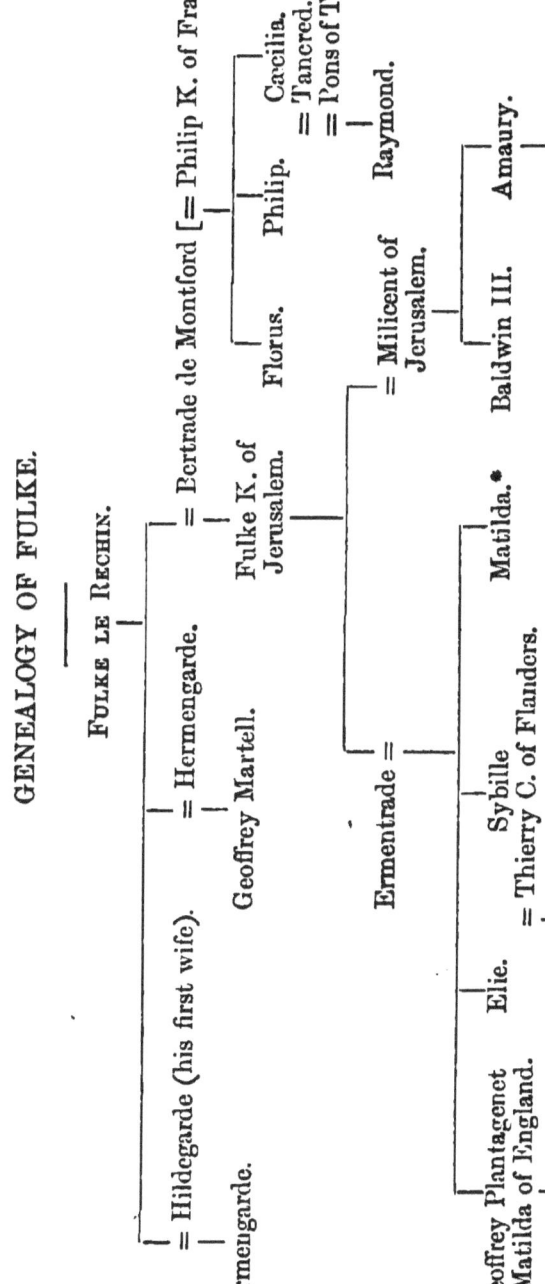

CHAPTER XI.

KING BALDWIN III. AND THE SECOND GREAT CRUSADE.
A.D. 1144—1162.

> "Seigneurs, je m'en voiz outre mer, et je ne scais se je revendré. Or venez avant : se je vous ai de riens mes fait, je le vous desferai l'un par l'autre, si comme je ai accoutumé à tous ceulz qui vinront riens demander ni à moy ni à ma gent."—*Joinville.*

"HITHERTO," says William of Tyre, whom we have been principally following, "hitherto the events I have described were related to me by others. All that follows I have either seen with my own eyes or have heard from those who actually were present. I hope, therefore, with the assistance of God, to be able to relate the facts that I have yet to put down with greater accuracy and facility."

He was a young man when Fulke died, and preserves in his history that enthusiasm for his successor which one of his own age would probably entertain, and which Baldwin's early death, if not his admirable qualities, prevented from dying out. He writes of him as one might have written of Charles I., had he died five years after he came to the throne, or of Louis XIV., had he finished his reign thirty years earlier.

Baldwin was only thirteen when with his mother, Milicent, as Queen and Regent, he was crowned king. Like his great ancestors, the young king grew up taller and stronger than the generality of mankind; his features were firm and undaunted, and a light beard covered his lips and chin; he was not "too fat like his brother, nor too thin like his mother." In short, Baldwin, when he grew up, was a tall and handsome man. As for his mental qualities, his biographer exhausts himself in praises. He was prompt to understand; eloquent and fluent of speech; affable in manners; full of compassion and tenderness; endowed with an excellent memory (in which he must have presented a pleasing contrast to his father); tolerably well educated—"better, that is, than his brother"—the biographer's standard of education is difficult to catch, because he afterwards tells us of Amaury that he was educated, "but not so well as his brother:" he was fond of having read to him the lives of great kings and the deeds of valiant knights; he knew thoroughly the common law of the realm; his powers of conversation were great and charming; he attached to himself the affections of everybody high and low. "And," says the worthy bishop, "what is more rare in persons of his age, is that he showed all sorts of respect for ecclesiastical institutions, and especially for *the Prelates of the Churches.*" Where could a finer king be found?

If he had a fault it was that he was fond of gaming and dice. As the greater part of his life was spent on horseback, it was only occasionally that he could indulge in this vice. Another fault he had as a youth which he entirely renounced in later years. To the credit of King Baldwin it is recorded that he was, after his marriage, entirely blameless in respect of women. Now by this time the morals of the Kingdom of Jerusalem were in an extremely bad way, and the example of the young king could not fail of producing a great and most beneficial effect.

Queen Milicent was an ambitious woman, like her sister Alice, and had no intention at all of being a puppet.

She accordingly insisted on being crowned together with her son. The kings of Jerusalem had ceased to affect that proud humility which made Godfrey refuse to wear a crown when his Lord had only worn thorns, and sent Baldwin I. to Bethlehem to be crowned, as it were, out of sight of the city of Christ's sufferings. Now the ceremony was held in the very church of the Holy Sepulchre, which was the cathedral of the Christian city. In the king's hands was placed the sword, with which to defend justice and Holy Church; on his finger they put the ring of faith; on his head the crown of honour; in his right hand the sceptre of authority and the golden apple of sovereignty.

Mother and son were crowned together, and the unhappy state, which wanted the firm hand of a Godfrey, found itself ruled by a boy and a woman. The barons began to take sides and form parties. There was no leader in the councils, none to whom they could look to as the common head, and if one advanced above the rest they regarded him with suspicion and envy. Worst of all, they began to fight with each other. In the north, Raymond of Antioch and young Jocelyn of Edessa looked upon each other as enemies, and spent most of their time in trying to devise means of mutual annoyance. Jocelyn. who ought to have been occupied in organising means for the defence of his dominions against the formidable Zanghi, when he was not harrying Raymond, lay inactive at Tellbasher, where he indulged in his favourite pleasures, hoping to spend the rest of his life in ignoble ease, looking out upon the world with those goggle eyes of his, the only feature, and that not a lovely one, recorded of this prince.

But he was to be rudely shaken from his slumber. It was in the early winter of 1144, the year of Baldwin's accession, when news came to him that Zanghi was before the walls of Edessa with an immense army. Jocelyn, roused too late, sent everywhere for assistance. Raymond would not help him; his own knights reproached him with his indolence and apathy, and declared that they would not march to certain death. Queen Milicent issued orders for the army to move northwards, which were not obeyed; and Edessa was doomed.

Zanghi, finding success almost certain, redoubled his efforts, and sent for reinforcements in all directions. He even offered favourable terms of surrender; but these were refused. Zanghi's plan of siege was the ordinary one, quietly to undermine the towers, propping up the earth as it was removed with timber. When the proper time arrived, the timber would be set fire to, and of course the tower would fall. The Latin archbishop, who appears to have been in command, would hear of no surrender, and exhorted the people daily, holding forth the promise of the crown of martyrdom. But on the twenty-second day of the siege the towers which had been undermined fell with a crash, and the enemy poured in. The first thought of the people was to fly for shelter to the citadel. Many were crushed or trampled to death in the attempt, among whom was Archbishop Hugh, who had been storing up gold, and now tried to carry it into the citadel. The weight of his treasure helped to bear him down. The enemy were before them at the gates of the citadel, and the slaughter of the helpless people commenced, with all the horrors usual after a siege. Islam was triumphant; Christendom in despair.

But Zanghi died next year, being assassinated by his own slaves, and a lively joy was diffused throughout Palestine. "A certain Christian," says William of Tyre, with admirable modesty, for, of course, he was himself the accomplished poet, directly he heard of this event, delivered himself of the following melodious impromptu :*

"Quam bonus eventus ! fit sanguine sanguinolentus
　　Vir homicida, reus, nomine sanguineus."

King Baldwin won his spurs while yet a boy, first by

* The chroniclers wrote his name Sanguin.

a short and successful expedition beyond the Jordan, and next by his Quixotic attempt on the town of Bozrah, in the Hauran. It was an attempt undertaken in haste and without reflection, and doomed from the outset to failure. A certain Armenian, governor of the town, influenced probably by some private motives of revenge, came to Jerusalem and offered to put the town in the hands of the Christians, if they wished to have it. There was still lingering, in spite of the fall of Edessa, some remains of the old spirit of conquest, and, regardless of the dangers which hovered round the kingdom, and of the pressing necessity for consolidating all their strength for purposes of defence, the Christians tumultuously demanded to be led to the attack, and an army was called together. Baldwin went with them. The troops assembled in the north and started full of vainglorious confidence. On the second day they found themselves surrounded with clouds of enemies, who assailed them with showers of darts. The country was a desert; as the only means of getting water the people had formed artificial cisterns, in which the winter rains were stored. But they were filled with dead bodies of locusts, and the water was too bad even for men parched with thirst. The Christians struggled on. They arrived at Edrei. Here, at least, they would get water. But at Edrei as well the water was all stored in large cisterns. They let down buckets by ropes: men hidden below cut the ropes. For four days they pressed on, however, while the enemy was reinforced hourly, and by day and night a continuous hail-storm of arrows and projectiles was showered into the camp, so that neither man nor beast among the Christians escaped without some wound. On the fourth day, they were cheered by the sight of the town of Bozrah, and by the discovery of certain small rills of water, which they fought for, and won at the cost of many lives. But in the dead of night a messenger of very evil tidings came into the camp. The wife of the

T

Armenian had refused to be a partner in her husband's treachery: the enemy occupied the city in force, and all hope was to be given over of taking it by storm. Then the Christians despaired. Some of them advised the king to mount the fleetest horse—that of John Gomain—in the camp, and make his way back alone, so that at least *his* life might have a chance of being saved. But Baldwin, brave boy that he was, refused. He had not had the stories of valiant knights read to him for nothing. He would remain with his army and share their fate. At break of day the camp was broken up and the retreat commenced. Orders were given to lay the dead and the wounded, as they fell, on the beasts of burden, so that the enemy might not know the havoc they were making, and then, for Nûr-ed-dín was already on the alert, they started on their disastrous and melancholy retreat. The heat was oppressive; there was no water; clouds of dust hung over the little army; clouds of Saracens rode round them firing arrows into their midst. And yet the Christians moved on in good order. More wonderful still, there was not a single dead body behind them. Were they, then, protected by some unknown power? The Saracens hesitated. Thinking that their arrows had no effect, and ignorant of the ghastly load under which the camels were groaning, they tried another method. The whole country was covered with dry bushes and grass. They set fire to it, and the wind blew the flames and smoke directly upon the Christians. And then the people turned to Archbishop Robert of Nazareth, who bore the Holy Cross. "Pray for us, father, pray for us in the name of the wood of the Cross that you bear in your hands, for we can no longer bear our sufferings." It was high time that Robert should pray: the faces and hands of the army were blackened with smoke and dust; "they were like blacksmiths working at the forge:" their throats were dry with heat and thirst.

The archbishop prayed, and at his prayer the wind shifted, and the flames were blown towards the enemy. The Christians resolved to send a messenger to the Saracens. They chose a knight who had been suspected of treachery, but they had no other choice, because he alone spoke the language of the enemy. They asked him if he would faithfully perform his mission. "I am suspected," he said, "unjustly. I will go where you wish me. If I am guilty of the crime you impute to me, may I never return—may I perish by the enemy's weapons!" He went, but before he had gone far the poor wretch fell dead, pierced by a hundred arrows.

Then the Christians pressed on. Arrived near Damascus, the Emir of that city sent a messenger to them. If they would halt, he would feed and entertain them all. Worn, thirsty, and wearied as they were, they suspected his loyalty, and hurried on. In after times it was related that a knight, whom none had seen before, appeared every morning at the head of the army, guided them during the day by roads unknown to the enemy, and disappeared at night. Doubtless, St. George. We have said before that the time for saints' help ended with Godfrey. A saint appears again, it is true, but with how great a change! the last time Saint George fought for the Christians, he led them on to victory after victory. Now he shows them a way by which, broken down and utterly beaten, they can escape with their lives.

There was great rejoicing in Jerusalem when the remnant of the army, with the young king, came back. Those who had been wont to sing psalms for the defeat of the enemy, sang them now for the safe return of the defeated king. "This our son," they chanted, "was dead, and is alive again: he was lost, and is found."

After the death of Zanghi, who had repeopled the city of Edessa, the ill-advised Jocelyn instigated the people to revolt against their new masters. All the Turks in the place were put to death, and Jocelyn, once more reinstated in the city of his father, sent messengers in all directions, asking for help. No help came, for it was impossible that any one should send help. Nûr-ed-dín came to the town with ten thousand men before Jocelyn had held it for a week. He vowed to exterminate the Christians, and these were too few in number to make any resistance. They threw open the gates, and all sallied forth together, with the resolution to fight their way through the beleaguering army. Jocelyn got through, and, with a few knights, reached Samosata in safety. The rest of the people were all massacred.

Some years after this, Jocelyn himself was taken prisoner, and spent the rest of his life, nine years, in captivity, far enough removed from any chance of indulging in those vices which had ruined him, and perilled the realm. It was a fitting end to a career which might have been glorious, if glory is a thing to desire; which might have assured the safety of the Christian kingdom, if, which is a thing to be questioned, the Christian kingdom was worth saving.

And now hostilities on both sides seem to have been for a time suspended, for the news reached the East how another Crusade had been preached in the West, and gigantic armies were already moving eastwards to protect the realm, and reconquer the places which had been lost. Signs, too, were not wanting which, though they might be interpreted to signify disaster, could yet be read the other way. A comet, for instance; this might portend evil for the Saracens—Heaven grant it was intended to strike terror into their hearts. But what could be said of the lightning which struck, of all places in the world, the very church of the Holy Sepulchre itself? Nothing but the anger of God could be inferred from a manifestation so clear, and the hearts of all were filled with terror and forebodings.

The details of the second Crusade, as it is called, unhappily resemble those of the first. It is not necessary that we should do more than follow the leading incidents which preceded the arrival of the soldiers—all who were left—in Palestine.

It was exactly fifty years since Peter the Hermit went through France, telling of the indignities offered to the pilgrims, and the sufferings of the faithful. But in fifty years a vast change had come over the West. Knowledge had taken the place of ignorance. No fear, now, that the rude soldiery would ask as every fresh town rose before their eyes, if that was Jerusalem. There was not a village where some old Crusader had not returned to tell of the long march, the frightful sufferings on the way, the obstinacy of the enemy, the death of his friends. From sea to sea, in France at least, the East seemed as well known as the West, for from every province some one had gone forth to become a great man in Palestine. Fulke from Anjou, Godfrey from Lorraine, Raymond from Toulouse, another Raymond from Poitou, Robert from Normandy, another Robert from Flanders, Hugh le Grand from Paris, Stephen from Blois, and fifty others, whose fame was spread far and wide in their native places, so that men knew now what lay before them. They went, if they went at all, to fight, and defend, not to conquer. The city was Christian; but there was plunder and glory to be got by fighting beyond the city.

Bernard proclaimed the Crusade. He preached the necessity of going to the assistance of a kingdom dear to all Christian eyes, tottering to its fall. He called attention to the corruption of morals, which he declared to be worse than any state of things ever known before; he forbore from promising easy conquests and victories where all the blood would be that of the infidel; on the contrary, he told the people that the penances inflicted by God Himself for their sins were the clash of arms, the fatigues and dangers of war, the hard fighting and physical suffering of a campaign under the sun of Syria; and, which is very significant, he appears to have invoked a curse upon all who refused to obey the summons, and follow to the Holy War.

The first Crusaders set off with light and buoyant hearts; they were marching, they thought, to certain conquest; the walls would fall down before them: it was a privilege and a sacred pleasure to have taken the sign of the Cross. The second army started with gloomy forebodings of misery and suffering; they were going on a penitential journey; they were about to encounter perils which they knew to be terrible, an enemy whom they knew to be countless as the sands of their own deserts, not because they wanted to fight, but because Bernard, who could not err, told them that God Himself laid this penance on their shoulders. Every step that brought Peter's rough and rude army nearer to Constantinople was a step of pleasure: every step that the second army took was an addition to the weariness and boredom of the whole thing. The most penitential of all was the young king, Louis VII. of France,. upon whose conscience there lay the terrible crime of having burned the church at Vitry. For in the church, which he had fired himself, were thirteen hundred men, women, and children, who were all burned with it. The king would fain have saved them, but could not, and when he saw their blackened and half-burned bodies, his soul was sick within him for remorse and sorrow. It was a calamity—for which, however, the king was not, perhaps, wholly responsible—worse than that modern burning of the women of Santiago. In Germany they began to expiate their sins by murdering the Jews, a cheap and even profitable way of purifying the troubled conscience, because they plundered as well as murdered them. Bernard, to his infinite credit, stayed the hand of persecution, and showed the people that this was not, hateful as a Jew must always be to a Christian, the way pointed out by Heaven. The preaching of Bernard was seconded by the exhortations of the poets, who united in singing the praises of those who take the Cross, and in denouncing those who refused. "Rise," says one bard,

> "Rise, ye who love with loyal heart;
> Awake, nor sleep the hours away:
> Now doth the darksome night depart,
> And now the lark leads in the day:
> Hear how he sings with joyous strain
> The morn of peace which God doth give
> To those who heed nor scathe nor pain;
> Who dare in peril still to live;
> Who, night or day, no rest may take,
> And bear the Cross for Christ's own sake."

The Crusade consisted wholly of Germans and French. The former went first, headed by Conrad, King of the Romans, who left his son Henry in charge of his dominions. They got through the Greek emperor's dominions with some difficulty, being unruly and little amenable to discipline, but were at last safely conveyed across the straits to Asia Minor, where they waited the arrival of King Louis.

In France an enormous army had been collected, by help of the old cry of "Dieu le veut," the magic of which had not yet died out; there must have been men, not very old, who remembered the preaching of Peter, and the frantic cries with which the Cross was demanded after one of his fiery harangues. Bernard wrote to the pope, with monkish exaggeration, that "the villages and the castles are deserted, and one sees none but widows and orphans whose husbands and fathers are yet living." Most of them, alas! were to remain widows and orphans indeed, for the husbands and fathers were never destined to return. And, as in the First Crusade, many of those who joined ruined themselves in procuring the arms and money necessary for their outfit. The Church, as before, kindly came to their assistance by buying the lands of them at a nominal value.

The gravest mistake was that made at the very outset when the barons were permitted to take with them their wives. Queen Eleanor, who afterwards married our Henry II., went with her husband, accompanied by a great number of ladies, and the presence of large numbers of women in the camp caused grave disorder, and subsequently great peril, both to the French and German armies.

It was in the early winter of 1147 that the Crusaders crossed the Hellespont. Without waiting for the French, the Germans, divided into two bodies, had pushed on. They reckoned on the friendship of the Greeks, but they were grievously disappointed. Extravagant prices were demanded for the most inferior food; lime was put into the bread, which killed many; the Turcopoles hovered about and cut off the supplies; but, in spite of these obstacles, a portion of the army, under the Bishop of Freisingen, managed to reach Syria. As for the larger part, under Conrad, they were guided as far as Dorylæum, where the first Crusaders had so hard a battle. Here the guides ran away, and the Turks fell upon them. The army consisted of seventy thousand horse, and a vast multitude of foot soldiers, of women, and of children. About seven thousand horse escaped with King Conrad. All the rest were slaughtered. No greater calamity had ever happened to the Christian arms. Conrad got back to Nicæa, where Louis, who had just arrived, was encamped. The French resolved to take the way by the sea-shore. We need not follow through all the perils of their march. They fought their way to Ephesus; thence, crossing the Mæander, they came to a place called Satalia, at the western extremity of Cilicia; and here Louis left them, and went by sea to Antioch. The plague broke out among the troops: the Greeks refused them any help, which they got from the very Turks whom they came to fight, and finally, out of the hundreds of thousands who had left the West a year before, a few thousands only struggled into Syria. Of the women who went with them, their wives and mistresses, not one got to Palestine, save only Queen Eleanor and her suite.

Raymond of Antioch was the cousin of Eleanor. He welcomed Louis and his queen to his little court, and immediately began to cast about for some way of making their visit to Palestine serviceable to himself. It was the way of all these Syrian knights and barons. Every man looked to himself and to his own interests; no man cared about the general interest. Jocelyn of Edessa, who was not yet put into prison, Pons of Tripoli, Raymond of Antioch, all hoped to catch the great kings of the West on their way to Jerusalem, and to turn the Crusade into such channels as might advance their own interests.

Suspecting nothing, Louis made a lengthened stay at Antioch, waiting for the remains of his great army. Raymond, thinking the best means of getting at the king was through his consort, employed every means in his power to amuse Eleanor. She, who had no kind of sympathy with the piety or remorse of her royal husband, preferred the feastings and amusements of Antioch to anything else, and would gladly have protracted them. But her own conduct and the levity of her manners caused grievous scandal, and effectually prevented her from having any influence over the king, who, when pressed to help Raymond, coldly replied that, before anything else, he must visit the holy places. Raymond, who had succeeded in pleasing the queen, if he had not won her heart, by way of revenge, persuaded Eleanor to announce her intention of getting divorced from the king on the ground of consanguinity, while Raymond declared that he would keep her, by force, if necessary, at his court. Louis took council of his followers, and by their advice, carried off his queen by night, and made the best of his way to Tripoli, where he was met by an emissary of Queen Milicent, who was afraid he would be drawn into some enterprise by the count, urging him to come straight on to Jerusalem.

In June, 1148, a great council of the assembled kings and chiefs was held at Acre. At this meeting were present King Baldwin, Queen Milicent, the Patriarch of Jerusalem, the barons of the kingdom, and the Grand Masters of the two great orders of the Temple and St. John, on behalf of the Christian kingdom; while the Crusaders were represented by Kings Conrad and Louis, Otto Bishop of Freisingen, brother of Conrad, Frederick (afterwards Barbarossa), his nephew, the Marquis of Montferrat, Cardinal Guy of Florence, Count Thierry of Flanders, and many other noble lords. Only it was remarked, by those who were anxious for the future, that the Counts of Tripoli, Edessa, and Antioch were not present, while it was ominous that Eleanor of France did not take her seat with the other ladies who were present at the council.

There were several courses open to the Crusaders. They might retake Edessa, and so establish again that formidable outpost as a bulwark to the kingdom. They might strengthen the hands of Raymond, and so make up for the loss of Edessa. They might take Ascalon, always a thorn in the side of the realm; or they might strike out a new line altogether, and win glory for themselves by an entirely new conquest, an exploit of danger and honour. Most unfortunately, they resolved upon the last, and determined on taking the city of Damascus. Such a feat of arms commended itself naturally to the rough fighting men. They despised Jocelyn; they resented the treatment of Raymond; and therefore they could not be got to see that to strengthen the hands of either of these was to

strengthen the power of the Christians, while to conquer
new lands was to increase their weakness and multiply
the hatred and thirst of revenge of their enemies. And
with that want of foresight which always distinguished
the Crusaders, they followed up their resolution by immediate action, and started on their new enterprise with
the eagerness of children, in spite of a burning July sun.
The King of Jerusalem marched first, because his men
knew the roads. Next came King Louis, with his French,
and lastly, the Germans, under Conrad. On the west side
of Damascus lay its famous gardens, and it was determined first to attack the city from this side. The paths
were narrow, and behind the bushes were men armed with
spears, which they poked through at the invaders as they
passed. The brick walls which hedged in the gardens
were perforated, with a similar object. There was thus a
considerable amount of fighting to be done in dislodging
these hidden enemies before the Christians managed to
make themselves masters of the position, It was done
at last, all the leaders having performed the usual
prodigies of strength and valour—Conrad himself cut a
gigantic Saracen right through the body, so that his head,
neck, shoulder, and left arm fell off together, a clean
sweep indeed—and the Damascenes gave themselves up
for lost. And then happened a very singular and inexplicable circumstance. The Christians deliberately abandoned a position which had cost them so much to win, and
resolved to cross over the river to the other side, where
they were persuaded that the attack would be much
easier. They went across. They found themselves
without water, without provisions, and in a far worse
position for the siege than before. The Damascenes
received reinforcements, closed up the approaches to the
gardens, and quietly waited the course of events. There
was nothing left but to retreat; and the Christians,
breaking up their camp in the middle of the night,

retreated, or rather fled, in disgrace and confusion. This was the end of the second Crusade.

Why did they leave the gardens? Many answers, all pointing to treachery, were given to the question. Some said that Thierry of Flanders wanted the city, and because the chiefs would not promise it to him, preferred seeing it remain in the hands of the enemy, and so became a traitor. Others told how the Templars arranged the whole matter for three great casks full of gold byzants, which, when they were examined, turned out to be all copper. Raymond of Antioch, according to a third story, managed the false counsels out of revenge to the king. And so on. Talk everywhere, treachery somewhere, that was clear, because treachery was in the Syrian air, and because knights, and barons, and priests were all alike selfish and interested, rogues and cheats—all but King Baldwin. "Whoever were the traitors," says the historian, "let them learn that sooner or later they shall be rewarded according to their merits, unless the Lord deign to extend them his mercy." He evidently inclines to the hope that mercy will not be extended to them.

· Disgusted with a people who would not be served, and wearied of broken promises and faithless oaths, the chiefs of the Crusade made haste to shake off the dust of their feet, and to leave the doomed kingdom to its fate. Some of their men remained behind, a reinforcement which enabled Baldwin to keep up his courage and show a bold front to the enemy so long as his life lasted.

Nûr-ed-dín, directly they were gone, invaded Antioch, and Raymond was killed in one of the small skirmishes which took place. At this time, too, Jocelyn of Edessa fell into the hands of the Turks, and was put into prison. It was almost impossible for Baldwin to defend Antioch alone. Nevertheless, he held it manfully, and it was not till after his time that it was ceded to the Greeks, who in their turn surrendered it to the Turks. Tripoli, the count of which town was himself assassinated, remained the only bulwark of the kingdom. The eyes of Palestine were turned again upon Europe. But from Europe little help could now be expected. Louis, returning defeated and inglorious, had been hailed as a conqueror. Medals were struck in his honour, with the lying legend—

> Regi invicto ab Oriente reduci
> Frementes lætitiâ cives.

And, though he promised to lead another Crusade, his conscience was appeased by his pilgrimage, and his love of praise was satisfied by the honours he received. Therefore he went no more. Moreover, two new methods of crusading were discovered, nearer home, and far more profitable. In the north of Germany lay a large and fertile country, inhabited wholly by pagans. Why not conquer that, and reduce so fair a land to Christianity? And in Spain, so close at hand for pious Frenchmen, were vast provinces, rich beyond measure, all in the hands of those very Saracens whom they were asked to go all the way to Palestine in order to fight. And then there died both Bernard and Suger, the sagacious Suger, who saw the disgrace which had fallen on the Christian arms, and wished to repair it by sending out another army in place of that which Louis had madly thrown away.

The boundaries of poor young Baldwin's kingdom were greatly contracted. Nothing now remained but what we may call Palestine proper, with a dubious and tottering hold on a few outlying towns. Fifty years had been sufficient to turn the sons of the rough and straightforward soldiers of Godfrey, whose chief fault seems to have been their ungovernable fits of rage, into crafty and double-faced Syrians, slothful and sensual, careless of aught but their own interests, and brave only when glory, to which they still clung, could be got out of it. Nor was the kingdom itself free from discord and variance. Queen Milicent retained her authority, nor could she be persuaded to give it up. It was the most monstrous thing—it shows, however, how the feudal ideas had become corrupted—that she should insist on holding part of the realm in her own name. She did so, however, giving Baldwin Tyre as his principal place, and retaining Jerusalem as her own. She had a following of barons, who preferred, for many reasons, to be under the rule of a woman. The reins of government were confided to her own cousin, one Manasseh, and Baldwin had the mortification of finding himself in times of peace, few enough, it is true, only the second man in a country of which he was the nominal king. He claimed his rights; these were refused. He besieged Manasseh in his castle; he even besieged his mother in hers. The patriarch acted as mediator, and, after long negotiations, a compromise was effected, by which Milicent, more fortunate than her equally ambitious sister, Alice of Antioch, received the city of Nablous to hold as her own for the rest of her life.

It was during these negotiations, or at their close, that the king held a great council at Tripoli on the state of the kingdom. And it was while the council was sitting that Count Raymond was assassinated—no one knew at whose instigation, because the murderers were instantly cut to pieces.

The Turks made an attempt upon the kingdom of Jerusalem itself, and while the knights were gone to defend Nablous, they encamped on the Mount of Olives. Then the people of Jerusalem went out, as full of courage as Gideon's three hundred, and drove them off with great slaughter. Their success—success was now so rare— raised the spirits of all the Christians, and the king resolved to follow it up by laying siege to that old enemy of Christendom, Ascalon, which was to Jerusalem even as the mound which Diabolus raised up against the city of

Mansoul in Bunyan's allegory. It was in 1153 that this strong place, which ought to have been in the hands of the Christians fifty years before, had it not been for the jealousy of Count Raymond, fell at last. Baldwin marched against it with all the forces he could command. A fleet watched the port from the sea, while the siege was hurried on by land. Every ship that brought pilgrims was ordered to proceed southwards, and the pilgrims were pressed into the service. Nevertheless, the work went on slowly, and after more than four months, reinforcements were received from Egypt, and the besieged were as confident as ever. Accident gave the Christians the town. They had a moveable tower, higher than the walls, with which they were able to annoy the enemy almost with impunity. One day, when it was laid alongside the wall, the besieged threw a vast quantity of wood, on which they poured oil and sulphur, between the ramparts and the town. This they set fire to; but, unfortunately for themselves, without first considering which way the wind was blowing. It was a strong east wind, and the flames were blown towards the walls. They blazed all day and all night, and when they ceased, at length, the stones were calcined, and that portion of the wall about the fire fell down with a crash. The Christians wanted nothing more. At daybreak the soldiers were awakened by hearing the noise, and rushed towards the spot. They were too late. The Templars were already crowding in at the breach, and, *in order to get all the plunder for themselves*, these chivalrous knights had stationed men to prevent the army from following them.

Non habet eventus sordida præda bonos,

remarks the historian. Their cupidity proved the death of a great many of their body, for they were too few to carry everything before them, as they had hoped. Forty Templars perished in this attack, and the rest were not able to get in at all, for the people drove them back, and in an incredibly short time fortified the broken wall with great beams of timber; and then, safe for a time behind their rampart, they tied ropes to the corpses of the knights, and dangled them up and down outside the wall, to the indignation of the Christians. After deliberation, confession, and a grand mass, a general assault was ordered, and for a whole day hand-to-hand fighting was carried on. And then the city yielded, and obtained fair terms. Provided they evacuated the town within three days, their lives were to be spared. And at last, in delusive imitation of the glories which were never to return again to the Christian arms, the standard of the Cross floated from the towers of Ascalon, the "Bride of Syria." The unfortunate people, with their wives and children, made what haste they could to get ready, and in two days had all left their city, carrying with them all their portable goods. The king honourably kept his word with them, and gave them guides to conduct them to Egypt across the desert. All went well so long as their guides were with them. But these left them after a time, and gave them over to a certain Turk, who had been with them in Ascalon—" valiant in war, but a perverse man, and without loyalty "—on his promise to conduct them safely to Egypt. But on the way he and his men fell on them, robbed them of all their treasures, and went away—whither, history sayeth not—leaving them to wander helplessly up and down the desert. And so the poor creatures all perished. It is a pity that we cannot ascertain what became of the admirable Turk who knew so well how to seize an opportunity.

During the siege of Ascalon, the Lady Constance of Antioch, whom the king had been anxious to see married for a long time, chose, to everybody's astonishment, a simple knight, one Renaud de Chatillon, as her husband. The king, anxious above all that a man should be at the head of Antioch, consented at once, and Renaud, of whom we shall have more to say, wedded the fair widow. Although the king approved of the marriage, it appeared that the Patriarch of Antioch did not, and trusting to the sacredness of his person went about the city spreading all sorts of stories about the fortunate young bridegroom. Renaud dissembled his resentment, and invited him to the citadel, and then, by way of giving the reverend bishop a lesson as to the punishment due to calumniators, set him in the sun all day, with his bald head covered with honey to attract the wasps. After this diabolical audacity, as William of Tyre calls it, there was nothing left for the patriarch but to pack up and get away to Jerusalem as fast as he could. The king reprimanded Renaud, but too late, for the mischief was done, and the head of the prelate already painfully stung.

Internal troubles occupied the king for the next year or two. These were caused by the quarrels between the two military orders and the Church of Jerusalem. We hear only one side of the story, which throws the whole blame upon the knights. No doubt the clergy were also in some way to blame. By special permission of the pope, no interdict or excommunication could touch the Knights of St. John or the Knights Templars. They were free from all episcopal jurisdiction, and subject only to the pope. It pleased Raymond, Grand Master of the Hospitallers, for no reason given by the chronicler, to raise up all sorts of troubles against the Patriarch of Jerusalem and the prelates of the Church, on the subject of parochial jurisdiction and the tithes. The way they showed their enmity is very suggestive of many things. "All those whom the bishops had excommunicated, or interdicted, were freely welcomed by the Hospitallers, and admitted to the celebration of the divine offices. If they were ill, the brothers gave them the viaticum and extreme unction, and those who died received sepulture. If it happened that for some enormous crime"—probably the withholding of tithes—" the churches of the city were put under interdict, the brothers, ringing all their bells, and making a great clamouring, called the people to their own chapels, and *received the oblations themselves;* and as for their priests, they took them without any reference whatever to the bishops." Obviously, therefore, the quarrel was entirely an ecclesiastical squabble, due to the desire of the Church to aggrandize and preserve its power. The knights, *ecclesia in ecclesiâ*, a church within a church, would not recognise in any way the authority of the patriarch. For this they had a special charter from the pope. But they would not pay tithes, and they were constantly acquiring new territories. We may have very little doubt that it was the question of tithes on the knights' lands which caused all the quarrel. But it is very remarkable to note the way in which the historian speaks of interdicts and excommunications. In the West an interdict was a great and solemn thing. In England only one interdict, at the memory of which the people shuddered for many years to come, was ever laid upon the country, while, though English kings have been excommunicated, it has happened rarely. In Palestine the custom of debarring offenders, whether towns or individuals, from the privileges of the Church, is spoken of as quite a common practice. The thing, evidently, was often happening. The patriarch was handy with his interdicts, and it must have galled him to the very soul to find that the people cared nothing for them, because they could get their consolations of the Church just as well from the knights.

One cannot, however, defend the manner in which the knights vexed the heart of the patriarch in other ways. For whenever he went to the Church of the Holy Sepulchre, the knights, who had a great building opposite (in what is now called the Muristàn), began to ring all their bells at once, and made so great a noise that he could not be heard. And once, though one can hardly believe this, they went to the doors of the church and shot arrows at the people who were praying. Probably they pretended to shoot them in order to frighten the priests. Such a practical joke, and its effect in the skurrying away of people and priests, would be quite in accordance with the spirit of the times.

The patriarch, though now nearly a hundred years of age, went himself to Rome, but got no satisfaction. He had with him six bishops and a band of lawyers to plead his cause; but he was badly received by the pope and badly treated by the cardinals. And after being put off from day to day, finding that he could get no redress, he retired in shame and confusion, and probably patched up some sort of peace with his enemies the knights.

And now followed a sort of lull before the storm, three or four years of actual peace and internal prosperity. Renaud de Chatillon disgraced the cause of Christianity by an unprovoked attack upon the Isle of Cyprus, which he overran from end to end, murdering, pillaging, and committing every kind of outrage. Nûr-ed-dín made himself master of Damascus, an event which more than counterbalanced the loss of Ascalon. And Baldwin committed the only crime which history can allege against him. For he had given permission to certain Turcomans and Arabs to feed their cattle on the slopes of Libanus. Here, for a time, they lived peaceably, harming none and being harmed by none. But the king was loaded with debts which he could not pay. Some one in an evil hour suggested to him an attack upon this pastoral people. Taking with him a few knights, the king went himself and overran the country sword in hand. Some of them escaped by flight, leaving their flocks and herds behind; some buried themselves in the forests; some were made slaves; and some were mercilessly slaughtered. The booty in cattle and horses was immense, and Baldwin found, by this act of iniquity, a means of paying off, at least, the most pressing of his creditors. But his subsequent misfortunes were attributed to this perfidy, the worst which a Christian king of Jerusalem had as yet displayed.

Nûr-ed-dín laid siege to the castle of Banias, into which Count Humphrey had introduced the knights of St. John on conditions of their sharing in the defence. Baldwin went to its assistance. Nûr-ed-dín raised the siege and retired. The king, seeing no use in staying any longer, began his southward march. They encamped the first night near the lake Huleh, where they lay without proper guards, believing the enemy to be far enough away. The king's own body-guard had left him, and some of the barons had left the army altogether, followed by their own men. In the morning the enemy fell upon them all straggling about the country. Baldwin retreated to a hill-top with half a dozen men, and gained in safety the fortress of Safed. And then the historian adds a sentence which shows how utterly rotten and corrupt was this kingdom, founded by the brave arms of Godfrey and his knights. "There was very little slaughter, because everybody, not only those who were renowned for their wisdom and their experience in war, but also the simple soldiers, eager to save their miserable lives, gave themselves up without resistance to the enemy like vile slaves, feeling no horror for a shameful servitude, and not dreading the ignominy which attaches to this conduct."

Is it possible to imagine a knight of the First Crusade, or even a simple soldier, preferring to surrender at once than to risk the chance of life in the battle? And when the news came south, which happened soon enough, instead of flying to arms, the men flew to the altars, chanting the psalm "Domine, salvum fac regem."

Fortunately one of those little crusades, consisting of a fleet and a few thousand men, arrived at this juncture, headed by Stephen, Count of Perche. Baldwin welcomed them with delight, and made the best use of them, defeating by their help the Saracens at every point in the county of Tripoli and the principality of Antioch, and lastly gave the Damascenes the most complete defeat they had ever experienced. It must always be remembered that it was by such windfalls and adventitious aids as these that the kingdom of Jerusalem was maintained. The pilgrims who came to pray fought in the intervals of prayer; a small percentage of them always remained in the country and attached themselves to the fortunes of king or baron. When the influx of pilgrims was great the new blood kept up the stamina, physical as well as moral, of the Syrian Christians; when the influx was small the king had to depend upon the *pullani*, the Syrian born, the creoles of the country, who were weedy, false, and cowardly, like those knights and soldiers who surrendered, rather than strike a blow for their lives, to Nûr-ed-dín.

In 1160 died Queen Milicent. Against her moral character, since the scandal about Hugh of Jaffa, no word had been breathed. But she was ambitious, crafty, and intriguing, like her sisters, not one of whom lived happily with her husband. She founded a convent on the Mount of Olives, in return for which the ecclesiastical biographers, as is their wont, are loud in their praises of her. Her youngest sister was made its first abbess. She died of some mysterious malady, for which no cure could be found. Her memory failed, and her limbs were already long dead when she breathed her last. No one was allowed to go into the room where she lay save a very few, including her two sisters, the Countess of Tripoli, widow of Raymond, and the Abbess of Saint Lazarus of Bethany. Probably the disease she suffered from was that which broke out in her grandson, Baldwin IV., leprosy. The year before her death the king had contracted a splendid marriage, advantageous from every point of view. He married Theodora, niece to the Emperor of Constantinople. The new queen was only thirteen: she was singularly beautiful, and brought, which was of more importance, a large dowry in ready money. Baldwin was passionately fond of his young bride, and from the moment of his marriage gave up all those follies of which he had been guilty before. But he had a very short period of this new and better life. Renaud de Chatillon, who had made his peace with the emperor, by means of the most abject and humiliating submissions, got into trouble again, and was taken prisoner by the Mohammedans. Baldwin, affairs in the north falling into confusion in consequence of this accident, went to aid in driving back the enemy. Here he was seized with dysentery and fever, diseases common enough in the Syrian climate. His physician, one Barak, an Arab, gave him pills, of which he was to take some immediately, the rest by degrees. But the pills did not help him, and he grew worse and worse. They said he was poisoned. Some of the pills were given to a dog, which died after taking them—the story is, however, only told from hearsay, and is probably false. He was brought to Beyrout, where he languished for a few days and then died, in his thirty-third year, leaving no children.

Great was the mourning of the people. Other kings had been more powerful in war; none had been braver. Other kings had been more successful; none had so well deserved success. And while his predecessors, one and all, were strangers in the land, Baldwin III. was born and brought up among them all; he knew them all by name, and was courteous and affable to all. In those degenerate days he was almost the only man in the kingdom whose word could be trusted; moreover, he was young, handsome, bright, and generous. The only faults he had were faults common to youth, while from those which most degrade a man in other men's eyes, gluttony and intemperance, he was entirely free. Even the Saracens loved this free-handed chivalrous prince, and mourned for him. When some one proposed to Nûr-ed-dín to take advantage of the confusion in the country and invade it, he refused, with that stately courtesy which distinguished even the least of the Saracen princes. "Let us," said he, "have compassion and indulgence for a grief so just, since the Christians have lost a prince such that the world possesses not his equal."

The wiseacres remembered how, when he stood godfather to his brother's infant son, he gave him his own name, and on being asked what else he would give him, "I will give him," said the king, with his ready laugh—it was his laugh which the people loved—"I will give him the kingdom of Jerusalem." The gossips had shaken their heads over words so ominous, and now, with that melancholy pleasure, almost a consolation, which comes of finding your own prognostications of evil correct, they recalled the words of fate and strengthened themselves in their superstition.

Ill-omened or not, the words had come true. Baldwin was dead, his brother was to succeed him, and his nephew was to come after. And henceforth the days of the kingdom of Jerusalem are few, and full of trouble.

The kingdom of Jerusalem, like a Roman colony, was founded by men alone. Those women who came with the Crusaders either died on the way, unable to endure the fatigue, heat, and misery of the march, or fell into the hands of the Turks, whose mistresses they became. The Crusaders therefore had to find wives for themselves in the country. They took them from the Syrian Christians or the Armenians, occasionally, too, from Saracen women who were willing to be baptized. Their children, subjected to the enervating influences of the climate, and imbibing the Oriental ideas of their mothers, generally preserved the courage of their fathers for one or two generations, when they lost it and became wholly cowardly and sensual and treacherous. But the kingdom was always being reinforced by the arrival of new knights and men at arms, so that for all practical purposes it was a kingdom of the West transplanted to the East. All the manners and customs were purely European. Falconry and hunting were the most favourite sports. They amused the Saracens, when they came to have friendly relations with them, by tournaments and riding at the quintain. Indoors they beguiled the time which was not taken up by eating, drinking, or religious services, in chess, dicing, and games of chance. They were all great gamblers, and forgot in the chances of the dice all their misfortunes and anxieties. Those who were rich enough entertained minstrels, and had readers to read them the lives of illustrious warriors and kings. Later on, but this was always done with the greatest secrecy, even by Frederick II., who cared little enough what was said of him, they learned to admire the performances of dancing girls. Richard of Cornwall was so delighted with their voluptuous dances that he carried a number of them to England. As for their manner of living it was coarse and gross. They brought their Western appetites to the East, and, ignorant of the necessity of light food and temperance in a hot climate, they made huge meals of meat and drank vast quantities of wine. This was probably the main cause of their ungovernable temper, and the sudden outbursts of rage which sometimes made them commit acts of such extraordinary folly. And this was most certainly the cause why they all died young. And though they imbibed every other Oriental habit readily—Oriental voluptuousness, Oriental magnificence, Oriental dress—they never learned the truth that Mohammed enforced so rigidly, that to preserve life we must be temperate. Fever destroyed them, and leprosy, that most miserable of all diseases, crept into their blood, possibly through the eating of pork, of which they were inordinately fond.

For the rest, they swore enormous oaths, vying with each other in finding strange and startling expressions; they were always rebelling against the authority of the Church, and always ready to be terrified by the threats of the priests and to repent with tears. In religion they exercised a sort of fetish worship. For it was no matter what odds were against them so long as the wood of the True Cross was with them; it mattered little what manner of lives they led so long as a priest would absolve them; there was no sin which could not be expiated by the slaughter of the Mohammedans. Every Crusader had a right to heaven; this, whatever else it was, was an escape from the fires of hell. The devil, who was always roaming up and down the world, appearing now in one form and now in another, had no power over a soldier of the Cross. Everybody, for instance, knows the story of the Picard knight. He had made a bargain with the devil, to get revenge—this obtained, he could not get rid of his infernal ally. He took the Cross and the devil ceased to torment him. But when Jerusalem was taken, and he returned home, he found the devil there already, awaiting him in his own castle. Therefore he took the Cross again, went *outre mer*, stayed there, and was no more troubled. And every Crusader was ready to swear that he had never himself met any other devil than the black Ethiopians of the Egyptian army. The saints, on the other hand, frequently appeared, as we have seen.

Such, in a few words, were the manners of the Christians over whom ruled Baldwin III.; an unruly, ungodly set, superstitious to their fingers' ends, and only redeemed from utter savagery by their unbounded loyalty to their chiefs, by their dauntless courage in battle, and by whatever little gleams of light may have shone upon them through the chinks and joints of the iron armour with which they had covered, so to speak, and hidden the fair and shining limbs of Christianity.

CHAPTER XII.

KING AMAURY. A.D. 1162—1173.

"I had thought I had had men of some understanding
And wisdom, of my council; but I find none."
Henry VIII.

AT the death of King Baldwin the personal unpopularity of his brother among the barons caused at first some hesitation as to his election, but this was overruled by the influence of the clergy, and Amaury was duly crowned in the Church of the Holy Sepulchre. He was at the time of his succession to the crown twenty-seven years of age. He had been named by his brother first Count of Jaffa, and afterwards, when the place was taken, Count of Ascalon. He was a man somewhat above the middle height; like his brother he had an aquiline nose, brown hair falling back from his forehead, and would have been as handsome as Baldwin but for his premature corpulence. He was inordinately fat, in spite of extreme temperance in eating and drinking. As for his faults, they were many. He was morose and taciturn, rarely speaking to any one, and never showing any desire to cultivate friendships; he was avaricious, always trying to accumulate treasure, a habit which he defended, honestly enough, on the ground that it was the duty of a king to provide for emergencies, a duty which he was the first King of Jerusalem to recognise. At the same time, he was always ready with his money in cases of necessity. He seldom laughed, and when he did, he seemed to laugh all over, in a manner as undignified as it was ungraceful. He had, too, a slight impediment in his speech, which prevented him from speaking freely, and was probably the main cause of his taciturnity. He was unchaste, and made no secret of his incontinence. He was a violent enemy of what his biographer calls the liberty of the Church—in other words, he insisted on the property of the Church bearing the burden of taxation equally with all other property. He had little education, but loved reading, especially the reading of history, and was fond of asking questions on curious and recondite questions. Thus, he once startled William of Tyre by asking him if there was any proof, apart from revelation, of the doctrine of a future world. The priest proved to him, by the Socratic method, he says, that there was; but he confesses that he was greatly exercised in spirit at the king's asking such a question. He was well versed in all questions of law, and in military matters was generally a prudent leader, and always patient of fatigue and suffering. " Being so fat," we are told, "the rigours of cold and heat did not trouble him"—a very odd result of corpulence. He obeyed all the ordinances of the Church, and showed his magnanimity by never taking the least notice of things said in his disfavour, when they were reported to him. He loved not dice or gambling, and had, indeed, but one sport of which he was really fond, that of falconry. Evidently a gloomy kind of prince, with his mind overwhelmed by all sorts of doubts and questions of morality and religion, perplexed by the cares and anxieties of his position, void of enthusiasm for the crown which he wore, but resolute to do the best he could for his kingdom; more prudent and far-seeing than any who had preceded him, but without the dash and vigour of his ancestors, slow of thought, and consequently liable to ill-success for want of promptness, a man something like our William III., who had a few who admired and respected him, but who, to the many, was unpopular and distasteful.

He had married Agnes, the daughter of Jocelyn the younger, by whom he had three children, Baldwin, afterwards king, Sybille and Isabelle. On his accession it was discovered, one wonders why the Church had not interfered earlier, that the marriage was unlawful, because his own and his wife's grandfather, Baldwin du Bourg, and Jocelyn the elder, had been first cousins. He was therefore compelled to get a divorce from Agnes, who married again, first Hugh of Ibelin, a gallant fighting man, and afterwards Renaud of Sidon, also a marriage within the limits, only this time the Church did not think proper to interpose her authority.

Like all the kings of Jerusalem, Amaury began his reign with an expedition, by way of winning the spurs of gallantry. The Egyptians—the Fatemite dynasty being now in its last stage of decay—failed to pay the tribute which had been agreed upon after the taking of Ascalon. Amaury led an army to Pelusium, which he took and plundered, and returned home laden with spoils and glory.

The Fatemite Caliphs, degenerate now, and sunk in sloth, left the whole government of their rich empire to their viziers, who had taken the title of sultan. Dhargam, the vizier at this time, had a powerful rival named Shawer, whom he managed to turn out of his government and banish from the kingdom. Shawer repaired to Damascus, and representing to Nûr-ed-dín the weakened state of the kingdom, urged him to send an army which should in the first instance place himself in the seat of Dhargam, and in the next make Egypt a sort of appanage to Damascus. The project was tempting. If Egypt could be made even an ally of Damascus, or more properly speaking, of Baghdad, to which Caliphate Nûr-ed-dín belonged, the way was clear for united action against the Christian kingdom on three sides at once. Nûr-ed-dín did not hesitate long. Deputing his ablest general, Shírkoh, to lead his forces, he despatched a formidable army to Egypt, to support the rebellious claims of Shawer. But Dhargam in his turn was not idle. He sent messengers to King Amaury, offering conditions, almost any which the king might dictate, in return for assistance. But while the negotiations were pending, and Amaury was making up his mind how to act, Shírkoh and his army were already in Egypt. Dhargam led his troops to meet the enemy, and in a first engagement entirely routed the Syrians. The next day, however, these rallied, and the unfortunate Dhargam was killed by a chance arrow in the battle. Shawer entered into Cairo in triumph, killed all Dhargam's relations—a summary and efficacious way of preventing any possible future claims on the part of his descendants—and allowed Shírkoh to establish himself in Pelusium, where the Syrians settled down, and refused either to quit the kingdom, or to acknowledge the authority of the caliph. Shawer found himself thus in the position of one seeking to be delivered from his friends, and saw no way of escape but by the intervention of the Christians. He sent ambassadors to Amaury, making overtures similar to those proposed by his late rival, even offering greater advantages if the previous terms were not sufficiently liberal; but Amaury accepted them, and marched with all his forces into Egypt. These allied forces of Shawer and Amaury besieged Shírkoh in Pelusium, but were not strong enough to get more than a conditional surrender, the Syrian general being allowed to depart with all the honours of war, and to return to Damascus. And at the same time Nûr-ed-dín received a defeat near Tripoli, which raised the spirit of the Christians to the highest point. Next year, however, he avenged himself by defeating young Bohemond of Antioch, Raymond of

Tripoli, the Greek governor of Cilicia, and the Armenian prince Toros. It was a shameful rout. "No one bethought him of his former courage, or of the deeds of his ancestors; no one sought to avenge the insults of the enemy, or to fight gloriously for the liberty and honour of his country. Each, on the other hand, hastening to throw away his arms, endeavoured by indecent supplications to preserve a life which it would have been a thousand times better to sacrifice by fighting valiantly for his country. Toros the Armenian got away by flight: Bohemond and the rest were all taken prisoners, while they were shamefully running away." In the midst of the consternation produced by this disaster, Thierry, Count of Flanders, who was continually coming into the country like a *Deus ex machinâ* in the midst of calamities, arrived opportunely with a small following of knights. He could not, however, prevent Nûr-ed-dín from taking the Castle of Banias, which in the absence of its seigneur, Humphrey, who was away in Egypt, had been consigned to the care of one Walter of Quesnet. Walter gave up the place, which he was too weak to defend, and in these degraded times was of course accused of having received bribes for the purpose from Nûr-ed-dín. Perhaps he did.

The king came back glorious with his Egyptian exploit, only to hear of these reverses, and to march north in hopes of repairing them. He could do no more than place the best men he had in the fortresses, while Shírkoh gained possession of a stronghold named the Grotto of Tyre, by treachery, as was alleged—at least the Christian governor was hanged for it at Sidon. The fortress of Montreal, in Moab, fell at the same time, and the king was so indignant that he hung up twelve of the Templars who had been among the besieged, and had consented to its capitulation. Nothing, in fact, can explain the continual reverses of the Christians except the fact of their utter demoralization and cowardice, and the dwindling away of that full stream of pilgrim soldiers who had formerly flocked yearly to the East. The Second Crusade, indeed, was productive of the greatest harm in this respect to the Christian kingdom. It drained the West of all the men who wished to become pilgrims; and the fact that so few returned deterred effectually those who would otherwise have wished to go. Other causes, of course, were at work. Of these, the chief were the crusades against the Moors in Spain and the Pagans in Germany, and the development of pilgrimages to local shrines and saints. It was much easier and a great deal pleasanter, though not so glorious, to ride across a friendly country to a saint not many hundreds of miles away, than to journey in peril and privation along the long and weary road which led to Jerusalem.

But there was a lull in the incursions of Nûr-ed-dín. He and Shírkoh had other and vaster projects on hand. They sent to the caliph at Baghdad, and pointed out the manifest advantages which would accrue from the extinction of the Fatemite power, the union of both caliphates into one, and the possession of a country so rich and so fertile as Egypt, the people of which were enervated by pleasure and luxury, and absolutely unfitted for any kind of resistance. The caliph listened. Surrounded as he was by every luxury that the heart of man could desire, it mattered little to him whether another rich country was added to his nominal rule or not. But it mattered greatly that the divided allegiance of Islam should be made to run again in one stream, and he consented to give all his influence provided the war were made a religious war. To this Nûr-ed-dín and his general eagerly assented, and the caliph wrote to all the princes who owned his sway, commanding them to assist Shírkoh in his intended invasion of Egypt.

Amaury possessed prudence enough to know that if the Syrians conquered Egypt his own position would be far worse than before; and he collected his forces and marched southwards, in hopes of intercepting the Syrian army in the desert. He missed them; but Shawer, full of admiration for the good faith which seemed to him to have actuated the Christians, welcomed them with every demonstration of gratitude when they arrived in Egypt, and placed, to use the phrase of the historian, all the treasures of the country at their disposal. Amaury established his camp near Cairo, on the banks of the Nile, and then held counsel what next to do. He determined to make another attempt to intercept Shirkoh, and though he again missed the main army, he came upon a small rear-guard, which he either killed or made prisoners. From the prisoners he learned that a great disaster had befallen the Turks on their way across the desert. South of Moab there had arisen a frightful storm and whirlwind, in which the sand was driven about like the waves of the sea. To escape it, the troops dismounted and crouched behind the beasts, covering their faces; they lost all their camels, most of their provisions, and a vast number of their men. Amaury came back again in good spirits at this intelligence, and thinking of returning home again, the tempest having done the work of his own sword. But he overrated the power of the Egyptians, and Shawer, knowing how utterly unable his own forces were to cope with those of Shírkoh, shattered as these were, implored the king to remain in Egypt and help him to drive off the invader. He undertook to give the Christians a sum of four hundred thousand gold pieces, half to be paid on the spot, half when the work was done, provided that the king undertook not to leave Egypt till the enemy had been driven out. The terms were agreed to; the king gave his right hand, in token of fidelity, and sent Hugh of Cæsarea, accompanied by a Templar named Foucher, to receive the personal promise of the great and mysterious caliph himself, whom no one had yet seen.

The two knights, with Shawer, proceeded to the palace. They were preceded by a number of trumpeters and swordsmen, and led through dark passages where gates, at each of which were Ethiopian guards, continually barred the way. Having passed through these, they found themselves in an open place, surrounded by galleries with marble columns, with panels of gold, and pavements of curious mosaic. There, too, were basins of marble filled with pure and sparkling water; the cries and calls of birds unknown to Europeans, of strange shape and glorious plumage, saluted their ears; and going farther on they found themselves in a menagerie of strange beasts, "such as the painter might imagine, or the poet, with his lying license, might invent, or the imagination of a sleeper could fancy in dreams of the night."

Passing on still through more corridors, and along other passages, they arrived at last in the palace itself, where were armed men, and guards whose arms and martial bearing proclaimed the power, even as the splendour of the place proclaimed the wealth, of the sovereign who owned it. They were shown into an apartment one end of which was hidden by curtains, embroidered with gold and precious stones. Before the curtain Shawer, the sultan, prostrated himself twice, and then took the sword which hung from his neck and humbly laid it on the ground. At that moment the curtains drew apart, and disclosed the caliph himself, seated on a golden throne, in robes more splendid than those of kings, and surrounded by a small number of his domestics and favourite eunuchs. Then the sultan advanced and explained the object of this visit, and the reasons which had led to the treaty with the Christians. The caliph replied in a few words that he agreed to the treaty, and promised to interpret all the conditions in the manner most favourable to the king.

But Hugh demanded that the caliph should ratify the treaty by giving his hand, after the manner of the

Christians, a proposition which was received with the greatest horror; nor was it till the sultan had urged the point with vehemence that the caliph consented, presenting his right hand covered with a handkerchief. Again the sturdy Hugh expostulated. "Sir," said he to the caliph, who had never been addressed in such a manner before; "loyalty knows no concealments. Let everything between princes be bare and open. . . . Give me your uncovered hand, or I shall be constrained to think that you have some secret design, and possess less sincerity than I wish to experience from you." The caliph yielded, smiling, and with a good grace, while his courtiers were dumb with amazement, and repeated, in the same words as Hugh, the oath to adhere to the conditions in good faith, without fraud or evil intention.

"The caliph was in the flower of youth, tall, and of handsome appearance; he had an infinite number of wives, and was named El "Adhid li dín illah. When he sent away the deputies, he gave them presents whose abundance and value served at the same time to honour him who gave them, and to rejoice those who received them from so illustrious a prince."

The terms of alliance being thus agreed upon, Amaury proceeded with his campaign. But Shírkoh was too wary to give him an opportunity of fighting, and after playing with him a little, withdrew into the desert, and the Christians occupied the city of Cairo, where they were allowed to go everywhere, even into the palace of the caliph, a mark of the highest favour. Shírkoh returned, and trusting to his superiority of numbers, forced on a battle. He had with him—of course the numbers must be taken with some reserve—twelve thousand Turks and ten thousand Arabs, the latter armed with nothing but the lance. The Christians had three hundred and sixty knights, a large body of Turcopoles, and the Egyptian army, the numbers of which are not given.

The battle was fought at a place called Babain, "the two gates," about two leagues from Cairo, on the borders of the desert, where sand-hills encroach steadily on the cultivated soil, and form valleys between themselves, in which the Christians had to manœuvre. No ground could have been worse for them. The battle went against them. At the close of the day Hugh of Cæsarea had been taken prisoner, the Bishop of Bethlehem, Eustace Collet, Jocelyn of Samosata, and many other knights, were killed, the Christians, fighting still, were scattered about the field, and the king found himself on one of the sand-hills, master of the position for which he had fought, but with a very few of his men round him. He raised his banner to rally the Christians, and then began to consider how best to get away from the field, for the only way was through a narrow pass, threatened on either side by a hill on which the Turks were crowded in force. They formed in close array, placing on the outside those who were the best armed. But the Turks made no attack upon them, probably from ignorance of the result of the day, or from fatigue, and the Christians marched all through the night. It was four days before they all came back to the camp, and it was then found they had lost a hundred knights on the field.

Shírkoh, whose losses had been very much greater, rallying his men, marched northwards on Alexandria, which surrendered without striking a blow. By Amaury's advice, an Egyptian fleet was sent down the river to intercept all supplies, and as Alexandria was without any stores of corn and provisions, it was not long before Shírkoh, starved out, left the city in the charge of his nephew, afterwards the great and illustrious Saladin, with a thousand horse, while he himself took up his old position near Cairo. Thereupon Amaury moved north to invest Alexandria. The Egyptian fleet held the river and commanded the port; the allied armies blocked up all the avenues of approach; the orchards and gardens round the walls, which had been the delight and pride of the Alexandrians, were ruthlessly destroyed: fresh recruits poured in from all parts of Palestine, and the besieged began to suffer from all kinds of privation. Saladin sent messengers to his uncle, urging him to bring assistance. Shírkoh, too weak to send any, thought it best to make favourable terms while he could. Sending for his prisoner Hugh of Cæsarea, he made proposals of peace. "Fortune," he said, "has not been favourable to me since I came into this country. Would to God I could see my way out of it! You are noble, a friend of the king, and weighty in counsel; be a mediator of peace between us. Say to the king, 'We are losing our time here; it passes without bringing any profit to us, while there is plenty for us to do at home.' And why should the king lavish his strength upon these cowardly Egyptians, to whom he is trying to secure the riches of the country? Let him have back all the prisoners whom I hold in irons; let him raise the siege, and give me back my men who are in his hands, and I will go out of the country."

Hugh took the message, and gave the advice that the Saracen wished. A council was held, and the terms were agreed to. The gates were thrown open, provisions taken in, and besiegers and besieged mingled on those friendly terms which were now common in the East. Saladin went to the camp of Amaury, who received him as a friend, and the Vizier Shawer entered into the city, and began the administration of justice; that is to say, he hanged all those who were unlucky enough to be in power when Shírkoh entered the city, and who had surrendered a place they had no means whatever of holding. Examples such as these, common enough in the Middle Ages, might have been expected to bring civic distinctions into disrepute. Ambition, however, was probably stronger than terror.

All being finished, the king returned to Ascalon, not entirely covered with glory, but not without credit.

On his arrival he learned that a bride was waiting for him at Tyre, Maria, niece of the Greek Emperor, who had been wooed and won for him—the young lady's wishes were not probably much consulted in the matter—by the Archbishop of Cæsarea. He hastened to Tyre, and on the 29th of the month, nine days after his arrival at Ascalon, he was married in great state and ceremony. And now there was peace in Palestine for a brief space. The young Count of Nevers arrived in Jerusalem, with a numerous following, intending to offer his arms to the king, and dedicate his life to fighting the Mohammedans. But a sudden illness struck him down, and after languishing a long time, he died. A secret embassy was also sent to Amaury from Constantinople. The emperor had learned the feeble and enervated state of Egypt, and ignorant that Nûr-ed-dín, a greater than he, had his eyes upon the same country, sent to expose his own ambition to Amaury, and to propose terms of common action. The idea was not new to the long-sighted king, the most clear-headed of all the kings of Jerusalem. He had had plenty of opportunities, during his Egyptian campaign, of contrasting the riches of Cairo with the poverty of Jerusalem, the fertility of Egypt with the sterility of Palestine. Little as he cared about the Church, of which he was the sworn defender, it could not but occur to him to contrast Jerusalem with Mecca, and to consider that while Mecca was the Holy City, Baghdad and Cairo were the capitals of the sovereign caliphs. Why should not Cairo be to Jerusalem what Baghdad was to Mecca? Why should not he, the caliph of Christianity, sit in that gorgeous palace behind the gold-embroidered curtains, dressed in robes of purple and satin, with his guards, his life of indolence and ease, and—his seraglio? For the customs of the East had struck the imaginations of these descendants of the

Crusaders. They, too, longed for the shady gardens, the fountains, the sweet scent of roses—and the houris of the world with whom the happy Turks anticipated the joys of heaven. Many of them, in their castles far away in the country, imitated, so far as they were able, the customs of their enemies; notably young Jocelyn of Edessa. Some of them became renegades, and going over to the Saracens, got riches, and therefore luxury, at the point of the sword. All of them—except perhaps the Templars and Hospitallers, who might do so in secret—openly maintained friendly relations with the Mohammedans, and partook freely of their hospitality.

And now Amaury was guilty of an act of perfidy which brought about, or rather accelerated, the final fall of the Christian kingdom. Tormented by his own ambitious designs, and the thought of that rich Empire of Egypt, which seemed to wait for the first hand strong enough to seize it—without waiting for the Greek Emperor, perhaps, however, acting in secret concert with him—he declared that Shawer had been sending secret messages to Nûr-ed-dín, and had thereby infringed the treaty of alliance. For this reason, as he alleged, he proclaimed war against Egypt, and led his army against Pelusium. One voice only was raised against the enterprise. Cruel, ambitious, avaricious, and haughty as the Templars were, they were never capable of deliberately breaking their word. The Grand Master of the Order, Bertrand de Blanquefort, spoke loudly against the expedition. He, for one, would not allow his knights to join an army which set out to carry war into a kingdom friendly to their own, bound by acts of solemn treaty, which had committed no offence, which had continued loyal and true to its engagements. The Templars remained behind at Jerusalem. The Hospitallers went with Amaury and his host, one of the finest armies that the kingdom had ever produced. They began by taking Pelusium, after a ten days' march through the desert along a road which they knew well by this time. The resistance made by Pelusium was very short, lasting only three days, when the Christians took the place, and slaughtered, at first, every man, woman, and child who fell into their hands.

The Vizier, Shawer, was thrown, at first, into the wildest terror. In the disorganised state of his army there was absolutely nothing to prevent the Christians from marching directly upon Cairo, and gaining possession by a single assault of the whole realm of Egypt. All seemed lost, and Shawer was already preparing for flight, when it occurred to him to tempt the king, whose cupidity was notorious, by the offer of money.

Nullum numen abest, si sit prudentia.

Everything is preserved, if only forethought remains. Shawer sent his messengers. Amaury listened to them. At the same time, as a last resource, Shawer sent couriers in hot haste to Nûr-ed-dín, exposing the critical state of the kingdom. To keep the Christians from advancing, he kept his messengers backwards and forwards, offering, declining, renewing, increasing the advantages of his terms. Amaury was to have a quarter of a million, half a million, a million, two million pieces of gold, on condition that he would give him back his son and nephew, and quit the kingdom. All this time, the negotiations being entirely secret, the king was pretending to advance, but very slowly, and the Christians, not knowing the cause of the delay, were eager to be led. After eight or nine days of negotiations, which the sultan had occupied in getting into Cairo every fighting man upon whom he could reckon, the king moved his forces to a village five or six miles from Cairo, where he pitched his camp. Here messengers from Shawer met him, imploring him not to advance nearer the city, as he was engaged in collecting, with all possible speed and diligence, the sum of money which he had promised. Shawer had already got back his son and nephew, giving in return two grandchildren—children of tender age. Amaury was completely deceived. Lulled by the assurances of Shawer, dazzled by his own golden dreams, he saw himself, the successful violator of a solemn treaty, returning laden with a treasure of gold such as no king of the West could boast; with this he would bring knights from Europe; with this he would beat off the Saracens, conquer Damascus, reconquer Edessa and the strong places of the north; and having successfully used this mighty treasure, he would violate another solemn treaty, return to Egypt with a larger and more powerful army and make himself master of Cairo and all its wealth. There was plenty of time; he was not yet thirty; life was all before him, and many years of enjoyment.

But there came a rude awakening to the dream. Núr-ed-dín, hearing of the expedition of Amaury, and getting the messengers of Shawer, had for himself two courses open to him. He might take advantage of Amaury's absence, and pour all his troops together into Palestine, so as either to annihilate the kingdom of Jerusalem, or cripple it beyond power of recovery; or he might send Shírkoh again to Egypt, this time as the ally of Shawer, and with secret instructions as to the nature of the alliance. He preferred the latter course. Egypt was a prey that required courage and promptness; Palestine could wait; like an over-ripe pear, it was certain, sooner or later, to drop at his feet. Shírkoh arrived in Egypt. Shawer dropped the veil, and laughed at Amaury. The king, in an agony of rage and mortification, hastily broke up his camp and retired to Pelusium. Thence, seeing that there was nothing more to be done, he returned in disgrace and confusion to his own kingdom.

As for Shírkoh, he had no intention whatever of going home again without getting something substantial out of the expedition. He established his camp before Cairo, and encouraged Shawer to look on him as one of his best friends, inviting him to enter his camp at all times, and come without escort. And one day, when Shawer, relying on the friendliness of his ally, rode in accompanied only by two or three of his sons and friends, he was seized by the guards of Shírkoh and beheaded, without any resistance being possible. Shírkoh, meantime, was taking a walk on the banks of the Nile, so as to be able to say that he was innocent of the murder. Shawer's sons fled to the caliph. But the caliph could do nothing; the house of Shawer were all cut off, like the house of Saul; and the representative of the Fatemites was compelled to acknowledge the servant of his rival as his sultan and vizier, the real master of Egypt.

"Oh, blind cupidity of men!" cries William of Tyre; "all the treasures of Egypt were lying at our feet. . . . There was safety for those who travelled by sea; there was trade for those who wished to enrich themselves in Egypt; there was no enemy for us in the south; the Egyptians brought us their merchandize, and spent their gold in our country. And now all is changed; sad are the notes of our harps; the sea refuses us peaceful navigation; all the countries around us obey our enemies; every kingdom is armed for our ruin. And the avarice of one man has done this; his cupidity has covered over with clouds the clear bright sky which the goodness of the Lord had given us."

It was some comfort to the Christians to hear that Shírkoh, a year after his accession to power, was gone out of the world. But a mightier than Shírkoh came after him, his nephew, Saladin.

And now, indeed, the situation of the Christian kingdom was precarious. With the exception of Tyre and the towns to the north, the kingdom consisted of nothing but Palestine between Tiberias on the north and Ascalon on the south. All the outlying forts, or nearly all, were already gone. The prestige of Amaury, which had been raised by his first successful expedition, was entirely gone by the ill-success of the second. Moreover, Egypt, which had been a friendly power, was now hostile. By means of a fleet from Egypt the country might be menaced from the sea as well as from the land; reinforcements, supplies, might be cut off; pilgrims intercepted. Under these circumstances, it was resolved to send letters at once to all the Western kings and princes, calling for assistance. The patriarch, the Archbishop of Cæsarea, and the Bishop of Acre were selected to be the bearers of these. The deputies, armed with these despatches, embarked in a single ship. A frightful storm overtook them; the oars were broken; the masts all went by the board; and on the third day, more dead than alive with sickness and fright, the unlucky ambassadors put back to port, and refused to venture themselves again upon the sea. The Archbishop of Tyre took their place, and went away, under better auspices, accompanied by the Bishop of Banias, who died in France. He was away for two years, but did not effect anything. Europe, in fact, was growing tired of pouring assistance into a country, which, like the sea, swallowed everything, gave nothing back, and still demanded more.

The Emperor of Constantinople, however, who was perfectly aware of the importance of keeping the Turks employed in fighting against Palestine, and knew well that, Jerusalem once gone, Asia Minor was at their mercy, and Constantinople would be the object of their ambitions, sent a fleet of a hundred and fifty galleys of war, with sixty large transports, and ten or twelve *dromons*, filled with all sorts of instruments of war. It would have been better for King Amaury had this gift, a white elephant, which had to be fed, never been sent. As it was come, however, he proceeded to make use of it by invading Egypt a third time. And this time they determined on besieging Damietta, and Amaury led his army from Ascalon, on the 10th October, 1169, on the most useless expedition that he had yet undertaken.

A bar, formed by an iron chain, ran across the river, which prevented the Christian fleet from advancing to the town; they therefore took up their station outside. The troops on land formed the siege in regular form, and, if Amaury had given the word, the town might have been carried by assault ; but he let the moment pass, and reinforcements of Turks poured into the place by thousands. Towers were constructed and sorties made by the besieged, but no advantage on either side was gained. But now began the misfortunes of the Christians. The Greeks had no provisions. They subsisted for a while by eating that portion of the palm which is cut from the top of the trunk at the branching out of the leaves, no bad food provided enough can be obtained, the worst of it being that each palm contains no more than enough for a single salad (as the palmiste is now used), and costs the life of a tree. And when the forest of palms was cut down round Damietta there was no more food of any kind to be had, while the soldiers of Amaury were unable to help their allies, having to consider the probability of being in a few days without food themselves. Then heavy rains fell and swamped the tents, and even a broad ditch round each one did not wholly keep out the water. The Greek fleet, too, was nearly destroyed by a fire boat, which was sent down the river. It set fire to six of the galleys, and would have destroyed all the rest but for the king himself, who mounted his horse, half dressed, and rode down to the bank shouting to the sailors. The assaults were continued, but there was no longer any heart in the Christian camp, and Amaury signed a treaty of peace and withdrew his troops to Ascalon, which he reached on the 21st of December, having been engaged for two months in convincing the Saracens of his feebleness even when backed by the Greeks. The fleet was overtaken by a storm, most of the ships were lost, and of all the magnificent array of galleys that sailed from Constantinople in the spring, but very few remained after the campaign of Damietta. The failure of the expedition was probably due to the fact that the Greek Emperor, who had promised a large sum of money sufficient for the maintenance of the army, allowed it to go without any. And the Greek generals, the first to find themselves in want of provisions, not only had no money to buy them, but could find no one to lend them money.

The following year was marked by disasters of quite another kind. A great earthquake, or rather a succession of earthquakes, passed through Palestine, and by its violence and the frequency of its attacks, for it returned again and again during a space of three or four months, filled all men's hearts with fear; hundreds perished in the ruin of their houses; grief and consternation spread everywhere. Antioch, with nearly its whole population, was entirely destroyed, even its strong walls and towers being all thrown down; Laodicea, Emesa, Aleppo, and Hamath shared the fate of Antioch. Tripoli presented the appearance of a heap of stones, and Tyre, more fortunate than the rest, had yet some of its towers overthrown. Amid these disasters there was no thought of war, and for some months, at least, there was peace. But in December, news came that Saladin was invading Christian territory in the south. Amaury hastened to Ascalon, and called all his chivalry together. They assembled at Gaza, and he found that he could muster two hundred and fifty knights and two thousand foot. Saladin was besieging the fort of Daroum, which the king had himself built. But leaving Daroum, Saladin advanced to Gaza. The Christian army fought their way through to the citadel, and Saladin, after pillaging the city, retired with his forces. Probably his object was to accustom his men by small successes with overwhelming forces for the greater efforts he intended to make when the prestige of the Christians should have sunk lower, and the dread which the Saracens still felt for the strong-armed knights in steel should have wholly, or in great measure, passed away.

Early in the following year Amaury called a council of his barons to deliberate on the precarious state of the kingdom. Every day the number of the enemy increased, every day their own resources diminished. There was, of course, but one way to meet the dangers which menaced them, the only way which the kingdom had ever known, the arrival of aid from Europe. It was resolved to send ambassadors with the most urgent letters to all the powers, and to Constantinople a special ambassador begging for instant aid. Who was to go? The king, after a short parley with his advisers, declared that he would go himself. The barons cried out, on hearing this announcement, that they could not be deprived of their king, that the realm would fall to pieces without him—to all appearance seriously alarmed at the prospect of being left alone, or else every man hoping himself to be appointed as ambassador. But Amaury terminated the discussion in a manner characteristic of himself. "Let the Lord," he said, "defend His own kingdom. As for me, I am going." It is tolerably clear that the sovereign who could permit himself to have doubts on the subject of a future world, might well have doubts as to whether a kingdom, so harassed as his own, so devoured by greed, selfishness, and ambition, so corrupted by lust and licence, was really the kingdom of the Lord. If it was, of course the Lord would look after His own; if not, why then Amaury's hands were well washed of the responsibility. He went to Constantinople, where he was received with every demonstration of friendship, and William of Tyre exhausts himself in describing the favour shown to him. One thing is noticeable, that the splendour of the Greek emperor rivalled that of the caliph. On the occasion of the first interview of Amaury with the emperor, there were suspended before the hall of audience curtains of precious stuff and rich embroidery, exactly like what we are told of the Caliph of Cairo, and as soon as the king arrived the curtains were withdrawn and the emperor disclosed sitting on a throne of gold, and dressed in the Imperial robes. Great fêtes were given to celebrate the arrival of Amaury and his train; all the sacred relics, including the wood of the Cross, the nails, the lance—was this the lance found by Peter at Antioch, or another?—the sponge, the reed, the crown of thorns, the sacred shroud and the sandals, were shown to the Latins; games and spectacles were invented for their amusement, including choruses of young girls and theatrical displays, in which, says the Archbishop of Tyre, careful lest the king's example should be taken as a precedent among his own flock, the greatest propriety was observed; and at last, treaties having been signed and promises made, Amaury departed, laden with valuable presents of gold and other valuables. Alas! it was not gold that he wanted, but stout hearts and strong hands, and of these he brought back none but his own.

He returned for more fighting and more disappointment. Nûr-ed-dín was reported near Banias with an army, and Amaury had to fix his camp in Galilee to watch his movements. The object of the sultan, however, seems to have been, like that of Saladin, to accustom his men to face the Christians, and not yet to force on a decided engagement.

The Archbishop of Tyre at this time returned from his embassy. Nothing had been effected. The princes of the West would promise no help, would give no help. He brought with him Stephen, son of Count Thibaut of Blois, whom the king intended to make his son-in-law. But Stephen, after coming to Jerusalem, declined the king's offer, led a wild and licentious life for a few months, to the general scandal, and then returned to Europe.

Then followed three years of war. Toros, the Armenian prince, and the firm ally of the Christians, died, and was succeeded by his nephew, Thomas. His brother, Melier, wishing to obtain the dominion for himself, repaired to Nûr-ed-dín, obtained his help on certain conditions, and expelled his nephew, with all the Latin Christians who were in Armenia and Cilicia. The prince of Antioch declared war against him, and the king marched his army north. But while he was on the road, news came that Nûr-ed-dín was attacking Kerak in Moab. Before Amaury could get to Jerusalem, whither he hastened on receipt of this news, the Saracens were defeated, and the siege raised by Humphrey the Constable.

Then came Saladin with a large force. It was decided that the Christian army was not strong enough to meet him, and the troops were marched, on pretence of seeking the Saracens, to Ascalon, where they remained, while Saladin went round the south of the Dead Sea and laid siege to the fortress of Montreal. This proved too strong for him, and he returned to Egypt. The year after he made another unsuccessful attempt in Moab, in which, however, he burned the vineyards and ravaged the country, the king not being strong enough to follow him. And now follows the most extraordinary and inexplicable story in the whole history of Jerusalem. We give it in the words of the historian himself (an account of the sect of Assassins will be found p. 322).

"During forty years the Assassins followed the faith of the Saracens, conforming to their traditions with a zeal so great that, compared with them, all other people would be esteemed prevaricators, they alone exactly fulfilling the law. At this time they had for chief a man endowed with eloquence, ability, and enthusiasm. Forgetting all the customs of his predecessors, he was the first who had in his possession the books of the Gospels and the Apostolic code: he studied them incessantly and with much zeal, and succeeded at length, by dint of labour, in learning the history of the miracles and precepts of Christ, as well as the doctrine of the Apostles.

"Comparing this sweet and fair teaching of Christ with that of the miserable seducer, Mohammed, he came in time to reject with scorn all that he had been taught from the cradle, and to hold in abomination the doctrines of him who had led the Arabs astray. He instructed his people in the same manner, ceased the practices of a superstitious worship, removed the interdiction from wine and pork, abolished the Mohammedan fasts, and overthrew the oratories. He then sent a messenger, one Boaldel, to King Amaury with the following offer. If the Templars, who possessed strong places in his neighbourhood, would remit an annual tribute of two thousand pieces of gold which they exacted from the people round their castles, he and his would be converted to the faith of Christ, and would all receive baptism.

"The king received the ambassador with a lively joy. He went so far, in his readiness to close with the offer, as to hold himself prepared to indemnify the Templars for the sum which they would lose. And after keeping the messenger a long time in order to conclude an arrangement with him, he sent him back to his master, with a guide to watch over the security of his person. They had already passed the city of Tripoli, and were on the point of entering into the country of the Assassins, when suddenly certain men, brethren of the Temple, drawing their swords and rushing upon the traveller, who advanced without fear and under the protection of the king, massacred the messenger of the sheikh."

Thus was lost the most splendid opportunity that ever Christian king of Jerusalem had. There cannot be the least doubt that, had the messenger arrived home in safety, a large army of men devoted to any cause which their chief embraced, sworn to obey or to die, trained in close discipline, fanatic to the last degree, would have been transferred to the Christian camp. Moreover, there would have been a precedent which history lacks of the conversion of a whole tribe or nation from Islamism to Christianity. What sort of religion the sheikh of the Assassins contemplated is difficult to tell. But he could not have been a worse Christian than the defenders of Palestine. And then comes the question, why did the Templars kill the messenger? what reason had they for thwarting the sheikh and the king? why, considering the indemnity they were to receive, should they wish to prevent the arrangement? And what could have been their motive for preventing the conversion of the Assassins to their own religion? One answer only occurs to us. It has always seemed to us that the Templars, towards the close of the Christian rule in Palestine, were actuated by a deep and firmly rooted ambition. They proposed, seeing the weakness of the kingdom, and the worthlessness of its barons, to acquire for themselves castle after castle, strong place after strong place, till, when King Amaury was dead, and his son, already known to be tainted with leprosy, was on the throne, the kingdom would drop quietly into their own hands, the only strong hands left in the country. With this end in view they were acquiring forts in Cilicia and Armenia, all over Phœnicia, and across the Jordan. Palestine proper was dotted with their manors and fiefs. Nor was this all. In Europe their broad lands increased every day, and their income, even now, one hundred and fifty years before their dissolution, was enormous. There can be no doubt that the Templars, had they chosen to concentrate their forces, and to get together all the knights they could muster, might have deferred for long, and perhaps altogether, the final fall of the kingdom. But they did not perceive the immediate danger, and while the Mohammedan forces were uniting and concentrating, they probably still believed them to be divided and dissentient.

On no other ground than the hypothesis of this ambition

can we explain the singular murder of this ambassador. *The Templars did not wish to see the king's hands strengthened.*

As this strange association, the Order of Assassins, played a most important part in the political events of the period of which we are speaking, a more detailed account of their origin and tenets may not be out of place here.

The national aversion of the Persians from the religion of their Mohammedan conquerors gave rise to a number of secret sects and societies having for their object the subversion of Islam, and in the hatred which already existed between the two great divisions of that creed, the Sunnís and Shiahs, the leaders and originators of these sects found a ready means of securing proselytes and adherents. In the year 815, a chief named Babek founded a new religious order and waged an open war against the Caliphs, by whom he was, however, defeated and exterminated. But while his partisans fell beneath the sword of the executioner there was living at Ahwas, in the south of Persia, a certain 'Abdallah, grandson of Daisán the dualist, who had inherited the hatred which his grandfather had sworn against the faith and power of the Arabs. Warned by the fate of Babek's followers, he determined to undermine insidiously what he could not with safety openly attack. He accordingly formed a society into which proselytes were only admitted upon proof, and after being sworn to the profoundest secrecy. The initiation consisted of seven degrees, in the last of which he taught—that all religions were mere chimeras and human actions indifferent. His missionaries spread over the whole of the East, and carried their peculiar doctrines into Syria, where one of them, named Ahmed ibn Eshkâas el Carmatí, founded the sect of Carmathians, whose history has been already traced. 'Obeid allah el Mehdí, the founder of the Fatemite dynasty, was a follower of El Carmatí, and from the moment when El Mehdí made himself master of Egypt the Carmathian tenets prevailed in that country, under the name of the Ismáilíyeh. They were propagated by official agents, of whom the chief was named *dái ed doát*, "missionary of missionaries," and *cádhí el codhát*, " judge of judges." In the year 1004, they held public assemblies in Cairo under the presidency of the last-mentioned officer. These meetings were called *mejális el hikmeh*, or "scientific meetings," and were devoted to instructing those present in the mathematical and other sciences; but such as were considered worthy, were admitted to a more intimate participation in their mysteries, and were taught the secret doctrines of the sect, consisting of a strange *mélange* of Persian and Gnostic ideas.

We have already seen how this institution was made to subserve the interests and pander to the mad fanaticism of El Hákem bi amri 'llah, and indirectly gave birth to the powerful sect of the Druzes.

During the last half of the eleventh century one of the Ismaelite missionaries, Hassan ibn Subáh el Homáirí, became the founder of the new sect of the Ismaelites of the East, or Assassins. Hassan was born in Khorassan; in his youth he contracted an intimate friendship with Nizám el Mulk and 'Omar el Kheiyám, and the three associates took a solemn oath mutually to advance each other's prospects in after life. 'Omar el Kheiyám became celebrated as an astronomer and poet;[*] and Nizám el Mulk attained to the office of grand vizier, under the Seljukian Sultán Melik sháh. Hassán es Subah sought and obtained the assistance of his former companion, and was promoted to high office in the court. Prompted, however, by ambition, he endeavoured to supplant his benefactor, but Nizám el Mulk discovered and counteracted his designs, and Hassan was driven in disgrace from the king's presence. Not long afterwards he founded the order of Assassins, and Melik

---

[*] His 'Quatrains,' stanzas of exquisite polish, but breathing the most sensual and atheistic philosophy, have been recently published by M. Nicholas, Paris, 1867.

Sháh and his vizier were among the first of his victims. In 1090, he made himself master of the fortress of Alamút, built on the summit of a lofty mountain, with steep escarpments, a little distance from Casbín in the Persian province of 'Irák. This castle he fortified and supplied with water, partly from artificial and partly from natural springs, and, by compelling the inhabitants to cultivate the surrounding land and store the produce in the subterranean granaries of the castle, he rendered it capable of sustaining a protracted siege.

Although the secret doctrines of the Ismaelites were taught in nine degrees, there were but two ranks in the order, namely the *refik*, or "companion," and *dáï*, or "missionary." Hassan instituted a third class, that of the *fedawí*, or "devoted one." For them the secrets of the order were always covered with an impenetrable veil, and they were but the blind instruments of vengeance or aggression in the hands of their superior. They composed the body-guard of the grand master, and were never for a single moment without their daggers, so as to be ever ready to perpetrate murders at his command.

Marco Polo gives us a substantial, and doubtless exact, account of the ceremonies which took place upon the initiation of a *fedawí* into the order. Within the precincts of their impregnable fortresses were gardens furnished with all that could delight the eye or appeal to the sensual taste of the voluptuary. Here the neophyte was led, delicious meats and wine of exquisite flavour were set before him, girls as beautiful as the houris of the prophet's paradise ministered to his pleasures, enchanting music ravished his ears, his every wish was gratified almost before it was uttered, and, intoxicated with delight, he fancied that he had really entered upon the joys of the blessed. An intoxicating drug had in the meanwhile been mixed with the wine, and, by producing a sort of delirium, for a time enhanced his enjoyment, but as the satiety and languor consequent upon excess crept over him he fell back stupefied and insensible, in which state he was carried out of the place. On awaking he found himself beside the grand master, who told him that all the joys he had experienced were but a foretaste of what was destined for those who yielded implicit obedience to his commands. The alternative for those who doubted or hesitated was instant death.

The youth thus "devoted" to the service of the order was carefully trained in all the arts of deception and disguise; he was taught to speak various languages, and to assume a variety of dresses and characters; and, loosed from all trammels of conscience or of creed, he went forth, prepared to plunge his dagger into the breast of his dearest friend, and even into his own, at his superior's command. Such an association could not but prove a formidable political agent in those troublous times, and the sovereigns of the East feared the secret dagger of the order more than the armies of their foes, and rendered to the grand master whatever tribute and homage he chose to demand. Towards the middle of the twelfth century the power of the Assassins had extended itself from Khorassan to the mountains of Syria, from the Mediterranean to the Caspian. All trembled before it, and submitted more or less to its will. Hassan died in 1124, after having chosen for his successor Kia Buzur-gumíd, one of the most strenuous of his *daïs*; and the dignity of grand master became ultimately hereditary in his family. The order of Assassins continued in its integrity until 1254, when Manjou Khan, grandson of the celebrated Jenghíz Khan, put an end to its existence. As for the association of the Ismaelites in Cairo, the *Mejális el Hikmeh*, or scientific lodges, they were finally suppressed by Saladin in the year 1171 A.D.

The Grand Master of the Assassins was called simply *sheikh*, "elder," or "chief;" and from his rocky fortresses of Alamút and Maziatt he was known as Sheikh el Jebel,

"Sheikh of the Mountain." The Crusaders, misinterpreting the title, always spoke of him as the "Old Man of the Mountain."

There is little doubt but that the order of Knights Templars, who figure so largely in the history of the Crusades, were a society closely akin to the Assassins. The different grades of rank amongst them correspond exactly with the several degrees of the Ismaelite fraternity. Their dress, white with a red cross, symbolizing innocence and blood, is almost identical with the garb of the Fedawís, while the irreligious practices and secret murders, which are clearly proved against them, all tend to establish the conviction that they were rather Knights of the Dagger than of the Cross.

But to return to our history.

Amaury, the poor harassed king, all whose projects failed, and none of them through his own fault, fell into a fit of rage which nearly killed him, when he heard the news of the murder of the ambassadors of the "Old Man of the Mountain." What was to be done? what revenge could be taken for a mischief which was irremediable? He called his barons, and poured the whole story into their indignant ears. They chose two of their own body, and sent them to Odo de St. Amand, Grand Master of the Templars, to demand satisfaction in the name of the king and the realm for a crime so extravagant. One Walter du Mesnil was suspected, a stupid man, likely to do whatever others told him without inquiry or doubt. And here appears the pride of the Templars. Odo coldly sent back word that he had "imposed a penance" on the criminal, and that he should send him to the pope. The king went to Sidon himself, seized the suspected man by force, and threw him into prison, in spite of the protestations and fury of Odo. Then followed protest, appeal, and protest again. Amaury succeeded in making the sheikh himself believe in his own innocence, but the sheikh's enthusiasm for the religion of Christ was quenched, and the opportunity gone by.

The significance of Odo's reply to Amaury lies in his promise to send the criminal to the pope. Just as the Templars, from the very beginning, were free from any episcopal jurisdiction, and owned no authority in ecclesiastical matters in other than the pope himself, so they now arrogated to themselves freedom in things temporal. They would have no king but their grand master, no bishop but the pope; they would have no interference in the government of their own castles and places from any sovereign at all. And this seems the main reason—their assumption of independence—why their destruction was determined on by King Philip of France.

In the year 1173 * died Nûr-ed-dín, the greatest man of Saracen story, next to Saladin.

Directly Amaury heard of his death, he laid siege to Banias—it will be remembered how Nûr-ed-dín refused to take advantage of Baldwin's death—but raised the siege after a fortnight in consequence of entreaties and the offer of large sums of money from Nûr-ed-dín's widow. On his return he complained of indisposition. This became worse, and a violent dysentery set in. They carried him to Jerusalem, where he died, after all the doctors, Greek, Syrian, and Latin, had been called in successively. He was then in his thirty-eighth year. One feels pity for Amaury, more than for any other of the Kings of Jerusalem. He was, at the same time, so long-headed and so unlucky; so capable, yet so unsuccessful; so patient under all his disasters; so active in spite of his corpulence; so careful of the kingdom, yet so unpopular; so harassed with doubts, yet so loyal to his oaths; and so hopeful in spite of all his disappointments, that one cannot help admiring and sympathising with him. He committed the

* According to William of Tyre. Others place his death a year later.

most gross act of perjury in invading Egypt on pretence of Shawer's disloyalty. But he was punished for it by the destruction of the fairest dream of conquest that ever man had.

For one thing the present writers must, at least, be thankful to him. He it was who instigated William of Tyre to write that admirable history from which a large part of these pages are taken.

In 1163 the city of Jerusalem was visited by the Jewish traveller Benjamin of Tudela. He tells the following curious story concerning the tombs of the kings. "On Mount Sion are the sepulchres of the house of David, and those of the kings who reigned after him. In consequence of the following circumstance, however, this place is at present hardly to be recognised. Fifteen years ago, one of the walls of the place of worship on Mount Sion fell down, and the patriarch commanded the priest to repair it. He ordered stones to be taken from the original wall of Sion for that purpose, and twenty workmen were hired at stated wages, who broke stones from the very foundation of the walls of Sion. Two of these labourers, who were intimate friends, upon a certain day treated one another. and repaired to their work after their friendly meal. The overseer accused them of dilatoriness, but they answered that they would still perform their day's work, and would employ thereupon the time while their fellow-labourers were at meals. They then continued to break out stones, until, happening to meet with one which formed the mouth of a cavern, they agreed to enter it in search of treasure, and they proceeded until they reached a large hall, supported by pillars of marble, encrusted with gold and silver. and before which stood a table, with a golden sceptre and crown. This was the sepulchre of David, king of Israel, to the left of which they saw that of Solomon in a similar state, and so on the sepulchres of all the kings of Juda, who were buried there. They further saw chests locked up, the contents of which nobody knew, and were on the point of entering the hall, when a blast of wind like a storm issued forth from the mouth of the cavern so strong that it threw them down almost lifeless on the ground. There they lay until evening, when another wind rushed forth, from which they heard a voice like that of a man calling aloud, 'Get up, and go forth from this place.' The men rushed out full of fear, and proceeded to the patriarch to report what had happened to them. This ecclesiastic summoned into his presence R. Abraham el Constantini, a pious ascetic, one of the mourners of the downfall of Jerusalem, and caused the two labourers to repeat what they had previously reported. R. Abraham thereupon informed the patriarch that they had discovered the sepulchres of the house of David and of the kings of Juda. The following morning the labourers were sent for again, but they were found stretched on their beds and still full of fear; they declared that they would not attempt to go again to the cave, as it was not God's will to discover it to any one. The patriarch ordered the place to be walled up, so as to hide it effectually from every one unto the present day. The above-mentioned R. Abraham told me all this."

To enable the reader better to understand what has gone before, it will be as well to review the position of the Turks in Syria during this and the immediately preceding reigns.

By the taking of Jerusalem, and the flight of its Egyptian governor, El Afdhal, the kingdom of Syria was lost for ever to the Fatemite Caliphs. They yet retained possession of Egypt, but the remaining princes of the house were mere tools in the hands of designing ministers, and gave themselves up to luxurious ease in their palaces at Cairo. Nor were their opponents, the 'Abbassides, in much better case, but lingered idly on in Baghdad, wielding the shadow of their former power, while rival vassals fought and struggled for the substance.

The Seljukian sultans, after lording it over their imperial masters, had shared the same fate; and, having yielded themselves up to the enticements of luxury and wealth, were in turn tyrannized over by their more vigorous Turkish slaves the Atabeks. The founder of this family, a favourite slave of Melik Sháh, had been promoted to the governorship of Aleppo, but perished in the civil disorders consequent on the death of the sultan and the final division of the Seljukian kingdom. His son Zanghí did good service against the Franks at Antioch, and was rewarded by the caliph with the sovereignty of Aleppo and Mosul. His career was one of uninterrupted success, and, in a comparatively short space of time, he had taken Edessa, and wrested from the Franks their possessions beyond the Euphrates. His son Núr-ed-dín completed the work which his father had begun; he once more raised the prestige of the Mohammedan name, and added the kingdom of Damascus to that of Aleppo and Edessa, which he had inherited. Christian and Mohammedan authors alike testify to the uprightness and integrity of his character, to his impartial justice, and to the austere simplicity of his manners. He rigorously proscribed the use of wine, he wore neither gold nor silk, and on one occasion when his favourite wife requested the indulgence of some feminine fancy, he bestowed upon her "three shops in the city of Hums," alleging that he had no other private property, and that he dared not alienate the public funds, which he considered as a sacred trust. He is usually designated by Moslem writers by the title of Shehíd the Martyr, not because he fell fighting for the faith, but because his life was spent in one continuous series of holy works.

The Frank occupation of Syria and the Holy Land had spread dismay throughout the whole of Islam; in their distress the followers of the prophet turned to Damascus, and saw in the rising greatness of its sovereign a fresh hope of retrieving their fortunes. Nûr-ed-dín did indeed become the instrument of the final overthrow and expulsion of the Christians; but a slight digression is necessary to explain the circumstances which led to his introduction upon the scene.

Dargham and Shawer, rival aspirants to the dignity of prime minister to El "Adhid le dín Allah, last of the Fatemite caliphs of Egypt, had, by their struggles for power, involved that country in civil war. Shawer, finding himself unable to cope with his more powerful foe, applied for assistance to Nûr-ed-dín, who sent Esed-ed-dín Shírkóh, governor of Edessa, with a large army into Egypt. Dargham was defeated and slain, and the victorious Shírkóh claimed for his master Nûr-ed-dín the reward which Shawer himself had proposed, namely, a third of the revenues of the country; and, on payment being delayed, proceeded to occupy Bilbeis, the capital of the eastern province, as security. Shawar, as perfidious as he was ambitious, invited Amaury, King of Jerusalem, to aid him in ejecting his creditor. Shírkóh was obliged to relinquish Bilbeis; but, having received reinforcements from Damascus, he speedily returned, marched upon Cairo, and defeated the troops of the Fatemite caliph, and made himself master of Upper Egypt. His nephew Yusuf had been, in the meanwhile, sent against Alexandria, which place he captured, and gallantly defended for more than three months, against the combined forces of the Egyptians and Crusaders. At last, both the Christian and Damascene troops consented to evacuate Egypt, on consideration of receiving each a large sum annually out of the revenues; and articles of peace were solemnly drawn up, and ratified by all the contending parties; the Crusaders were, moreover, allowed to maintain a garrison at Cairo, ostensibly for the purpose of protecting the Egyptian government from aggression on the part of Nûr-ed-dín. Fortunate would it have been for the Christian kingdom of Jerusalem had Amaury held to his agreement; but the favourable terms which had been accorded him inspired him with an undue confidence in his own strength, and, blind alike to his interests and his honour, he determined upon a fresh invasion. Accordingly, in the latter end of the year 1168, he led an army into Egypt, took possession of Bilbeis, and marched upon Cairo. The greatest consternation prevailed in the capital at the treacherous conduct of the Christian monarch, and the savage cruelty of his troops. Cairo was hastily surrounded with a wall and fortifications, and the old city was set on fire at the approach of the invaders, the conflagration raging for fifty-four days. In this extremity the Egyptian caliph piteously besought Nûr-ed-dín to lend him his aid; and, in order still further to excite his compassion, and depict the miserable plight to which they were reduced, and the danger to which they were exposed from the unbridled licentiousness of the invaders, El "Adhid enclosed locks of his women's hair in the letter which contained his appeal. Shawer, in the meantime, endeavoured to avert the immediate calamity by making terms with Amaury, and the latter, dreading the arrival of the Damascene reinforcements, consented to raise the siege on receiving an indemnity of a million *dinárs*; a hundred thousand were paid down in ready money, and the Crusaders retired, in order to give the vizier time to collect the remainder. Nûr-ed-dín, on receipt of El "Adhid's letter, at once despatched Shírkóh to the relief of Cairo, with an army of eight thousand men, six thousand of whom were Syrians, and the remainder Turks, and a sum of two hundred thousand *dinárs*, as well as a large supply of clothes, arms, horses, and provisions. Shírkóh requested his nephew Yusuf Saláh-ed-dín (Saladin) to accompany him upon this expedition; but the latter, remembering the difficulties and dangers he had experienced at Alexandria, begged to be excused, and was only induced to accept a commission by an exercise of authority on the part of the sultan Núr-ed-dín. El ″Adhid met Shírkóh on his arrival with every mark of respect and gratitude, and conferred upon him a magnificent robe of honour. The vizier Shawer was also a frequent visitor to the Damascene general's tent; and assured the latter that although appearances had been against him, he had not willingly broken faith with him, and promised that the former agreement to pay Núr-ed-dín a third of the revenue should now be complied with. At the same time he was plotting how he might best dispose of so troublesome a visitor; and, having determined upon his assassination, invited Shírkóh, his nephew, and the rest of his staff, to a banquet, at which he hoped to execute his treacherous project. Saladin, however, received intelligence of the conspiracy, and prevented his uncle from accepting the fatal invitation. Shawer, furious at being thus foiled sought the tent of Shírkóh, under pretence of a friendly visit, and would doubtless have murdered him had he not fortunately been at that moment on a visit to the tomb of the celebrated Mohammedan saint Es Shafíí.* Returning from his fruitless visit, Shawer was met by Saladin and his party, who threw him from his horse, and carried him to Shírkóh's camp. El ″Adhid, on hearing the news, sent to demand the head of his treacherous vizier, whom he justly regarded as the cause of all the troubles that had recently fallen upon Egypt. Shírkóh gladly acceded to the request, and was installed by the Fatimite caliph into the vacant post of prime minister, and received the honorary title of El Melik el Mansúr, "the Victorious King." and Emír el Jayúsh, "Commander-in-chief of the Forces." He did not,

---

* On page 204 we gave William of Tyre's version of this event; the Mohammedan authors from which the foregoing account is taken regard it in a somewhat different light.

however, live long to enjoy his newly-acquired dignity, but died within two months and four days after his appointment. He was succeeded by his nephew Saláh-ed-dín Yúsuf ibn Aiyúb (the Saladin of European historians), whose life and exploits we shall relate in a future chapter.

CHAPTER XIII.

KING BALDWIN THE LEPER. A.D. 1173—1186.

> "Would I were dead, if God's good will were so,
> For what is in this world but grief and woe?"
> *King Henry VI.*

THE only son of Amaury, by his first wife Agnes, daughter of the younger Jocelyn of Edessa, was placed, at the age of nine years, under the charge of William of Tyre. He was a studious bright boy, and at first raised the highest hopes of his future. But his tutor discovered by accident that he was afflicted with that dreadful and incurable disease which was beginning to be so prevalent among the Syrian Christians. In his boyish sports with the children of his own age, his tutor remarked that when the boys pinched each other in the arm, little Baldwin alone was able to bear the pain without any cry or apparent emotion. This awakened his suspicions, and he took the child to be examined by physicians. It was found that his right arm, of which he had appeared to have perfect command, was half paralysed. All sorts of fomentations and frictions were tried, but all proved fruitless, and it was soon apparent that the future king was a confirmed leper. Day by day the disease gained ground, seizing on his hands and feet, and gradually gaining hold of his whole body. He was handsome, too, and an accomplished horseman, passionately fond of reading history and hearing the stories of valiant knights, like his father and uncle. In person he exactly resembled his father, and, like him, he was troubled with an impediment of speech.

He was thirteen when his father died, and four days after that event he was crowned in the Church of the Sepulchre with all the ceremonies customary at this important event. The regency was at first confided to Milo de Plancy, in spite of the opposition made by Raymond, who pleaded vainly his relationship to the king, his long services, and the importance of his dignity as Count of Tripoli. Milo was a native of Champagne, and a distant cousin of King Amaury. He was popular, because he was prodigal of promises, and full of that *bravoure* which catches the eyes of the people. But he was arrogant, presumptuous, and full of ambition. Drawing upon himself the hatred of all the barons by his manifest contempt for them, he was set upon one night, by order of some unknown person, probably one of the barons, and murdered, after which Raymond succeeded as regent with no opposition. Raymond had spent nine years of his life in prison at Aleppo, and had employed the dreary years of his captivity in study, so that he was learned above the generality of laymen. He was a man of courage in action, of prudence, and of extreme sobriety in life. To strangers he was generous and affable: to his own people he was neither one nor the other.

An important change had meantime occurred in the fortunes of Saladin. The death of Nûr-ed-dín left his kingdom to a boy, named Malek-es-Saleh, who was received as his successor, while the Emir, Abu-Mokaddem, was appointed regent. But the new regent gave little satisfaction to the people, and a secret message was sent to Saladin urging him to come to Damascus and take the regency. He went, Abu-Mokaddem himself yielding to the storm, and inviting him to take the reins of office.

He very soon became master of the situation, and, marrying the widow of Nûr-ed-dín, he assumed the title of Sultan, and henceforward ruled the East. During the settlement of his affairs there was comparative peace for the kingdom, what little fighting went on being mostly in favour of the Christians. The Emperor of Constantinople, however, experienced, near Iconium, a defeat so disastrous that any help from that quarter was not to be looked for, and Manuel himself, heart-broken at the loss of his splendid army, and the capture and ill-treatment of his brother, never recovered his cheerfulness: the memory of his misfortune perpetually troubling him and depriving him of all repose and tranquillity of spirit.

In the third year of the king's reign arrived in Jerusalem William Longsword, son of the Marquis of Montferrand. He had been invited to marry Sybille, sister of the king, and a few weeks after his arrival the marriage was celebrated. The greatest hopes were entertained of this prince. He was strong, brave, and generous. He was of the noblest descent, his father having been maternal uncle to King Philip of France, and his mother being the sister of Conrad. He had grave faults, however: he could not keep any counsel, but was perpetually telling of his projects; he was passionate and irascible to the last degree, and he was addicted to intemperance in eating and drinking. This probably proved fatal to him, for he died three or four months after his marriage, leaving his wife pregnant.

This was another calamity to the kingdom, which was sorely in want of a man strong enough to organize a combined stand against the rising power of Saladin. Philip, Count of Flanders, who came to make an expiatory pilgrimage, was next received with hope, and the king offered him the command of all his forces; but Philip failed in the single enterprise he undertook, and returned home with little addition to his glory. While Raymond, the regent, was with Philip in the north, Saladin, who had returned to Egypt, led one of his periodical incursions into Palestine, and fell to ravaging and pillaging the south country. Baldwin, leper as he was, did not want courage. If he could not fight, he could at least go out with his men. He had with him Raymond, who had hastened to join him; Count Jocelyn, his uncle, son of Jocelyn the younger, and three hundred and seventy-five knights in all. It was judged prudent at first to retire to Ascalon, but the people growing so infuriated at the sight of the destruction of their property, the little Christian army went out to attack the mighty force of Saladin. It was the last of those wonderful battles where the Christians, frightfully overmatched, bore down their enemies by sheer bodily strength, and carried the day in spite of numbers. The historian puts down Saladin's army at twenty-six thousand, besides many thousands of light armed men. Of course, the number is exaggerated, but there can be no doubt of the paucity of the Christian army and the victory won by Baldwin. Saladin escaped with a hundred horsemen in all, mounted on a camel: his men were dispersed in all directions: heavy storms of rain and an intensity of cold, to which they were unaccustomed, fell upon them in the desert, and the Bedawín, learning their misfortunes, plundered and murdered them. But the Christians were too weak to follow up the victory by invading Egypt, and contented themselves with building a fort at the ford over the Jordan. They also took the opportunity of a little leisure to repair the walls of Jerusalem, which were falling down with age. And at this time died stout old Humphry, Constable of the kingdom, after a life spent in incessant conflicts. His death was a great loss to the kingdom, which could not now spare a single man. And after a grievous defeat near Banias, where Odo, the Grand Master of the Templars, was taken prisoner, the king concluded a treaty of peace with Saladin.

Baldwin's disease had now assumed its most violent form. He could use neither hand nor foot, he was half blind, and rapidly losing his eyesight altogether. But he clung to the crown, and learning that the Count of Tripoli was coming to Jerusalem with a large following, he feared that his intention was to depose him, and hastened to marry his sister Sybille, widow of William Longsword, to Guy of Lusignan. It was an unfortunate marriage, for Guy had no virtue of any kind. He was handsome and personally courageous, but quite unfit for the burden that this position threw upon him. And now everything went wrong. There was no longer any self-restraint, any concord, any noble aims among the Christian knights. The patriarch himself, Heraclius, led openly a life of flagrant immorality; the Count of Antioch, Bohemond, a degraded descendant of the great Bohemond, divorced his wife without any grounds, and married a woman of ill repute: Raymond of Tripoli quarrelled with the king; on all sides were drinking, dicing, vice, and self-indulgence. Nothing was more certain than that the fall of the kingdom was a matter of time only, and Saladin, taking advantage of the treaty, which was as useful to him as it was necessary to the Christians, was training his men for the final effort by which he was to win Jerusalem.

Renaud de Chatillon, the restless adventurer who had married Constance of Antioch, was the actual cause of the fall of the kingdom. His wife being dead, and her son become the Count of Antioch, he married again, this time the widow of Humphry the Constable. By his second marriage he became the seigneur of Kerak and other castles situated beyond the Jordan. He had with him a large number of Templars, and when the treaty with Saladin was concluded, he announced his intention of not being bound by it, and continued his predatory excursions. Saladin complained to Baldwin, but the hapless king was powerless. Then Saladin arrested eighteen hundred pilgrims, who had been wrecked on the shores of Egypt, and declared his intention of keeping them in irons until Renaud gave up his Mohammedan prisoners. Renaud and the Templars only laughed at the threats of Saladin, and went on as before. The treaty being thus openly broken, Saladin had no other course open but to recommence hostilities, but after ravaging Galilee and laying siege to Beyrout, the affairs of his own kingdom compelled him to retire, in order to make war with the Attabegs, masters of Mossoul.

Guy, meantime, too weak for the position he held, had not been able to prevent Saladin's ravages in Galilee, and when the sultan attacked the fortress of Kerak could not go out to the assistance of Renaud. Yielding to the pressure of his barons, the king deprived Guy of the regency, and associated his nephew, a child of five years old, with him on the throne, under the title of Baldwin the Fifth. Poor little Baldwin the Fifth died very soon after, however, and had very little enjoyment of his dignity. He was the son of William Longsword and Sybille. Baldwin then summoned Guy de Lusignan before him to answer for his many sins of omission. Guy refused to obey, and took refuge in Ascalon, of which he was count. The king, who was now quite blind, was carried to that city, and personally summoned him to surrender. The gates were closed. Baldwin, thinking they would not dare to refuse him admission, knocked at the gate with his own helpless hands. But no answer was given. Then the poor blind king, impotent in his rage, called Heaven to witness the outrage to his authority, and was carried back to Jerusalem, swearing to punish the audacity of Guy. All he could do was to deprive him of his dignities, and to hand the regency over to Raymond of Tripoli.

In the desolated state of the country, nothing could be thought of but, as usual, to send to Europe for help. The patriarch Heraclius, the Grand Master of the Temple, and the Grand Master of the Hospitallers, were sent on an urgent embassy to ask for help. They went first to Rome. The pope had been driven out of Rome and was now at Verona, trying to re-establish peace throughout the whole of Christendom. With him was Frederic, Emperor of Germany. They next went to France. Philip Augustus received them with every kind of distinction, but would promise no help. He had only recently mounted the throne, and his own affairs required care. Next, and as a last resource, they went to England. Henry II. was full of domestic trouble at the time. He had taken, he acknowledged, an oath to defend the kingdom of Jerusalem, but he could not go now, it was impossible; he would, however, help them with treasure. The patriarch lost his temper at this, the last of the repeated refusals. "You were sworn," he cried, "to take your army to the Holy Land. Ten years have passed without your doing anything to redeem your promise. You have deceived God: know you not what God reserves for those who refuse to serve him? I see," he went on, "that I am exciting your wrath; but you may treat me as you treated my brother, Thomas of Canterbury; it is all the same to me whether I die in Syria by the hand of infidels, or whether I am murdered by you, more cruel than any Saracen." Henry took no notice of these angry words, and declared his resolution not to abandon the kingdom, and allowed those of his subjects who wished to take the Cross. But the zeal for crusading had died out, and very few went to defend the Church of the Sepulchre.

As for the kingdom of Jerusalem, it was fast tottering to its fall. The country* was dotted over with castles and strongholds, the owners of which had learned, since the death of Amaury, to despise the authority of the king. Moreover, the pride and power of the Templars set up a sort of rival

---

* See Michaud, Vol. ii., p. 306.

authority. Every baron fought for his own land and for his own aggrandisement. There was no more thought of conquest and glory: they fought now for plunder only. When pilgrims arrived from the West they were made use of by the Syrian barons for their own purposes; and when they were strong enough to fight the Saracens, no treaty was sacred, no convention was kept. The cities, especially those of the sea-shore, were divided into nations, such as the Pisans, the Genoese, and the Venetians, all of whom contended with each other over their privileges, and often fought out their quarrels in the streets. The Templars and the Hospitallers bargained for their arms by demanding the cession of half a town, or a fort, in return for their services. They quarrelled with each other, with the Church, and with the king. And with the depravation of morals had come a total neglect and contempt of religion, with—of which there are a few traces—the birth of the spirit of infidelity. Men had begun to question and to compare. There were not wanting renegades to be found among the Mohammedan armies. Islam received its converts from the Christians, but it gave back none in return.

The Crusaders had embarked upon an enterprise which rested on religious enthusiasm. Religion was the salt of the kingdom which they founded. While this lasted—it lasted till the reign of Baldwin the Third—there was hope. When this died—it died in the reign of Amaury —the kingdom was lost. Every baron and every soldier was in a sense a special soldier of Christ, a kind of lay priest of the altar. He had ever before his eyes those sacred places at sight of which his fathers had wept aloud. But the handling of sacred things is profitable only so long as the heart is open to their influences. To the impure the most holy things are a mockery, the highest aims are a subject of derision. And just as a worthless priest is generally worse than a worthless layman, because he has deadened his conscience more, and religion, a familar thing, has no longer any power to move his soul, so the degenerate soldiers of Jerusalem were worse than their fellows, coarse, rude, and sensual though these might be, beyond the sea, because for them there was nothing left which was able to touch their hearts.

Our history of the Christian kingdom draws to a close. In the midst of these troubles, the miserable king, who had mercifully been deprived of his senses, for the disease, when it has devoured the fingers and toes, and eaten into the vigour and strength of a man, fastens mysteriously on his intellect, and devours that too, died, or rather ceased to breathe, and was buried with his fathers. We are not told what epitaph was chosen for him. Surely, of all men, on Baldwin's tomb might have been carved the word, "Miserrimus."

Little Baldwin the Fifth died a day after his uncle, poisoned, as was supposed, by his mother and Guy de Lusignan. It is possible. The women whom Baldwin the Second left behind him, his daughters Milicent, Alice, Hodierne, were bad themselves, and the mothers of worse daughters. Of Sybille we can say little, except that she was known to have had a guilty love for Guy before their marriage—the king was actually uncertain at one time whether to stone to death his sister's paramour, or to make him her husband!—that she was completely under his rule, and that she was ambitious, bold, and intriguing.

CHAPTER XIV.

KING GUY DE LUSIGNAN. A.D. 1186—1187.

> Heu ! voce flebili cogor enarrare
> Facinus quod accidit nuper ultra mare,
> Quando Saladino concessum est vastare
> Terram quam dignatus est Christus sic amare.
> *Contemporary Poem.*

WHEN the little King Baldwin had been buried,* Sybille went to the Patriarch, the Grand Master of the Templars, and the Grand Master of the Hospitallers, to ask their advice and assistance. The first two bade her be under no anxiety, because they would procure her coronation, the former out of love for her mother, the Lady Agnes, and the latter out of the great hatred he bore for Raymond of Tripolis. And they advised her to send at once for Renaud de Chatillon, as a man likely to be of great service to her. Unluckily for Renaud, he came. At the same time she was to send to the Count of Tripoli and the barons, summoning them to her coronation, because the crown had devolved upon her. These, however, refused to be present, and sent a formal protestation against the coronation. Heraclius and the Master of the Templars laughed at the protest, but the Master of the Hospitallers refused to attend the ceremony. The gates of the city were shut, and no one allowed to enter or go out. The

---

* The history of William of Tyre, from which most of the preceding account of the Christian kingdom has been taken, ends abruptly just before the death of Baldwin. This chapter is mainly taken from Bernard the Treasurer.

barons, who were at Nablous, sent a trustworthy messenger, disguised as a monk, to see what went on. Denied admittance at the gates, he went to the lazar house, which was close to the walls, and where he knew of a little postern. Here he was admitted, and, like a modern reporter, went to the church and took notes of the proceedings. The Queen elect was brought into the church by Renaud and the Master of the Templars. The patriarch asked the latter for his key—there were three—of the treasury, where were laid up the crowns. He gave it up. Next he asked the Master of the Hospitallers for his. He refused to give it up. Now, without the three keys, those in the hands of the grand master and that kept by the patriarch, the coronation could not proceed, for the simple reason that the crown and sceptre were not to be got at. The Master of the Hospitallers, when they pressed him, declared that he had hidden the key. They searched for it, but could not find it. Then they pressed him again, the coronation ceremony waiting all this time in the church, until, in a rage, he dashed his key down on the ground, and told them they might do as they pleased.

The patriarch brought out two crowns: one he placed on the altar, the other he placed on the head of Sybille. When she was crowned he said to her, "Lady, you are a woman, and it is fitting that you have with you a man, who may aid you to govern the realm. Take this crown, and bestow it upon one capable of ruling."

It must be mentioned that, previous to her coronation, Sybille, in the hope of conciliating the barons, had announced her intention of getting a divorce from her husband. In this hope she was deceived, for not one was present. There was therefore no occasion for further pretence. Taking the crown she called Guy de Lusignan, and said to him, "Sir, advance and receive this crown, for I know not how better to bestow it."

He knelt before her, she placed the crown upon his head, and so Guy de Lusignan became King of Jerusalem, the only incapable king the little kingdom had, the only worthless king. When his brother Geoffrey heard of the election, he remarked, "If they have made him a king, I suppose they would have made me a god had they known me."

When the spy got back to Nablous, and told what had happened, Baldwin of Ramleh offered to lay a wager that he would not be king for a year, a bet which he would have won, as the event proved.

"As for me," said Baldwin, "the country is lost, and I shall go, because I do not wish to share the shame and disgrace of having assisted in the ruin of our kingdom. And for you, my lords, do what you please."

"Sir Baldwin," cried Raymond, "have pity on Christianity and remain to help us. Here is Count Humphry with his wife Isabelle, also the daughter of King Amaury. Let us go to Jerusalem and crown them there. We shall have with us at least all the knights of St. John. And I have a truce with the Saracens, who will even help us if we want them."

It was decided to make Humphry King: but Humphry had no mind for a crown which brought with it so many anxieties and troubles as that of Jerusalem. In the dead of night he rode off to Queen Sybille; and when the barons came to crown him in the morning, they found to their great disgust that he was gone.

He went straight to his sister-in-law, and, being brought into her presence, saluted her as Queen. But she took no notice of him, because he had not been present at her coronation. "Whereupon Humphry began to scratch his head like a child that is ashamed of himself, and said, 'Dame! I could not. Why, they wanted to make me king in spite of myself. That is why I ran away!'"

Evidently a simple straightforward knight, this Humphry of Toron and of sound, rather than brilliant, parts.

"Since it is so," said the queen, "I have no longer any animosity towards you. But first do homage to the king."

Which Humphry did.

The barons, acting on the advice of Raymond, were not slow in coming to tender their allegiance, with the exception of Sir Baldwin of Ramleh, who only sent his little son, praying Guy to receive his homage, which the king refused to do. Thereupon Baldwin came himself, and went through the necessary forms, saying, "Sir Guy, I do you homage, but as a man who would rather not hold lands under you."

It was for his son's sake, for the knight would not remain any longer in the country, and went away, "to the great joy of the Saracens."

Raymond, meantime, was gone to Tiberias, where he waited to see what would happen. The first thing that happened was a succession of signs from heaven, manifestly importing disaster. As they happened on Mohammedan soil as well as Christian, it is presumed that the followers of Islam interpreted them in a contrary spirit. There were tempests and impetuous winds, hail as big as hens' eggs, earthquakes, great waves, and *rades de mer*, while fire ran across the heavens, "and you would have sworn that all the elements were wrathful, detesting the excesses and vices of man." It will be observed that even in portents there is a decadence in the Christian kingdom. Time was when knights in armour assailed cities in the heavens, and when great comets blazed in the east like swords hanging over a doomed country. We fall back now on hail and storm.

Raymond called in Saladin on learning that it was the king's intention to besiege Tiberias. Saladin was glad of an excuse, and sent his son in command of a small army— Bernard says of seven thousand.*

The Grand Master of the Templars went out to meet

* Others say five hundred, which is more probable.

them. He had in all one hundred and forty knights with whom to confront this host. The knights fought, as they always did, gallantly and bravely; so bravely that they perished almost to a man, only the Master himself and a very few escaping. One knight, Jacques de Maillé, a Templar, performed such prodigies of valour that after he had fallen, the Turks cut up his garments and divided them, in memory of so valiant a man. It was in May that this disaster happened, the result of internal dissension. "And in this month," says a chronicler, "when it is most fitting that roses should be gathered, the people of Nazareth went out to gather together the dead bodies of their valiant knights, and to give them burial."

The Master of the Templars had got hastily back to Nazareth, and sent out messengers in all directions that he had gotten a signal victory over the Turks, and that all who wanted booty must hasten to his standard. They all flocked to him, like vultures, at the mention of booty, and he led them to the field where the dead bodies of his knights lay, the flower of the two orders. It is the keenest sarcasm on the cowardice and meanness of the people that we read of.

"Pudet hæc opprobria nobis
Et dici potuisse et non potuisse refelli."

But after this misfortune, further quarrels between king and barons were useless, and Raymond hastened to make his submission. He met the king at the Castle of St. George, at Ramleh, where a reconciliation was effected, real and complete, so far as Raymond was concerned, half-hearted and suspicious on the part of the weak-minded king.

Raymond, whose advice was generally sound, recommended Guy to convoke all the forces at his disposition, and meet at the fountain of Sefúríyeh. He also advised that the wood of the Cross should be brought out by Heraclius, as the emergency was great. Heraclius, who was afraid and probably foresaw disaster, declined to come, alleging illness, but sent it by two of his bishops.

Meantime, the king, by permission of the Master of the Templars, had laid hands upon the treasure which Henry II. of England had sent year by year, since the death of Thomas-à-Becket, to be used when he should find time to accomplish his vow of a crusade. By means of this money Guy found himself, when Saladin sat down before Tiberias, at the head of the finest army which had marched under the banner of the Cross since Godfrey besieged Jerusalem. The Countess of Tripoli was in Tiberias, with her four sons, all knights. She wrote to Guy saying that unless assistance came she must surrender the place. Guy called a council and read the letter. Raymond was the first to advise.

"Sir," he said, "let them take Tiberias, and I will tell you why. The city is mine, and my wife is in it; if it is lost no one, therefore, will lose so much as I. But if the Saracens take it, they will occupy it, and will not come here after us, and then I shall get it back again whenever I please. Now I prefer to lose my city for a time than that the whole country should be lost, and between this place and Tiberias there is not a drop of water. We shall all die of thirst before we get there."

Thereupon, quoth the Master of the Templars, "Here is some of the hair of the wolf." But Raymond took no notice of this offensive remark. "If it is not exactly as I have said," he went on, "take my head and cut it off."

All agreed that the advice given was sound and just, except the Master of the Templars, who in his blind rage against Raymond could not agree that anything he said was right. And in the night he went to the king's tent, just as he was going to bed. "Do you believe," he said, "in the advice of Raymond? It was given for the sole purpose of bringing shame and disgrace upon us all. . . . Strike your tents, call to arms, and march at once."

The king who owed to this man his crown, and the money with which the army was raised, obeyed immediately, and to the grief and surprise of the barons, the order was given to break up the camp. And on this sad night, the 1st of July 1187, the Christian host marched in silence and sadness to its fate.

The Count of Tripoli led the first division; in the centre was the king with the Holy Cross, borne by the Bishops of Acre and Lydda; and the Templars, with Balian of Ibelin, brought up the rear. The whole army consisted of twelve hundred knights, a considerable body of light horse, and about twenty thousand foot. The words of Count Raymond proved exactly true: there was no water at all on the way. The Christians were harassed by the Turkish cavalry, by the heat of the day, by the clouds of dust, and by the burning of the grass under their feet, which was set fire to by the enemy as they marched along. They halted for the night, and the camp of the Saracens was so close to that of the Christians that "you could have seen a cat run from one to the other." It was a night of dreadful suffering for want of water, and when the morning dawned some of those who could bear their sufferings no longer went over to the camp of Saladin, and threw down their arms, begging for a drink of water. "Sir," said one of these deserters to Saladin, "fall on them—they cannot help themselves—they are all dead already." King Guy, in hopes of ending the sufferings of his men by victory, gave the signal for the battle to commence. It was lost as soon as begun. For men, who had not quenched their thirst for nearly four and twenty hours, had no 'last' in them. The knights, as usual, fought manfully, but even these soon gave way. All round them was an arid plain or arid rocks, while beneath their feet, and hardly a mile away, lay the calm and placid Lake of Galilee, mocking their thirst by the serenity of its aspect. The Holy Cross was lost in the midst of the fight, and when the news went through the army there was no longer any hope. Some tossed away their arms and sat down to be killed or to be taken prisoners; some threw themselves upon the swords of the Mohammedans. A little band of a hundred and fifty knights gathered round the royal standard and defended the king to the last. Raymond, with Balian of Ibelin, and a few more, cut their way through and escaped to Tyre; but at last all resistance ceased, and King Guy, his brother Geoffrey, with Renaud de Chatillon, the Grand Master of the Templars, and all the chivalry of Palestine that were not killed, were taken prisoners and brought before Saladin.*

As for the wood of the Holy Cross, some years after the battle of Tiberias had been fought and lost, a brother of the Temple came to Henry, Count of Champagne, and told him that, in order to save it from falling into the hands of the Saracens, he had himself buried it with his own hands, and that he knew where to look for it. He took with him certain men to help in digging, and they searched for three consecutive nights, but failed to find it. So, that for a time, there was an end of one mischievous imposture at least.

And now the highest ambition of Saladin was to be crowned with success. Of all the holy places of his religion, only one was more sacred than Jerusalem. It was destined for him to restore that sacred Dome of the Rock which Omar had founded to the purposes for which it was built, and to remove from the midst of the Mohammedan Empire that hornet's nest of Christians which, for nearly a hundred years, had checked their conquests, insulted their faith, and perpetually done them injury.

The gates of the cities of Palestine flew open at the approach of the conqueror. Tiberias yielded at once, and Saladin sent Raymond's wife to her husband. Raymond, however, was dying, and of a broken heart. Almost alone among the chiefs he had still some nobility left, and he

* See also Chapter xvi., page 380.

could not bear to survive the fall of the country, his country, and the end of so many high hopes and glorious achievements. Acre resisted two days, and then opened its gates. Nablous, Ramleh, Cæsarea, Jericho, Jaffa, Beyrout, had no knights left to make defence with, and perforce capitulated. Tyre, Tripoli, Ascalon, alone remained to the Christians. Saladin vainly attempted the first, and desisted from the siege for more important matters. But Ascalon was too necessary, in consequence of its communications with Egypt, to be passed over, and he laid siege to the place in due form. Guy was with him, in fetters. A breach was effected in the walls, and Guy was put forward to urge upon the inhabitants not to make a useless resistance. These sent deputies to the Sultan. "On these conditions only shall you enter Ascalon, except across our bodies. Give life to our wives and children, and restore the king to liberty. Else we will fight." Saladin granted the conditions. Guy was to be set at liberty within a year; the people of Ascalon were to leave the city freely and to carry with them all that they pleased.

And now, at length, came the turn of Jerusalem. Balian of Ibelin had obtained of Saladin a safe conduct to the city, in order to take out his wife and children, but on the sole condition that he was not to stay there more than one night. He promised, and went. He found the city defended by women and monks. A few pilgrims were there, and some fugitive soldiers who had escaped the slaughter of Tiberias. The people pressed round him with tears, cries, and lamentations, when he told them of his word given to Saladin. "Sir," said the patriarch, "I absolve you from your oath; know well that it would be a greater sin to keep it than to break it, for great shame would it be for you and for your heirs, if you were thus to leave the city in its hour of danger." Then Balian of Ibelin yielded, and sent to Saladin that he had been forced to break his word. Saladin by this time was used to the perjury of Christians. For some years the Mohammedans, simple in their faith, could not understand a religion which permitted the most solemn treaties to be broken whenever a priest could be prevailed on to give absolution for the perjury. But they were wiser now. Raymond and Jocelyn, Renaud and Amaury, had taught them the worth of a Christian's promise, the value of a Christian's oath. Still, in Balian's case there was much to be said. It was not in human nature to resist the pleadings of the women and the sight of all these helpless beings whose fate seemed placed in his hands.

There were only two knights in all the city. Balian knighted fifty sons of the bourgeois. There was no money, because Guy had taken it all Balian took off the silver from the Holy Sepulchre, and coined it into money for his soldiers. Every day all the men that he could spare rode out into the country and brought in provisions, of which they might have direful need, because the city was so full of women and children that the houses were crowded and the unfortunate creatures were lying about in the streets. Some sparks of courage lived yet among the defeated soldiers, and all swore to defend the city to the last. Balian, of course, knew perfectly well that the cause was hopeless, and only remained to make what terms he could for the people. But it was necessary to make at least some resistance for the sake of honour, barren honour though it might be.

Before the siege began, Saladin sent a message to the city to the effect that if they made any resistance he had sworn to enter it by assault only. Before this message, and after the taking of Ascalon, his offers there were those which nothing but the most extreme confidence in his own power would justify. "I know," he said, "that Jerusalem is the house of God: that is a part of my religion. I would not willingly assail the house of God, if I can get possession of it by treaty and friendship. I will give you thirty thousand byzants if you promise to give up this city. You shall be allowed five miles all round the city as your own ground to cultivate and use as you please, and I will cause such an abundance of provisions to be sent in that yours shall be the cheapest market in the world. You shall have a truce from now to Pentecost; if, after that time, you seem to see hope of success, keep your town if you can : if not, give it up, and I will see you all safe and sound on Christian soil." But the deputies went away with many boasts that they were going to die for the glory of God. In the end, nobody died who could by any means avoid it. But at first, when Saladin's camp was fixed to the west, where, nearly a hundred years before, had been that of Godfrey de Bouillon, the Christians made gallant sorties, and the Saracens could do nothing against the impetuosity of their charges. They observed, however, that after midday the sun was at their own backs and in the faces of the enemy; and they reserved their attacks for the afternoon, throwing dust in the air and into the eyes of the besieged.

After eight days of ineffectual fighting, Saladin changed his camp to the east side, pitching it at the gate of St. Stephen, where the valley of the Kedron has no great depth. In this new position, Saladin was able to erect machines for casting stones and arrows into the city. He also set his men to work undermining the walls. In two days they had undermined fifteen toises of the wall, the Christians not being able to countermine "because they were afraid of the showers of missiles from the mangonels and machines." The Saracens fired the supports of their mines, and as much of the wall as had been mined fell down.

Then the besieged, finding that no hope remained of holding the town, held a hasty council as to what should be done. For now a universal panic had seized the soldiers; they ran to the churches instead of to the ramparts, and while the defenders of the city prayed within the walls of the church, the priests formed processions and walked round the streets chanting psalms.

Let Bernard the Treasurer tell this story in his own words:

"The bourgeois, knights, and men of arms, in the council, agreed that it would be better to sally forth and for all to die. But the patriarch advised them to the contrary. 'Sirs, if there were no other way, this would be good advice, but if we destroy ourselves and let the lives perish which we may save, it is not well, because for every man in this town there are fifty women and children, whom, if we die, the Saracens will take and will convert to their own faith, and so they will all be lost to God. But if, by the help of God, we can gain permission, at least, to go out from here and betake ourselves to Christian soil, that would seem to me the better course.' They all agreed to this advice. Then they took Balian of Ibelin and prayed him to go to Saladin and make what terms of peace he could. He went and spoke to him. And while he was yet speaking with Saladin about delivering up the city, the Turks, bringing ladders and fixing them against the walls, made another assault. And, indeed, already ten or twelve banners were mounted upon the ramparts, or had entered where the wall had been undermined and had fallen down. When Saladin saw his men and his banners on the walls, he said to Balian, 'Why do you talk to me about delivering up the city, when you see my people ready to enter? It is too late now; the city is mine already.' And even while they spoke, our Lord gave such courage to the Christians who were on the walls, that they made the Saracens thereon give way and fall to the ground, and chased them out of the moat. Saladin, when he saw it, was much ashamed and troubled. Then he said to Balian that he might go back, because he would do nothing more at the time, but that he might come again the next day, when he would willingly listen to what he had to say. . . . The ladies of Jerusalem took cauldrons and placed them before Mount Calvary, and having filled them with cold water, put their daughters in them up to the neck, and cut off their tresses, and threw them away. Monks, priests, and nuns went barefooted round the walls of the city, bearing in procession the said Cross before them. The priests bore on their heads the *Corpus Domini,* but our Lord Jesus Christ would not listen to any prayer that they made, by reason of the stinking luxury and adultery in the city which prevented any prayer from mounting up to God. . . . When Balian came to Saladin, he said that the Christians would give up the city if their lives were saved. Saladin replied that he spoke too late; but he added, 'Sir Balian, for the love of God and of yourself, I will take pity on them in a manner, and, to save my oath (that he would only take them by force), they shall give themselves up to me as if they were taken by force, and I will leave them their property to do as they please, but their bodies shall be my prisoners, and he who can ransom himself shall do so, and he who cannot shall be my prisoner.' 'Sire,' said Balian, 'what shall be the price of the ransom?' Saladin replied that the price should be for poor and rich alike, for a man thirty byzants, for every woman and every child, ten. And whoever could not pay this sum was to be a slave. . . .

"Balian went back with these hard terms, and during the night prevailed upon the Master of the Knights Hospitallers to give up, for the ransom of the poor, all that was left of the treasure of King Henry of England. And the next day he obtained of Saladin a reduction of the ransom by one half.

"Then said Balian to Saladin, 'Sire, you have fixed the ransom of the rich; fix now that of the poor, for there are twenty thousand who cannot pay the ransom of a single man. For the love of God put in a little consideration and I will try to get from the Temple, the Hospitallers, and the bourgeois, as much as will deliver all.' Saladin said that he would willingly have consideration, and that a hundred thousand byzants should let all the poor go free. 'Sire,' said Balian, 'when all those who are able have ransomed themselves, there will not be left half of the ransom which you demand for the poor.' Saladin said that it should not be otherwise. Then Balian bethought him that he should not make so cheap a bargain by ransoming all together as if he ransomed part at a time, and that by the help of God he might get the rest at a cheaper rate. Then he asked Saladin for how much he would deliver seven thousand men. 'For fifty thousand byzants.' 'Sire,' said Balian, 'that cannot be; for God's sake let us have reason.'

"It was finally arranged that seven thousand men should be ransomed for thirty thousand byzants, two women or ten children to count as one man. When all was arranged Saladin gave them fifty days to sell and mortgage their effects and pay their ransom, and announced that he who should be found in the city after fifty days should belong to the conquerors, body and goods.

"All the gates were closed except that of David. Guards were placed at this to prevent any Christian from going out, the Saracens being admitted to buy what the Christians had to sell. The day on which the city was given up was Friday, the 2nd day of October, 1187. Saladin placed officers in the town of David to receive the ransom, and ordered that no delay was to be granted beyond the fifty days. The patriarch and Balian went immediately to the Hospital and carried away the thirty thousand byzants for the ransom of the poor. When this was paid, they summoned the bourgeois of the city, and, choosing from their body the two most trustworthy men of each street, they made them swear on the relics of saints that they would spare neither man nor woman through hatred or through love, but would make one and all declare on oath what they had, and would allow them to keep back nothing, but would ransom the poor with what remained after their own ransoms had been paid. They took down the number of the poor in each street, and making a selection, they made up the number of seven thousand, who were allowed to go out of the city. Then there was hardly anything left for the remainder. . . . But when all those who were ransomed were out of the city, and there remained yet many poor people, Seif-ed-dín went to Saladin, his brother, and said to him, 'Sire, I have helped to conquer the land and the city. I pray you to give me a thousand slaves of those that are still within it. Saladin asked him what he would do with them. Seif-ed-dín replied that he would do with them as seemed him best. Saladin granted his request, and his brother released them all. When Seif-ed-dín had taken out his thousand captives, the patriarch prayed Saladin to deliver the poor which yet remained. He gave the patriarch seven hundred. Then Balian asked Saladin for some of those left. He gave Balian five hundred. 'And now,' said Saladin, 'I will make my own alms.' Then he commanded his bailiffs to open the postern towards Saint Lazarus, and to make proclamation through all the city that the poor might go out by this way, only that if there were among them any who had the means of ransom, they were to be taken to prison. The deliverance of the poor lasted from sunrise to sunset, and yet there were eleven thousand left. The patriarch and Balian went then to Saladin and prayed him that he would hold themselves in hostage until those who were left could obtain from Christendom enough to pay their ransom. Saladin said that he would certainly not receive two men in place of eleven thousand, and that they were to speak no more of it."

But Saladin was open to prayers from all quarters.

The widows and children of those who had fallen at Tiberias came to him weeping and crying. "When Saladin saw them weeping, he was moved with great pity; and, hearing who they were, he told them to inquire if their husbands and fathers were yet living, and in prison, those who were his captives he ordered to be released; and, in those cases where it was proved that their husbands were dead, he gave largely from his own private purse to all the ladies and the noble maidens, so that they gave thanks to God for the honour and wealth that Saladin bestowed upon them." Clearly a magnanimous prince, this Saladin, and one who was accustomed to return good for evil.

There were so many Christians who came out of the city that the Saracens marvelled how they could have all got in. Saladin separated them into three divisions; the Templars led one, the Hospitallers another, and Balian the third. To each troop he assigned fifty of his own knights to conduct them into Christian territory. . . . These, when they saw men, women, or children fatigued, would make their squires go on foot, and put the wearied exiles on horseback, while they themselves carried the children. Surely this is a tender and touching picture of the soft-hearted soldiers of Islam, too pitiful to let the little children cry while they had arms to carry them, or to drive the weary forward while they could walk on foot themselves.

When the exiles got to Tripoli they found themselves worse off than on the march. Raymond would not let them enter, but sent out his knights, who caught all the rich bourgeois, and brought them prisoners into the city. Then Raymond deprived them of all that they brought out of Jerusalem. The poorer of them dispersed into Armenia and the neighbouring countries, and disappear from history. The names of the Christians linger yet, however, in the Syrian towns, and many of their descendants, long since converted to the faith of the country, may be found in every town and village between Antioch and Ascalon.

Jerusalem was fallen, and the kingdom of the Christians was at last at an end. It had lasted eighty-eight years. It had seen the exploits of six valiant, prudent, and chivalrous kings. It was supported during all its existence solely by the strength and ability of its kings; it fell to pieces at once when its king, a poor leper, lost his authority with his strength. Always corrupt, always self-seeking, the Christians of the East became a by-word and proverb at last for treachery, meanness, and cowardice. It was time that a realm so degraded from its high and lofty aims should perish; there was no longer any reason why it should continue to live; the Holy City might just as well be kept by the Saracens, for the Christians were not worthy. They had succeeded in trampling the name of Christian in the dust; the Cross which they protected was their excuse for every treachery and baseness which a licentious priest could be bribed to absolve. The tenets and preaching of their faith were not indeed forgotten by them, for they had never been known; there was nothing in their lives by which the Saracens could judge the religion of Christ to be aught but the blindest worship of a piece of wood and a gilded cross; while the worst among them —the most rapacious, the most luxurious, the most licentious, the most haughty, the most perjured—were the very men, the priests and the knights of the orders, sworn to chastity, to self-denial, to godliness. It appears to us that Christianity might have had a chance in the East against Islam but for the Christians; and had men like Saladin been able to comprehend what was the religion which, like an ancient painting begrimed and overladen with dirt and dust, lay under all the vices and basenesses of the Christianity they witnessed, the world would at least have been spared some of the bitterness of its religious wars.

As for Guy de Lusignan, it matters very little what became of that poor creature. He made one or two feeble attempts to get back something of his kingdom, but always failed. He finally sold his title to King Richard, in exchange for that of King of Cyprus, and ruled in great tranquillity in his new kingdom for a year, when he died.

So disastrous an event as the fall of Jerusalem must needs be accompanied by signs and wonders from heaven. On the day that the city surrendered, one of the monks of Argenteuil, as he remembered afterwards, saw the moon descend from heaven to earth. It is remarkable that nothing was said at the time of this very curious phenomenon. In many churches the crucifixes shed tears of blood, which was their customary and recognised way of expressing regret when the monks thought anything was going wrong with the power of the Church. And a Christian knight saw in a dream an eagle flying over an army, holding seven javelins in its claws, and crying, "Woe, woe to Jerusalem."

CHAPTER XV.

THE THIRD CRUSADE.

"Signor, saciez, ki or ne s'en ira
  En cele terre, u Diex fu mors et vis,
  Et ki la crois d'outre mer ni prendra
  À paines mais ira en paradis."
  Thibault de Champagne.

We are not writing a history of the Crusades, and must hasten over all those episodes in the long struggle of three hundred years which do not immediately concern the Holy City. It is with regret that one turns from the glowing pages of Vinsauf, Villehardouin, and Joinville, with the thought that they have little to do with our subject, and that we must perforce leave them for other pastures, not so fair.* But a few words to show the progress of events, if it is only to make us understand the story of Saladin, are indispensable.

The news of the fall of Jerusalem was received in Europe with a thrill of horror and indignation. From every pulpit, preachers thundered in the ears of the stupefied people the intelligence that the city for which so much had been risked and spent was fallen, and that it

* Why has no English historian treated of the Crusades? Besides the scattered notices in Milman there is only the work of Knightley, meritorious in its way, but as dry as sawdust; spoiled, too, by the accident that it was written for the Society for the Promotion of Christian Knowledge, and the author seems always horribly afraid of saying something which might offend the Committee.

was the judgment of God upon the sins of the world. Terrified and conscience-stricken, all Europe repented and reformed. Luxury was abandoned, mortifications and self-denial were practised; every sinner looked on the fall of the city as partly caused by himself; nothing but prayers and lamentation were heard through all the cities of Western Europe. And then when Pope Gregory sent his circular letter exhorting the faithful to take up arms for the recovery of Jerusalem, and when William of Tyre, eloquent, noble in appearance, illustrious for learning and for virtues, came to Europe to pray for help in the name of Christianity, kings forgot their quarrels, nobles their ambitions, and it seemed as if, once more, the cry of "Dieu le veut" would burst spontaneously from the whole of Western Europe. It might have done had there been a man with the energy and eloquence of Peter the Hermit. But the moment of enthusiasm was allowed to pass, and Philip Augustus after taking the Cross, delayed his Crusade, while he renewed his quarrel with Henry the Second.

In England and in France, in order to defray expenses, a tax called the Tithe of Saladin, consisting of a tenth part of all their goods, was levied on every person who did not take the Cross. The clergy, with their usual greed, endeavoured to evade the tax, on the ground that the Church must keep her property in order to preserve her independence. They were overruled, however, and had all to pay, except a few of the poorer orders, and the Lepers' Hospitals. In every parish the Tithe of Saladin was raised in the presence of a priest, a Templar, a Hospitaller, a king's man, a baron's man and clerk, and a bishop's clerk. As this did not produce enough, Philip Augustus arrested all the Jews, and forced them to pay five thousand marks of silver. In order to prevent such a rush of villagers as might lead, as it had already led, to the desertion of the fields, every one had to pay the tithe except those who took the Cross with the permission of their seigneur. And when the money had all been collected, war broke out again between the two kings of France and England. Peace was made between them by aid of the pope's legate, but Henry died in the midst of his preparations. Richard saw in the death of his father the consequence of his own unfilial conduct, and took the Cross as a sign of his unfeigned repentance. Baldwin, Archbishop of Canterbury, preached the Crusade throughout England. It was the first time that it had been preached here, and the old enthusiasm of the French was aroused among the English. All wanted to take the Cross; wives hid their husbands' clothes; they ran naked to Baldwin. Everywhere all sorts of miracles took place; the people gathered the very dust which the bishop had trodden on as a holy relic; they flocked together from every part of England, Wales, Ireland, and Scotland, and if the numbers were less than those which went from France it was because a selection was made, and only those went who obtained permission to go. The religious zeal of the English found its first exercise in the famous massacre of the Jews. From them Richard got large sums of money, and as, with all his resources, he could not get enough, he mortgaged a large part of his estates, sold the dignities of the crown, and was quite ready to sell the city of London itself, could he have found a purchaser.

In one respect this Crusade started with far better prospects of success than any which had preceded it. They went by sea, thus avoiding the horrible sufferings inevitable in crossing Asia Minor; and they established a code of laws, to maintain discipline and order in the army. Whosoever struck another was to be dipped three times in the sea; whosoever drew his sword upon another was to have his right hand cut off; whosoever swore at another was to be fined an ounce of silver for every oath; if a man were convicted of theft he was to be shaven, hot pitch was to be poured on his head, which was then covered with feathers, and he was to be put upon the nearest shore; while if a man murdered another, he was to be tied to the corpse, and both bodies thrown together into the sea. No woman was to go with the Crusaders at all, save such as were necessary for the service of the camp, and those only who were of sufficient age to be above suspicion. No one was to practise gaming in any shape whatever; and all luxury in dress or in the table was forbidden. Thus the army started with the most admirable intentions as regards virtue. It was to be a camp where there was no vice, no gaming, no swearing, no violence—under penalties of boiling pitch and feathers, abandonment on a savage coast, the loss of the right hand.

Richard started from Marseilles; Philip Augustus from Genoa; Frederick Redbeard from Germany followed the old course of Bulgaria and Asia Minor. He had with him a hundred thousand men; and he refused to allow any man to join the army who was not possessed of at least three marks of silver. Frederick had the courtesy to send an ambassador to Saladin, announcing his intention of making war upon him.

He fought his way across Asia Minor to Iconium, which surrendered. The old terror which Godfrey and Baldwin had been able to inspire among the Saracens was inspired again by Frederick. The Mohammedans expected his arrival in Syria with the liveliest apprehensions. But he never got there, for bathing in the river Selef he was seized with a chill, and died. After his death large numbers of his men deserted; the rest fought their way under the Duke of Swabia; and at length, out of the one hundred thousand who had followed Frederick, there entered into Palestine six hundred horse and five thousand foot.

Saladin, meantime, had besieged Tyre and Tripoli, both ineffectually. He had, however, got possession of the strong post of Kerak, after a siege of more than a year.

The Christian defenders actually sold their wives and children to the besiegers, in order to save them from starvation. Saladin gave them back again after the capitulation. He also, in 1189, two years after his capture, restored liberty to Guy de Lusignan, on his taking a solemn oath never to go to war with him. Guy swore, and directly after he returned to Christian soil got the oath annulled, and returned to besiege Acre. This was the crime which, above all things, enraged the Saracens, and made a man like Saladin unable to understand a religion which permitted it. Here was a captive king released from his prison by the clemency of his conqueror, and without ransom, solely on the condition that he would leave it to others to make war upon him. Yet the very first thing he does is to break his oath, and get up an army to attack him. Conrad de Montferrat, who was in Tyre, refused to admit Guy, not thinking it necessary to acknowledge a king who was unable to defend himself. But Guy, who was not without courage, found means to raise a small army, and with it sat down before Acre. He nearly took it by assault, when an alarm was spread that Saladin was coming, and his men fled in a panic. It was not Saladin who was coming from the land, but the first reinforcement of the Crusaders from the sea. The Frisians and Danes, twelve thousand in number, came first, and camped with Guy. Next came the English and the Flemings. And then Saladin, becoming aware of the new storm that was rising against him, came down from Phœnicia, and prepared to meet it. Every day the Crusaders arrived; before Richard and Philip were even on their way there were one hundred thousand of them, and the hearts of the Mohammedans sank when they beheld a forest of masts, always changing, always being renewed as the ships went away and others came. The Christians, on the other hand, were confident of success; a French knight, looking on the mighty host about him, is reported to have cried out, blasphemously enough, "If God only remains neuter the victory is ours." Saladin forced on a battle, and experienced a disastrous defeat. The Saracens fled in all directions, and already the Christians were plundering their camp, when a panic broke out among them. Without any enemy attacking them, they threw away their arms, and fled. Saladin stopped his men, and turned upon them. The rout was general, and victory remained with Saladin, but a victory which he could not follow up, in consequence of the confusion into which his camp had been thrown. He withdrew, and the Crusaders, recovering from their panic, set to work, fortifying their camp, and besieging Acre. They passed thus the winter of 1189-90, without any serious success, and contending always against Greek fire, which the besieged threw against their movable towers. In the spring came Saladin again; the Crusaders demanded to be led against the Saracens, the chiefs refused; the soldiers revolted, and poured forth against the enemy, only to experience another defeat, exactly similar to the first. And then the leaders, despondent at their ill-success, endeavoured to make peace with Saladin, when the arrival of Henry, Count of Champagne, followed by that of Frederick, Duke of Swabia, raised their hopes again. But then came famine, winter, and disease. Worse than all these, came dissension. Queen Sybille died with her two children. Conrad of Tyre resolved to break the marriage of her sister Isabelle, now the heiress to the crown of Jerusalem, with Humphrey de Toron, and to marry her himself. He did so, and claimed the throne; so that the camp was split into two parties, that of Guy, and that of Conrad. It was resolved to submit the matter to the arbitration of the kings of England and France. The two kings were quarrelling on their way. Richard refused to espouse Alice, Philip's sister, to whom he was betrothed, and married in her place Berengaria. He further offended Philip by his conduct in Sicily, and by his conquest of Cyprus, which island he refused to share with Philip. Of course, therefore, directly Richard declared for Guy, Philip took the part of Conrad; and it was not till after long discussions that it was decided that Guy should hold the crown during his life, after which it was to descend to Conrad and his children. Then both kings fell ill; Saladin also was ill, with continual fevers, and constant messages were sent to and from the Christian and Saracen monarchs, which were construed by the savage soldiers into proposals of treachery. Acre fell, after a two years' siege, and the loss of sixty thousand Christians by the Saracens' swords. Philip went home after this, and Richard, pleased to be left without a rival, began his ferocious course in Palestine by the cold-blooded slaughter of two thousand seven hundred Saracens.

From Acre, after a short rest, devoted to those very pleasures against which such stringent edicts had been passed, Richard led his army to Cæsarea. In the midst was a sort of *caroccio*, a sacred car, in which was the standard of the Cross, whither the wounded were brought, and where the army rallied. The Saracens hung upon the march, shooting their arrows into the ranks of the Christians. If one was killed he was buried there and then. At night, when the camp was fixed, a herald cried aloud three times, to remind the soldiers of their vows, " Lord, help the Holy Sepulchre." And at break of day the march was resumed. They moved slowly, only performing about ten miles a day. And then came the great battle of Assur, when Saladin lost eight thousand of his men, and ought to have lost Palestine, if Richard had been as good a Crusader as he was a general. Had they marched upon Jerusalem there was nothing in their way. But they stopped at Jaffa. Richard made propositions to Saladin. Would he give up Jerusalem? The Saracen replied that it was impossible to abandon a city whence the prophet had mounted to heaven. Then Cœur de Lion made a proposition which called forth, to his extreme astonishment—for the strong-armed king had but little insight into the intricacies of theology—such vehement opposition, that he was forced to abandon it. It was nothing less than to marry his sister Jane, widow of William of Sicily, to El Melik el "Adil, Saladin's brother. Both were to govern Jerusalem together. El Melik el "Adil, who was on terms of personal friendship with Richard, was perfectly willing to arrange the marriage; but it was impossible to meet the objections of imams as well as bishops, and the negotiations were broken off, Richard proving thereupon his zeal for the faith by murdering his captives. He then gave orders to march, declaring that he was going to deliver Jerusalem. They started, but on the way he changed his resolution, and determined to rebuild Ascalon, to the chagrin and even despair of the common soldiers. And then the chiefs quarrelled. Peace was reestablished. Guy de Lusignan was made king of Cyprus, and Richard gave the crown of Jerusalem to Conrad of Tyre. But the latter was murdered by two emissaries of the sheikh of the Assassins, "the old man of the mountains."* Henry of Champagne then married his widow Isabelle, and received the title of king.

The next winter passed, and in the spring Richard, who had spent his time in small skirmishes, whence he usually returned with half-a-dozen heads at his saddle bow, declared his intention of returning to Europe. He was persuaded to remain, and once more led the army in the direction of Jerusalem. But he stopped some twenty miles from the city. And the army, like the people of Israel, murmured against him. There must, it seems to us, have been some secret reason why he never marched upon Jerusalem. Could it have been some superstitious one? Joachim, the hermit of Calabria, had prophesied

* See p. 410.

that Jerusalem should be taken seven years after its capture by Saladin. It was now only five years. Was he waiting for the fulfilment of the prediction? From his vacillation, it would almost appear so. One day he rode within sight of the city. And then this great knight, this type of his age; wild beast and murderer in and after battle; illiterate and rude; yet full of noble impulses, and generous above his peers, burst into bitter weeping, and covering his face with his shield, cried aloud that he was not worthy even to look upon the city of his Saviour. He could not bear the thought of giving up the conquest of the Holy Land. On the other hand, if we are right in our conjecture as to his motives for delay, he could not possibly, with everything in his own kingdom going wrong in his absence, wait two years more. He shut himself up in his tent and passed hours alone, with pale and gloomy countenance. A temporary relief to his sorrow was afforded by the successful cutting off of the caravans which were going to Saladin from Egypt. He got, too, a piece of the True Cross, which was paraded through the camp with great rejoicing.

Then, for the whole army looked to him for advice and guidance, he called a council, and exposed certain reasons which made him hesitate before advancing on Jerusalem. Of these, the principal were, want of knowledge of the country, and its arid and thirsty nature. He proposed to submit the matter to a council of twenty, of whom half should be Templars and Hospitallers, and to be guided by their advice; but the council could not agree, and dissension broke out between the Duke of Burgundy and King Richard. The design of besieging Jerusalem was given up, and the army slowly and sadly returned to Ramleh, and thence to Jaffa.

A peace was concluded shortly after between Richard and Saladin, in which it was agreed to destroy Ascalon entirely, by the joint labour of Christians and Mohammedans; the Christians were to have all the coast between Tyre and

Joppa; peace was to be enforced in the north of Syria; pilgrimages were to be freed from the former tax, and a truce for two years was to be agreed upon.

The English Crusaders, divided into three bodies, all went up unarmed to Jerusalem. They were received with kindness, and the Bishop of Salisbury, who came last, with distinction, being entertained by Saladin himself, who showed him the wood of the True Cross, and granted him, as a favour, that two Latin priests should be permitted to serve at the Church of the Sepulchre. And then, all being arranged, Richard embarked at Acre. The people crowded to the shore, weeping and crying over the loss of their champion, the most stalwart warrior that ever fought for the Cross. The king himself could not restrain his tears. Turning to bid farewell to the country, he cried, "Oh, Holy Land! God grant that I may yet return to help thee!" And his last message was one to Saladin, telling him that he was only going home to raise money in order to complete the conquest of the land. "Truly," said the courtly Saladin; "if God wills that Jerusalem pass into other hands, it cannot fall into any more noble than those of the brave King Richard."

Such, briefly and baldly told, is the picturesque crusade of Cœur de Lion. Of the terror which his name inspired; of his many and valiant gests, of his personal strength, his chivalrous generosity, we have not room to speak. Nor can we do more than allude to those other qualities for which he made his name known; his ferocious and savage cruelty; his pleasure in fighting for love of mere butchery; the ungovernable rage which sometimes seized him; his want of consideration for others; his "masterfulness;" the way in which he trampled on, careless over whose body he passed, provided he attained his ends. For these, and the other stories which can be told about him, we refer our readers to the chronicles, and to that book on the Crusades which has yet to be written.

CHAPTER XVI.

SALADIN.

"Sans peur et sans reproche."

SALADIN has already appeared upon our pages, but hitherto scarcely more than incidentally. The reader will, no doubt, be glad to have a consecutive account of the career of this illustrious prince, as told by the historians of his own nation.

We must go back to the time of the invasion of Egypt by King Amaury. On Shírkoh's death, many of the chief officers of Nûr-ed-dín's army were desirous of succeeding to the important post of grand vizier; but the Caliph, El 'Adhid, himself sent for Saladin, and conferred the office upon him, together with many privileges and titles of honour. He was designated El Melik en Násir, "the Victorious King," and Sipáh-sálár, a Persian title, signifying generalissimo of the army; and his standard, or coat of arms, was placed instead of his name at the head of all official communications—a form made use of only in the case of royal personages. In writing to him, however, the Egyptian Caliph did not address his letters to Saladin individually, but inscribed them "To the Emír Saladin, and all the princes in the land of Egypt." This was doubtless in order to assert his own prerogative and superior authority; but the young Kurd, having once placed his foot upon the steps of the throne, was not to be deterred from mounting to the summit of his ambition by mere scruples of etiquette. He was, moreover, a rigid follower of the Shafi'ite sect, and therefore no friend to the pretensions of the sons of 'Alí; indeed, he had already received the commands of Núr-ed-dín to depose the Ismaelites from all religious and judicial offices, to appoint orthodox doctors in their stead, and to insert the name of the Abbaside Caliph of Baghdad in the Friday prayer in the place of that of the Fatemite Caliph of Egypt.

In 1169 the Franks made their final effort for the possession of Egypt, and besieged Damietta; but Saladin had garrisoned and provisioned the town so well that it was enabled to hold out until a fresh attack by Núr-ed-dín upon the Syrian possessions of the Christians compelled them to abandon the attempt and return home bootless. The next year Saladin himself invaded their territory, and, after plundering the neighbourhood of Ascalon and Ramleh, returned to Egypt. His next expedition was against Ailah ('Akabah), which he blockaded by land and sea, and conquered with little difficulty.

For some time Saladin was prevented from carrying out Núr-ed-dín's injunctions respecting the abolition of the Fatemite sect and authority, through fear of an insurrection; but towards the end of the year 1171 an opportunity offered itself in the sudden illness of El 'Adhid li dín allah. Of this Saladin at once availed himself, and the name of El Mostadhí bi amr illah was solemnly proclaimed in the mosques of Cairo.

This great *coup d'état*, which won Egypt over to the orthodox Mohammedan sect, and ultimately enabled Saladin to grasp the independent sovereignty of the country, was effected, as an Arab historian quaintly observes, "so quietly, that not a brace of goats butted over it." The last of the Fatemites died only ten days afterwards, in happy ignorance of the downfall of his dynasty. The news was hailed with great demonstrations of joy in Baghdad, and 'Emád-ed-dín Sandal, a confidential servant of Saladin's, was despatched to Cairo with dresses of honour for the emir, bearing also the black flag, the famous standard of the house of Abbas.

But Saladin was flying at higher game; and when news reached him of the death of Núr-ed-dín, in August 1174, he at once set out for Damascus. El Melik es Sálíh Ismáïl, who had succeeded his father upon the throne, was absent at Aleppo when Saladin arrived, and the latter established himself without opposition in the government of the town. Hums and Hamah (the Hamath of the Bible) next yielded to his authority, but Aleppo still held out, and warmly supported the cause of El Melik es Sálíh the legitimate heir to the kingdom. After an unsuccessful attempt to reduce the place by blockade, Saladin made terms with his rival, and each agreed to leave the other in quiet possession of the districts of Syria which he then actually held. Having concluded this arrangement, he returned to Egypt. El Melik es Sálih died in 1181, and was succeeded by his uncle, 'Ezz-ed-dín Masúd, who, however, exchanged by mutual consent the throne of Aleppo with Maudúd, lord of Sanjár.

In May, 1182, Saladin once more set out for Damascus, ravaging the country of the Crusaders by the way, and obtaining a large amount of booty. He never afterwards returned to Egypt, but from that moment devoted himself to the task of reconquering the Holy Land for the Mussulmans.

In the following month he began his campaign, and, pitching at Tiberias, harassed the neighbourhood of Beisán, Jaibín, and the Ghor, causing much loss to the Christians, both of property and life. Beirút and the sea coast were next attacked, and, even where the towns themselves held out, the country around suffered severely from his depredations, for he seldom returned empty handed from a raid.

It was in this same year, 1182, that the Frank occupants of Kerek and Shobek determined to make an expedition against Medinah itself, and thus to attack the Mohammedans in the very birthplace and stronghold of their faith. They had even sworn that they would dig up the body of the Prophet, and carry it off to their own country, in order to put a stop to pilgrimages once and for all. That this was no idle threat was clear from the fact that the Prince Renaud of Kerek had caused ships to be constructed and carried over land to the Red Sea, and that troops had been transported in these vessels, and were actually on their way to Medinah.

Saladin was at Hauran when the news of the intended invasion reached him. He was furious at the insult offered to his religion, and sent orders to his lieutenant in Egypt to despatch the Emír Hisám-ed-dín Lúlú in pursuit of the enemy. The Franks, rather more than three hundred in number, besides a body of rebellious Bedawín which had joined their ranks, had advanced within a day's march of Medinah when Lúlú caught them up. Despairing of being able to resist the Egyptian troops, who were superior to themselves both in numbers and discipline, they sought refuge upon a mountain difficult of access, while the Bedawín, with their usual discretion in cases of danger, took to their heels. Lúlú, however, followed them to the heights, captured, and sent them in chains to Cairo. They were given over for execution "to the dervishes, lawyers, and religious persons," who put them all to a cruel death, reserving only two of the most conspicuous members of the band, "who were sent to Mecca to have their throats cut, like the beasts who are sacrificed before the Ka'abah."

In 1183 Saladin obtained possession of Hums, Amed, 'Aintáb, and other places. He next besieged Aleppo, which he took after a short siege; though, to compensate the sovereign of that place, 'Emád-ed-dín ibn Maudúd, for its loss, he bestowed upon him the territory of Sanjár. The conquest of Aleppo took place in the month Safar, and a poet of Damascus (Muhíy-ed-dín), celebrating the event in an ode addressed to the Sultan, " declared that the capture of Aleppo in Safar was a good augury for that of Jerusalem in Rejeb"—a verse which seems to have been prophetic, for Jerusalem fell in the month Rejeb of the year 1187 A.D.

The next year the Sultan made a fresh attack upon Kerek. A severe conflict took place between his forces and the Christians, and some of the forts fell into his hands. He did not, however, follow up his advantage, but returned to Damascus, having first marched upon Nablús, which he plundered and burnt.

In 1186 Diyár Bekr also yielded to his arms, and his kingdom was now becoming so extensive that he found himself obliged to make some different provision for the government of the various provinces. Sending for his son, El Melik el Afdhal, from Egypt, he assigned him the *seigneurie* of Damascus; Egypt, Hamah, Diyár Bekr, &c., he allotted to other members of his family.

We now come to 1187, the year of the fall of Jerusalem, and the most important era in Saladin's career. His operations against the Franks, though generally successful, had as yet partaken rather of the character of border forays than regular warfare, and, although they harassed and annoyed the Crusaders, they did not materially weaken their position in the country. Jerusalem was defended by the flower of the Christian chivalry, and as yet appeared too strong for him to attack; but his determination had long been taken, and he merely waited for an opportunity to strike a decisive blow. An appeal was, moreover, made to him, artfully calculated to inflame his religious zeal, and sting his personal pride. An aged native of Damascus had been taken prisoner by the Franks and carried to Jerusalem. From the place of his captivity he sent a copy of verses to the Sultan, in which the Holy City was made to address him thus:

> Just sovereign, mighty monarch! thou
> To whom the Crosses' standards bow!
> There cometh up before thee now .
>   Jerusalem's piteous plaint.
> "Elsewhere are idols overthrown—
> Shall I, the Holy House, alone,
> The Muslim's noblest temple, groan
>   Beneath so foul a taint?"

The verse had its effect, and later on, Saladin rewarded the author with the deanery (if I may so translate the word *khatábeh*) of the Masjid el Aksa.

In the month of March he addressed letters to all parts of his dominions calling on his subjects to rally round his standard, and follow him to the "Holy War." Setting out from Damascus with such men as he could raise, he began himself to beat up recruits, and persuaded even the most unwilling to take up arms in the cause of their faith.

Renaud, Prince of Kerek, had resolved upon attacking the Mohammedan pilgrims on their return from Mecca, and carrying them into captivity; but Saladin encamped near Bosra until the caravan had passed, and so thwarted his designs. Renaud was one of the fiercest and most implacable antagonists the Muslims had to contend with, and he, knowing that he had little chance of quarter if he fell into Saladin's hands, withdrew into his fortress at Kerek. As the Egyptian contingent for which he was waiting did not arrive so soon as he had expected, Saladin commanded his son, El Melik el Afdhal, to remain at Rás el·Má, and collect an army, while he himself occupied his leisure by plundering and burning the villages in the neighbourhood of Kerek. Here he was at last joined by the Egyptians, and things remained *in statu quo* for two months. Meanwhile El Afdhal had executed his father's commands, and collected a large body of men, with whom, in the absence of other orders, he marched upon Tiberias. At Sefúríyeh they were met by the Christian troops, who sallied forth in great numbers from the town and gave them battle. Fortune, however, declared for the Muslims, and the Crusaders retired with great loss. Saladin, on receiving the news of this victory, left Kerek and joined his son. The combined forces now amounted to an immense number of men, all ardently desiring to do battle with the "infidels," and the Franks, sensible of the approaching danger, made overtures for peace. But Saladin continued his march upon Jerusalem. On the 27th of June he pitched at Jaibín, and on the following morning reached the Jordan.

In the meantime the Crusaders endeavoured to stop his progress, and had assembled (according to the Arab authorities) to the number of fifty thousand in the plain of Sefúríyeh, where for some days continuous but unimportant skirmishes took place. Saladin determined first to attack Tiberias itself, and, sending a party of sappers and miners stealthily to undermine the walls, he approached and entered the town at nightfall. The Franks knew that the loss of this important place would be fatal to their cause. The next morning, therefore, as soon as they got information of the movement, they beat to arms, and proceeded with all speed to endeavour to oust Saladin from his position. It was a Friday morning, but, rigid Mussulman as the Sultan was, he did not, on this occasion at least, allow his scruples to interfere with his plan of action. Leaving some men in charge of the castle of Tiberias, he sallied out, and gave battle to the enemy. The conflict raged fiercely, neither side gaining a decisive advantage, until night coming on put a stop to the encounter. In the morning, both sides prepared to resume the fight, and the Muslims rushed to the attack shouting like one man. At this a sudden panic seized upon the Christian ranks, and they retired in disorder to Jebel Hattín, a village in which is the reputed tomb of Jethro, the father-in-law of Moses. The Count of Tripoli, foreseeing that defeat was imminent, withdrew with his followers before the general rout began, and fled to Tyre.

And now was enacted a scene of indescribable carnage and confusion. The Muslims, who had followed in hot pursuit, came suddenly upon the retreating host, and, having surrounded them on all sides, so as to make escape impossible, set fire to the dry herbage beneath their feet. The flames spread instantly, and the Christians, scorched by the burning grass, and fainting under the scarcely less fierce rays of a Syrian midsummer sun, fell, huddled together like sheep, beneath the swords and darts of their assailants. No less than thirty thousand of their bravest soldiers are said to have perished on the field, and many others were taken captive. So entirely were they cowed and demoralized that one peasant alone is related to have taken thirty prisoners, and tied them in his tent, and to have sold one of them for an old boot!

Amongst the prisoners were the king himself, and his brother Godfrey, Odo, Lord of Jebeil, Count Humphrey, the Grand Masters of the Templars and Hospitallers, together with many knights of both orders, and Prince Renaud of Kerek, who was one of the first captured. Saladin had sworn that if ever Renaud fell into his power he would slay him with his own hand, for he was incensed against him not only for his meditated attack upon Medinah, but because he had violated the truce and treacherously murdered some Egyptians who were passing by Shobek, answering them by coarse jests upon Mohammed when they appealed to his honour and the articles of peace.

The Sultan was sitting in the threshold of his tent,

which was not yet completely set up, and the captives were arrayed before him one by one. When King Guy was brought out he courteously invited him to sit down by his side, and perceiving Renaud immediately after, he made him sit down beside the king, and commenced upbraiding him with his former breach of faith and with his attempt upon the sanctuary of Medinah. Renaud excused himself, saying, through the interpreter, "that he had only acted after the manner of princes." At this moment the king gave signs of being greatly distressed by thirst, and Saladin ordered iced sherbet to be brought for his refreshment. Having quenched his own thirst, the king handed the cup to Renaud; but as the latter raised it to his lips, Saladin exclaimed, "Thou hast given him to drink, not I." This sentence was equivalent to Renaud's death knell, for Saladin thereby disclaimed the obligation he would have been under (according to the laws of Arab warfare) to spare the life of a captive who had eaten or drunk with him. As soon as the tent was pitched the Sultan again ordered Renaud to be brought before him, and told him he was "going to help Mohammed against him this time." He then gave the Prince of Kerek one last chance for his life, offering to spare him if he would embrace Islam. Renaud, whatever his other faults, was no coward, and as he returned a proud refusal to the offer, Saladin smote him to the ground, and commanded the attendants to cut off his head. The order was promptly executed, and the reeking corpse was dragged by the feet to where the king was standing. The latter, who had witnessed the incident, made sure that his own turn was to follow next, and could not conceal his agitation; but Saladin assured him that he had no cause to fear, that "it was not the custom amongst his people for one king to injure or insult another, and that Renaud had only met the fate which all such traitors deserved."

The capture of the king was, however, of less importance in the eyes of the Christians than that of the "True Cross," which fell into the hands of the Mussulmans on this occasion. The native writers describe with great glee the costly covering of gold and precious stones in which the relic was encased, and the despair of the Christians at its loss. This victory, which completely crushed the Christian power, and paved the way for Saladin's future successes, took place on the 14th of June.

Saladin, by his manœuvre of the previous Friday, had only possessed himself of a portion of the town of Tiberias. Raymond's wife had moved all she possessed to the castle, and prepared to defend it against the invaders, but, when she saw the turn which affairs had taken, she very wisely withdrew with her immediate followers and rejoined her husband at Tyre. The Mohammedans were thus enabled to occupy the fort.

Having appointed Sárim-ed-dín Caimázá Sanjí as governor of Tiberias, Saladin pitched his tent outside the town, and commanded the Templars and Hospitallers who had been taken prisoners to be brought before him. No less than two hundred of these were found distributed amongst the soldiery, and Saladin ordered them to be immediately beheaded. There were a number of "doctors and philosophers" present with the Mohammedan troops, and these petitioned as a particular favour to be allowed to perform the office of executioners, and permission being accorded them, the learned gentlemen each selected a knight and butchered him, as a practical comment upon the Ovidian maxim—

> Ingenuas didicisse fideliter artes
> Emollit mores nec sinit esse feros!

The grand masters of the two orders were spared and sent, together with the king, his brother Godfrey, and the Lord of Jebail, to Damascus, where they were thrown into prison.

On the following Tuesday the Sultan resumed his march, and on the Thursday morning encamped before the walls of Acre. The inhabitants made no resistance, but came out of the city and met him with prayers for quarter. This he granted them, and, having given them the option either of remaining in the city or removing from it, and giving those who chose to withdraw time to enable them to do so, he took possession of it with his troops on the 9th of July. While here, Saladin received intelligence that his brother, El Melik el 'Adil, had left Egypt, and was on the road to join him, having conquered the fortress of Mejdel Yaba and the city of Jaffa by the way.

Making Acre his head-quarters, the Sultan dispersed his emírs over the country in different directions for the purpose of attacking the castles and fortified towns. Nazareth was taken after a slight resistance, men and women were carried into captivity and their property plundered. Sefuríyeh was found to be entirely deserted, the inhabitants having decamped after the disastrous battle of Hattín. Cæsarea, Arsúf, Sebastiyeh, and Nablús were next added to the list of Saladin's conquests; the last named place fell an easy prey, as all the principal inhabitants, both of the town and its vicinity, were Mohammedan, and consequently disaffected to the Christian rule.

Fúleh was one of the most important fortresses of the Crusaders, and a depôt both for their stores and men. Against this the Sultan next directed his attention, and succeeded in reducing it after some days' siege. He did not, however, derive as much advantage from the conquest of this place as he had expected, for its defenders had found means of withdrawing with the greater part of their arms and provisions; so that the Sultan found no one there when he entered it but a few of the lower class of the population. It was, nevertheless, important in its results, for the conquest of the other principal forts of the neighbourhood followed as a matter of course, and Dabúriyeh, Jaibín, Towáliyeh, Lejún, Beisán, and other places fell into the Saracens' hands, including the entire provinces of Tiberias and Acre.

The Sultan then ordered his nephew, El Melik el Muzaffar to march upon the fortress of Tibnín. After a week's siege the inhabitants were obliged to sue for quarter. The request was referred to Saladin personally, who granted quarter to the defenders of the town, taking hostages for their good conduct, on condition of their entirely surrendering it within five days, and setting free all the Mohammedan captives who remained in their hands. This plan he adopted thenceforth with all places which he conquered, and thus set at liberty a large number of prisoners, many of whom were doubtless fighting men, and would add greatly to the numerical strength of his army.

The occupation of Tibnín by Saladin's troops took place on the 26th of July, 1187, and three days afterwards the Muslim flag was flying from the walls of Sidon.

Saladin next attacked Beirut, which place prepared for a long resistance; but his sappers and miners having succeeded in undermining the wall and weakening the foundations of the tower, the besieged deemed it better to capitulate, and the town was occupied by the Saracens on the 6th of August.

While he was at Beirut a letter came to the Sultan from one of his officers at Damascus, informing him that Odo, Lord of Jebail, who, it will be remembered, was taken prisoner at Hettín, had consented to surrender his town on condition that he should be himself released from captivity. Saladin ordered him to be brought to Beirút in chains, and having concluded the bargain and obtained possession of Jebail (August 14th), he set Odo at liberty. The arrangement was not a politic one for the Mussulmans, for Odo was an active and influential chief, and was destined to give them much trouble. The greater part of the inhabitants of Beirút, Sidon, and Jebail were Mohammedans, which may account for the easy conquest of those places. The Christian part of the population, who had received permission to withdraw on the entry of the Sultan's troops, removed to Tyre, where the Count of Tripoli had retired after the defeat of the Christians at Tiberias. Hearing that Saladin was marching upon him, the count vacated the city and fled to Tripoli, where he died. The Marquis of Montferrat, who had only arrived that year on the coast of Syria, happened at this time to put into the port of Acre, not knowing that it was in the possession of the Muslims. He was at first surprised that no demonstration of joy greeted his arrival, but quickly perceiving the real state of the case, he would willingly have sought safety in flight. The wind, however, being unfavourable, he asked for quarter and requested that he might be allowed to land. Permission was given him, but he pretended that he dare not trust himself ashore without a safe-conduct in the Sultan's own handwriting, and gaining time by this and similar devices, he took advantage of a favourable wind springing up and sailed away to Tyre. Here he landed, and at once set about fortifying and entrenching the town, and, being joined by the fugitives from all the towns conquered by the Mussulmans, he succeeded in establishing himself in an almost impregnable position.

After the conquest of Beirút and Jebail, Saladin returned by way of Sidon and Sarfend, and, passing by Tyre without attempting to assault it, he proceeded to the coast of Philistia, and, having taken Ramleh, Yabneh, Bethlehem, and Hebron on his way thither, sat down before Ascalon and prepared to bring his engines of war to bear upon the walls. For fourteen days the city held out, at the end of which time the inhabitants surrendered on the urgent representations of the king and the Grand Master of the Templars, to whom Saladin had given a promise that he would release them from captivity so soon as he should have mastered the forts and towers which still remained in the hands of the Crusaders. Ascalon was enabled to make very good terms with its conqueror, all the residents being permitted to leave unmolested, and taking with them all their property and possessions. It surrendered on the 5th of September, 1187, having been in the hands of the Crusaders for nearly thirty-five years. At Ascalon Saladin was joined by his son, el Melik El 'Azíz 'Othmán, from Cairo, who brought with him a contingent of troops, and information of the departure of the Emír Lúlú with the Egyptian fleet to intercept the arrival of reinforcements to the Crusaders by sea.

And now came the supreme moment for the Christian power; the Sultan gave orders to march upon Jerusalem, and the greatest consternation prevailed within the Holy City.

On the evening of Sunday, the 20th of October, the Mohammedan army arrived in front of the town on the west side, where it was met by a large sortie, and a fierce and sanguinary conflict took place. On the 25th, the Sultan moved his camp to the north side of the city, and began to set up his engines and battering rams, and shortly effected a slight breach; at the same time his sappers were undermining the wall which runs parallel to the Wády Jehennum. The Christians, few in numbers and disheartened, made one or two sorties, but victory inclined to the Mussulmans. Balian of Ibelin now sallied forth with a flag of truce, and besought the Sultan to allow them to capitulate, but Saladin would hold no parley with him, and swore that "he would capture the city by the sword, as the Franks had taken it from the true believers." The Frank leaders, finding entreaties of no avail, swore that

2 c

if terms were not granted them they would sell their lives as dearly as might be, utterly destroy the city, and the Cubbet es Sakhrah with it, and murder every Mohammedan who remained in their power.* As there were some thousands of Muslim prisoners in the city, this last threat induced the Sultan to reconsider his determination, and a council of war was called, at which it was resolved that the peaceable capitulation of the town should be received upon certain conditions. These were, that the Christians should pay ten dínars for every man, five for a woman, and two for a child, and that those who could not pay were to surrender as prisoners. There were said to be more than sixty thousand fighting men in the town, besides women and children and other non-combatants; the sum of money demanded was therefore immoderately large. Balian disbursed thirty thousand dínars on behalf of the poor, and the Grand Masters of the Hospitallers and Templars, as well as the Patriarch, came forward nobly to the relief of their poorer brethren both with money and security. The Mohammedans entered the city on the 1st of November, just before noon-day prayer, and at once took precautions for ensuring the due performance of the stipulation, by locking the gates of the city and allowing no one to leave without payment of the required sum, and, moreover, appointing officers to collect the poll-tax from the inhabitants.

The Mohammedan historians themselves allow that great corruption prevailed amongst these officers, and that for a small consideration they connived at the escape of many Christians by the breaches which had been made during the siege, or even let them down themselves in buckets from the walls. Some of the more distinguished, especially of the women, experienced the Sultan's clemency; amongst these was a princess of great wealth, who had resided in Jerusalem as a nun, and who was allowed to leave with her property intact. Sybille, the queen consort of the captive king, and the Princess of Kerek, daughter of Philip and mother of Humphrey, were also excused the tax, and permitted to depart. Zeha, one of the Saracen generals, sought and obtained the release of over five hundred Armenians, alleging that they belonged to his country and were only present as pilgrims; and a thousand more Armenians were set at liberty on a similar representation being made in their favour by Muzaffer-ed-dín Kokabúrí, another of Saladin's officers. Committees were established in various parts of the town where payments were received, and a passport from any of these boards was sufficient to procure the bearer a free passage out of the city. As might be expected much peculation went on amongst the inferior officers, in spite of which nearly one hundred thousand dínars were brought into the public treasury, while many Franks still remained prisoners in default of payment. The Franks were anxious to clear out of the place as soon as possible, and sold their lands and effects at ruinous prices to the Mussulmans, while the patriarch stripped the Holy Sepulchre and other churches of the plate, gold and silver ornaments, and other valuables, and prepared to carry them off with him. El 'Emád, the Sultan's secretary, saw with displeasure the disappearance of all this treasure, worth, we are told, more than two hundred thousand dínars, and advised Saladin to forbid its removal, declaring that the privilege extended to private property alone. But the Sultan declared that the Christians should never have occasion to charge the Muslims with a breach of faith, and allowed the Franks to carry off all the portable articles they pleased. Those who were enabled to leave made the best of their way to Tyre; but there still remained over fifteen thousand defaulters, of whom eight thousand were women and children. When the Mussulmans were quietly settled in the possession of Jerusalem the Christians asked and obtained permission to return, on payment of the usual tax.

A curious reason is given by the Arab historians for the strong feeling which the taking of Jerusalem excited throughout Europe. The Christians, say they, made an image of Christ and Mohammed, the latter holding an upraised stick and the former fleeing away, and carried it about with them in Christian countries to induce their co-religionists to revenge their quarrel by a new crusade.

The first Friday after the taking of Jerusalem was a memorable one for Islam; Saladin himself was present at the public service and prayed in the Cubbet es Sakhrah, where a most eloquent sermon (*khotbah*) was delivered by the poet Muhiy-ed-dín (whose verse prophetic of the occasion has been already alluded to*) and the concourse of people was so great that there was scarcely standing room in the open court of the Haram Area.

The Franks had built an oratory and altar over the Sakhrah itself, and "filled it with images and idols;" these Saladin removed, and restored it to its original condition as a mosque. The Christians are also said to have cut off portions of the Sakhrah and sold them in Sicily and Constantinople for their weight in gold.

A great cross, plated with gold and studded with jewels, was found on the holy rock when Saladin entered the Temple; this the Muslims pulled down and dragged with great glee round the city, to the intense horror of the Christians, who expected some dreadful visitation to follow such profanity. Saladin's first care was to uncover the *mihráb* or "prayer niche,"† in front of which the Templars had

---

* Page 77.

† The *mihráb*, that is, of the Jámi' el Aksa, as being that of the congregational building, and therefore the principal one in the enclosure. It is necessary to bear in mind a few facts, which are perfectly clear from the statements of the Arab historians (in the original), but which are either neglected or misinterpreted by many European writers, and notably by Mr. Fergusson. These are:
1. That the *Masjid el Aksa* is the *whole* Haram Area, including the Jámi' el Aksa and Cubbet es Sakhrah, as well as all the smaller

built a wall, leaving an empty space between;"* they had also built a spacious house and a chapel on the west of the kiblah. He pulled down the wall, covered the *mihráb* with marble, thoroughly cleansed the place, and supplied it with lamps, costly carpets, and other furniture. The Sultan Nùr-ed-dín had himself resolved upon the conquest of Jerusalem, but the expedition was prevented by his sudden death. He had ordered a magnificent pulpit (*mimbar*) to be executed by a celebrated artist at Aleppo, intending to present it to the mosque; this Saladin sent for and placed in the Jámi' el Aksa, where it remains to the present day, and forms one of the principal objects of attraction to the visitor, being one of the most exquisite pieces of carved wood-work in the world. Both the Cubbet es Sakhrah and El Aksa were furnished by the Sultan with copies of the Coran, doubtless from the celebrated library at Damascus, the remains of which are preserved in the little dome (called Cubbet el Kutub) in the Jámi' el Omawíyeh of that city.

The princes of Saladin's family personally assisted in the work of restoration and purification, and it is related that El Melik el Muzaffar himself headed the attendants

---

oratories, mosques, minarets, &c. 2. That *all these* were built by 'Abd el Melik (see p. 77), and that the Cubbet es Sakhrah is only mentioned more specially than the other buildings erected by that prince because of its magnificent proportions and the peculiar sanctity of the spot it covers. 3. That the Cubbet es Sakhrah is only a supplementary building (see p. 83). 4. That when *the* pulpit, *the* "kiblah," &c., of the Masjid el Aksa is spoken of it must always be referred to that of the Jámi' el Aksa; just as when speaking of the chancel of an English cathedral we should mean that of the main building, and not that of the lady chapel, and still less of any oratory, however large, that might exist in another part of the close. The account in the text is taken from Mejír-ed-dín. The inscription recording Saladin's restorations may still be seen in letters of gold over the *mihráb* of the Jámi' el Aksa.

* Some say it had been even turned into a *latrina*.

who swept out and washed the sanctuary. The process must have cost a considerable sum, for after thoroughly cleansing it with water they deluged every portion, even to the walls and pavement, with rose water.

The *mihráb*, or, as it is sometimes called, the Tower of David, near the Jaffa Gate, was also refurnished as a mosque, and endowed with funds.

These more important buildings provided for, he turned his attention to the other churches and sacred places in the town. The church of Sion was occupied by El Melik el "Adil and his staff officers, the soldiery being encamped at the gate. The church of St. Hannah was turned into a college for the doctors of the Shafiite sect; and the Patriarch's house adjoining, and partly built on the church of the Holy Sepulchre, was made use of as a cloister for the Sufí monks and philosophers; both of these establishments were liberally endowed, and afterwards became celebrated schools of Mohammedan learning. As for the church of the Holy Sepulchre it was locked up, and no Christian allowed to enter it. It had indeed a narrow escape, as many of Saladin's officers counselled him to destroy it; thanks, however, to the Sultan's moderation and the noble example of 'Omar, which he adduced, their advice was not carried out. The whole of the wealth which he had acquired by this conquest he distributed amongst the most deserving of his followers, disregarding the advice of some more prudent minds to keep it against future emergencies. He also collected all the Mohammedan captives, and fed them, clothed them, and sent them to their homes at his own private expense.

Saladin, having written to the caliph to acquaint him with the victory, remained for some time at Jerusalem to complete the reduction of the fortresses in the neighbourhood and to tranquillise the country; while his generals El Melik el Afdhal and El Melik el Muzaffer, proceeded to Acre. The Emír 'Alí ibn Ahmed el Mashtúb, governor of Sidon and Beyrout remained behind with the Sultan. Hearing that the Marquis of Montferrat had taken advantage of the concentration of their attention upon Jerusalem to strengthen his position at Tyre, he began to tremble for the safety of his own towns, and continually urged Saladin to resume his campaign in Syria.

Accordingly, on the 26th of October, Saladin once more set out for Acre, and reached that city on the 3rd of November. In eight days more he had moved off to Tyre, and, encamping at some distance from the walls, awaited the arrival of the rest of his forces. On the 25th of November the reinforcements came up, under the command of his son, El Melik ed Dháhir Ghiyás ed-dín Ghází, from Aleppo, and the siege was commenced in right earnest, all the wood in the neighbourhood being cut down for the construction of the battering rams and other engines. But Conrad defended the place skilfully and gallantly, and it withstood all attempts to take it by storm.

Hitherto we have seen Saladin prosecuting a career of victory unsullied by a single defeat; the tide of war now began to turn for a time in favour of the Franks.

The first disaster which the Muslims experienced was by sea. The Sultan had ordered all the ships of war to come up and assist in the blockade of Tyre, and those which were at Acre, ten in number, quickly appeared upon the scene, and were joined in a few days by the fleet from Beirút and Jebail. The marquis, seeing that this manœuvre was likely to cause him some trouble, determined to counter it, and accordingly sent out his own vessels to give them battle. The Muslim ships were drawn up in line close upon the shore and immediately protected by their own troops. The sailors, confident in the security of their position, neglected to remain upon the alert, and thus gave the marquis his opportunity, of which he was not slow to avail himself. On the night of the 8th of December, a number of the Sultan's ships were riding at anchor near the entrance to the harbour of Tyre; the sailors and marines were tranquilly sleeping in happy ignorance of the enemy's movements, when, just before morning, they were rudely awakened to find themselves surrounded and at the mercy of the ·Christians, by whom they were at once boarded and captured. The Mohammedans were paralysed at this sudden and unexpected reverse, and the remainder of the fleet were hastily ordered off to Beirút, towards which they made the best of their way, the army riding alongside of them upon the shore to cover their flight. Before, however, they had got far, the Frank vessels came suddenly down upon them, and the Mohammedan sailors, precipitating themselves into the water, made hastily for the shore, leaving their vessels without a soul on board. One schooner alone managed to elude her pursuers, and got off with all her crew. When the Christians came upon the deserted vessels (which they still believed to be full of men) they fancied that the Mohammedans were too terrified to give them battle, and poured tumultuously out upon the shore and attacked the main body of Saladin's troops. The latter had by this time somewhat recovered their presence of mind, and gave them a warm reception; a desperate conflict took place, and the Franks were at last driven back towards the town. Two of their leaders fell into the enemy's hands, and " a great count " was also taken prisoner. El Melek ed Dháhir, who had not taken part in any of the previous engagements, at once ordered the last mentioned prisoner to be beheaded, and the Mohammedans, believing him to be the Marquis of Montferrat himself (whom he did resemble in form and features) were greatly delighted at the supposed death of so formidable an antagonist. But they had experienced a very heavy blow, and would fain have compelled the Sultan to relinquish the enterprise against Tyre and return home. Saladin, however, reproached them with their faint-heartedness, and, partly by bribes, partly by persuasion, induced them to persevere.

As a slight compensation for his recent losses and defeats he received news about this time of the capitulation of the Fortress of Honein, which had been for some time besieged by one of his officers.

The troops now began to suffer so severely from the winter cold and rains that Saladin was obliged, though with extreme reluctance, to raise the siege of Tyre. He had expended immense sums of money upon his engines of war; but these were for the most part too bulky to remove, while to leave them behind would be to strengthen the hands of the besieged. Some, therefore, which it was possible to take to pieces and pack up, were sent on to Sidon, while others, which could not be so provided for, were set fire to and destroyed. The army then broke up into several divisions, and departed with the understanding that they were to come back again in the early part of the spring and resume the siege. The Sultan himself moved on to Acre and camped outside the city; but the cold presently became so intense that he was compelled to seek shelter within the walls. Remaining here in winter quarters, he occupied himself in regulating and improving the public institutions of the town. With the first mild days of spring Saladin was again on the move, and as the whole complement of the army had not yet come up, he determined to commence the new campaign by laying siege to the fortress of Kokeb; but this proved a longer and more difficult task than he had anticipated.

While the Sultan was at Kokeb he received a visit from the widow of Renaud, Prince of Kerek, who came to beg for the release of her son Humphrey. She was accompanied by the queen and her daughter, who had also married Renaud's son. Saladin received them with great courtesy, and agreed with the Princess of Kerek for the release of her son on condition that the two fortresses of

Kerek and Shobek should surrender at discretion to his arms. Having exacted a promise from her to this effect, Humphrey was sent for from Damascus, and proceeded with his mother and a detachment of Mohammedan troops to arrange for the fulfilment of the terms of the contract. But the people of Kerek were by no means disposed to become a ransom for the young count, and met the widow's demand for them to lay down their arms with coarse jeers and opprobrious language. At Shobek she fared no better, and was after all constrained to return to the Sultan with the humiliating confession that she had not sufficient authority over her troops to carry out the stipulations. Saladin, like a true and noble gentleman as he was, disdained to take a mean advantage of her failure, and allowed both the lady and her son to proceed to Tyre. In the meantime he sent troops to reduce Kerek and Shobek. Kokeb still maintained an obstinate resistance, and Saladin, leaving an officer with five hundred men behind him to continue the siege, and posting a regiment of five hundred cavalry at Safad to harass the Christians in that quarter, left for Damascus, which he reached on the 5th of March, 1187. Here he received intelligence of the approach of his army from the east, and, remaining only a week in his capital, he again set out for Baalbekk, whence he marched on to Lebweh, and was there joined by 'Emád-ed-dín, Lord of Sanjár, with his division. Disencumbering themselves of all the heavy baggage, the combined forces hurried on to the sea coast. Several months were consumed in military operations against the Franks without any decisive engagement taking place, though one after another, Jebeleh, Laodicea, Sion, Bekas, and other towns and fortresses fell into the Sultan's hands, and materially increased his resources by the quantity of arms and provisions which they contained. The fort of Burzíyeh gave him more trouble. This castle enjoyed the reputation of being the strongest in Palestine: and was situated upon a lofty mountain nearly 1700 feet high, with steep escarpments, and surrounded by deep valleys. Notwithstanding its formidable character Saladin determined to attack it, and on the morning after his arrival (21st August) he ascended the heights with his troops, both cavalry and infantry, and the whole of his siege train, and surrounded the fortress on every side. For two days and nights a continuous assault was made upon the walls with the battering rams, and projectiles were thrown into the midst of the castle without intermission. On the morning of the 23rd, preparations were made for taking the place by storm: the whole army was divided into three parts, each of which was to carry on the assault for a portion of the day, so as to give the besieged no interval of rest. The first division, under 'Emád-ed-dín, commenced the attack with the early morning light, and the contest raged on both sides with unexampled fury; at last, 'Emád-ed-dín's men beginning to flag, were relieved by the second division, commanded by the Sultan in person. Placing himself at the head of the storming party, Saladin called out to his soldiers to follow him to victory: answering his appeal by a long and enthusiastic shout, they swarmed like one man up the rocks and battlements, carrying everything before them, and poured into the fortress. The defenders, driven back from the walls, now began to cry out for quarter; but it was too late, the blood of the Muslims was fairly aroused, and even Saladin's presence and authority could not for some time stop the indiscriminate slaughter. At last order was partially restored, the prisoners—an immense number—were secured, and the soldiers, loaded with booty, returned in triumph to their tents. Amongst the captives were the sister of the Prince of Antioch (to whom the castle belonged), her husband, daughter, and son-in-law; these were all treated by the conqueror with the greatest kindness and consideration, and were, together with a few of their immediate followers, allowed to depart free and unmolested. The fall of Burzíyeh was closely followed by that of Diresak and Bukrás, both strongholds of the Templars, near Antioch. The last of the two was a great depôt of provisions, and by its capture a large quantity of grain fell into the Saracens' hands.

Saladin next turned his attention to Antioch itself, but the prince of that town, knowing that it was not sufficiently well furnished either with provisions or arms to support a long siege, deemed it more prudent to come to terms. A truce was therefore concluded for five months, and an exchange of prisoners made.

At Bukrás the Sultan took leave of 'Emád-ed-dín, Zanghi, and the Syrian contingent, who had done him good service in the late campaign. Both the chief and his soldiery received substantial marks of Saladin's gratitude, who bestowed upon them liberal presents in addition to the share of prize-money which had been already allotted to them.

Saladin then proceeded with his own army by way of Aleppo, Hamath, and Baalbekk to Damascus, whither his men were desirous of returning in time to keep the fast of Ramadhán. Anxiety, however, for the success of the military operations which he had confided to his various generals, would not allow him to remain long in idleness, and in the beginning of October he set out for Safad. On the way he was joined by his brother El Melek el 'Adil, who had just concluded the siege of Kerek in Moab, that place having capitulated after a protracted resistance. Safad held out until the 30th of November, when it was ceded to Saladin's forces; the defenders obtained quarter by the release of a number of Muslim prisoners, who were in their hands, and received permission to withdraw to Tyre. The Christians hoped to make up for the loss of this important stronghold by strengthening their position at Kokeb, which was blockaded by one of Saladin's generals. They accordingly despatched two hundred picked men to lie in wait for the Muslims at a certain difficult part of the road and attack them at a disadvantage. But a company of Mohammedan troops happened to come across a straggler from this party, who, to save himself, betrayed his companions, and pointed out the ambuscade in the valley.. The whole two hundred were captured and brought to the Saracen leader. Amongst the prisoners were two chiefs of the Knights Hospitallers, and being carried before the Sultan one of them said, "Thank God, we shall come to no harm, now that we have looked upon your highness's face."

"This speech," says the Arab writer, "must have been dictated by divine inspiration, for nothing else could have induced the Sultan to spare their lives; as it was, he set them both at liberty."

The great addition to the besieging force, combined with the extreme cold and scarcity of provisions, proved too much for the endurance of the garrison of Kokeb, and in the beginning of January, 1189, it was added to the list of the Sultan's conquests. After this, Saladin and his brother returned to Jerusalem, where the latter took leave of him and set out for Egypt with his division of the army.

The Sultan then proceeded to Acre, and spent some time in fortifying and otherwise providing for the safety and good government of the town, which he handed over to the care of one Bahá-ed-dín Caracosh, who had, in the meantime, arrived from Egypt with a large following. Towards the end of March he commenced a tour of inspection throughout his Syrian dominions, visiting in turn, Tiberias, Damascus, and other places. On the 21st of April he reached the Shakíf Arnon, near which he encamped in the plain called Merj 'Ayún. The fortress of the Shakíf was in the hands of Renaud, Lord of Sidon, who came in person to the Sultan, and begged for three months' grace to enable him to remove his family from

Tyre, alleging that, if the Marquis of Montferrat should get intelligence of what he had done, his family would be detained there as hostages. The Sultan acceded to his request, and refrained from attacking his castle. Renaud, however, took advantage of this leniency to strengthen his own position, and made secret but active preparations for war. Saladin discovering the treachery, gave orders for blockading the fort, whereupon Renaud again endeavoured to induce him to grant a year's cessation of hostilities; but the Sultan was not to be deceived a second time, and, some officers he had sent to inspect the castle reporting that the work of fortification was still being carried on, arrested the count, and sent him a prisoner to Banias. Sending for him a few days afterwards, he upbraided him with his perfidy, and despatched him for safe keeping to Damascus. As for the castle, the Sultan established a close blockade, although it was full twelve months before it was finally ceded to his lieutenant. While the Sultan was encamped in the Merj 'Ayún, the Frank forces were concentrating around Tyre, which the marquis had contrived to make the greatest stronghold in Syria, and in which the last hope of the Christian arms was placed.

On the 3rd of July they made an attempt upon Sidon, but were repulsed by Saladin—whose scouts brought him timely notice of the manœuvre—though not without considerable loss on either side.

After this Saladin retired to Tiberias, and occupied some time in making preparation for a decisive attack upon the Christian camp. Meanwhile, the Christians were by no means idle, but dispersed themselves over the country in various directions, committing much depredation, and harassing the Mohammedan troops, who were continually falling into their ambuscades.

On the 22nd of August Saladin received news that the Franks had collected their forces by land and sea, and were bearing down upon Acre, a detachment having already reached Alexandretta, where they had had a slight skirmish with the Muslims. The Sultan hastily issued orders for collecting the army together, and hurried off to the relief of the town. Having arrived at Sefúríyeh he left his heavy baggage, and pushed on to Acre with all speed; but the Franks were before him, and had already invested the place, rendering the approach impossible for his troops.

On the 13th of September he made a desperate onslaught upon the besieging lines, drove the Franks to a hill called Tell es Siyásíyeh, and thus established a free communication with the city on the north side.

On the 21st of September the Franks assembled towards the close of the day and attacked the Muslims in full force; the latter, however, withstood the shock, and both sides fought with great fury, but night coming on compelled them to desist from hostilities.

On the 24th the Sultan moved to Tell es Siyásíyeh, which, from its commanding position, appeared to him a very important post to occupy. Here information was brought him that the Franks were dispersed over the country in foraging parties, and, without loss of time, he despatched companies of Arabs, whose familiarity with guerilla warfare peculiarly adapted them for such service, to intercept them. The Bedawin horsemen bore down upon the small detached parties, cut them off from the camp, and, slaughtering them almost without resistance, carried their heads in triumph to Saladin.

On the 3rd of October the Franks made a desperate onslaught upon Saladin's troops; a fierce battle ensued, in which victory inclined to the Christians, and the Muslims were compelled to flee, some to Tiberias, and others to Damascus. While the victors were occupied in pillaging the Sultan's camp a panic suddenly seized them; the Muslims rallied, and attacked their left, completely defeating them, and killing more than five thousand cavalry, amongst whom was the Grand Master of the Templars. The bodies of the Franks lay in such numbers on the field of battle that the Muslims were much annoyed by the stench, and the soldiers were employed for some days in throwing the carcasses into the sea.

Saladin now dismissed the Egyptian contingent, bidding them return in the spring, and both sides prepared for the winter, which was already setting in with great severity. The Franks fortified their camp, and dug a fosse round the town of Acre, extending from sea to sea. The Sultan had, in the meantime, removed to his old camp at Kharúbeh, where the heavy baggage lay. The news that the Emperor of Germany, Frederick Barbarossa, was *en route* for Syria stimulated both parties to further exertions, and the warlike preparations went on with greater activity than ever.

On the 13th of December the Egyptian fleet—which the Sultan had ordered to be prepared on the first landing of the Franks at Acre—arrived, with a complement of more than ten thousand men. This reinforcement gave great confidence to the Muslim troops, and constant raids were made by the new comers upon the Christian lines. The arrival of a Frank ship, laden with women, about this time, seems to have demoralized both armies; for the ladies appear to have been somewhat indifferent as to religion and nationality, and to have bestowed their favours upon Christian and Muslim alike, according as one or the other happened to meet them on landing. The Arab writers, however, speak of many Christian women, who were animated by the true Crusading spirit; and it was no uncommon occurrence to find upon the field of battle, or amongst the prisoners, many champions of the softer sex. The new year, A.D. 1190, came in, and found things *in statu quo*, the town besieged by the Franks, and the latter in turn hemmed in by the Sultan's forces.

Saladin himself, ever actively engaged in inspecting his lines, was exposed to constant dangers; on one occasion, having ventured out hunting on the beach, he would inevitably have been taken prisoner by a party of the enemy, had not the advanced guard of his own army, which was stationed in the neighbourhood, luckily come up in time to effect a rescue. Constant communications were kept up between the town and the Sultan's army by means of carrier pigeons and of divers, who managed to swim past the enemy's lines, and carry letters and money to and fro between them. The Franks had constructed towers, battering-rams, and other engines of war, with great skill, and would have, no doubt, accomplished the taking of the city by storm, had it not been for a certain cunning artificer from Damascus, who succeeded in destroying them one by one with rockets, naphtha, and other combustibles, which he directed upon the works.

The winter and spring passed away without any decisive change in the relative position of the two armies; but on the 13th of June, 1190, a second naval reinforcement arrived from Egypt, and the Sultan endeavoured, by an attack by land, to divert the attention of the enemy, and enable the marines to land. The Frank ships, however, were not idle, and several severe engagements took place by sea, in which the Muslims had decidedly the disadvantage. Presently news arrived that the Emperor of Germany had crossed over from Constantinople, and had been for more than a month, during the severest season of winter, in great straits, his army being compelled to devour their cavalry horses for want of food, and to burn their pontoons in the absence of fire-wood.

On reaching Tarsus the army halted to drink at the river which flows by the city, and the Emperor being driven, in the crowd and confusion, to a deep part of the stream, where there was a rapid current, was hurried away by the force of the stream, received a blow on the head from an overhanging bough, and was taken out in an insensible and almost lifeless condition. A violent chill and fever was the result, which terminated after a few hours in his death. His son succeeded him in the command, and arrived at Acre with the remnant of a fine army in a miserable plight, and entirely dispirited by such a succession of reverses.

The Franks, when they heard of the approach of the son of the Emperor of Germany, were afraid that he would appropriate all the credit of the campaign, and determined to make a final effort before he arrived. Accordingly at noon, on the 25th of July, they attacked the camp of El Melik el "Adil. He withstood the charge, and managed to drive back the enemy without waiting for the rest of the troops to come up. At this juncture the Sultan arrived upon the scene with a large number of men, and attacked the Franks in the rear. A complete victory for the Muslims was the result, more than ten thousand of the enemy falling, with a loss, it is said, of only ten men on the other side.

The arrival of Count Henry with a large following and much wealth, gave fresh courage to the disheartened Christian forces. The count distributed large sums amongst the soldiery; and the siege of Acre was prosecuted with more vigour than ever. Provisions now became very scarce and dear in the Christian camp, and many of the soldiers, compelled by actual starvation, came over as deserters to the Mohammedan lines.

A few battles were fought, always with disadvantage to the Franks, many of whom were also killed or taken prisoners in the ambuscades which the Muslims were continually laying for them. On the 31st of December, seven ships arrived from Egypt with provisions for the relief of the town, and while the inhabitants were engaged in assisting them to escape the enemy's fleet and get into port, the Christians took advantage of the walls being partially deserted, to make a desperate effort to take the place by storm. The scaling ladders, however, broke with the weight of the men; the storming parties were thrown into disorder, and the Muslims, on the alarm being given, left the ships to themselves, and rushing up to the walls drove back or cut to pieces their assailants. The incident was disastrous to both sides, for a sudden storm coming on carried the seven ships out to sea, where they perished with all the crews and supplies. A few nights afterwards a portion of the eastern wall of the city fell down, but the defenders thrust their bodies into the breach so promptly, that the Franks were unable to take advantage of the opportunity.

Two curious stories are told of this period of the war. One is, that a party of Frank renegades having obtained possession of a small vessel, landed upon the island of Cyprus during the celebration of a feast. They immediately proceeded to the principal church of the place, entered it, and mixed with the congregation who were assembled there in prayer. Suddenly they started up, locked the door, and completely sacked the building, carrying away more than twenty-seven prisoners, women and children, whom they sold at Laodicæa. The other story is, that some Mohammedan looting the Christian camp, had stolen an infant, three months old, from its mother's arms. The bereaved parent rushed over to the enemy's camp, and, before she could be stopped by the guards and chamberlains, appeared before the Sultan's tents, lamenting her loss, and beseeching him to restore her child. Saladin caused inquiries to be made, and finding that the infant had been purchased by one of his soldiers, ransomed it with his own hand, and gave it back to its mother.

A brig belonging to the Mohammedans and bound for Acre, with seven hundred men on board and a large quantity of arms and munitions of war, came into collision with one of King Richard's English vessels. The Mohammedan captain, finding himself worsted in the fight, burnt his ship, which perished with all hands. This was the first serious disaster which the Mohammedans had experienced. In June, 1190, hostilities were carried on with renewed vigour, and engagements were of daily occurrence. On one occasion, after a slight skirmish, the Franks retired with a single capture, and having got out of bow shot of the Muslim camp they made a bonfire and roasted their prisoner alive. The Muslims, maddened at the insult and barbarity, brought out one of their Frank prisoners, and, by way of reprisal, burnt him in front of their lines. El 'Emád, Saladin's secretary, who relates the incident, describes with much feeling the effect produced upon the minds of all the spectators by this exhibition of savage ferocity.

The crisis was evidently approaching. The Franks endeavoured to delude the Sultan into inactivity by proposals for peace, while they were at the same time hastening on their preparations for a final assault upon Acre. Saladin, however, was constantly informed of the state of things within the city, and knew that it could not hold out much longer; he, therefore, refused to listen to terms, but used all means in his power to force on a battle, and on the night of the 2nd of July he attacked the enemy's trenches, and succeeded in forcing a position at one, though not a very important point.

At this juncture, Seif-ed-dín el Mashtúb, momentarily expecting the city to be taken by storm, came out with a flag of truce to make an offer of capitulation, and demand quarter on behalf of the inhabitants. King Richard received him with his usual bluntness, and refused to grant the request. When El Mashtúb reminded him of the clemency which his master Saladin had exercised upon similar occasions, Richard answered curtly: "These kings whom thou seest around me are my servants; but as for you, ye are my slaves; I shall do with you as I please."

The Saracen emír returned to Acre highly indignant at this discourteous treatment, and swore that the fall of the city should cost the victors dear.

When El Mashtúb made known the ill success of his errand many of the chief men and emírs of Acre deserted the city, to the great chagrin of the Sultan, who condemned them to forfeiture of their estates, and other pains and penalties. This severity, and the charge of cowardice, induced some to return and take part once more in the defence of the town.

On the 4th of July a great battle took place, and lasted until the morning of the 5th, but without any decided advantage on either side. Evening again came and found them in the same position; the city surrounded by the enemy, and the enemy surrounded by Saladin's army. But on Saturday the 6th, the Prince of Sidon sallied forth from the trenches with about forty knights, and rode into the Sultan's camp carrying a flag of truce. Saladin sent Najíb-ed-dín, one of his confidential officers, to arrange with him the terms on which the city should be capitulated. At first the Franks refused to listen to any other terms than the complete surrender of all the Christian possessions in Syria and Palestine, and the release of all the captives. It was then proposed that Acre should be ceded to the Christians, that its garrison and inhabitants should be allowed to leave unmolested, and that an exchange of prisoners should be made, one Christian being released by the Muslims for every one of their own men given up by the Christians. These terms were also refused, and Saladin's magnificent offer to throw the "True Cross" into the bargain could not induce them to agree. Perhaps the relic had fallen into disfavour after its failure at Tiberias, or it might be that the Crusaders were beginning to rely more upon their own military prowess than upon the childish superstitions of the fetish-worshipping monks.

On the 22nd of July the Christians effected a breach in

the walls, and were with difficulty prevented from entering the city. El Mashtúb again sought Richard's camp with offers of capitulation, and this time with better success. It was agreed that the lives and property of the defenders of Acre should be spared on condition of their paying two hundred thousand dínárs, releasing five hundred captives, and giving up possession of the True Cross.

Suddenly, therefore, much to the Sultan's surprise and annoyance, the Christian standards were seen flying from the walls of Acre. He immediately despatched Bahá-eddín Caracosh to make the best arrangements possible, and promised to pay half the amount of the indemnity at once, and give hostages for the settlement of the remainder of the claim within a month. Hostilities were not suspended in the meantime, and the Franks having made several sallies from their new position at Acre, suffered severely from the Arab horsemen, who continually came down unexpectedly on them and cut off their retreat.

In the beginning of August messengers came from the Christian camp to demand payment of the sum agreed upon. The first instalment of a hundred thousand dínárs was given up to them, but Saladin refused to pay the rest, or to hand over the captives until he had received some guarantee that the Christians would perform their part of the contract, and allow the prisoners from Acre to go free. After numerous delays and disagreements everything appeared at last likely to be satisfactorily arranged; the money was weighed out and placed before Saladin, the captives were ready to be delivered up, and the "True Cross" was also displayed. Richard was encamped close by the Merj 'Ayún, and had caused the Acre captives to be ranged behind him on the neighbouring hill side. Suddenly, at a signal from the king, the Christian soldiers turned upon the unhappy and helpless captives, and massacred them all in cold blood. Even at such a moment as this Saladin did not forget his humane disposition and his princely character. The proud Saladin disdained to sully his honour by making reprisals upon the unarmed prisoners at his side; he simply refused to give up the money or the cross, and sent the prisoners back to Damascus.

Which was the Paynim, and which the Christian then?

In the first week of September the Franks determined to march upon Ascalon, and, having provided for the safety of Acre, set off in that direction. El Afdhal, who was in command of the advanced guard, intercepted them on their road, and managed to divide them into two parties. He then sent off an express to his father Saladin, requesting him to come to his assistance, but the officers of the Sultan represented to him that the army was not yet prepared to move; the opportunity was therefore lost, and the Franks were enabled to pass on to Cæsarea. The Muslims, however, shortly afterwards started in pursuit, and on the 11th of September they came up with the enemy, and a bloody battle was fought by the Nahr el Casb near Cæsarea. The next day both armies moved off to Arsúf; a battle took place on the road, and the Franks retired with considerable loss into the town, while the Muslims encamped on the banks of the river 'Aujeh.

In a few days they again fought their way along the coast, and on the 19th of September the Christian army succeeded in reaching Jaffa, while the Sultan with his troops encamped at Ramleh on the afternoon of the same day.

Here he waited for the heavy baggage, and when this arrived, in charge of his brother, El "Adil, he moved on to Ascalon. A council of war was immediately held, at which it was decided to destroy the fortifications of the last named town. As the Franks were in possession of Jaffa, which lies about half way between Ascalon and Jerusalem, it was clearly impossible to defend both towns without the maintenance of an overwhelming force in each, and as Saladin felt sure that Ascalon, if besieged, would share the fate of Acre, he determined to raze it to the ground, and concentrate his efforts upon the defence of Jerusalem. The work of demolition was at once commenced, and the city, one of the finest in Palestine, soon became a mass of ruins; the inhabitants suffered severely by this transaction, for they were obliged to sell their property at ruinous prices, and dispersed themselves over the country, to find a home where best they could.

The intermediate fortresses of Lydda, Ramleh, and Natrún were next destroyed, and on the 14th of October the Sultan camped on a high hill near the latter town. A few unimportant engagements had in the meantime taken place between the two armies, in one of which Richard narrowly escaped being taken prisoner.

Negotiations were now reopened between El Melik el 'Adil and King Richard, and a peace was actually arranged, upon the stipulation that Richard should give his sister in marriage to El 'Adil, and that the husband and wife should occupy the throne of Jerusalem, and jointly rule over the Holy Land. The Grand Masters of the Templars and Hospitallers were to occupy certain villages, but they were not to retain possession of any of their castles. The queen was to have no military attendants in Jerusalem, although a certain number of priests and monks were still to be allowed there.

El 'Adil called the principal men of the army around him, El 'Emád, Saladin's secretary, amongst the number, and deputed them to consult the Sultan's wishes upon the subject. The latter agreed to the conditions, and on the 30th of October the messengers returned to King Richard to inform him of the acceptance of his proposal.

The Frank chiefs, however, strongly opposed the match, while the priests poisoned the princess's mind, and induced her to withdraw from the engagement, except on the condition that El 'Adil should embrace the Christian religion. This, of course, he declined to do, and the negotiations fell through. The Sultan then moved off to Ramleh, so as to be nearer the enemy. Here news was brought him that the Franks had made a sortie at Barzur; hastening against them he approached their camp and completely surrounded it, but the Christians charged fiercely and suddenly, and broke through the Mohammedan ranks.

On the 18th another conference was held between El "Adil and the King of England, but again their attempts at negotiations failed. The Lord of Sidon, who had come from Tyre, was more fortunate, and concluded a peace with the Sultan, hoping by this means to strengthen his own hands against Richard. The latter, on this, again renewed his proposals, but they, as usual, came to nothing, for whenever an arrangement was on the point of being concluded his bad faith or stupidity rendered it abortive.

There was now no longer any doubt but that the Franks were bent upon the conquest of the Holy City, and as winter was coming on apace, the Sultan retired, on the 14th of December, within the walls of Jerusalem, and occupied himself with the fortification of the town. He, however, provided for the safety of the country between Jerusalem and Jaffa by posting brigades of soldiers in the various passes and defiles upon the road.

A party of workmen opportunely arrived at this time from Mosul, despatched by the sovereign of that place, who also sent money to pay them. These were employed in digging the trenches, and remained six months engaged upon the work. In addition to this, Saladin built a strong wall round the town, at which he compelled more than two thousand Frank prisoners to labour. He repaired the towers and battlements between the Damascus and Jaffa gates, expending upon them an immense sum of money, and employing in their construction the large stones which were quarried out in cutting the trench. His sons, his brother, El 'Adil, and other princes of his court, acted as overseers of the work, whilst he himself daily rode about from station to station encouraging the labourers, and even bringing in building stones upon the pommel of his saddle. His example was followed by all classes of inhabitants, and the work of fortification went on with great rapidity. By the beginning of the year 1192 the wall was completed, the trenches were dug, and the inhabitants awaited with complacency the arrival of the besieging army. On the 20th of January the Franks left Ramleh, and had advanced as far as Ascalon, when they suddenly changed their intention of marching upon Jerusalem and stayed to rebuild the demolished city. El Mashtúb, who had been taken prisoner by the Franks, but had purchased his ransom for the sum of fifty thousand dínárs, of which he had actually paid thirty thousand (and given pledges for the rest), came to Jerusalem on the 18th of March. The Sultan received him graciously, and gave him the town of Nablús and its vicinity as a compensation for his heavy pecuniary loss. The general did not, however, live long to enjoy his good fortune, but died in the course of the year, bequeathing a third of his estate to the Sultan, and leaving the rest to his son.

On the 29th of March the Marquis of Montferrat was assassinated at Tyre by two men as he was leaving the house of the bishop, where he had just been entertained at a repast. The murderers were at once arrested, and put to an ignominious death; not, however, until they had confessed that it was the King of England who had instigated them to the deed. Many attempts have been made by historians to clear King Richard's character from this foul blot, and a letter purporting to come from the " Old Man of the Mountain " accepting the responsibility of the act is triumphantly appealed to. The document in question is, however, a transparent forgery, and the unscrupulous character and savage brutality of the lion-hearted king afford only too good reason for believing the dying testimony of the actual perpetrators of the crime. At any rate, Richard alone profited by it, and obtained possession of Tyre, which he subsequently made over to Count Henry of Champagne. On the death of the marquis, Richard again endeavoured to come to terms with Saladin, proposing to divide the country equally between the latter and himself, and to leave all Jerusalem and its fortifications in possession of the Muslims, with the sole exception of the Church of the Holy Sepulchre.

A great reverse was experienced by the Mohammedans about this time by the fall of Dárúm, a strong fortress, situated on the border of the Egyptian territory beyond Gaza. The Franks stormed the town after having effected a breach in the walls, and refused quarter to the inhabitants. The governor, finding all hope of further resistance gone, escaped to Hebron; the superintendent of stores, however, remained, and, determining that the besiegers should reap as little profit as possible from their conquest, hamstrung all the beasts of burden and burnt them. When the Christians entered the city they put nearly every one of the inhabitants to the sword, reserving only a few prisoners, for whom they thought they might obtain a heavy ransom. Several other engagements took place in the same neighbourhood, in which the Franks were not so successful, and on the 3rd of April they divided their camp into two parties, the one making its head-quarters at Ascalon, and the other pitching at Beit Jibrín. Jerusalem was now threatened with an immediate attack, but the vigilance of the Sultan warded off the blow, and a determined sortie compelled the enemy to retire to Colonia.

The Sultan had sent frequent messengers to Egypt to hurry on the departure of the army which was being levied in that country for the relief of Jerusalem. Faleked-dín, El 'Adil's brother, who was in command, pitched his tents at Bilbeys; whence, as soon as his numbers were complete he set off, followed by an immense concourse of merchants and traders who had taken advantage of the military escort across the desert. On the 23rd of June news reached the Sultan that the Egyptian contingent was on the march, but that, relying on their numbers, they were proceeding without due caution, while the King of England with a large force was lying in wait for them upon the road. Saladin sent off an officer at the head of a division to meet the approaching force, with orders to conduct them round by the desert, and take them over the river of El Hesy before the enemy should come upon them. Falek-ed-dín, however, did not take any means to inform himself concerning the place of rendezvous, but taking the shortest road, and sending his heavy baggage round by another way, he called a halt, and encamped for the night beside a stream called El Khaweilifeh. With the early dawn next morning the enemy came suddenly upon them, and a scene of indescribable confusion ensued. The Muslims started up from their sleep, ran frantically off in any direction that was open to them, and thus escaped in the twilight. Their baggage, arms, and equipments fell, of course, into the enemy's hands; this was so far fortunate, for if the Franks loved slaughter well they loved plunder better, and there was sufficient to turn their attention from pursuing the fugitives of the Egyptian force thus completely broken up and routed; some wandered back to Egypt, not a few were lost in the desert, and a miserable remnant found their way by Kerek to Jerusalem, where the Sultan received them kindly and condoled with them upon their misfortune.

The Crusaders, being unsuccessful against Jerusalem, determined to make an expedition against Beirút, as the occupation of that port was most important for their communications with home, and its conquest seemed likely to prove an easy matter.

But they had miscalculated the tactics of the man with

whom they had to deal; Saladin, who appears throughout to have possessed the fullest information respecting their movements, sent orders to his son, El Afdhal, at Damascus, to prepare for their reception. Accordingly, when they reached the sea coast of Syria they found Beirút occupied by the Damascene troops, and a large army awaiting them in the Merj 'Ayún, which prevented the Franks in Acre from coming to the assistance of their comrades. Taking advantage, also, of their absence, Saladin bore down upon Jaffa, which, in the absence of King Richard, could not hold out for long. The Muslims had already effected an entry into the city, and were about to take possession of the fortress, when Saladin, who could never refuse a petition for quarter, and whose experience of the Crusaders' good faith had not yet taught him prudence, allowed himself to be prevailed upon by promises of submission on the part of the patriarch and other chief men of the town to grant a day's delay and treat about the terms of capitulation. Of this concession the Christians, as usual, took a mean advantage, and while they deluded the Sultan with false oaths and promises, they were sending express messengers to hasten the return of Richard, who unexpectedly arrived by sea in the very midst of the negotiations and took possession of the citadel. The Muslims thus lost much of the advantage which their victory gave them, but they still retained possession of the town itself, and recovered the greater part of the property which had been plundered from the Egyptian contingent.

Both parties were now at a dead lock; the Franks on their side could not hope to take Jerusalem, and the Muslims on theirs were unable to drive the Christians out of the country. Richard was the first to propose an armistice; but Saladin still held out, and strenuously urged upon his officers the necessity for continuing the *jehád*, or "Holy War." But the Mohammedan chiefs were weary of continued fighting without decisive results, and as strongly urged upon the Sultan that the army required rest, and that peace was absolutely necessary to enable the country to recover its industrial activity, the repression of which had already caused so much misery to the inhabitants. An appeal to Saladin on behalf of a suffering community was never made in vain, and he consented to forego the attractions of military glory for the sake of his people's prosperity. A truce of three years and eight months, both by land and sea, was ultimately agreed upon, commencing 2nd of September, 1192. The crusading princes and generals took solemn oaths to observe the conditions of the treaty, with the sole exception of King Richard, who held out his hand to the Saracen Sultan, and said that "There was his hand upon it, but a king's word might be taken without an oath." Saladin returned his grasp, and professed himself satisfied with that mode of ratifying the truce. He probably felt that in this frank and cordial demonstration he had a better guarantee of Richard's good faith than any oath would have afforded; for bitter experience had taught him that so long as an unscrupulous priest remained to give the sanction of the Church to an act of perfidious meanness, a Crusader's oath was of little value. The terms of the truce were, that the sea-board from Jaffa to Cæsarea, and from Acre to Tyre, should remain in the hands of the Franks, and that Ascalon should not be rebuilt; the Sultan, on his side, insisted that the territory of the Ismaelites should be included in the truce, and the Franks on theirs demanded a similar privilege for Antioch and Tripoli; Lydda and Ramleh were to be considered common ground. Saladin, on the conclusion of the truce, occupied himself in strengthening the walls and fortifications of Jerusalem; and the Crusaders, having free access to the city, commenced visiting the Holy Sepulchre in crowds, and, to judge from the accounts given of their behaviour, this privilege, for which they had been fighting so long, was after all but lightly esteemed. King Richard begged Saladin not to allow any one to visit the city without a written passport from himself, hoping by this means to keep up the devotional longings of his followers, and so to induce them to return at the expiration of the truce. Saladin's keen penetration at once detected the impolicy of such a step, while his sense of honour revolted against its discourtesy, the request was, therefore, refused. Richard shortly after this fell ill, and leaving the government in the hands of his nephew, Count Henry, he sailed away, and left the Holy Land for ever. Saladin, whose restless energy and religious zeal would not allow him to remain long in idleness, prepared for a pilgrimage to Mecca, and had actually written to Egypt and to Arabia to make the necessary arrangements; but at the instance of his officers, who represented to him the urgent need which the country stood in of his presence, he relinquished his intention.

After a tour through Syria, in the course of which he provided for the safety and good government of the towns through which he passed, redressing the wrongs of the people, punishing those who exercised injustice or oppression, and rewarding all whose administration had been moderate and just, he returned to Damascus, after an absence of four years, during the whole of which time he had been incessantly occupied in the prosecution of the Holy War. His arrival was hailed with the greatest demonstrations of joy; the city was illuminated, and for days the people made holiday to celebrate the return of their beloved sovereign, the saviour of El Islam. But their joy was short-lived, for on the 21st of February, 1193, he was seized with a bilious fever, and after lingering for twelve days he expired, and was buried in the citadel of Damascus, in the apartments in which he died. A short time afterwards the Sultan's remains were removed to the tomb which they now occupy, in the vicinity of the Great Mosque, and which had been prepared for their reception by his son, El Afdhal. Saladin was nearly fifty-seven years old when he died; his father, Aiyúb, was the son of a certain Kurd, a native of Davín, named Shádí, and a retainer of 'Emad-ed-dín Zanghí, father of the celebrated Sultan Núr-ed-dín, of Damascus. From him the dynasty was called the Kurdish or Aiyubite dynasty. At the outset of his career Saladin delighted to emulate his great namesake, Yúsuf es Sadík, the Joseph of Scripture story; in pursuance of this idea he sent for his father to Egypt, immediately upon his accession to power, and offered to give up all authority into his hands. This Aiyúb declined, and contented himself with the honourable and lucrative post of Controller of the Treasury, with which his son entrusted him. The old gentleman died of a fall from his horse while his son was absent upon one of his expeditions against the Christians at Kerek. No better proof can be given of the respect and esteem which Saladin's many virtues naturally commanded than the terms upon which he lived with his brother and other relatives. In spite of the too frequent application of the proverb which says that "the Turk can bear no brother near the throne," we do not hear of a single instance of jealousy or insubordination being exhibited against his authority by any member of his house or court, while his subjects absolutely idolized him. Saladin knew how to win the affection of his troops while he made his authority felt, and his example restrained in them that license which war too often engenders. Courteous alike to friend and foe, faithful to his plighted word, noble in reverses and moderate in success, the Paynim Saladin stands forth in history as fair a model of a true knight *sans peur et sans reproche* as any which the annals of Christian chivalry can boast.

CHAPTER XVII.

THE MOHAMMEDAN PILGRIMS.

"Proclaim unto the people a solemn pilgrimage; let them come unto thee on foot, and on every lean camel, arriving from every distant road; that they be witnesses of the advantages which accrue from visiting this holy place."—Cor'án, cap. xxii. vv. 28, 29.

THERE are two kinds of pilgrimage in Islam, the *Hajj* and the *Ziyáreh*. The first is the greater pilgrimage to the shrine of Mecca, and this it is absolutely incumbent upon every Muslim to perform once at least in his life. As the injunction is, however, judiciously qualified by the stipulation that the true believer shall have both the will and the power to comply with it, a great many avoid the tedious and difficult journey. The second, or *Ziyáreh*, consists in "visiting" the tombs of saints, or other hallowed spots, and is an easier and more economical means of grace, as the pilgrim can choose his shrine for himself. Next to that of Mecca and Medina, the pilgrimage to Jerusalem is most esteemed by Mohammedan devotees; and, as we have already seen, political exigencies have, on more occasions than one, caused it to be substituted for the more orthodox and genuine *Hajj*. While all Muslims are enjoined to visit Mecca, they are recommended to go to Jerusalem. Plenary indulgence and future rewards are promised to those who visit the Holy City, and the effect of all prayers and the reward or punishment of good or evil works, are doubled therein. Such as are unable to accomplish the journey may send oil to furnish a lamp, and as long as it burns the angels in the place will pray for the sender. As for those who build, repair, or endow any portion of the Mosque, they will enjoy prolonged life and increased wealth on earth, as well as a reward in heaven. The Roman church is not singular in its successful dealings with rich and moribund sinners.

The pilgrim, in entering the Haram, puts his right foot forward, and says, " O Lord, pardon my sins, and open to me the doors of thy mercy." As he goes out he repeats the customary benediction upon Mohammed, and exclaims, " O Lord, pardon my sins, and open to me the doors of thy grace." In entering the Cubbet es Sakhrah he should be careful to keep the Holy Rock upon his right hand, so that in walking round it he may exactly reverse the proceedings in the case of the Tawwáf, or circuit of the Ka'abeh at Mecca. He should then enter the cave which is beneath the Sakhrah with humility of deportment, and should first utter the formula called "the Prayer of Solomon," viz., " O God, pardon the sinners who come here, and relieve the injured." After this, he may pray for whatsoever he pleases, with the assurance that his request will be granted.

As he is conducted about the Haram es Sheríf the various sacred spots are pointed out to him, and when he has performed the requisite number of prostrations, and repeated the appropriate prayer dictated by his guide, the story or tradition of each is solemnly related to him. Thus, on approaching the "Holy Rock" he is told that it is one of the rocks of paradise; that it stands on a palm-tree, beneath which flows one of the rivers of Paradise. Beneath the shade of this tree Asia, the wife of Pharaoh, who is said to have been the most beautiful woman in the world, and Miriam, the sister of Moses, shall stand on the Day of Resurrection, to give drink to the true believers.

This Sakhrah is the centre of the world, and on the Day of Resurrection the angel Israfíl will stand upon it to blow the last trumpet. It is also eighteen miles nearer heaven than any other place in the world; and beneath it is the source of every drop of sweet water that flows on the face of the earth. It is supposed to be suspended miraculously between heaven and earth. The effect upon the spectators was, however, so startling that it was found necessary to place a building round it, and conceal the marvel.

The Cadam es Sheríf, or "Footstep of the Prophet," is on a detached piece of a marble column, on the south-west side of the Sakhrah. It is reported to have been made by Mohammed, in mounting the beast Borák, preparatory to his ascent into heaven on the night of the "M'iráj."

Before leaving the Cubbet es Sakhrah the pilgrim is taken to pray upon a dark coloured marble pavement just inside the gate of the Cubbet es Sakhrah, called Báb el Jannah; some say that this is the spot upon which the prophet Elias prayed, others that it covers the tomb of King Solomon. All agree that it is a stone which originally formed part of the pavement of Paradise.

A descent into the Maghárah or cave beneath the Sakhrah—a reverential salutation of the "tongue of the rock," a broken column slanting against the roof of the cave—a prayer before the marks of the Angel Gabriel's fingers—and, if he be a Shi'ah, a fervent prostration before a piece of iron bar which does duty as the sword of 'Alí ibn Abi Tálib "the Lion of God." These, with a few others of less interest, complete the objects of special devotion in the Cubbet es Sakhrah itself.

On issuing forth into the open court more wonders meet his eye. First, there is the beautiful Cubbet es Silsileh*

* Also called Mahkemet Da'ád, or the Tribunal of David.

or Dome of the Chain; it derives its name from a tradition that in King Solomon's time a miraculous chain was suspended between heaven and earth over this particular spot. It was possessed of such peculiar virtue that whenever two litigants were unable to decide their quarrel they had but to proceed together to this place, and endeavour each to seize the chain, which would advance to meet the grasp of him who was in the right, and would elude all efforts of the other to catch it. One day two Jews appealed to the ordeal, one accused the other of having appropriated some money which he had confided to his keeping, and, swearing that he had not received it back, laid hold of the chain. The fraudulent debtor, who had artfully concealed the money in the interior of a hollow staff upon which he was leaning, handed it to the claimant, and swore that he had given back the money. He also was enabled to seize the chain, and the bystanders were hopelessly perplexed as to the real state of the case. From that moment the chain disappeared, feeling doubtless that it had no chance of supporting its character for legal acumen in the midst of a city full of Jews.

The place, however, still retains some of its judicial functions, and, if we are to credit Arab historians, perjury is an exceedingly dangerous weapon in the neighbourhood of the Sakhrah. It is related that the Caliph 'Omar ibn 'Abd el 'Azíz ordered the stewards of his predecessor Suleimán, to give an account of their stewardship upor oath before the Sakhrah. One man alone refused to swear and paid a thousand dínárs rather than do so; in a year' time he was the only survivor of them all. The Constan tinople cabinet might take a hint from this.

On the right hand of the Sakhrah, in the western part the court, is a small dome called the Cubbet el M'iráj, "Dome of the Ascent," which marks the spot from whic Mohammed is supposed to have started upon his "heaven' journey." It is, of course, one of the principal objects the Muslim pilgrims' devotion. The present dome was erected in the year 597, on the site of an older one which had fallen into ruins, by a certain governor of Jerusalem named Ez Zanjelí.

The Macám en Nebí, or "Prophet's Standpoint," is celebrated from its connection with the same event. It is now occupied by an elegant pulpit of white sculptured marble.

At the end of the Haram Area, on the eastern side, is a spot known as Súk el Ma'rifah (Market of Knowledge), behind the praying place of David. The tradition attaching to this spot is, that when any of the ancient Jewish occupants of the city had committed any sin, he wrote up over the door of his own house a notice of the fact, and came to the Market of Knowledge to pray for forgiveness. If he obtained his request he found the written confession obliterated from his door, but if the writing still remained the poor Jew was rigorously cut off from all communication with his kind until the miraculous signature of pardon was accorded him. A little lower down on the same side is a small apartment containing an ancient marble niche, resembling in shape the ordinary Mohammedan *mihráb*; this is usually known as 'Mehd ·Eisá or "Jesus' Cradle," although some of the Muslim doctors, with greater regard for the antiquarian unities, call it "Mary's Prayer-niche." The pilgrim enters the place with reverence, and repeats the *Súrat Miryam*, a chapter of the Coran which gives the Mohammedan account of the birth and ministry of our Lord.

By the Jámi' en Nisá, or "Woman's Mosque," forming part of the Jámi' el Aksa, is a well, on the left of the great entrance, called Bir el Warakah or "Well of the Leaf." The story goes that during the caliphate of 'Omar a man of the Bení Temím, named Sherík ibn Haiyán, dropped his bucket into this well, and climbing down to fetch it up found a door, into which he entered. Great was his surprise at seeing a beautiful garden, and having walked about in it for some time he plucked a leaf and returned to tell his companions of his strange adventure. As the leaf never withered, and the door could never again be found, no doubt was entertained but that this was an entrance into Paradise itself, and as such the well is now pointed out to the pilgrim.

The bridge of Es Sirát, that will be extended on the Day of Judgment between heaven and hell, is to start from Jerusalem, and the pilgrim is shown a column, built horizontally into the wall, which is to form its first pier.

The Muslim guide will wax eloquent upon this, his favourite subject, the connexion between the Day of Judgment and the Masjid el Aksa; and as the pilgrim stands upon the eastern wall he will hear a circumstantial account of the troubles and the signal deliverance which shall come upon the true believers in the latter day.

Dajjál, or Antichrist, (he learns), will not be allowed to enter Jerusalem, but will stop on the eastern bank of the Jordan while the faithful remain on the western side. Then Christ, who will reappear to save the true believers, will take up three of the stones of Jerusalem, and will say as he takes up the first, "In the name of the God of Abraham;" with the second, "In the name of the God of Isaac;" and with the third, "In the name of the God of Jacob." He will then go out at the head of the Muslims, Dajjál will flee before him, and be slain by the three stones. The victors will then proceed to a general massacre of the Jews in and around the Holy City, and every tree and every stone shall cry out and say, "I have a Jew beneath me, slay him.". Having done this the Messiah will break the crosses and kill the pigs, after which the Millenium will set in.

The last sign which is to precede the day of resurrection is that the Ka'abeh of Mecca shall be led as a bride to the Sakhrah of Jerusalem. When the latter sees it, it will cry out, "Welcome thou Pilgrim to whom Pilgrimages are made." No one dies until he has heard the sound of the Muezzin in Jerusalem calling to prayer.

The pilgrims to the Haram es Sherif differ but little from those of the Holy Sepulchre. Both endure great hardships, exhibit intense devotion and ostentatious humility; and both believe that by scrupulous practice of the appointed rites and observances they are advancing a claim upon the favour of heaven which cannot be repudiated. Both delight in assuring themselves and others that it is love for the stones on which the saints have trodden which brings them there, but if their satisfaction could be analysed it would be found to consist in a sense of religious security, which a learned Muslim doctor has quaintly expressed: "The dwellers in Jerusalem are the neighbours of God; and God has no right to torment his neighbours."

As with us in Europe, the only notices of Jerusalem during the Middle Ages are derived from the Crusaders and early pilgrims, so the various accounts of the Holy City, with the quaint stories and traditions attaching to it, with which Mohammed's writings teem, are all due to the early warriors and pilgrims of Islam.

Of these, and their name is legion, I will select a few of the most eminent in order that the reader may form some idea of the sources from which the Arab historians have drawn their information.

The Mohammedan pilgrims to Jerusalem range themselves naturally into two great classes or periods, namely, those who "came over with the conqueror" 'Omar, or who visited the city between the date of his conquest and the second Christian kingdom, and those who were posterior to Saladin. Of all the Mohammedan pilgrims to Jerusalem the first and most distinguished was Abu 'Obeidah ibn el Jerráh, to whom, as has already been shown, the conquest of Jerusalem was due.

He died in the great plague at 'Amwás, (Emmaus) A.D. 639, in the fifty-eighth year of his age, and was buried in the village of Athmá, at the foot of Jebel 'Ajlún, between Fukáris and El "Adilíyeh, where his tomb is still pointed out. In this plague no less than twenty-five thousand of the Muslim soldiery perished.

Bellál ibn Rubáh, Mohammed's own " Muezzin," accompanied 'Omar to Jerusalem. He·was so devoutly attached to the person of the Prophet that he refused to exercise his office after Mohammed's decease, except on the occasion of the conquest of the Holy City, when he was prevailed upon by the Caliph once more to call the people to prayers in honour of so great an occasion.

Khálid ibn el Walíd, surnamed the "Drawn Sword of God," was also present with the victorious army of 'Omar ; he died in the year 641 A.D., and was buried, some say, at Emessa, and others, at Medínah.

'Abúdat ibn es Sámit, the first Cádhí of Jerusalem, arrived with 'Omar, he was buried in the Holy City, but his tomb disappeared during the Christian occupation.

Another interesting member of the first pilgrim band was Selmán el Fársí, one of the early companions of Mohammed. Although he does not play a very conspicuous part in Mohammedan history, his name has acquired a strange celebrity in connexion with the mysterious sect of the Nuseiríyeh in Syria. The tenets of this people are so extraordinary and so little known that I cannot refrain from giving a slight account of them here.

The Nuseiríyeh worship a mystic triad, consisting of and represented by 'Alí, the son-in-law and successor of Mohammed, Mohammed himself, and Selmán el Fársí. These are alluded to as '*Ams*, a mystical word, composed of the three initial letters of their names; 'Alí being, moreover, called the Maná, or "meaning," *i.e*, the object implied in all their teaching, Mohammed, the chamberlain, and Selmán el Fársí, the door. To understand this we must remember that Eastern sovereigns are never approached except through the mediation of their chamberlains; and the three offices will therefore correspond with those of the Holy Trinity, the King of Kings, the Mediator, and the Door of Grace. From this triad proceed five other persons, called *aitám*, or monads, whose function is that of creation and order. Their names are those of persons who played a conspicuous part in the early history of Islám; but they are evidently identical with the five planets known to the ancients, and their functions correspond exactly to those of the heathen deities whose names the planets bear.

The Nuseiríyeh hold the doctrine of a Fall, believing that they originally existed as shining lights and brilliant stars, and that they were degraded from that high estate for refusing to recognise the omnipotence of 'Alí.

The mystic Trinity, 'Ams, is supposed to have appeared seven times upon the earth, once in each of the seven cycles into which the history of the world is divided. Each of these manifestations was in the persons of certain historical characters, and each avatar was accompanied by a similar incarnation of the antagonistic or evil principle.

The devil of the Nuseiríyeh is always represented as a triune being, and, carrying out the principle of affiliating their religious system upon the history of Mohammedanism, they have made the opponents of 'Alí represent the personification of evil, as he himself and his immediate followers are the personification of good. Thus Abu Bekr, 'Omar, and 'Othmán, are considered by the Nuseiríyeh as the conjunct incarnation of Satan.

They believe in the transmigration of souls, and that after death those of Mohammedans will enter into the bodies of asses, Christians into pigs, and Jews into apes. As for their own sect, the wicked will become cattle, and serve for food; the initiated who have given way to religious doubts will be changed into apes; and those who are neither good nor bad will again become men, but will be born into a strange sect and people.

The religion professed by the great mass of the Nuseiríyeh is, indeed, a mere *mélange* of doctrines, dogmas, and superstitions, borrowed from the various creeds which have at various times been dominant in the country; and yet this incongruous jumble serves as a cloak for a much more interesting creed, namely, the ancient Sabæan faith.

The Nuseiríyeh conceal their religion from the outer world with the greatest care, and do not even initiate their own sons into its mysteries until they have arrived at years of discretion; the women are never initiated at all.

In the first degree or stage of initiation, they are made acquainted with the doctrines of which I have given a sketch; in the second they are told that by 'Ams the Christian Trinity is intended; and in the last, or perfect degree, they are taught that this Trinity, the real object of their worship, is composed of Light, or the Sky, the Sun, and the Moon, the first being illimitable and infinite, the second proceeding from the first, and the last proceeding from the other two.

The five monads are, in this stage, absolutely declared to be identical with the five planets.

In their religious ceremonies they make use of hymns, libations of wine, and sacrifices; to describe them in detail would be out of place in this work, I will, therefore, only mention one, which has an exceptional interest.

Amongst the ceremonies observed at their great feast is one called the "Consecration of the Fragrant Herb." The officiating priest takes his seat in the midst of the assembly, and a white cloth, containing a kind of spice called mahlab, camphor, and some sprigs of olive or fragrant herb, is then placed before him. Two attendants then bring in a vessel filled with wine, and the master of the house in which the ceremony takes place, after appointing a third person to minister to them, kisses their hands all round, and humbly requests permission to provide the materials necessary for the feast. The high priest then, having prostrated himself upon the ground, and uttered a short invocation to certain mystic personages, distributes the sprigs of olive amongst the congregation, who rub them in their hands, and place them solemnly to their nose to inhale their fragrance.

This ceremony would alone furnish evidence of the antiquity of the Nuseiríyeh rites, for it is unquestionably the same as that alluded to by Ezekiel (viii. v. 17), when condemning the idolatrous practices of the Jews. In that passage the prophet (after mentioning "women weeping for Tammúz," the Syrian Adonis, "twenty-five men with their backs toward the temple of the Lord, and their faces to the east, worshipping the sun in the east," and thus showing beyond question that the particular form of idolatry which he is condemning is the sun worship of Syria) concludes with the following words: "Is it a light thing which they commit here? For they have filled the land with violence, and have returned to provoke me to anger: *and, lo, they put the branch to their nose.*"

The more sober Muslim historians tell us that Selmán el Fársí died at the age of ninety-eight or ninety-nine years; but some do not scruple to assert that he was over six hundred years old, and had personally witnessed the ministry of Christ. Nothing certain seems to be known of him, except that he died in the year A.D. 656, and no reason appears for his deification by the Nuseiríyeh except the fact that he was a Persian, and a friend of 'Alí ibn Abí Talib. Abu Dhurrá is another of the companions of Mohammed, deified by the Nuseiríyeh (in whose pantheon he appears as the representative of the planet Jupiter), and is also said to have entered Jerusalem with the army of 'Omar. He is buried at Medinah.

Sheddád ibn Aus. It is related that Mohammed, some little time before his death, predicted that Jerusalem would be conquered, and that Sheddád, and his sons after him, would become Imáms (or high priests) there, which prediction came to pass. Sheddád died in Jerusalem, A.D. 678, at the age of seventy-five, and was buried in the cemetery near the Bab er Rahmah, close under the walls of the Haram es Sheríf, where his tomb is still honoured by the faithful.

The Caliph Mo'áwíyeh also visited Jerusalem before his accession to the throne, and it was in that city that the celebrated compact was made between him and "Amir ibn el "As to revenge the murder of 'Othmán. He died in Damascus, on the 1st of May, A.D. 680.

One of the most distinguished of Mohammedan pilgrims to Jerusalem was Ka'ab el Ahbár ibn Máni', the Himyarite, familiarly called Abu Is'hak. He was by birth a Jew, but had embraced the Muslim religion during the caliphate of Abu Bekr, in consequence, as he alleged, of his finding in the Book of the Law a prophecy relating to Mohammed. He is chiefly remembered as having pointed out to 'Omar, whom he accompanied to Jerusalem, the real position of the Sakhrah. The following tradition is also ascribed to him: that "Jerusalem once complained to the Almighty that she had been so frequently destroyed; to which God answered, 'Be comforted, for I will fill thee, instead, with worshippers, who shall flock to thee as the vultures to their nests, and shall yearn for thee as the doves for their eggs.'" He died at Hums in A.D. 652.

Sellám ibn Caisar was one of the companions of Mohammed, and acted as governor of Jerusalem under the Caliph Mo'áwíyeh.

The position of women amongst the first professors of Islám appears to have been much more honourable than amongst their later successors, and the early annals of the creed contain many notices of gifted and pious women who appeared to have exercised no small influence over the minds of their contemporaries. One of these distinguished females was Umm el Kheir, a freed woman of the noble family of 'Agyl, and a native of Basora. She visited Jerusalem, where she died about the year 752. Her tomb is still to be seen on the Mount of Olives, in a retired corner south of the Chapel of the Ascension; and is much frequented by pilgrims. It is related that Umm el Kheir, one day, in the course of her devotions, cried out, "Oh, God, wilt thou consume with fire a heart that loves thee so?" When a mysterious voice replied to her, "Nay, we act not thus; entertain not such evil suspicions of us." The precept, "Conceal your virtues as you would your vices," is also attributed to the same saint.

Safíyah bint Hai, known as "The Mother of the Faithful," was amongst the earliest pilgrims to Jerusalem, having visited it with the army of 'Omar. To her is attributed the tradition that the division of the wicked from the good on the Day of Judgment will take place from the top of the Mount of Olives. She died about the year 670.

An anecdote related of the celebrated Sufyán eth Thorí, affords a good example of the devotion and fervour of these early Mohammedan pilgrims. He is said to have repeated the whole of the Coran at one sitting in the Cubbet es Sakhrah, and on one occasion, when he had prayed until he was completely exhausted, he bought a single plantain and ate it in the shade of the mosque, apologising for even this indulgence by the remark, "The ass can do more work when he has got his fodder." He died at Bosrah A.D. 777.

Al Imám es Sháfíi', one of the most learned of the Mohammedan doctors, and the founder of one of the chief sects into which the religion is divided. He was born in 767 A.D., the same year in which Abu Hanífeh, the founder of the Hanefite sect, died. His works, which are very voluminous, and considered by his followers as next in authority to the Coran itself, are said to have been all written within the space of four years.

The following *fatwa*, or legal decision, attributed to him

during his stay at Jerusalem, not only evinces the great erudition and readiness for which he was so celebrated, but affords an amusing specimen of the trifling minutiæ upon which the Mohammedan doctors often consent to dispute. Having established himself in the Haram es Sheríf, he professed himself ready to answer any question that might be put to him, concerning either the Coran or the Sunneh, that is, the written or oral law. "What should you say," said a person present, "respecting the legality of killing a wasp, when one is engaged in the rites of the pilgrimage." Without a moment's hesitation the Imam replied, "The Coran itself tells us that we are to accept whatsoever the prophet hath granted us, and to abstain from what he has forbidden us. (Coran, 59. 7.) Now, Ibn 'Aiyinah had it from 'Abd el Melik ibn Amír, who had it from Huzaifah, that the prophet said, 'Be guided in all things by my immediate successors, Abu Bekr, and 'Omar.' But Ibn 'Aiyinah further relates that Mas'úd told him that Cais ibn Musallim was informed by Tárik ibn Shiháb, that 'Omar bade the pilgrim slay the wasp." Es Shafií died at Carafah es Sughra, in Egypt, on the 20th December, A.D. 819.

Mohammed ibn Karrám, the founder of the Karramíyeh sect, resided at Jerusalem for more than twenty years, and died there in the year 869 A.D. His doctrines are considered by the majority of Mussulmans as heterodox and pernicious. He was said to have been buried by the Jericho gate, near the tombs of the prophets, but neither the gate nor the sheikh's tomb exist at the present day.

Abu 'l Faraj al Mucaddasí, Imám of the Hambileh sect, and the founder of that of Imám Ahmed. He is the author of very esteemed and voluminous works upon theology and jurisprudence. He died the 9th of January, 1094, and was buried at Damascus, in the cemetery near the Bab es Saghír, where his tomb is still frequented by the faithful.

Sheikh Abu 'l Fath Nasr, a celebrated recluse and theologian, fixed his residence at Jerusalem, living the life of an ascetic, in the building to the east of the Báb en Rahmah, which was called after him En Násiríyeh. He was a friend of the eminent philosopher El Gházali, whom he met at Damascus. He died in the last named city in the year 1097, A.D.

Abu 'l Ma'álí el Musharraf ibn el Marján Ibrahím el Mucaddeú. He is the author of a celebrated treatise upon the history and antiquities of Jerusalem, entitled *Fadháïl Bait el Mucaddas w es Sakhrah*, "The Virtues of Jerusalem and of the Rock." Little or nothing is known of him beyond this composition; the date of his decease is also uncertain, but it is ascertained that he was contemporary with Sheikh Abu 'l Cásim, who was born about 1040, A.D.

This Sheikh Abu 'l Cásim er Rumailí, was a celebrated doctor of the Shafiite sect. He established himself at Jerusalem, and was so renowned for his great knowledge of religious jurisprudence, that difficult points of law from all quarters of the Muslim world were sent to him for his opinion, and his decision was always considered final. He is also the author of an excellent treatise on the history of Jerusalem. On the capture of the city by the Crusaders, in the year 1099, he was taken prisoner, and his ransom fixed at one thousand dínárs. The Muslims did not however, appear to set a very high value upon their learned doctor, for the sum demanded for his release was never raised; and the reverend gentleman was stoned to death by the Franks at the gate of Antioch. Some authorities say that he was put to death in Jerusalem.

Abu 'l Cásim er Rází was by birth a Persian, and studied jurisprudence at Ispahan, from which place he removed to Baghdad, and ultimately proceeded to Jerusalem, where he adopted the life of a religious recluse. He was slain by the Crusaders on their entry into Jerusalem in July, 1099.

The renowned philosopher, El Ghazálí himself, was also a pilgrim to Jerusalem, in which city he composed the magnificent work for which he is chiefly celebrated, namely the *Muhyi 'l úlúm*, "The Resuscitation of Science." He occupied the same apartments in which Sheikh Násir had formerly resided, and the name was changed in consequence from that of En Nasiríyeh to El Ghajálíyeh. The building, however, has long since disappeared. El Ghazáli died at Tús, his native town, in the year 1112.

Dhíá-ed-dín 'Eisá studied Mohammedan literature and jurisprudence in Aleppo, and was attached to the court of Esed-ed-dín Shírkoh, Saladin's uncle, with whom he visited Egypt. On the death of the former, it was principally owing to the exertions made by him, and Bahá-ed-dín Caracosh, that Saladin was appointed to succeed him as Grand Vizier of Egypt. In the year 753, Dhíá-ed-dín accompanied Saladin upon an expedition against the Franks, in the course of which he was taken prisoner, though subsequently ransomed for sixty thousand dínárs. He was a great favourite with Saladin, and, as has been before mentioned, preached the first sermon in the Masjid el Aksa after the conquest of the Holy City. He was of noble birth, and great learning, and while accompanying Saladin in his "Holy War" he combined the ecclesiastical with the military character, wearing the armour and uniform of a soldier, and the turban of a priest. He died during the siege of Acre, in the year 583, and his remains were sent to Jerusalem, and buried in the cemetery of Mamilla.

Sheikh Sheháb-ed-dín el Cudsí was also a *Khatíb*, or preacher, in Jerusalem; he was present with Saladin at the taking of the city, and received the *soubriquet* of Abu Tor, "The Father of the Bull," because he was in the habit of riding upon one of those animals, and fighting from its back. Saladin bestowed upon him a small village, near the Jaffa gate, in which was the monastery of St.

Mark, where he lived and died. Both the monastery and the hill upon which it stands are now called after him, Abu Tor. It is related of him, that when he wanted any provisions he used to write an order and tie it on the neck of his favourite bull, which would go straight to the bazaars and bring back the articles required.

After the death of Saladin the list of eminent Muslims whose names are connected with the history of Jerusalem becomes too formidable in its dimensions to admit of more than a brief notice of a few of the most important. I will commence with the kings and princes.

El Melik el Moázzem was a son of El 'Adil, Saladin's brother, and succeeded his father in the government of Syria, in August, 1218, A.D. He was a Hanefite (departing in this from the traditions of his house, which had all along professed the doctrines of Es Shafíí), and founded a college for the sect in the Masjid el Aksa. He was a great patron of Arabic philosophy, and erected the building called the "Dòme of the Grammarians," on the south side of the court of the Sakhrah; to him is also due the construction of the greater number of carved wooden doors which adorn the Haram building, and which still bear his name. We have already alluded in a former chapter to the operations of this prince, and his brother, El Melik el Kámil, against the Franks, as well as to the invasion of the Khárezmians, and other troubles which overtook Jerusalem.

After this we hear no more of victories or crusades, and the connection of the succeeding princes with the history of Jerusalem is chiefly derived from their benefactions to the Haram es Sheríf. I will mention only a few of these, whose munificence is recorded on the numerous tablets which adorn the buildings in the sacred area.

El Melik ed Dhaher Beybers, Sultan of Egypt, visited Jerusalem in 1269, on his return from a pilgrimage to Mecca. Passing by the "Red Hill," between Jericho and

Jerusalem, which is, according to the Muslims, the traditional site of Moses' grave, he erected the building to which devotees yearly flock in crowds, to the present day. He repaired the Mosque El Aksa, and the Cubbet es Silsilah, and completely renovated the interior of the Cubbet es Sakhrah, which was in a very dilapidated condition. He died at Damascus in June, 1277.

Es Sultán Caláűn, originally a Memlúk, purchased for one thousand dínárs, ascended the throne of Egypt in 1279. He repaired the roof of the Jámi' el Aksa, and erected a cloister called El Mansúrí, near the Báb en Názir.

El Melik el 'Adil Ketbegha began to reign in 694, and repaired the eastern wall of the Haram by the Golden Gate. Es Sultán Lajein, who succeeded him, also executed many repairs in the mosque. Sultán Mohammed, son of Caláŏn, who had succeeded his father, but been twice compelled to abdicate, at last succeeded in establishing himself on the throne of Egypt in A.D. 1310. He repaired the south wall of the Haram, coated the inside of the mosque with marble, and regilded the domes of El Aksa, and the Cubbet es Sakhrah. So beautifully was this gilding executed, that Mejír-ed-dín, writing one hundred and eighty years afterwards, declares that it looked as though it had been but just laid on. Even now, in the records of Saladin's restoration which exist upon the dome of the Cubbet es Sakhrah, and over the Mihráb of the Aksa, the gold remains untarnished.

Mohammed ibn Caláŏn also repaired the arches over the steps leading up on the north side to the platform on which the Dome of the Rock stands, and executed many useful works in and around Jerusalem, he died in A.D. 1340.

Es Sultán el Melek el Ashraf Shábán, grandson of the preceding, repaired the Bal el Esbát, put new wooden doors in the Jámi' el Aksa, and repaired the arches over the steps on the west side of the Sakhrah platform, by the Báb en Názir. Sultán Abu Sa'íd Barkúk was the first of the Circassian dynasty in Egypt, he ascended the throne in 1382. To him is due a portion of the wood-work around the Sakhrah.

In 1393, his lieutenant, El Yaghmúrí, came to Jerusalem, and set right the numerous abuses which had crept into the administration of the city in the time of his predecessor. These reforms he proclaimed by causing an account of them to be engraved upon a marble tablet, and hung up in the Haram es Sherif. The governors of Jerusalem would seem to have been rather prone to relapses in this respect, for we find El Yaghmúrí's example followed by many of the succeeding viceroys.

Sultán en Násir Farj succeeded to the throne of Egypt in the year 1399, when only twelve years old. He separated the government of Jerusalem and Hebron from that of Mecca and Medína, which had hitherto been exercised by one official. During his reign occurred the incursions of the Tartars, under Timour or Tamerlane.

Sultán el Melik el Ashraf Barsebáï, a freedman of Barkúk's, becoming Sultán in 1422, followed his former master's example, and expended some money upon the repair of the mosque at Jerusalem. He presented a beautiful copy of the Coran to the Mosque of El Aksa, and appointed and endowed a reader and attendant to look after it.

In the year 1447, during the reign of El Melik ed Dháher Chakmak, a portion of the roof of the Cubbet es Sakhrah was destroyed by fire. Some say the accident was caused by lightning, others, by the carelessness of some young noblemen, who clambered into the roof in pursuit of pigeons, and set fire to the woodwork with a lighted candle which one of them held in his hands. The Sultan repaired the damage, and also presented to the Sakhrah a large and magnificent copy of the Coran. This prince was a great champion of the faith, and sent his agent, Sheikh Mohammed el Mushmer to Jerusalem for the purpose of destroying all the newly erected Christian buildings in the place, and of clearing out the monasteries and convents. Some new wooden balustrading which was found in the Church of the Holy Sepulchre was carried off in triumph to the Mosque of El Aksa; and the monastery, or Tomb of David, was cleared of its monkish occupants and appropriated by the Mohammedans, while even the bones in the adjoining cemetery were dug up and removed.

The so-called Tomb of David was originally a convent of Franciscan monks, who believed it to be the site of the Cœnaculum, and their traditions mention nothing of an underground cavern such as is now said by the Mohammedans to exist. The tradition which makes it the tomb of David is purely Muslim in its origin, and does not date back earlier than the time of El Melik ed Dháher Chakmak. Oral tradition in Jerusalem says that a beggar came one day to the door of the monastery asking for relief, and in revenge for being refused went about declaring that it was the tomb of David, in order to incite the Muslim fanatics to seize upon and confiscate the spot. His plan, as we have just seen, succeeded.

El Ashraf also gave a great Coran to the Jámi' el Aksa, which was placed near the Mosque of 'Omar, by the window which overlooks Siloam. Sultán el Ashraf Catibáï, in the year 1472, widened and improved the steps leading up to the platform of the Sakhrah, and furnished them with arches like those on the other sides. He also re-covered the roof of El Aksa with lead. A notice of the events which happened in Jerusalem during the reign of this sovereign will be found in the account of Mejír-ed-dín (p. 439).

The names of a great number of learned men are mentioned in the Mohammedan histories of Jerusalem, either as pilgrims or as preachers, cádhís or principals of colleges. Of these the majority would be unknown to, or possess but little interest for, the European reader, I will therefore content myself with mentioning a few who have written upon or otherwise distinguished themselves in connection with the Holy City.

Sheikh el Islám Burhán-ed-dín, chief Cádhí of Jerusalem, died in 1388. The marble pulpit in the Cubbet es Sakhrah, from which the sermon is preached on feast days, was the gift of this divine. Es Saiyid Bedr-ed-dín Sálem, a lineal descendant of 'Alí ibn Abi Tálib, was also connected for some time with the Haram at Jerusalem. He was esteemed a great saint, and was visited as such by pious Muslims even during his lifetime. Many miracles are recorded of him, and it is said that the birds and wild beasts came to make pilgrimages to his tomb and those of his sons—at Sharafát in the Wády en Nusúr, about three days' journey from Jerusalem—and prostrate themselves with their faces on the ground at the door of the small building which covers the graves. They are still objects of great veneration to Muslim pilgrims in Palestine. Es Sheikh Abu 'l Hasan el Magháferí exercised the office of Khatíb, or preacher, in Jerusalem. He studied the celebrated history of the city by Ibn 'Asáker, under the direction of its author, in A.D. 1200. Shems-ed-dín el 'Alímí accepted the office of chief Cádhí of Jerusalem in 1438, towards the end of the reign of Sultan Barsebaí. An incident is related in the notices of his life which throws some light upon the condition of the Christians in the city. A church of large dimensions, and furnished with a magnificent dome, existed on the south side of the Holy Sepulchre, in close proximity to the Haram es Sheríf. This was a favourite place of worship with the Christian inhabitants, and the chaunting of the priests could be heard in the Cubbet es Sakhrah itself, to the great scandal of the "Faithful." While they were concerting measures for putting a stop to the services without infringing the law, an earthquake happened, which threw down the dome of the church, and completely dismantled the building. The Christians applied to the governor of the city and the Cádhí of the Hanefite sect for permission to restore the building, and, by dint of heavy bribes, obtained it. El 'Alímí, who was Cádhí of the Hambelite sect, was furious at this, and declared that as the church had been destroyed by the act of God for the express convenience of the Muslim worshippers in the Cubbet es Sakhrah, it was sheer blasphemy to allow it to be rebuilt. An indignant letter written by him to Cairo brought a special commissioner with orders from the Sultan el Ashraf Einál to stop the building and pull down what had been already erected. This was probably the commencement of the general Crescentade against the churches and monasteries of Jerusalem, which took place under the jurisdiction of El 'Alímí, in the reign of Sultán Chakmak, to which I have already alluded in my notice of that prince. The Cádhí was also in the habit of seizing upon the children of deceased Jews and Christians, who were tributaries of the State, and of compelling them to be trained up in the Mohammedan religion. The Shafiite Cádhí disputed the legality of this, and the question was warmly disputed by the Mohammedan doctors, both in Jerusalem and Cairo. Although the decision was not favourable to his view of the case, he continued to follow the same course until he was removed from the office in 1468. Amongst the Mohammedan viceroys and governors of Jerusalem may be mentioned the following: El Emír 'Ezz-ed-dín es Zanjeilí, who repaired the Cubbet el Míraj in the year 1200. El Emír Hisám-ed-dín, who restored the Cubbet en Nahwíweh in 1207. El Emír Zidugdi was governor of Jerusalem during the reigns of the Sultans Beibars and Cala'on. He built a cloister by the Báb en Názir and paved the court of the Sakhrah. El Emír Násir-ed-dín made extensive restorations in the Haram

Area, and opened the two windows in the Aksa which are on the right and left of the Mihráb, and coated the interior of the mosque with marble in 1330. The well-known author, Mejír-ed-dín, resided for some time in Jerusalem, and has given us the best history of the Holy City extant in Arabic. The following is a brief extract of his own very graphic account of the events which happened there during the reign of the Sultán El Ashraf Catibái, in whose service the writer was. As a picture of the state of things in Jerusalem in the fifteenth century it may not prove uninteresting to our readers.

In the year 1468 a severe famine occurred in Jerusalem and its neighbourhood in consequence of the unusual drought of the preceding winter. The people began to exhibit signs of dissatisfaction, and matters were not improved by a quarrel which took place between the Názir el Haramain, or Superintendent of the Two Sanctuaries (Hebron and Jerusalem), and the Náïb, or Viceroy. These two officials came to an open rupture, and as the Názir and his men were engaged in laying in water from the Birket es Sultán to some buildings upon which they were employed, the Náïb with a company of attendants came suddenly upon them, and a fierce fight took place. The city was immediately divided into two factions, some taking the part of the Názir and others of the Náïb, and even the presence of a special commissioner from Cairo failed to quell the disturbance. The plague, with which Syria had been for some time visited, next attacked Jerusalem, and raged from the 17th of July, 1469, until the middle of September.

The next year (1470) was more propitious, but the great people of the city still seemed unable to agree. On the 12th of February, Cádhí Sherf-ed-dín came to Jerusalem, and was visited, immediately on his arrival, by Ghars-ed-dín, chief Cádhí of the Shafiite sect. Now Sheikh Sheháb-ed-dín el 'Amírí, principal of one of the colleges attached to the Haram, also happened to drop in, and, either through ignorance or inadvertence, took a seat in the assembly above the Cádhí. The two reverend gentlemen entered into a warm dispute, in the course of which the Sheikh threatened to tear the Cádhí's turban off his head. The Cádhí retorted that the Sheikh "did not know the meaning of a turban," implying that he did not know how to conduct himself as became his office. Both parties then left the assembly, and the matter being referred to arbitration, certain learned gentlemen adjourned to the Cubbet es Sakhrah to discuss it, accompanied by a crowd of idlers. The people of Jerusalem, determined to defend their fellow-citizen, attempted to decide the question by pillaging the Cádhí's house and maltreating his wives. The day was a very rainy one, which circumstance increased the bad temper of the mob, and it was at one time more than probable that the sanctuary would become the scene of anarchy and bloodshed. In a subsequent appeal, made to the Sultan himself at Cairo, the Cádhí got scant satisfaction, and was so laughed at and ridiculed on his return to Jerusalem that he was ultimately obliged to resign his office and leave. The atmosphere of Jerusalem appears to have a particularly unfortunate effect upon the temper of theologians.

The winter of 1472-3 was exceedingly severe, and the rains so incessant that the foundations of the buildings were, in many instances, undermined; three hundred and sixty houses are said to have fallen down from this cause, but one woman, who was buried in the ruins of her dwelling, was the only person killed.

About the end of the year 1475 the Sultan himself, El Ashraf Catibái, performed the pilgrimage to Jerusalem on his return from Mecca. Immediately upon his arrival in the city he held a court, on which occasion the inhabitants crowded round him to present petitions against the Viceroy, whom they accused of all manner of injustice and oppression. The chief Cádhí was also included in the indictment, as having given corrupt decisions in the interests of the governor. The latter purchased immunity by paying off upon the spot all claims that were made against him, and was retained in his office by the Sultan, who, however, intimated that if a single complaint were again made he would have him cut in halves. The Cádhí narrowly escaped corporal punishment, and was dismissed ignominiously from his office, and compelled to leave the city.

In May, 1476, orders came from the Sultan to arrest all the Christians connected with the Churches of the Holy Sepulchre, Sion and Bethlehem, in revenge for the capture of four Muslims by the Franks at Alexandria. The orders were executed, but we are not told what became of the prisoners. Towards the end of 1477 the plague, which had been raging for some time in Syria, reached Jerusalem, and lasted for more than six months, causing a terrible mortality.

In 1480 a great disturbance took place in Jerusalem in consequence of the governor having imprisoned and put to death some Bedawín of the Bení Zeid tribe. A crowd of ferocious Arabs bore down upon Jerusalem determined to revenge the death of their comrades, and the governor, who was riding outside the city at the time of their arrival, narrowly escaped falling into their hands. Setting spurs to his horse he dashed through the Báb el Esbát, rode across the courtyard of the Mosque, and escaped through the Báb el Magháribeh. The Bedawín swarmed in after him with drawn swords, utterly regardless of the sacred character of the place. Finding that their victim had escaped they followed the method adopted on similar occasions by European agitators, broke into the houses and shops of the neighbourhood and plundered all that they could lay their hands on, and then broke open the jail and let loose the prisoners.

In 1481 a number of architects and workmen were sent to Jerusalem by the Sultan to repair the Haram, and to rebuild the various colleges which had fallen into decay. In 1482 a messenger arrived bearing the Sultan's order that the Christians were to be permitted to take possession once more of the Church of the Holy Sepulchre, and exhibit therein the customary Easter pyrotechnic display. The order was at first disputed by the Muslim officials, but as the commissioner threatened to indict them for contempt of authority they were obliged to give way.

In 1491, Jerusalem was again visited by the plague; at first from thirty to forty people died of it daily, but in a little time the average rate of mortality was increased to a hundred and thirty.

The winter of this year was very severe, and a snow-storm occurred, which lasted several days, and lay upon the ground to the depth of three feet, greatly incommoding and frightening the inhabitants. When it began to melt, the foundations of many of the houses gave way, and serious disasters were the result.

Mejír-ed-dín's history of this period is very diffuse, and is chiefly devoted to an account of the various Cádhís, and other religious or legal functionaries in Jerusalem. But the ascendency of the Shafiite or Hanefite doctrines, or the intense devotion of an old gentleman who had learned a whole commentary upon the Coran by heart, are not subjects of much general interest; we have, therefore, confined ourselves to stating the few facts above detailed.

We ought, perhaps, to include in our list of Mohammedan pilgrims those from whom all our information is gleaned,— Ibn 'Asáker, and the later Arabic writers who have written on the subject; their names, however, and the names of their books, although of high authority to the Oriental scholar, could have but little weight with the English reader.

CHAPTER XVIII.

THE CHRONICLE OF SIX HUNDRED YEARS.

"Oh! yet we trust that somehow good
 Will be the final goal of ill,
 To pangs of nature, sins of will,
Defects of doubt, and taint of blood."

In Memoriam.

THE Christian kingdom, reduced after Saladin's conquest to a strip of land along the coast, with a few strong cities, depended no longer on the annual reinforcement of pilgrims, but on the strength and wealth of the two military orders. Unfortunately these quarrelled, and the whole of Syria became divided, Mohammedans as well as Christians, into partisans of Knights Templars, or of Knights Hospitaliers. Henry of Champagne, the titular king, was only anxious to get away, while Bohemond, the Prince of Antioch, was only anxious to extend his own territories. In Germany alone the crusading spirit yet lingered, and a few Germans flocked yearly to the sacred places. Germany did more. The emperor, with forty thousand men, went to Palestine by way of Italy. When he arrived, he found, to his amazement, that the Christians did not want him—the truce concluded with the Mohammedans being not yet broken. The barons and princes had resolved not to break it at all; but rather to seek its renewal. But the Germans had not accomplished their long journey for nothing. They issued from their camp at Acre in arms, and broke the truce by wantonly attacking the Saracens. Reprisals at once followed, as a matter of course. Jaffa was attacked. Henry of Champagne hastened to its defence. There he fell from a high window, and was killed. The arrival of more Crusaders enabled the Christians to meet El Melik el "Adil in open field, and to gain a complete victory. They followed it up by taking the seaboard towns, and the whole coast of Syria was once more in the hands of the Christians. Of Jerusalem no one thought except the common soldiers, with whom the capture of the city remained still a dream. Isabelle, the widow of Henry, was married a fourth time, to Amaury de Lusignan, who had succeeded his brother Guy on the throne of Cyprus, and now became the titular king of Jerusalem, a shadowy title, which was destined never to become a real one, except for a very brief interval.

When the Germans went away, the Christians of Palestine were once more at the mercy of the Saracens, with whom they had broken the treaty. The Bishop of Acre was sent to supplicate help from Europe. He was shipwrecked and drowned almost immediately after leaving port. Other messengers were sent. These also were drowned in a tempest. So for a long time news of the sad condition of the Christians did not reach Europe. But, indeed, it was difficult to raise the crusading spirit again in the West. Like a flame of dry straw it had burned fiercely for a short time, and then expired. Jerusalem was fading from the minds of the people. It was become a city of memories, round which the glories of those myths which gathered about the name of Godfrey and Tancred were already present. Innocent III., a young and ardent pope, wrote letter upon letter. These produced little effect. He sent preachers to promise men remission of sins in return for taking the Cross. But it was a time when men were not thinking much about their sins. Priests imposed the penance of pilgrimage to Palestine; but it does not appear that many pilgrims went; and boxes were placed in all the churches to collect money; but it is not certain that much money was put into them. Then Fulke de Neuilly, the most eloquent priest of the time, was sent to preach a crusade, and succeeded in fanning the embers of the crusading enthusiasm once more into an evanescent and short-lived flame. How little of religious zeal there was in the movement may be judged by the sequel, and we cannot here delay to detail the progress of the Crusade which ended in the conquest of Constantinople. No history can be found more picturesque, more full of incident, and more illustrative of the manners and thoughts of the time; but it does not concern Jerusalem. An old empire fell, and a new one was founded, but Christendom was outraged by the spectacle of an expedition which started full of zeal for the conquest of the Holy Land, and was diverted from its original purposes to serve the ambition of its leaders, and the avarice of a commercial city.

Egypt and Syria, meantime, were kept quiet from war by troubles not caused by man. The Nile ceased for a time to overflow, and a fearful famine, a famine of which the records speak as dreadful beyond all comparison, set in; during this men kept themselves alive by eating the flesh of those who died, while the cities were filled with corpses, and the river bore down on its tide dead bodies as numerous as the lilies which bloom on its surface in spring. And before the famine, which extended over Syria as well, had ceased, an earthquake shook the country from end to end. Damascus, Tyre, Nablous, were heaps of ruins; the walls of Acre and Tripoli fell down; Jerusalem alone seemed spared, and there the Christian and the Mohammedan met together, still trembling with fear, to thank God for their safety. The sums of money which Fulke de Neuilly had raised in his preaching were spent in repairing the walls which had fallen, and the knights sent messengers in all directions to implore the assistance of the West.

Amaury, a wise and prudent chief, died, leaving an infant son, who also died a few days after him, and Isabelle was a widow for the fourth time. Pope Innocent III. could find none to go to the Holy Land but those whom he ordered to go by way of penance. Thus, the murderers of Conrad, Bishop of Wurtzburg, were enjoined to bear arms for four years against the Saracens. They were to wear no garments of bright colours; never to assist at public sports; not to marry; to march barefooted, and dressed in woollen; to fast on bread and water two days in the week, and whenever they came to a city to go to the church, with bare backs, a rope round the neck, and rods in the hand, there to receive flagellation. But their penance was not so cruel as that inflicted on the luckless Frotmond, described above (p. 124). Another criminal, one Robert, a knight, went to the pope and confessed that while a captive in Egypt, during the dreadful famine, he had killed his wife and child, and kept himself alive by eating their flesh. The pope ordered him to pass three years in the Holy Land.

The Crown of Jerusalem devolved, by the death of Amaury de Lusignan, on the daughter of Isabelle, by her husband, Conrad of Tyre. The barons, looking for a fit husband to share the throne with her, that is, to become their leader in war, selected John de Brienne. He was recommended by the King of France, "as a man good in arms, safe in war, and provident in business." And hopes were held out that another crusade would be sent from France. On the strength of this expectation, the Templars, in spite of contrary advice from the Hospitallers, broke the truce which yet existed with the Mahometans, and open war began again. King John de Brienne came with an army of three hundred knights, and no more; fortresses and towns were taken; the Christians began to drop off, and desert the falling country; and the new king soon found himself with no place that he could call his own, except the city of Acre. He sent to the pope for assistance. The pope could not help him, because there was a new and much easier crusade on the point of commencing, that against the Albigeois. And then happened that most wonderful episode in all this tangled story, the Crusade of the Children, "expeditio nugatoria, expeditio derisoria."

It had long been the deliberate opinion of many ecclesiastics that the misfortunes of the Christian kingdom, and the failure of so many Crusades, were due to the impure lives of the Christian soldiers. Since the First Crusade it had been the constant and laudable aim of the Church to maintain among the *croisés* a feeling that personal purity was the first requisite in an expedition inspired solely by religious zeal. All their efforts were vain; laws were made, which were broken at once. Shameful punishments were threatened, of which no one took any notice. Even the camp of Saint Louis himself was filled with every kind of immorality; while that of Richard's Crusade, spite of the strictest laws, became the scene of profligacy the most unbridled. For every one Crusader, in the later expeditions, who was moved by a spirit of piety, there might be found ninety-nine who took the Cross for love of fighting, for the sake of their *seigneurs*, for sheer desire of change, for a release from serfdom, for getting away from the burden of wife and family, for the chance of plunder and license, and for every other unworthy excuse. Thus it was that the religious wars fostered and promoted vice; and the failure of army after army was looked on as a clear manifestation of God's wrath against the sins of the camp.

This feeling was roused to its highest pitch when, in the year 1212, certain priests—Nicolas was the name of one of these mischievous madmen—went about France and Germany calling on the children to perform what the fathers, through their wickedness, had been unable to effect, promising that the sea should be dry to enable them to march across; that the Saracens would be miraculously stricken with a panic at sight of them; that God would, through the hands of children only, whose lives were yet pure, work the recovery of the Cross and the Sepulchre. Thousands—it is said fifty thousand—children of both sexes responded to the call. They listened to the impassioned preaching of the monks, believed their lying miracles, their visions, their portents, their references to the Scriptures, and, in spite of all that their parents could do, rushed to take the Cross, boys and girls together, and streamed along the roads which led to Marseilles and Genoa, singing hymns, waving branches, replying to those who asked whither they were going, " We go to Jerusalem to deliver the Holy Sepulchre," and shouting their rallying cry, " Lord Jesus, give us back thy Holy Cross." They admitted whoever came, provided he took the Cross; the infection spread, and the children could not be restrained from joining them in the towns and villages along their route. Their miserable parents put them in prison; they escaped; they forbade them to go; the children went in spite of prohibition. They had no money, no provisions, no leaders; but the charity of the towns they passed through supported them. At their rear streamed the usual tail of camp followers, those people who lived wherever soldiers were found, following in the track of the army like vultures, to prey on the living, and to rob the dead. Of these there came many, *ribauds et ribaudes*, corrupting the boys, and robbing them of their little means; so that long before the army reached the shores of the Mediterranean the purity of many was gone for ever.

There were two main bodies. One of these directed its way through Germany, across the Alps, to Genoa. On the road they were robbed of all the gifts which had been presented them; they were exposed to heat and want, and very many either died on the march or wandered away from the road, and so became lost to sight; when they reached Italy they dispersed about the country seeking food, were stripped by the villagers, and in some cases reduced to slavery. Only seven thousand out of their number arrived at Genoa. Here they stayed for some days. They looked down upon the Mediterranean, hoping that its bright waters would divide to let them pass. But they did not; there was no miracle wrought in their favour; a few, of noble birth, were received among the Genoese families, and have given rise to distinguished houses of Genoa; among them is the house of Vivaldi. The rest, disappointed and disheartened, made their way back again, and got home at length, the girls with the loss of their virtue, the boys with the loss of their belief, all barefooted and in rags, laughed at by the towns they went through, and wondering why they had ever gone at all.

This was the end of the German army. That of the French was not so fortunate, for none of them ever got back again at all. When they arrived at Marseilles, thinned probably by the same causes as those which had dispersed the Germans, they found, like their brethren, that the sea did not open a path for them, as had been promised. Perhaps some were disheartened and went home again. But fortune appeared to favour them. There were two worthy merchants at Marseilles, named Hugh Ferreus, and William Porcus, Iron Hugh and Pig William, who traded with the East, and had in port seven ships, in which they proposed to convey the children to Palestine. With a noble generosity they offered to take them for nothing; all for love of religion, and out of the pure kindness of their hearts. Of course this offer was accepted with joy, and the seven vessels, laden with the happy little Crusaders, singing their hymns, and flying their banners, sailed out from Marseilles, bound for the East, accompanied by William the Good and Hugh the Pious. It was not known to the children, of course, that the chief trade of these merchants was the lucrative business of kidnapping Christian children for the Alexandrian market. It was so, however, and these respectable tradesmen had never before made so splendid a *coup*. Unfortunately, off the Island of St. Peter, they encountered bad weather, and two ships went down, with all on board. What must have been the feelings of the philanthropists, Pig William and Iron Hugh, at this misfortune? They got, however, five ships safely to Alexandria, and sold all their cargo, the Sultan of Cairo buying forty of the boys, whom he brought up carefully and apart, intending them, doubtless, for his best soldiers. A dozen, refusing to change their faith, were martyred. None of the rest ever came back. Nobody in Europe seems to have taken much notice of this extraordinary episode, and its memory has so entirely died out that hardly a mention of it is found in any modern history of the period. Thousands of children perished. Probably their mothers wept, but no one else seems to have cared. And the pope built a church on the Island of Saint Peter, to commemorate the drowning of the innocents, with the cold remark that the children were doing what the men refused to do. It is, however, pleasing to add that the two honest merchants were accused some years afterwards of conspiring to assassinate the Emperor Frederick, and so perished on the gallows-tree.

In 1213, after the Children's Crusade, Innocent essayed once more to wake the enthusiasm of Christendom. He promised, as before, remission of sins to those who took the Cross: he wrote to the Sultans of Damascus and Cairo, informing them that the Crusaders were coming, and urged on them the advisability of giving up Jerusalem peaceably: and he informed the world that Islam was the Beast of the Apocalypse, whose duration was to be six hundred and sixty years, of which six hundred were already passed. Some, no doubt, of his hearers, thought that, such being the case, they might very well be quiet for sixty years more. At the same time he wrote to the Patriarch of Jerusalem with strict injunctions to

effect, if possible, a reform in the morals of the Syrian
Christians, as if that were a hopeful, or even a possible
task; and, as before, preaching was ordered through every
diocese, and collecting-boxes for every church. In England the preaching was a total failure. John saw a means
of reconciling himself with the Church, and took the
Cross. But the barons, in their turn excommunicated,
held aloof, and occupied themselves with their home
affairs. Philip Augustus of France, after giving the
fortieth part of his wealth to the expenses of the Crusade,
quarrelled with the Cardinal de Courçon over the powers
which he assumed to possess as the legate of the pope.
In Germany, Frederick II., recently crowned King of the
Romans, took the Cross in the hope of preserving the
support of the Church, Otho, his rival, being at war with
the pope. Then came the Council of Lateran, at which
Innocent presided. He spoke of Jerusalem and the Holy
Land. His address was received without any marks
of enthusiasm. Nevertheless a Crusade was actually
undertaken, partly against the Prussians, partly to Palestine. The latter was led by Andrew, King of Hungary.
It was conveyed in Venetian ships from Spalatro and
the towns of the Adriatic first to Cyprus, where they
were joined by the deputies of the king and patriarch,
and the military orders. Thence they sailed to Acre,
where they landed in 1217. Like all the crusading
armies, this was too big to be manageable, too diverse in
its composition to be subject to discipline, too unruly
to be led, and under too many leaders. They marched
straight across Palestine, avoiding Jerusalem and the
south. They bathed in the Jordan, and wandered along
the banks of the Sea of Galilee, singing hymns, making
prisoners, and plundering the towns, the Saracens not
striking a blow. Their only military exploit was an
attempt on Mount Tabor, on the top of which stood a fortress. There, too, were the ruins of a church and the

monasteries which the Mohammedans had destroyed. The Crusaders climbed the hill in the face of the enemy's arrows and stones, and would have carried the fortress easily by assault but for one of those panics which were always seizing the Christians at this period. They all turned and fled down the slope of the hill in the wildest confusion. On their return to camp the chiefs accused each other: the soldiers talked of treachery, and the patriarch refused any more to bring out the wood of the Cross—for this imposture had been started again. To revive the spirits of the army, Andrew ordered a march into Phœnicia. The time was winter: cold, hail, and rain killed the troops: on Christmas Eve a furious tempest destroyed their camp and killed their horses. Dejected and discouraged, the Christians returned to Acre. Famine began again, and it was resolved to separate into four camps. John de Brienne, King of Jerusalem, with the Duke of Austria, commanded the first, which lay in the plains of Cæsarea: the kings of Hungary and Cyprus the second, which was stationed at Tripoli: the Master of the Templars the third, at the foot of Mount Carmel: the fourth remained at Acre. The King of Cyprus died, and the King of Hungary went home again. He had got possession of the head of St. Peter, the right hand of St. Thomas, and one of the seven vessels in which the water had been turned into wine. His anxiety to put these treasures in a place of safety was the chief cause that led him to forsake the Crusade.

After his departure the Crusaders changed all their plans, and—it is very curious to observe how persistently they avoided Jerusalem, the pretended object of their aims—embarked at Acre for the siege of Damietta, which they took after nearly two years of fighting. This taken, they advanced on Cairo: on the way, for we have no space to follow all their misfortunes, the Nile overflowed, they were cut off from all hope of succour, assailed on every side by the enemy, and finally compelled to offer terms. During the negotiations they found themselves deprived of everything, encamped on a plain inundated by the waters of the Nile: worn-out by hunger and sickness. The King of Jerusalem went himself to the Sultan. "There he sat down and shed tears. 'Sire,' said the Sultan, 'why do you weep?' 'Sire,' replied the King, 'I do well to weep, for the people with whom God has charged me I see perishing in the midst of the waters and dying of hunger.' The Sultan had pity on the King, and wept himself, and for four days running sent thirty thousand loaves daily to poor and rich."

So ended a Crusade which showed neither prudence nor bravery, which began with an artificially-excited enthusiasm, and was carried on by the leaders in hopes of gaining personal distinction. There was no discipline, no strong bond of a common hope; the knights deserted the banners after a defeat and went home, some of them without even striking a blow; and even in this time of relic-worship the wood of the Cross failed to animate the spirits of the soldiers. Of all the Crusades, this was the least worthy of success, the least animated by religious ardour.

We are next to see the conquest of Jerusalem absolutely effected by a Crusader, but by a Crusader under excommunication and interdict, by means of a treaty with the Mohammedans, and actually against the will and wishes of the Church. It is a troubled and tangled web of dissimulation, ambition, and interested motives, into which we dare not venture.* On the one hand we have a sovereign, clear-sighted, gifted with a strong will, highly educated, equal at all points of scholarship and attainments to any Churchman, holding tolerant views as to differences of religion, a poet, a musician, and an artist:

* See Milman's 'Hist. of Latin Christianity,' vol. iv., p. 196 *et seq.*, for as clear a statement of the imbroglio between Frederick and the Pope as can well be looked for.

one, too, who loved to associate with poets and artists: a king who surrounded himself with Mohammedan friends, and made no sign of displeasure when they performed the devotions due to their religion in his very presence: a lawyer far in advance of his age, a gallant lover, and a magnificent prince. In his Sicilian Court he welcomed alike Christian, Jew, and Mohammedan—even Saracen ladies. Here the sturdy and uncompromising faith of Western Europe was shorn of its strength and sapped by the spirit of toleration, or even worse, by the spirit of free thinking. Frederick himself wrote and spoke Arabic: he corresponded with the Sultan of Damascus, receiving from him, and propounding himself, curious questions in geometry. Society, in fact, modern society, born before its time, was about to grow up amid the fostering influences of Frederick, when its growth was checked and destroyed by the interposition of the pope. For, on the other side, stood the Monk: cold, bigoted, cut off from social influences, old in the practice of austerities, fanatic in the cause of the Church, arrogating to himself the blind obedience of the whole world, claiming ever more and more the domination over men's hearts. The Monk, personified by Pope Gregory IX., formerly the Cardinal Ugolino, confronted the king, and bade him do his bidding; while, to his monastic eyes, the existence of such a court as that of Frederick's was blasphemous, devilish, and full of sin.

Frederick had taken the Cross. He had, moreover, pledged himself to embark for the Holy Land in August, 1227. The time approached. Frederick had already opened up negotiations with El Malek el Kamîl, the Sultan of Egypt. Presents had passed between them. Even an elephant had been sent, and the Church shuddered at this big and visible proof of treachery on the part of Frederick. Pilgrims meantime assembled by thousands and from all parts: Frederick failed in having provisions and ships for all the throng: the heats of summer came on with violence, and fever broke out. But the fleet sailed, with Frederick. Three days afterwards his ship came back. He was ill, and could not go.

Old Pope Gregory saw his opportunity. He would use his power. Frederick was not ill, but only pretending illness. He preached from the text, "It must needs be that offences come, but woe unto him through whom they come." He pronounced the sentence of excommunication. Frederick wrote, on hearing of this, in perfect good temper, calmly stating the fact of his illness: he took no notice of the excommunication; but, after holding a Diet of the Barons of Apulia, he issued an appeal to Christendom, calling on all the sovereigns of Europe to shake off the intolerable yoke of the priests, and declaring his own innocence in the matter of the broken covenant. He called to witness the ill-treatment and ingratitude with which the Church had always repaid those who submitted—the malice and bitterness with which the Church had always persecuted those who refused to submit; and he pointed to the power and wealth of Rome as contrasted with the poverty of the early Church. In the long history of the world's revolt against the pretensions of the priesthood, which has never for a moment ceased since these pretensions first began to make themselves heard, no more remarkable document has ever been issued, save only the famous theses of Luther.

Frederick was rewarded by a second excommunication, and the pope placed every town in which he might be under interdict. Then the people of Rome rose in insurrection, and the pope fled.

Frederick went to the Holy Land. If he wished to avoid fighting with his friends, the Saracens, he had certainly succeeded; because the Crusaders, forty thousand in number, on hearing of Frederick's return to Italy, all re-embarked and went home again. The king, notwithstanding a peremptory order from the pope forbidding him to embark so long as he was under the ban of the Church, set sail with a small fleet of twenty galleys, and six hundred knights. He arrived at Acre. The Knights Templars and Hospitallers received him as their king. Frederick was now married to Yolante, the daughter of John of Brienne, from whom he took the crown of Jerusalem, on the ground that he only held it in right of his wife, whose rights were now descended to her daughter. The clergy refused to meet him, and there came messengers from the pope, by whose command the knights of the orders withdrew their help. Frederick went his own way. He sent Balian, Prince of Tyre, as an ambassador to El Malik el Kamíl, who sent him back with valuable presents, Saracenic robes, singers, and dancing girls, and, above all, Frederick's old friend Fakhr-ed-dín. Then the Templars wrote to the Sultan proposing the assassination of the Emperor. Kameel quietly sent on the letter to his friend, who read it and said nothing. The negotiations between Frederic and Kameel went on in secrecy; they were so far advanced that the former found himself in a position to disclose to the barons the terms proposed. He sent for the Grand Masters of the two orders, and submitted his proposals to them. They refused to act without the patriarch. Frederick knowing well enough that the patriarch would refuse to act without the pope's consent, replied that he could do without that prelate. And then the treaty was signed. The Christians were to have Jerusalem, except the Mosque of Omar, where the Mohammedans were to worship freely; the Saracens were to have their own tribunal; the emperor, King of Jerusalem, was to send no succour to any who might attack the sultan; with some minor points. And as soon as the treaty was signed, the Germans set off with Frederick, and the Master of the Teutonic Knights, to the Holy City. The Christians had got back their city. The Church of Christ refused to have it, or to acknowledge, in any way, the treaty. Frederick rode into the city to find the church empty and deserted. With his knights and soldiers he marched up the aisle, took the crown from the altar, and put it on his own head, without oath or religious ceremony of any kind. Nor did he affect any religious zeal or manifest any emotion. "I promised I would come," he said, "and I am here." It was his answer to the world, and his defiance of the pope. His vow was fulfilled, in a literal sense; but the Crusade was ruined; he had done more than any other king since Godfrey; he had recovered the city, but without slaughtering the infidel, and subject to the conditions that the Mohammedans were to practise their religion within its walls. What did Frederick care for a religion which he confounded with the gloomy teaching of his ecclesiastical enemies? "I am not here," he confided to his friend Fakhr-ed-dín, "to deliver the Holy City, but to maintain my own credit."

And two days after his coronation he went away again, in cynical contempt of the city and its church. He wrote a letter to the pope and sovereigns of Europe, stating that he had, "by miracle," taken the city, which was henceforth Christian. The pope, in an agony of rage at the way in which his enemy had ignored his excommunication, foamed at the mouth, and called the treaty a treaty of Belial. Moreover, he could not but feel the awful irony of the situation, when Jerusalem itself, and the Church of the Holy Sepulchre, were forbidden to have the service of the Christian religion performed in them, because their deliverer, a Christian king, was under the interdict of the pope. And here, reluctantly, we must leave the fortunes of Frederick; not, perhaps, a good man, but a better man than the arrogant and implacable monk who opposed him; and, perhaps, from an unecclesiastical point of view, the best man in a high place at that time in all the world.

The treaty was signed in 1229. Frederick in leaving

Palestine, left the Christians without a chief, without a head. The Christians in Jerusalem, always dreading an attack from the Saracens, were constantly taking refuge in the tower of David, or the surrounding deserts. The patriarch, who had done most to estrange the emperor, wrote letter after letter, imploring for help. How many such letters had been sent since the Crusades had first commenced? Gregory had concluded some sort of reconciliation with Frederick, and now asked his help in an attempt to get up a new Crusade. It was left to the Franciscan friars—Saint Francis of Assisi had himself been present at the Crusade of King Andrew—to preach this. There were found a large number of barons in France to enrol their names; and by the Council of Tours it was resolved that the Cross should no longer be a pretext for the safety of every sort of criminal. But while the Crusaders were assembling came the news of the downfall of the Latin kingdom of Constantinople, and a discussion begun as to whether it were better to go to the help of that city instead of Jerusalem. And before they had decided, came a message from Frederick urging them to wait for him. While they waited, civil war broke out in Italy. The old animosity between Frederick and the pope was revived; and, worse than this, the treaty which Frederick had made with El Malik el Kamíl, which was for ten years only, expired; and the Saracens from Kerak, marching suddenly upon Jerusalem, took it without the least resistance, and razed the tower of David. The pope had forbidden the Crusaders to leave Europe; but in spite of his prohibition, a small army, under the Duke of Brittany and the Count of Champagne, landed in Acre. After a few ineffective forays, they experienced a defeat which cost them the loss of many of their leaders. So they all went home again, and were replaced by an English prince, Richard of Cornwall, who afterwards called himself Emperor of Germany. The Saracens thought that

Richard Lion Heart was coming back again, and awaited his approach with the keenest terror. But he did nothing. Abandoned both by Templars and Hospitallers, he contented himself with ransoming the Christian prisoners, and, after visiting Jerusalem, and worshipping at the Holy Places, Richard returned to Europe, and the turmoil of European wars.

And now a new enemy appeared in the field. The people of Kh'árezm, driven westwards by the Tartars, came into Syria, a wild and ferocious band, with their wives and children, sparing neither Mohammedans nor Christians. Had the forces in Syria been united, a successful stand might have been made against them. But the Mohammedans were divided amongst themselves, and the Sultan of Cairo offered the Kharezmians Palestine for their own, if they would conquer it. They accepted the offer with joy, and marched twenty thousand strong upon Jerusalem. All the people in the city abandoned it hastily, except the helpless poor and infirm. These the Kharezmians found in their beds, and after killing them, thirsting for more blood, they inveigled back the Christians by hoisting the flags of the Cross. The flying Christians, looking round from time to time, caught sight at last of the banner of victory. Satisfied that God had delivered the city by a special miracle, and hearing, moreover, the bell ring for prayer, they trooped back to the city. Directly they were within the gates, the Kharezmians, who had only withdrawn a short distance, returned and surrounded them. In the depth of night the unhappy Christians endeavoured to fly. They were all cut to pieces. None were spared. And the barbarians then turned their wrath upon the very tombs, and tore up the coffins of Godfrey and Baldwin, which they burned with all the sacred relics they could find.

The Templars at Acre called on the Saracen princes of Damascus, Emessa, and Kerak, to make common cause against their common enemy. They came to Acre, headed by the valiant El Melik el Mensúr, Prince of Emessa, whose entrance into the city was greeted with shouts of applause. The allied armies met the Kharezmians on the plain of Philistia, the battlefield of so many periods and so many peoples. A curious incident is told, which took place before the battle. The Count of Jaffa, an excommunicated man, asked the patriarch, who was there with his wood of the Cross, as usual, for absolution. He refused it. Again he asked, to be again refused. But then the Bishop of Rama, impatient of his superior's obstinacy, cried out, "Never mind. The patriarch is wrong, and I absolve you myself." Of course one priest's absolution is as good as another's, and the count went into battle, to be killed with a light heart. They fought all that day, and all the next day, with a ferocity which nothing could equal. But then the Mohammedans gave way, and the victory remained with the Kharezmians. Of the allies thirty thousand lay dead on the field, while of the Christian knights, there returned to Acre only the Prince of Tyre, the Patriarch of Jerusalem, with his wood, thirty-three Templars, twenty-six Knights of St. John, and three Teutonic knights. The Kharezmians came before Jaffa. They tied Walter de Brienne, who was their prisoner, to a cross, and told him that unless he exhorted the besieged to submission they would put him to death. He called on the garrison to defend themselves to the last extremity, and was sent to Cairo, where he was murdered by the mob. Palestine was relieved of the presence of the Kharezmians by the Sultan of Cairo, who sent them to Damascus, which they took and plundered. They then demanded the fulfilment of his promise as regarded the lands of Palestine. But the Sultan prevaricated, and refused, sending an army of Egyptians against them; they were defeated in ten battles, and perish out of history altogether, having only appeared for the brief space of three or four years.

The Kharezmians were gone; but the Christians, who had suffered most of any at their hands, were in a condition of terrible weakness. So threatening was the state of affairs, that they once more forced their claims on the pope, and showed how, without help, they were all undone. The pope renewed all the privileges accorded by his predecessor to those who took the Cross. And then followed the Crusades of Saint Louis. Of his expedition to Egypt, the siege of Damietta, the calamities which befel his army, his own captivity, his ransom and freedom, we cannot here speak. They belong to the special history of the Crusades.

It was in 1250, after his return, that Saint Louis visited Acre. He had with him a small number of knights, all in rags, and deprived of everything. A pestilence broke out in the city. Louis remained, endeavouring to ransom the twelve thousand Christian captives from the Sultan of Cairo. Meantime he was urgently wanted at home, where that most singular movement, known as the revolt of the *Pastoureaux*, was distracting his country. And all efforts failed to raise bands of new Crusaders. Some, however, went to join the king. Among them was a Norwegian knight, named "Alenar de Selingan," according to Joinville, who, with his companions, beguiled the time till they should be fighting the Saracens by slaying the lions in the desert. The Sheikh of the Assassins also sent an embassy with presents to Louis, asking for his friendship, and offering to remain as firmly allied to him "as the fingers on the hand or the shirt to the body." Ives, a monk who could speak Arabic, was sent back on the part of the king with a present of gold and silver cups and scarlet mantles. He brought back a confused and wondrous story of the religion of this sect (see p. 322). He described them, oddly, as having a wonderful veneration for Peter, whom they maintained to be still alive. And he told how a mournful silence reigned round the castle of the Sheikh, and how, when he appeared in public, a herald went before, crying out, "Whoever you are, fear to appear before him who holds in his hand the life and death of kings."

Louis, meantime, was repairing the fortifications of Cæsarea and Jaffa, and making severe laws against the dissolute morals of the Christians in the East and of his own men. His knights went on pilgrimages to Jerusalem, whither he refused himself to go. But he went to Nazareth, to Mount Tabor, and other sacred places.

After a little fighting, the news of his mother's death determined him to go home. He sailed in 1254, having been four years engaged in his disastrous expedition, which only had the effect of making the Mohammedans cautious how far they attacked the Christian settlements, and mindful of the exasperation into which their fall might throw the West of Europe. The subsequent efforts to raise a Crusade all failed. The poets as well as the priests did their best, but with no success. It is remarkable, however, that there is not a word about crusading in the whole of the Romance of the Rose, except a reference or two to the palm of the pilgrim. Neither of its writers, certainly, was at all likely to be touched by the crusading enthusiasm. Rutebeuf however, throws himself into the projected Crusade with extraordinary vigour. "Ha! roi de France!" he cries—

"Ha! roi de France!
Acre est toute jor en balance."

He laments that no one will come to the help of the sacred places.

Ah! Antioch; ah! Holy Land,
Thy piteous wail has reached this strand.
We have no Godfrey, brave and bold;
The fire of charity is cold
  In every Christian heart;
And Jacobin and Cordelier
May preach, but not for love or fear
  Will soldier now depart.

He shows, too, the change come over the thoughts of

men by giving a dispute between a *croisé* and one who refuses to take the Cross, in which the latter advances the startling proposition, not heard since the time of Origen, that a man can very well get to heaven without "pilgrimising," and without fighting for the Cross.*

But Rutebeuf is very urgent. He laments the decay of religious zeal.

> O'ergrown with grass the long road lies,
> Thick trodden once by eager feet,
> When men pressed on with streaming eyes,
> Themselves to offer at God's seat.
> They send, instead, wax tapers now;
> God has no true hearts left below.

The fatal thing, however, was a feeling slowly growing up that it was God's will that the Church of the Sepulchre should belong to the infidel; and a bishop of a somewhat later time gives three reasons for this; namely, first, as a plea for the Christians; second, for the confusion of the Saracens; and thirdly, for the conversion of the Jews. And for the first reason he argues that Christians will never be allowed to have the city again till they are sinless, because God will not have his children commit sin in such a place; as for the Saracens, they are, of course, only dogs; now the master of a house is not very careful about the behaviour of his dogs, but he cannot bear ill behaviour on the part of his children.

Little now remains to tell, because Jerusalem passes away from history, and the events which follow are hardly even indirectly concerned with the Holy City. Louis led another Crusade and met his death at Tunis. Edward of England, with his brother Edmund and eight hundred men came to Acre, but were, of course of little use with so small a reinforcement; and, after concluding a treaty with

---

* "Je dis que cil est foux nayx,
　Qui se mest en autrui servage
　Quant Dieu peut gaaigner sayx
　Et vivre de son heritage."

the Sultan of Egypt, they too departed. Then twenty years of expectation and fear pass away: Europe looks with indifference upon the Holy Land: Laodicea is taken: Tripoli is taken: and lastly, Acre itself is taken. The siege of this, the last place held by the Christians, lasted a month, when the Mohammedans entered the city after a furious assault. They were driven back by arrows and stones hurled from the houses: day after day they came on, were repelled with slaughter, and every day the Christians saw their camp growing larger and larger. The military orders fought with a heroism which caused the Saracens to think that two men were fighting in every knight. But the end came at length, with a great and terrible carnage. The nuns, trembling, and yet heroic, actually preserved their honour by cutting off their noses, so that the Saracens only killed them. The Patriarch of Jerusalem was put on board a ship, entreating to be allowed to die with his flock. The ship sank and he was drowned, so that his prayer was granted. A violent storm was raging. Ladies rushed to the port, offering the sailors all they had, diamonds, pearls, and gold, to be put on board. Those who had no money or jewels were left on the shore to the mercies of the victors. The Templars held out in their castle a few days longer and then fell. All were killed. So ended, after two hundred years of continued fighting, the Christian settlements in Palestine.* The West heard the news of the fall of Acre with a sort of unreasoning rage, and instantly set about mutual accusations as to the cause of its fall. And the wretched *Pullani*, the Syrian Christians, who had survived the taking of Acre, dropped over one by one to Italy and begged their bread in the streets while they told the story of their fall.

* In the same year the house of the Virgin was miraculously transferred from Nazareth to a hill in Dalmatia; whence, by another miracle, it came to Loretto. · Why did not the Holy Sepulchre come too?

Pilgrims and travellers continued to visit Jerusalem. Sir John Mandeville was there, early in the fourteenth century, and describes the churches and sacred sites, but says little enough about the condition of the people. Bertrandon de la Roquière was there a hundred years later. He says that though there were many other Christians in Jerusalem, the Franks experienced the greatest amount of persecution from the Saracens, and that there were only two Cordeliers in the Church of the Sepulchre. And in the same century Ignatius Loyola twice went on pilgrimage. He wished to end his days in Palestine, but this was, unhappily, denied him, and he returned, to be a curse to the world by establishing his society. Among other pilgrims, passing over various princes and kings, may be mentioned Korte, the bookseller of Altona early in the eighteenth century, who was the first to assail the authenticity of the sites, and that of Henry Maundrell, chaplain to the English factory at Aleppo.

But during the interval of five hundred years Jerusalem has been without a history. Nothing has happened but an occasional act of brutality on the part of her masters towards the Christians, or an occasional squabble among the ecclesiastics. Perhaps, some time, the day may come when all together will be agreed that there is no one spot in the world more holy than another, in spite of associations, because the whole earth is the Lord's. Then the tender interest which those who read the Scriptures will always have for the places which the writers knew so well may have a fuller and freer play, apart from lying traditions, monkish legends and superstitious impostures. For, to use the words which Cicero applied to Athens, there is not one spot in all this city, no single place where the foot may tread, which does not possess its history.

2 H

CHAPTER XIX.

THE MODERN CITY AND ITS INHABITANTS.

JERUSALEM stands upon a tongue of land, bounded on the west by the Valley of Hinnom, and on the east by the Valley of Jehoshaphat, two deep wádies, which, uniting at the southern extremity, under the name of the Kedron, flow down together to the Dead Sea. The promontory thus formed is divided again by a smaller valley, called the Tyropœon, bisecting the city from north to south, and running from the Damascus gate, by the Pool of Siloam, into the Kedron. Two hills, or spurs, thus project from the elevated ground on the north-west of the city, of which the western—the higher of the two—is called Mount Sion, and the eastern, Mount Moriah ; upon the last stood the Temple of the Jews, and upon it at the present day stands the far-famed Masjid el Aksa, better known as the Haram es Sherif, or "Noble Sanctuary." Between the valley of Hinnom and that of the Tyropœon a narrow neck of ground is occupied by the Citadel or "Tower of David."

In shape the city is an irregular rhomboid, the longest diagonal of which measures something less than a mile. It covers about two hundred and nine acres of ground, of which thirty-five are occupied by the area of the Haram es

Sherif. There are five gates: the Damascus gate in the centre of the north side; St. Stephen's gate on the east, a little to the north of the Haram; the Water or Dung gate, in the Tyropœon valley, with the Sion gate on the south side, and the Jaffa gate immediately under the walls of the city on the west. The main street is about three-fifths of a mile long, and bisects the city from north to south; from this the other streets run, for the most part, at right angles; that which follows the direction of the north wall of the Haram being called the Via Dolorosa, and containing the Roman archway known as the "Ecce Homo Arch." The city is divided into quarters, defined by the intersection of the principal street, and that which crosses it at right angles from the Jaffa gate to the Bab es Silsileh, one of the gates of the Haram; they are named after the different sects to whom they are appropriated.* The Mohammedan quarter comprises the north-east portion of the town, also, of course, including the Haram Area; the Christian quarter is in the north-west; the Jewish quarter consists of all the south-eastern part, except so much of it as it covered by the Haram; and the remaining quarter, the hill of Sion, on the south-west, is appropriated to the Armenians. The mountains which encompass Jerusalem are dull and unvaried in outline, and, being composed of white limestone, there is an utter absence of all pleasing variety of colouring. Nor does the intense clearness of the atmosphere add much to the general effect, diminishing as it does the distance, and dwarfing the proportions of all around. The view from the Mount of Olives, situated immediately to the east of the city, alone forms an exception to the monotony of the general appearance of the neighbourhood, and from this really fine views are obtained. Looking on the city itself, the eye rests upon the graceful form and rich colouring of the Dome of the Rock, standing in its

* For these particulars see the Ordnance Survey of Jerusalem, 1864-5.

picturesque and quiet enclosure, while the gilded dome of the Holy Sepulchre, the tapering minarets of numerous mosques, the massive walls and clustering buildings, combine to make a beautiful, and even impressive picture. Turning to look eastward, a scene no less grand and novel presents itself; before you, a little to the right, the mountains of Moab rise up high above the azure waters of the Dead Sea; the broad deep valley of the Jordan comes in from the left, the course of the stream just discernible by the thin fringe of verdure which lines its banks; while the blank dreary desert stretches almost to your very feet, making even the desolate hills of Jerusalem look green and fertile by the contrast.

There are many objects of interest outside the city walls, and a walk round the town, on the outside, furnishes food for much curious antiquarian speculation. Commencing with the head of the valley on the north-west side, you pass the upper and lower pools of Gihon, the former situated in the midst of a picturesque Mohammedan cemetery. Turning down into the Valley of Hinnom, and past the countless tombs excavated in the solid rock, you come to the well of Joab (the En-Rogel of Scripture), immediately opposite the queer little village of Siloam, which consists of caves faced with rude masonry or plaster.

In the Valley of Jehoshaphat—besides the modern Hebrew graves, which lie so thickly together that they appear almost to form one broad pavement—there are several curious monuments; the tomb of Jehoshaphat, of which nothing but a pediment rising a little out of the ground, and roughly bricked up, is now visible; the tomb of Zachariah, and the Pillar of Absalom, two monolithic monuments of uncertain date; and a little cave-chamber cut in the face of the rock, ornamented with two Doric columns, and leading into a sepulchral vault, which is said to have formed the hiding-place of St. James the apostle during the first Christian persecution. Then come the Fountain of the Virgin, the Garden of Gethsemane, and the site of the Ascension upon the Mount of Olives. All these, with many others, and the traditions which attach to each, have been too well and too frequently described by travellers to need that we should dwell upon them here.

The Cœnaculum, or Tomb of David, is situated at the south-west angle of the town, outside the city walls; the history of this has been already related on p. 436.

The olive groves by which the city is surrounded, and of which such glowing descriptions have been given by enthusiastic pilgrims, are scanty, and, like most other olive groves, exceedingly ugly and uninteresting; to tell the sober truth it is impossible to grow very rapturous over a stunted tree, with greasy, silver-grey foliage and dilapidated trunk. On a gala day, however, when a motley throng, dressed in bright colours and fantastic garb, crowd outside the Jaffa gate, disperse themselves amongst the tombs in the cemetery of the upper pool of Gihon, or cluster in animated groups beneath the olive trees, the scene is one which a lover of the picturesque might travel far to see.

The city is completely walled round, presenting the appearance of a huge fortress; by the Jaffa gate, where the tower of Hippicus rises above the walls, and the cypresses of the Armenian convent gardens peep over the battlements, they are pretty and picturesque, but, with this exception, there is nothing whatever in them to arrest the attention. Examining them more closely, you are struck with the great size of the stones used in their construction, many of which, especially in the lower portions, are doubtless of great antiquity. Captain Warren, in the course of his excavations at the south-east angle and elsewhere, has come upon blocks which may still occupy the place where Solomon's workmen laid them, but now that the excavations are discontinued and the shafts closed the pilgrim will be grievously disappointed if he expect to find a single stone *in situ*.

The houses are all built of roughly-hewn blocks of stone. Syrian houses have flat roofs, but the want of timber for beams renders this construction impossible in the southern part of Palestine, and the deficiency is supplied by furnishing the buildings with large stone domes. From the nature of the ground there is not a single level street in Jerusalem. The streets are paved with the hard limestone of the country, worn smooth with constant traffic, and this makes them cleaner than those of many other Eastern towns.

Nothing could be more out of harmony with all sacred associations than the interior appearance of modern Jerusalem. True, there is something picturesque and romantic about the narrow streets, the quaint old archways, and the ruins upon which you stumble at every turn; but the ruins are those of Saladin's city not of Herod's, while the Jerusalem of David and of Solomon lies crushed and buried twenty fathoms under ground.

Of course, the two principal objects of attraction in Jerusalem are the Church of the Holy Sepulchre and the Haram es Sherîf.

The actual Sepulchre is covered by a small chapel coated with reddish marble, and is surrounded by a circular building of fine proportions, with a magnificent dome. The Greek church is immediately to the east of this rotunda, and Calvary to the south-east, and some twelve or thirteen feet above it. The only entrance is by a door leading into an open court on the south, and this is never opened except by the Mohammedan official who has charge of it, and with the permission of the patriarch of one of the Christian sects.

On a bench inside the door sits a Turkish guard, whose duty it is to see that the Christians do not cut each other's throats in order to show their zeal for the faith, and the precaution is far from needless.

The open court in front of the entrance to the church is filled with native Christian pedlars from Bethlehem, who drive a thriving trade in crosses, rosaries, incense, and other devotional wares.

Of the various traditional sites within the church, and of the respective authenticity of each, it is not our province here to speak; suffice it to say, the priests have crowded into this small area every incident of the Passion and Crucifixion of our Lord, as well as a great many others of which the ordinary Christian has never heard.

It is refreshing to escape from the narrow streets and noisy stifling bazaars into the quiet shady close of the Haram es Sherif.

The engraving prefixed to this volume conveys a good idea of the general effect of the buildings and the enclosure in which they stand; but in order completely to realise the scene one must have the bright colours and the atmospheric effect: and, above all, the dim religious light streaming in through the gorgeous stained-glass windows of the Cubbet es Sakhrah and the Mosque of El Aksa. A few years ago the traveller was debarred from this enjoyment, and could not even venture near the sacred spot without danger to life and limb from the infuriated fanatics who guard it. Now, however, a *douceur* to the Sheikh, and the company of an attendant from the consulate, or police station, will be sufficient to procure the privilege. It is time that the jealous barbarity and insolent licence of the Turks should be modified by the good sense of civilized nations, and that sanctuaries such as these, which are common to Christian and Mohammedan, should be thrown open to both. Perhaps, some day, Europe may learn that it is scarcely worth while to make war upon a Christian power for the sake of upholding a rotten and corrupt government which repays the obligation by encouraging its own subjects to insult and murder the subjects of its allies.

The inhabitants of Jerusalem number about sixteen thousand, and the pilgrims and travellers who annually visit it at Easter time are reckoned at about fifteen thousand more.

The population is composed of such varied and discordant elements that to give an account of the different sects alone would occupy a volume. We do not profess to enter at all into the question from a theological point of view, but simply to give a brief account of the various peoples inhabiting Jerusalem as they appear to the traveller of the present day.

First in order come the Mohammedans, Turkish and native, who, although they give themselves the airs for which the true believer is distinguished, and look with ill-concealed aversion and contempt upon all besides themselves, yet are not, perhaps, quite so fanatical as those in other towns of the Holy Land. They are, for the most part, Orientals of the conventional type, leading lazy, useless lives, and dividing their time between smoking, praying, bargaining, and cursing. The Turks have the same stupid pasty look which all town-bred Turks have. The natives are remarkable for nothing but sturdy limbs, an inordinate appetite for brown bread and onions, and an incessant habit of reckoning up real or imaginary gains. If you see two Fellahín coming along the road you may venture anything that their conversation will be of piastres, and that the first word you hear will be a numeral. We must do the Mohammedans the justice to say that the bigotry is not all on their side, for a Jew's life is not safe if he so much as venture into the neighbourhood of the Holy Sepulchre.

The Christians are of so many different types and nations that it is almost hopeless to attempt to enumerate them all; the following are, however, the chief divisions:

The native Christians are chiefly from Bethlehem; they are a fine athletic race, much fairer than the Muslim peasantry, and exhibiting unmistakable traces of an admixture of European blood, dating back, no doubt, from the Crusading times. The women are sometimes exceedingly pretty, and their costume very picturesque; they wear a loose-fitting, coloured dress, and a saucepan-shaped cap upon their head, over which is thrown a white mantle. or veil, reaching almost to the feet.

The men wear enormous turbans and the ordinary striped *abbah*, or cloak, of coarse goat's-hair; this, with a linen shirt, leather belt, and enormous yellow slippers, completes their dress. They do a large trade in rosaries, crosses, carved shells, beads, and olive wood fancy articles, and are a quiet and industrious people.

The Syrians, or Jacobites, are a small body who occupy a monastery upon Mount Sion, called the House of St. Mark, The present bishop is an intelligent man, a native of Asia Minor; one or two monks of the monastery, and the old woman who cleans up the place, are natives of a village near 'Aintáb, on the banks of the Euphrates, the only spot where the Syriac language is spoken. In this little convent the traveller may still hear the accents of that ancient tongue, and, probably—as the old lady is no lover of monkish indolence—he will have the opportunity of judging of its capabilities as a scolding medium.

The Greek community consists mainly of monks, with a slight sprinkling of dragomen and wine-shop keepers. The Greek monk, with his handsome face, reverend beard, and severely simple costume, is a noble and saintly figure as to the outward man; but Greek monks, known more intimately, are found to be a drunken and sensual crew, devoid alike of honour and religion. We speak of the monks only, for the Patriarch of Jerusalem and one or two of his bishops are gentlemanly and even learned men, while amongst the laymen attached to the educational branch of the convent may be made some agreeable acquaintances. Although the blasphemous fraud of the "Descent of the Holy Fire" on Easter Sunday, is countenanced by the Armenians, it is really kept up by the Greeks, and performed by the Greek Patriarch. A more degrading spectacle than this can scarcely be imagined: the Church of the Holy Sepulchre crammed to suffocation with eager, half-mad pilgrims, and the Chief Dignitary of the Orthodox Church of Christ solemnly entering into His tomb to juggle with a box of lucifer matches! What wonder that the "infidel" soldiers, who keep the peace in the church, gaze on the scene with a supercilious and derisive smile.

About Easter time the city begins to swarm with Russian pilgrims. These are, perhaps, the only real religious enthusiasts among the crowds who annually come to worship at the Holy City, and no one who has seen the reverence with which they look upon everything in the place—even to the drunken monk who admits them into the church—or the genuine emotion and awe which they display when kneeling before the site of some absurd tradition, can doubt for one moment of their sincerity. Many a weary mile must they tramp along in their native land, many an unheard of hardship must they encounter before they can toil up the sides of Mount Sinai, or reach the foot of Calvary; and yet they never seem to grow sick or faint-hearted, but plod on with a marvellous steadiness of purpose, and whenever you meet a Russian pilgrim, whether it be in the midst of the scorching desert or by the shady banks of Jordan, he will greet you with a respectful salutation and a bright contented face. At Jerusalem itself they may well be content, for the Russian government has built a hospice near the Jaffa gate where thousands of these poor pilgrims are taken in and cared for. This immense establishment is furnished with dormitories, refectories, chapel, reading-rooms, hospitals, &c.,

and for cleanliness and good management would compare favourably with any institution of the kind in Europe.

The Copts have a large monastery of their own immediately contiguous to the Holy Sepulchre, and have contrived, by bribing a Turkish official, to appropriate a great portion of the funds and buildings belonging to the Abyssinians too. At the back of the chapel of the Holy Sepulchre, under the dome, is a little oratory belonging to this sect. The Copts of Jerusalem are little better than transplanted Egyptian Fellahín; their large round features and heavy looks easily distinguish them from the rest of the population.

The Abyssinians are an exceedingly gentle and inoffensive community. They are principally employed as domestic servants by the European residents in the city. They have a monastery, or, rather, a few cells amidst the ruins of what was once a monastery, in an open court over the Chapel of Helena, part of the buildings of the Holy Sepulchre. Here a few monks and a few nuns live in the utmost squalor and misery, subsisting on charity, and in a chronic state of fever. They exhibit great kindness and affection for their compatriots, and are always ready to assist from their own scanty means any Abyssinian who may come to them in distress. They are perhaps the only monks to whom can be conscientiously applied the name of men.

The Armenians are a thriving and industrious people, and their quarter is the only one in Jerusalem in which any regard is evinced for cleanliness or order. The large convent of St. James, the son of Zebedee, on Mount Sion, belongs to them, and the street immediately outside its gates might almost be mistaken for that of some European continental town. The church is the most richly decorated of any in the city, and, amongst other curiosities, possesses the chair traditionally supposed to have belonged to St. James. The patriarch is a gentleman and an accomplished man of the world, and even amongst the monks may be found some who devote themselves to photography and other useful arts. The Armenian is easily distinguishable by a florid complexion, very prominent nose, and dark hair.

The Georgians are a small and insignificant body, occupying the Convent of the Holy Cross outside Jerusalem, to the left of the Jaffa road.

Of the Occidental Christian communities need only be mentioned the Latins. Amongst a number of monks of the conventional low Romish type, there are a few intellectual men, who devote themselves to educating the poor peasantry of the neighbourhood. Their convents are more orderly, have more of life in them, than those of the Oriental Christians, and one is bound to say that the Latin clergy in Jerusalem do make the best of that parent of all social evils, the celibacy of the priesthood.

The Jews of Jerusalem are almost entirely supported by their co-religionists in Europe, upon whose charity they impose, and whose name they disgrace. They are divided into two classes: the Ashkenazim, who consist chiefly of emigrants from Germany and Poland, and the Sephardim, who claim connexion with the old Hebrew families of Spain. The Sephardim are far superior to the others, both in culture and in manners, and have occasionally a certain air of Oriental dignity about them. The Ashkenazim, on the contrary, are, for the most part, mean and disreputable in appearance, and apparently belong to the lowest orders of society. With his dull, exaggerated German-Jewish features, his ridiculous garb,—a long eastern *caftan*, or vest, and a broad-brimmed slouch hat, from which depend on either side of the face the Pharisaic lovelocks—the Ashkenaz Jew of Palestine resembles nothing so much as his representative in modern theatrical burlesque. The services in their synagogue are conducted in a shamefully careless and indifferent manner; and the weekly ceremony of "wailing over the stones of the Temple," when not regarded through that distorting medium of religious enthusiasm which too many travellers bring with them to the Holy Land, is simply a farce.

This picture is a melancholy one; much as one may wish that it could have been painted in brighter colours, it is best to present truthfully the impression which the modern city makes upon most travellers whose eyes are not blinded by the associations clinging to its soil. Filled with abuses, its sacred shrines defiled, and their worshippers exposed to constant danger and insult, Jerusalem is indeed "trodden down of the Gentiles until the time of the Gentiles be fulfilled."

APPENDIX.

THE POSITION OF THE SACRED SITES.

THERE are very many difficulties in the way of a reconstruction of the City of Herod. The course of the second and third walls, the position of Antonia, and even that of the Temple itself, have been made the subject of very keen and bitter controversy; and, coming to later times, the site of Constantine's buildings on and round the Holy Sepulchre has been assigned to two positions. Without attempting to go thoroughly into the question, which would not only take too much space, but would give this volume a character quite foreign to our purpose, let us only state the ground taken up as to the two chief sites only, that of the Temple and that of the Holy Sepulchre.

Everyone has seen plans of the modern city. The eastern side is mainly occupied by what is called the Haram Area, a four-sided space surrounded by vast walls, which are, in some places, buried a hundred feet deep in *débris*. One only of its angles is a perfect right angle, that at the south-west corner. In the middle is a platform constructed round a rough rock, projecting above the surface; in the rock is a cave. Above it is the Kubbet-es-Sakhrah —the Dome of the Rock—an octagonal building of very great beauty. Along the southern wall are various mosques and praying places, the most conspicuous being the Jámi‘-el-Aksa. Tradition has always assigned to the platform in the centre the site of Solomon's and Herod's Temples, but Mr. Fergusson, followed by Messrs. Lewin, Thrupp, and others, places the Temple in the south-west corner, measuring off six hundred feet from each angle to get its limits. We have thus, without considering minor points of difference, two sites for the Temple.

The so-called Church of the Holy Sepulchre is situated in the western part of the city, north of what is now called Mount Zion. There, according to the voice of tradition, were erected the buildings of Constantine, and there has existed, ever since, the cave which Christians have reverenced as the Sepulchre in which our Lord lay.

Mr. Fergusson maintains, on the other hand, that the Dome of the Rock is a building erected by Constantine to cover the Sepulchre of our Lord, and that the cave in the rock is the Sepulchre itself. To support this he endeavours to prove that the rock was not enclosed by the city walls at the time of the crucifixion ; that the cave may very well have been a tomb : and that, independent of all argument from architecture, the description of historians and pilgrims accord with his position of the church, up to the end of the tenth century, over the rock in the Haram Area. And at some period, most probably after the demolition by Hakem in 969, the Christians abandoned the old site, and collected money to build a new church on the present site, which they pretended was the real site.

There are three ways of considering the question : by excavation, by history, and by arguments derived from a study of the architecture. For the first, Captain Warren is the only person who has excavated, on a scale of sufficient magnitude to produce results which bear upon the question at all. We subjoin a few of his results and opinions, with one or two brief explanatory remarks :

(1.) He has made a contour map of the whole hill on which the Haram Area stands. From this, a most important contribution to the topographical question, it appears that the hill was, much as Josephus describes it, steep and almost precipitous. From the top of the rock to the lowest point in the south wall, a distance of seven hundred feet, there is a dip of one hundred and fifty feet, i.e., one in five.

This makes the altar of Solomon's Temple, provided that was in the south-west angle, some forty feet below the present surface. But was not the altar on the threshing-floor of Araunah? Further, the threshing-floors of Syria are now about the tops of high places, open to the four winds, and not on slopes, particularly steep slopes.

(2.) He thinks that the east wall is the most ancient, and the south-west angle a later addition, probably of Herod. His opinion is principally founded on the masonry of the stones laid bare at the foundations.

By Mr. Fergusson's theory, the east wall is more modern than the west; but see, below, the evidence of Josephus, p. 5.

(3.) He has found what he thinks was the old Ophel wall, running from the south-east angle round the ridge of the hill.

This wall, in Mr. Fergusson's plan, springs from the Triple Gate.

(4.) He has examined the Triple Gate for remains of the eastern wall *and finds none*.

(5). He has found what have been pronounced by an eminent authority to be Phœnician characters at the south-east and north-east angles.

Would Phœnician characters have been used by Herod's workmen?

(6.) He has found on the northside of the platform of the Dome of the Rock certain foundations, the remains of some older building. But as yet no further examination of the arches then discovered has been possible.

If Mr. Fergusson is correct, these may be remains of the Church of Justinian. But they may just as well prove to be part of the foundations of the Temple.

(7.) He discovered the actual remains of the great bridge which crossed the valley at the south-west corner.

The foundations of the wall were found to cross a carefully constructed older aqueduct. Now if the west wall was Solomon's, who built the aqueduct? It must have been either David or the Jebusites, and one always imagines that before Solomon's time there were few buildings or constructions, if any, in Jerusalem; certainly not aqueducts.

(8.) Jar handles were found at the south-east corner with inscriptions in Phœnician character of the same period as the Moabite stone.

Of course no direct inference can be drawn from the finding of anything small below the surface. Tobacco pipes were found thirty or forty feet below the surface, but no one has concluded therefrom that the kings of Israel smoked tobacco.

APPENDIX.

(9.) He thinks that "Solomon's Stables" are "a reconstruction from the floor upwards, and it is probable from the remains of an arch described by Captain Wilson at the south-east angle, that the original vaulting was of a much more solid and massive character."

If this is so, no argument can rest upon the manifest inability of the vaults as they now are to support the Royal Cloister.

Most of these results and opinions, it will be found, weigh very heavily in favour of the traditional view. At the same time an opinion may always be wrong.

II. Let us pass on to the evidence given by history.

The only historical evidence we can rely on as to the actual site of the Temple, on which subject little information can be found in the Bible itself, is to be obtained from Josephus. We refer to three passages :

(1.) Antiq. viii., 3, § 9.

"When Solomon had filled up great valleys with earth, and had elevated the ground four hundred cubits, he made it to be on a level with *the top of the mountain on which the Temple was built*, and by this means the outmost temple, which was exposed to the air, *was even with the Temple itself.*"

Solomon, therefore, following the practice common to all nations, built his temple in such a place, that it should occupy a commanding position, and should be an object of mark for the surrounding country.

(2.) Bell, Jud., v., ch. 5, § 1.

"Now this temple was built upon a strong hill. At first the *plain at the top was hardly sufficient for the holy house and the altar*, for the ground about it was very uneven, and like a precipice; but when King Solomon, who was the person that built the Temple, had built a wall to it on its east side, there was then added one cloister, founded on a bank cast up for it, and in the other parts the holy house stood naked; but in after ages, the people added new banks, and the hill became a larger plain. They then broke down the wall on the north side, and took in as much as sufficed afterwards for the compass of the entire Temple."

This is exactly confirmatory of the preceding. It proves that Josephus, and therefore the Jews, believed the altar, *wherever it really was*, to be the top of the hill.

See, however, above, Capt. Warren's results, No. 1.

(3.) Antiq. xx., ch. 9, § 7.

"They persuaded Agrippa to rebuild the eastern cloisters. These cloisters belonged to the outer court, *and were situated in a deep valley*, and had walls that reached four hundred cubits [in length], and were built of square and very white stones, the length of each of which stones was twenty cubits, and their height six cubits. This was the work of King Solomon, who first of all built the entire Temple. But King Agrippa, who had the care of the Temple committed to him by Claudius Cæsar, considering that it is easy to demolish any building, but hard to build it up again, and that it was particularly hard to do it to those cloisters, which would require a considerable time, and great sums of money, he denied the petitioners their request about that matter."

This evidence proves that a wall was built *before* the time of Herod, and traditionally by Solomon, *in a deep valley* east of the Temple. By reference to Capt. Warren's contour map, it will be observed that by no possibility can this be stated of a wall starting from the Temple gate.

Next, let us take the historical evidence from Eusebius downwards, as to the site of the Sepulchre. We adduce the principal passages which bear on the question.

First comes Eusebius. His evidence we have given in full (p. 57). It seems to us to amount to this:—

Constantine, taking down a temple to Venus which had been, according to tradition, built over the site of the Holy Sepulchre, and clearing away the earth, found a tomb, cut in the rock, still remaining. His workmen immediately concluded that this could be no other than the tomb of our Lord. He surrounded it with pillars and decorations. In front of it, or round about it, he made a level place. On the east side of the level place he built a magnificent church, the Basilica of the Martyrion, *the only church* which he erected at all. In front of this church was an open market-place. Market-places, it may be remarked, are always in the middle of towns, not on the outside.

Eusebius is contemporary with the event, and writes as if he actually witnessed the building of the church and the decoration of the tomb. His evidence is therefore of the highest importance; and from him it would appear that Constantine *built no church over the Sepulchre at all.*

We come next to the accounts left behind by pilgrims and others. First in order comes the Bordeaux pilgrim, who was in Jerusalem while Constantine's buildings were being erected. His account is as follows:—

"Also to you going out into Jerusalem, to ascend Sion, on the left hand and down below in valley by the wall in the pool which is called Siloam.... In the same way Sion is ascended, and then appears the place where was the house of Caiaphas the priest; and the column is still there at which they beat Christ with scourges. But within, inside the Sion wall, is seen the place where David had his palace, and [where were] seven synagogues, which once were there, [but] one only remains [standing], for the rest are ploughed up and sowed over, as Isaiah the prophet hath said. Thence, in order to go outside the wall, to those going to the Neapolitan gate, on the right hand, down in the valley, are walls where was the house or prætorium of Pontius Pilate. There our Lord was heard before He suffered. But on the left hand is the hill of Golgotha, where the Lord was crucified. Thence about a stone's throw is the crypt where His body was placed, and (from which) He rose again on the third day. There, lately, by order of Constantine, a Basilica has been built, that is, a church of wonderful beauty," &c., &c., &c.

(2.) St. Cyril. Fourth century.*
"The cleft (or entrance) which was at the door of the Salutary Sepulchre, was hewn out of the rock itself, as is customary here in the front of sepulchres. For now it appears not, the outer cave having been hewn away for the sake of the present adornment;† for before the sepulchre was decorated by royal seal, there was a cave in the face of the rock."‡

(3.) Antoninus Martyrus gives the following facts:—
"From the monument to Golgotha is eighty paces," *i.e.*, about two hundred feet. But between Siloam and Golgotha is a distance of about a mile.

(4.) Antiochus the Monk. A.D. 630.
Modestus ... templa Salvatoris nostri Jesu Christi, quæ quidem

---

* Taken from Williams' 'Holy City,' vol. ii., p. 80, and p. 172.

† Can this remark apply to the rock, rough and unshapen, in the Dome of the Rock? See Williams' 'Holy City,' vol. ii.

‡ It may be observed on this passage that the so-called Tomb of Absalom, as has been discovered by M. Clermont Ganneau, was originally a cave, but the rock has been cut away on all sides from it, so that it now stands out like a built monument.

barbarico igni conflagrarunt, in sublime erigit omni prorsus digna veneratione, puta ædes Calvariæ ac Sanctæ Resurrectionis; domum insuper dignam omni honore venerandæ crucis, quæ mater ecclesiarum est.*

(5.) Arculf. A.D. 695.

Bishop Arculf, returning from pilgrimage to the Holy Land to his bishopric in France, was wrecked and cast away in the Hebrides, whither contrary winds had carried the vessel. He was hospitably received by Adamnanus, the Abbot of Iona, and beguiled the winter evenings by narrating his adventures in Palestine, and describing the sacred sites. The abbot wrote down his account, and sent copies of it to different parts of England. Bede gives an abridgment. Arculf also made a plan of the Church of the Sepulchre, which has come down to our times.

" The Church of the Holy Sepulchre . . . . is supported by twelve stone columns of extraordinary magnitude. In the middle space is a round grotto (tegurium) cut in the rock itself, about a foot and a half higher than a man of full stature, *in which nine men could stand and pray.*† The entrance of the grotto is on the east side; on the north side, within, is the tomb of our Lord, hewn out of the rock, seven feet in length, and raised three feet above the floor. Internally the stone of the rock remains in its original state, and still exhibits the mark of the workman's tools. To this round church, which is called the Anastasis, that is, the Resurrection, adjoins on the right side the square church of the Virgin Mary, and to the east of this another church of great magnitude is built on the spot called in Hebrew Golgotha, from the roof of which there is hung by ropes a great brazen wheel with lamps. . . ."

And in another place, " In that famous place where was formerly the splendidly-built temple, in the neighbourhood of the eastern wall, the Saracens have erected a quadrangular house of prayer, . . . which house is able to contain about three thousand men at once."

(6.) Willibald. A.D. 765.‡

The Sepulchre had been cut out of the rock: and the rock itself stands out above the ground, and is square at the bottom and grows

---

* See Williams' 'Holy City,' ii., 263.

† The cave of the Sakhra contains an area of five hundred square feet; certainly one could hardly expect a writer having this area in his mind to say that it could only contain nine men.

‡ Given in Fergusson's 'Jerusalem,' p. 160, and in Bonney's 'Holy Places,' p. 23.

pointed at the top. On its summit is the Cross of the Sepulchre; and thereupon is built a beautiful house; and on the eastern side in that stone of the Sepulchre is a gate by which men enter within to pray; and there is within the couch on which lay the body of the Lord.

(7.) Bernhard the Wise. A.D. 807.

Bernhard* describes the group, as of " four churches connected together by walls, that is to say, one in the east, which has Mount Calvary: and one in the place in which the Cross of the Lord was found, which is called the Basilica of Constantine: another to the south, and a fourth to the west, in the middle of which is the sepulchre of the Lord. . . . Between these four churches is a Paradise without a roof, the walls of which shine with gold, and the pavement with precious marble. In the midst of it is an inclosure of four chains, which proceed from the aforesaid four churches, and in it said to be the centre of the world."

This account agrees with Arculf's. It is difficult to fit these churches into the Haram Area.

Building was always going on, which accounts for the difference between this story and that of Willibald's.

With a very few trifling exceptions, which may be found enumerated in the 'Bible Atlas,' p. 73, the whole voice of writers since the tenth century is clearly and unmistakably in favour of the present site.

We must not omit to notice the opinion of Mr. Lewin, that the Dome of the Rock was originally the Temple of Jupiter, which Dion Cassius tells us was built on the site of Herod's Temple. But he goes on to suppose that Hadrian was deceived as to the real situation of the Temple, a thing which seems to us impossible. The foundations which the Mohammedans found when they began to build, may very well have been those of the Temple of Jupiter, and many of the old pillars may have been used for the new Dome. The destruction of the Temple was probably due to Chosroes, who clearly left nothing standing at all. It may, however, have been destroyed by the pious zeal of the Christians.

So far therefore, as the historical evidence goes, it appears to us that the following facts come out with great clearness.

(1.) Josephus, and therefore the Jews generally, believed that Solomon's temple was built on the highest part of the hill, the ground being afterwards raised artificially.

* Williams' 'Holy City,' ii., 264.

(2.) Herod's temple was built, with greater magnificence, in the same spot.

(3.) Hadrian built a temple to Jupiter on the Temple Hill.

(4.) Julian attempted to rebuild the temple itself from its old foundations. Did he, to effect this object, first destroy the Temple of Jupiter? If not, who did?

(5.) For four centuries after this the place remained a receptacle for filth of all kinds, but not forgotten.

(6.) Omar erected a small mosque in front of it (p. 76).

(7.) 'Abd el Melik and his successors repaired the whole Masjid (the Haram Area), built the Mosque el Aksa, and the Dome of the Rock (p. 79).

(8.) The Crusaders called the Dome of the Rock, *Templum Domini*, the Temple of the Lord, to distinguish it from the Mosque el Aksa, which they called *Templum Solomonis*, the Palace of Solomon.

With regard to the Church of the Holy Sepulchre, we have the following data furnished us.

(1.) Constantine decorated the cave, and erected a magnificent Basilica over the site of the Crucifixion.

(2.) All Constantine's buildings were destroyed by Chosroes; and rebuilt, after a fashion, by Modestus, with the assistance of John Eleemon, Patriarch of Alexandria.

(3.) The Mohammedans at the taking of the city spared the Church of the Holy Sepulchre.

(4.) Hakem ordered the destruction of the church. This was done, and collections were made in every part of the Christian world to rebuild it.

(5.) This church was burned down in 1808.

With regard to the discrepancies in the accounts given by pilgrims, and the impossibility of completely harmonizing their descriptions with any theory of sites, this may be remarked: Too much stress must not be laid upon the accuracy or inaccuracies of stories told by early travellers. Why should we look for accuracy in the narrative of a pilgrimage spent in a state of mental *exaltation*, of which we cold-blooded Christians can have no possible idea? When the pilgrim, arrived at the goal of his journey, was crawling on his knees from site to site, praying and praising, abandoning himself to all the emotions which the memories of the places evoked, was it a time to pull out the measuring tape and to count the paces?

To sum up, next, the historical evidence as regards the Dome of the Rock.

(1.) When Mohammedan writers speak of the Masjid el Aksa, they mean, not the Mosque el Aksa, but the whole Haram Area, including all the oratories, mosques, minarets, &c.

(2.) All these were built, as has been related, chap. IV., by 'Abd el Melik.

(3.) The Dome of the Rock is only a supplementary building (see p. 83).

(4.) When the pulpit, the 'kiblah,' &c., of the Masjid el Aksa is spoken of, we must refer it to the Jami' el Aksa.

The Haram Area, when Omar visited it first, presented an aspect somewhat similar to what it has at present, so far as its outward walls, dimensions, and general level are concerned. In the centre was the rock, where, as everybody knew, had been the Temple. This was covered with rubbish and filth. And round the rock, and about it, were certain old foundations, most likely those of Hadrian's Temple to Jupiter, possibly those of the Temple of Herod. Along the south wall were extensive ruins. At the south-east angle lay arches and substructures overthrown; and further west the ruins of a Christian church, most probably that of Justinian's church, now the Jami' el Aksa. All these substructures were repaired by the Mohammedans, the position of the walls being, naturally, retained. Then, being desirous of building a dome over the Sacred Rock, 'Abd el Melik issued letters and collected money. He first designed and built a small dome, the same which is now called the Cubbet es Silsilah, for a treasury. He was so pleased with the work that he ordered his great dome to be built on the same model. The Dome of the Rock must not be compared with other mosques, because it is not one, and was never meant for one, but it may advantageously be compared with other *welis*, or Mohammedan oratories. Therefore no argument can be drawn from what would be an exceptional shape for a mosque.

It must be distinctly understood that Arabic historians are as clear and explicit as to the building of this splendid dome as we should be over the building of St. Paul's by Christopher Wren; and that in the account given by us (p. 79 *et seq.*) no single sentence is inserted for which there is not full authority in the Arabic historians.

The third and last method of argument is from architecture. History may be misinterpreted. It may even purposely deceive. But architecture cannot lie. Within limits, superior and inferior, the date of a building can be assigned to it. These limits approach each other more nearly as we come to modern times. Architects find no difficulty, for instance, in distinguishing buildings of the fifteenth from those of the sixteenth century. But the limits recede from each other as we go back. Therefore it is that this is an argument, as concerns the Holy Sepulchre, which can only be used by hands of the greatest experience. Nor ought any conclusion to be generally accepted by the world until it has been acceded to by a majority of that small number of architects competent to judge. Mr. Fergusson has written on the architecture of the Dome of the Rock; his conclusions however have not met with the approval of authorities, such as Professor Willis, or the Count de Vogüé, of equal rank with himself. Until architects agree, then, surely we have nothing to rest on but the historical evidence.

INDEX.

Abu Bekr, 66
Abu 'l Casím, 431
Abu 'l Faraj, 430
Abu 'l Fath Nasr, 431
Abu Ishak, 428
Abu Obeidah, 70, 423
Abu Saíd Barkúk, 435
Abu Táher, 95
Abúdat ibn es Sámit, 424
Abyssinians, 475
Acre, 367, 391, 406, 464
Adana, 166
Adhémar, 144, 145, 171, 173, 175
Ælia Capitolina, 54
Afdhal, 196, 330
Agrippa, chap. i.
Akiba (Rabbi), 51
Albinus, 8
Alexandria surrenders to Shirkoh, 307; taken by Amaury, 308
Alexis Comnenus, chap. vi.
Alice of Antioch, 253, 261
Alimi, El, 438
Al Imám es Shafi, 429
Amaury, King, chap. xiv.
Amaury de Lusignan, 444
Andrew's Crusade, 451
*Anselm, vision of, 178
Antioch, siege of, 170
Antoninus, 118
Arabs, their character and arts, 91
Armenians, 475
Arm of Ambrose, loss of, 207
Arnold, 176, 185, 216
Arnulphus, 118
Ascalon, 107, 287, 408
Ashraf Barsebai, Sultan, 435
——— Catibai, Sultan El, 439
——— Einál, Sultan El, 438
——— Shaban, Es Sultan, 434

Assassins, murder of messenger, 319; sect of, 322
Assises de Jerusalem, 202

Barain, battle of, 307
Baghi Seyan, 170
Baldwin I., chap. viii., 166, 201
——— II., chap. ix.
——— III., chap. xi., 269
——— IV., chap. xiii.
——— V., 343
Baldwin du Bourg, 225, 231, and chap. ix.
Balian of Ibelin, 352
Barcochebas, 52
Battle of Lake Huleh, 292
Bedawín in Jerusalem, 441
Beirût, attempt on, 413
Bellál ibn Rubáh, 424
Benjamin of Tudela, 328
Berenice, 14
Bernard, 277
Bertram of Tripoli, 227
Bertrand de Blanqueford, 310
Bether, 53
———, identification of, 54
Beyrout, 10
———, taking of, 228
Bir el Warakah (Well of the Leaf), 421
Bishop's Pilgrimage, 136
Blanchegarde, 267
Bohemond, 156, 224
Bordeaux Pilgrim, 116
Burham-ed-dín, Sheik, 437
Burzíyeh, castle of, 395

Cadam es Sheríf, 419
Cadhi of Jerusalem, 437
Cæsarea, 7, 16, 179, 219
Calaun, Es Sultan, 434
Caliph of Cairo, 305

2 K

Carmathians, the, 95
Carrier pigeons, 401
Cestius Gallus, 10 ; defeat of, 17
Chain, ordeal of the, 420
Charlemagne, 123
Chiefs of First Crusade, 135
Children's Crusade, 448
Chosroes takes Jerusalem and destroys Church of Holy Sepulchre, 63
Christians of city imprisoned, 441
Claudius Felix, 6
Clermont, Council of, 144
Cœnaculum, 436
Coloman, King, chap. vi.
Completion of Temple, 9
Conrad of Tyre, 367
Constance of Antioch, 288
Constantine builds Basilica, 59 ; decrees against Jews, 60
Copts, 475
Cruelty of Christians, 404, 406
Crusades, time ripe for, 169
Crusaders, return of, 199
Cubbet el Miráj, 420
Cuspius Fadus, 3

DAGOBERT, 201, 214, 216, 217, 222
Damascus, siege of, 283
Damietta, 452
————, Greek fleet at, 315
Darúm, capture of, 411
Dhaher Chakmak, El Melik, 435
————, El Melik el, 433
Dhia-ed-Dín, 432
Dome of the Rock, erection of, 79 ; repair of, 83, 93 ; inscription in, 86 ; not a mosque, 85
Druzes, their teaching, 106

EARTHQUAKE in Palestine, 316
Eastern Cloisters, 9
Edessa, fall of, 272
Edgar Atheling, 155
Edrei, 273
Effects of Christian occupation, 245
El Adhed, 332
El Arish, 233
El Emád, 387
El Ghazálí, 432
Eleanor, Queen, 281
Emico, 151
End of the world expected, 133
Es Sirát, Bridge of, 422
Eusebius, 57, et seq.

Eustace de Bouillon, 237
———— Garnier, 239
Ezz-ed-dín, 438

FAIR of September, 127
Fakhr-ed-dín, 456
Fálek-ed-dín, 411
Famine in Egypt, 445
———— in city, 439
Fatemite Caliphs, 300
Festus, 8
Florus, Gessius, 10, 11, 12, 13
Foulcher de Chartres, 213
Fragrant herb, consecration of the, 427
Francis of Assisi, 458
Frederic D. of Swabia, 367
Frederick II., 453
———— Redbeard, 365
Freisingen, Bishop of, 280
Frotmond, story of, 124
Fulke, chap. x. 254
———— the Black, 133
———— de Neuilly, 445

GARNIER DE GREY, 211
Georgians, 476
Gessius Florus, 10
Ghars-ed-dín, 439
Godfrey, chap. vii., 154, 181
Gorgona, disaster in Valley of, 164
Gotschalk, 151
Gregory IX., 454
Guy de Lusignan, chap. xiv. 339
Guymer, 167

HADRIAN, 51 ; builds Temple of Jupiter on site of Temple, 54
Hajj, the, 417
Hakem, el, 99, 129
Haram repaired, 442
Harûn Er Raschíd, 123
Helena, Life of, 55 ; Invention of the Cross, 56
Henry of Champagne, 367, 369, 443
Heraclius, 64, 67, 68
———— the Patriarch, 341
Hisam-ed-dín, 438
Holy Fire, miracle of, 216
Holy Grail, the, 219
Holy Lance, vision of the, 173 ; discovery of, 174
Holy Sepulchre, discovery of, 57 ; adornment of, 58

Hugh of Cæsarea, 304
—— of Jaffa, 263
—— Vermandois, 157, 205, 209
Humphrey de Toron, 346, 394

IDA OF AUSTRIA, 209
Ilgazi, 238
Imposture of Easter fire, 474
Innocent III., 445
Interdicts in Palestine, 290

JAMÍ-EN-NISÁ, 421
Jerome, 114
Jerusalem, Repair of the walls, 410
—————— Siege of, by Titus, chap. ii.
—————— Siege and fall of, 354
—————— Taking of, by Saladin, 585
Jesus, son of Ananus, 25
Jews, heroism of, 44
Jocelyn, 239, 241, 260
—————— II., 271
John de Brienne, 446, 452
—— Comnenus, 265
—— of Gischala, chap. ii.
Josephus, chap. ii
Judas the Galilæan, 3
Julian, attempts to rebuild the Temple, 61

KA'ADEH, the, desertion of, 96
Khalit ibn el Walíd, 424
Kharezmians, 459
Khotbah of Muhiy-ed-dín, 388
King, choice of, 191
Knights Hospitallers, foundation of, 247
—————— Templars, foundation of, 249
Kokeb, capture of, 397

LIETBERT, 135
Longsword, William, 337
Louis VII., chap. x.
—— IX., 461

MACÁM EN NEBÉ, 421
Macarias, 135
Maghárah, the, 419
Manahem, 15
Manners of the Syrian Christians, 295
Marin of Constantinople, 309
Masjid el Aksa, 75, 381
Mejír-ed-dín, 439
Milan, Bishop of, 206; his army entirely destroyed, 207
Milicent, 263, 270, 293

Milo de Plancy, 336
Moazzem, El Melik el, 433
Modern city, chap. xix.
—————— native Christians, 473
—————— Jews of Jerusalem, 476
Mohammedan beliefs, 422
—————————— pilgrims, chap. xvii.
Mohammed ibn Karrám, 430
——————, Sultan, 434
Montferrat, assassination of Marquis of, 369, 410
Montreal, capture of, 302
Mount Tarsus, passes of, 169

NAHR EL CASB, battle of, 407
Nasir-ed-dín, 438
Nasír Farj, Sultan, 435
Naval defeat of Mohammedans, 392
Nero, 8
Nevers, Duke of, 208; defeat of, 209
—————— Count of, 309
Nicæa, battle of, 153; siege of, 162
Nicephorus Phocas, 97, 128
Nicolas, preacher, 447
Nûr-ed-dín, 284, 292, 294, 301, 303, 309, 319, 327
Nuseiríyeh, doctrines of the, 425

ODOLRIC, 132
Omar, Caliph, 68, et seq.
Ordeal by fire, 177
Order of St. Lazarus, 247

PANCRATES, 168
Paula and Eudoxia, 114
Penances, 446
Peregrinationes, majores et minores, 121
Peter the Hermit, 141, and throughout chap. vi.
Philip Augustus, 365
—— of Flanders, 337
Pilgrim's Progress, The, 118
—————— service, the, 120
Pilgrimage, passion for, 113
Plague in Jerusalem, 441
Pons of Tripoli, 265
Population of Jerusalem, 23
Porphyry, 114
Position of sacred sites, *Appendix*
Pyrrhus, 171

RABBINICAL LAW, 48
Rains at Jerusalem, 440

Ramleh, 179, 220
Raymond, grand master of Hospitallers, 289
——— of Plaisance, 134
——— Poitiers, 262
——— Toulouse, 155, 198, 200, 206, 225
Relics, finding of, 126, et passim
Renaud de Chatillon, 288, 289, 291, 339, 371, 380
——— of Sidon, 398
Renegades, story of, at Cyprus, 403
Richard Cœur de Lion, chap. xv., and 404
——— of St. Vitou, 135
——— of Cornwall, 459
Robert of Flanders, 158, 172, 190
——— Normandy, 155, 171
——— Orleans, 130
Roger of Antioch, 230
Russian pilgrims, 475
Rutebeuf, 462

SAFIYAH BINT HAI, 429
Sakhrah, Mohammedan belief concerning, 419
——— purification of, by Saladin, 388
Saladin, 319, 338, 347, 350, 365, chap. xvi.
Saladin's holy war, 377
Samaritans, 5, 62
Second Crusade, 277
Seif-ed-dín, 358, 404
Selman el Farsí, 427
Sepulchre, Church of the, destroyed by Chosroes, 64; rebuilt by Modestus, 64; by Thomas, 93; destroyed by Hakem, 103
Shakíf, fortress of, 397
Sharafíl, 437
Shawer, 301, 311, 313
——— and Dhargam, 301
Sheddád ibn Aus, 427
Shehab-ed-dín, 439
Sherf-ed-dín, 439
Shírkoh, 312
Sicarii, 6
Sigard of Norway, 228
Simon Ben Gioras, chap. ii
Sophronius, 72
Stephanus, 5

Stephen of Blois, 155, 172, 205
———, Count of Perche, 292
Sufyan eth Thori, 429
Súkel Marifah, 421
Sybille, 337, 339, 367, chap. xiv.
Sylvester converts the Jews, 60

TANCRED, 157, 179, 225
Tell es Siyásíyeh, 399
Templars, defeat of, 348
Theodora of Constantinople, 293
Theudas, 4
Thierry of Flanders, 266
Thomas (patriarch) rebuilds Church of Sepulchre, 93
Tiberias, battle of, 350, 378
Tiberius, Alexander, 4
Tithe of Saladin, 363
Titus: his army, 19; number of, 20, 21; besieges Jerusalem, chap. ii.
Toghrul Beg, 109
Tomb of David, 436
Tours, Council of, 458
Trajan, revolt under, 49
Tripoli, 226
Truce between Saladin and Richard, 414
True Cross, Invention of, 56; discovery of piece of, 195
——— loss of, 381
Tutush, 111
Tyre, 243
——— siege of, 393

UMM EL KHEIR, 429

VENTIDIUS CUMANUS, 4, 5
Vespasian in Galilee, 17; taxes the Jews, 49

WALTER THE PENNILESS, 148
Walter of Cæsarea, 263
William of Cerdagne, 226
Willibald, 123

YAGHMÚRI, EL, 435
Yarmúk, battle of, 69

ZANGHI, 253, 262, 265, 270, 272, 330
Zidugdi, 438
Zimisces, 97, 129
Ziráyeh, the, 417

www.ingramcontent.com/pod-product-compliance
Lightning Source LLC
Chambersburg PA
CBHW020858020526
44116CB00029B/398